**Joseph J. Casino** studied at Villanova University and the University of Michigan and is presently archivist at Ryan Memorial Library and its historical collections at the Philadelphia archdiocesan seminary in Overbrook, Pa.

**Michael J. McNally** earned a Ph.D. in history from the University of Notre Dame. He is professor of church history at St. Vincent de Paul Regional Seminary at Boynton Beach, Fla. and the author of *Catholicism in South Florida, 1868-1968.*

**Charles E. Nolan** is associate archivist and records manager for the Archdiocese of New Orleans. He received a graduate degree from the Gregorian University in Rome and is the author of *A Southern Catholic Heritage*.

**Jay P. Dolan** is professor of history at the University of Notre Dame and director of the Cushwa Center for the Study of American Catholicism. His published books include *The Immigrant Church* (1975) and *The American Catholic Experience* (1985).

# The American Catholic Parish

*A History From 1850 To The Present*

*Edited by*

JAY P. DOLAN

VOLUME I

*Northeast • Southeast • South Central*

PAULIST PRESS
NEW YORK • MAHWAH

*Book design by Nighthawk Design.*

Copyright © 1987 by
Joseph J. Casino, Michael J. McNally
and Charles E. Nolan

Library of Congress Cataloging-in-Publication Data

The American Catholic parish.

    Includes bibliographies and indexes.
    Contents: V. 1. Northeast, Southeast, South Central—
v. 2. Pacific states, intermountain West, Midwest.
    1. Catholic Church—United States—History—19th
century. 2. Parishes—United States—History—19th
century. 3. Catholic Church—United States—History—
20th century. 4. Parishes—United States—History—20th
century. 5. United States—Church history—19th century.
6. United States—Church history—20th century.
I. Dolan, Jay P., 1936-
BX1407.P3A53    1987      282'.73      87-6865

Library of Congress Cataloging-in-Publication Data

ISBN 0-8091-0399-0 (v. 1)
ISBN 0-8091-0400-8 (v. 2)

Published by Paulist Press
997 Macarthur Boulevard
Mahwah, New Jersey 07430

Printed and bound in the
United States of America

# Contents

# Notes on the Contributors

JOSEPH J. CASINO (Northeast)
Joseph J. Casino is Archivist of the Ryan Memorial Library Archives and Historical Collections in Overbrook, Pa. Educated at Villanova University and the University of Michigan, Mr. Casino is the co-author of *The 41st International Eucharistic Congress: A History* (1978) and the author of other articles on early American history.

JAY P. DOLAN (General Editor)
is professor of history at the University of Notre Dame and director of the Cushwa Center for the Study of American Catholicism. His published books include *The Immigrant Church* (1975) and *The American Catholic Experience* (1985).

MICHAEL J. McNALLY (Southeast)
A priest of the Diocese of Palm Beach, and a graduate of the University of Notre Dame with a Ph.D. in History, Father McNally is a Professor of Church History at St. Vincent de Paul Regional Seminary, Boynton Beach, Florida, and the author of *Catholicism in South Florida, 1868–1968* (University Presses of Florida, 1984).

CHARLES E. NOLAN (South Central)
Charles E. Nolan is Associate Archivist and Records Manager for the Archdiocese of New Orleans. He received an H.E.D. from the Gregorian University. His published works include *A Southern Catholic Heritage* and *St. Maurice Parish of New Orleans*.

# Introduction

This two-volume study of the Roman Catholic parish in the United States is the first major publication of the Notre Dame Study of Catholic Parish Life. The Notre Dame Study was a research endeavor undertaken by a group of scholars from the University of Notre Dame. The goal of the project was to understand more thoroughly the American Catholic parish of the 1980s. The first phase of the project began in 1981 with a general survey of 1,850 parishes, 10% of the nation's total number of parishes at that time. The second phase began in 1982 and concluded in 1985. This part of the study was a more intensive examination of parish life by sociologists, political scientists, theologians, and historians. The final phase of the project is a joint effort by academic scholars and church leaders to interpret the significance of the study's findings for American Catholic parish life. The entire study was made possible by funding from the Lilly Endowment, Inc.[1]

The Notre Dame Study of Catholic Parish Life differed from all previous studies of the parish in a very significant way. It included history in its arsenal of intellectual analysis. At first glance this decision seems quite trivial. But it was hardly a trivial matter. It was a calculated choice made by the directors of the project so that a historical perspective and analysis would become an integral part of the study. Previous studies of the Catholic parish had neglected history and, thus, had unwittingly contributed to the historical amnesia so prevalent in American society.

An understanding of history is critical to a society's development and self-identity. This is so evident in European countries where historical monuments, some dating back more than a thousand years, vividly remind people of their rich cultural heritage. It is naive to believe that a person can understand contemporary English society without understanding the rise and fall of the British Empire. It is equally naive to think that someone can understand the meaning of the American experience without appreciating the cultural and political significance of the American Revolution. To say that 1776 is past history and has no contemporary relevance is to fail to grasp the influence that history has on the development of a people and their culture. To understand English history with its kings and lords, its feudal past, and its age of empire and triumphalism is essential to an understanding of contemporary English society. English people are the way they are because of who they were in ages past. The same is true of Americans. The Revolution of 1776, the settlement of the frontier, the Civil War, and the emergence

1

of the United States as an industrial giant were all phenomena that shaped the American personality. Americans are the way they are because of who they were. The differences between an Englishman and an American are very clear because their histories are so different. People can never understand who they are unless they understand who they were.

Catholics have a peculiar problem with history. They can point to a 2,000-year tradition that touches every continent of the earth. It is indeed an ancient and rich history. But in the nineteenth century Catholics began to believe that somehow, somewhere in the ancient past, history stopped and Catholicism became frozen in time. This view became so prevalent that many people believed that the Catholic religion was immune to the influence of history. This mentality persisted for well over one-hundred years, and only in recent times has it begun to lose its grip on the minds of people. Thus, the paradox—Catholicism has a rich and ancient past, but the Catholic faith is immune to the ebb and flow of historical developments. The Catholic God, in other words, is a God above and beyond history. In such a culture the study of history is not so central to a person's belief or self-understanding.

This attitude toward history and faith helps to explain the Catholic aversion to religious history. For Catholics the history of Catholicism is interesting but not personally significant. It really has nothing to do with a person's religion. This is erroneous. History does shape faith and to think that the faith of a German peasant in the fifteenth century is no different than that of an American astronaut in the twentieth century is to fail to understand the relationship between religion and history.

For Catholics in the United States the problem of history is even more serious. American Catholics have a very brief historical tradition, no more than 200 years old. Compared with Ireland or France, American Catholicism is still in its infancy. Thus, the weight of the past is quite light; it does not leave the imprint on contemporary Catholic culture in the same manner than an ancient Catholic tradition does in a country like Ireland. For this reason history does not have the same implications for American Catholicism as it does for Irish Catholicism. Nevertheless, the past, however brief it may be, has shaped the present. This is especially pertinent in the 1980s when the American Catholic community is in the midst of a major transformation. For anyone who wants to understand this present era of American Catholicism, an understanding of the past is essential. Catholics will never understand who they are as American Catholics unless they first know who they were.

A key to understanding the history of American Catholicism is the parish. In the nineteenth century the parish was the central gathering place for the people. This is where they manifested their beliefs and demonstrated their commitment to the Roman Catholic tradition. For many groups, such as the Polish in Chicago and the French Canadians in New Hampshire, even the neighborhood where they lived was named after the parish where they prayed. For these people and for many others the parish was clearly a central neighborhood institution. The spires of parish churches defined the boundaries of the city's neighborhoods. Oftentimes the neighborhood church took on a size and grandeur that rivaled, even occasionally surpassed, that of the bishop's cathedral. These monuments to the neighborhood God became the people's cathedral, striking reminders to them as well as to their American neighbors of the Catholic presence in the city.

As the Church developed in the nineteenth century, other institutions such as hospitals, orphanages, schools, and colleges were established. Nonetheless, the parish still remained the most important institution in the community. This was where the religion of the people was nurtured and strengthened; nineteenth-century Catholic education is the story of the emergence of the parish school; through their parish organizations Catholics first learned the lessons of benevolence and social concern. It is no exaggeration to say that in the nineteenth century the parish was the foundation of American Catholicism. Without it everything else would have collapsed.

In other countries where religion and culture were tightly bound together, the parish was not so central to the development of Catholicism. In Ireland, for example, Catholicism has been the religion of the vast majority of the people for over a thousand years. The main vein of the cultural bedrock of Ireland was and still is Roman Catholicism. In such an environment the parish was only one of many cultural institutions that encouraged the religious development of the people. In a country like Ireland the influence of Catholicism was and still remains inescapable. The situation in France, Spain, and Italy was similar. In the United States, however, Protestantism was the main vein of the nation's cultural bedrock. For that reason, Catholics had to establish their own institutions to nurture and sustain their religious tradition. The primary institution established by the people was the parish and in the United States, more so than in other nations, it took on an increased importance.

Because of its central importance in the community, the parish is a valuable analytical tool for the historian. It becomes the historian's magnifying glass and enables him or her to obtain a closeup view of the people and their religion. By focusing on the parish the historian can begin to sense the pulse of the people and understand more accurately the texture and quality of their lives. For anyone desirous of comprehending the history of the American Catholic people a study of the parish is essential. It was the hinge on which their religious world turned.

By concentrating on the parish community the historian necessarily broadens his or her range of interpretation. Rather than being limited to the lives of noteworthy individuals or important educational institutions, the parish enables the historian to examine a variety of issues that touched the lives of the people. This becomes especially evident in the essays gathered together in this collection.

With the parish community as their focal point, each historian was able to examine a broad range of issues over a century and more of time, from 1850 down to 1980. These issues included such topics as the involvement of lay people in the establishment and development of the parish community, as well as the religious world of the people. Ethnicity or nationality has been a major theme in American Catholic history, and these essays have examined that issue along with education and schooling, or the various ways immigrants handed on the faith to their children. In addition to the wide range of issues examined, these historical essays also offer the reader the unusual opportunity to compare the development of Roman Catholicism in various regions of the country. Because each essay follows the same thematic framework, a valuable comparative perspective is offered. Very few studies can claim this. Moreover, such a perspective should help people in different regions of the nation to understand more thoroughly the growth of Catholicism in their area and how this has differed from other geographical regions. Southeast Catholicism has a very different history than the Midwest; the history of the Western Mountain region is also very unique. Such regional diversity underscores the complexity of American Catholicism and should dispel any lingering belief in the myth that American Catholicism is Chicago or New York Catholicism writ large.

It should also be emphasized that these essays are not histories of a particular parish in a specific region. They examine the historical development in general rather than any one particular parish. Moreover, they use the parish as their focal point of analysis. In a very real sense, these essays represent a major attempt to write a new type of American Catholic history, a history based in a specific geographical region and rooted in the local parish community. In addition, this history is designed to provide a comparative regional analysis, something that has been missing until now.

In his essay on Catholicism in the Pacific Coast region, Jeffrey M. Burns points out how in each age a specific type of spirituality developed in the parish community. He also underscores the great financial pressure that plagued the Church on the West Coast as it sought to keep pace with the rapid population developments of the twentieth century. Upon turning to Carol L. Jensen's essay on the Western frontier, it is striking how different and unique Catholicism was in this region where it was commonplace for parishes to stretch across a territory as vast as any New England state. The boom and bust nature of life in the mining country was a situation that no New York pastor would ever have understood. Stephen J. Shaw's essay on the Midwestern heartland of the United States underlines the unusual ethnic diversity of American Catholicism. He also gives long overdue credit to the indispensable work of priests of various religious orders in establishing Catholicism in the frontier region of the Midwest. In addition, Shaw does a fine job of analyzing the changes that swept through the American Catholic community in the 1960s and 1970s. The Northeast region has been the population center of American Catholicism for decades. It has very rich resources and Joseph

J. Casino was able to use them very effectively. His work in parish financial records was especially revealing because it enabled him to examine the financial priorities of parish communities and demonstrate how central the school was in the parish. The history of Florida is quite different from that of New York or Pennsylvania and the effect of this on Catholicism was stunning. Michael J. McNally emphasizes the destructive effect of the Civil War on Southern Catholicism as well as the damage caused by the economic boom and bust environment of early twentieth-century Florida. The Hispanic transformation of post-World War II Southern Catholicism is also a major interest of McNally. Charles E. Nolan brings different talents and interests to his study of the South Central region. Covering an area that stretches from Kentucky to Texas he ranges far and wide in his essay. Surely one of the more interesting issues he examined was the effect of twentieth-century suburbanization on such regions as Texas and Louisiana.

These are but a few of the issues examined in the essays of this collection. The essays represent a new departure in American Catholic studies and will, henceforth, ensure that no history of American Catholicism can be complete without the comparative regional dimension that they offer. It is the hope of all of us associated with the Notre Dame Study of Catholic Parish Life that this collection of essays will provide people with a better, more informed understanding of the American Catholic parish, both past and present.

> Jay P. Dolan
> Charles and Margaret Hall Cushwa Center
> for the Study of American Catholicism
> University of Notre Dame
> February 1986

## Notes

1. For further information on the Notre Dame Study of Catholic Parish Life and the results of this study, consult the bimonthly reports issued by the Institute for Pastoral and Social Ministry, University of Notre Dame, 1201 Memorial Library, Notre Dame, Indiana 46556. These reports are edited by the project's directors, Professor David C. Leege and Monsignor Joseph Gremillion.

**PART ONE**

# From Sanctuary to Involvement: A History of the Catholic Parish in the Northeast

Joseph J. Casino

# Contents

# Preface

The Catholic parish has been, and continues to be, one of the most significant social institutions in a constantly changing American culture. Largely overlooked in the more conventional histories dealing with the development of the United States, the parish has done its work quietly and unobtrusively; and the society at large has been shaped, for better or for worse, by its strengths and weaknesses.

This is especially true in the Northeast region of the United States, that area bounded on the south by the cities and towns of Pennsylvania and the sandy beaches of New Jersey and on the north by the wilds of Maine. Running from the shores of the Atlantic Ocean to the widening spaces of the old Northwest Territory, the region encompasses geographically the early transit of Western civilization as it gained a foothold in the New World and then laboriously trudged its way westward toward the Great Lakes and the Ohio River Valley. Through its ports entered some of the first Catholics from Europe, largely Anglo-Saxon and Celtic, who would later meet and mix with other Catholic streams—the Gallic from the north and west, and the Hispanic from the south—to create the variegated Catholicism that we know today. Into this region would later pour the flood of Catholic immigrants from southern and eastern Europe, further adding to the amalgam. It quickly became, and still is, the most Catholic part of the country.

Despite so many differences in ethnicity and culture, all of these newcomers to America had one thing in common—they entered the American mainstream through the medium of the Catholic parish. They apparently wanted it that way, since one of their first acts in America was to obtain the services of a priest within the institutional framework of the parish. Thus, the immigrants themselves contributed to the transformation of the New World by the voluntary forming of communities and the construction of edifices through which ideas and practices that would otherwise never have had a hearing filtered into the mainstream culture.

As a social institution, however, the Catholic parish in the Northeast was also a *product* of the larger society in which it became embedded. That social matrix provided a regional element of diversity to be added to the ethnic. There was a world of difference between a small, isolated, sparsely populated parish in the forests of Maine and a large, bustling, overpopulated parish in downtown Manhattan, or between the grimy, impoverished parishioners of a coal-mining town in upstate Pennsylvania and the leisured, seasonal parishioners of a seaside vacation spot along the Atlantic coast. Moreover, there were great differences in the way non-Catholics received the newcomers and their churches, convents, and schools. One parish in urban Philadelphia could be the object of destruction for nativist incendiaries at the same time that non-Catholics in a rural Vermont village were contributing funds and labor for the construction of a church for their Catholic neighbors. Finally, the passage of time itself created diversity. American society has often been described as constantly revolutionary. Geographic and social mobility have been the main factors here, and Catholics in their parishes have not been exempt from such instability. Changes in the ethnic composition of neighborhoods and regions, and the upward social mobility of Catholics, have all created fluid populations in the parishes. Catholics changed and so did their parishes.

Unity and diversity, then, characterize the history of the Catholic parish in the Northeast. While the desire for parish life was universal, and the purpose and functions of parishes throughout the region were essentially the same, there never was anything that could be called the "typical" parish. Variety was evident from the beginning, and each parish saw considerable change and evolution over time. In a sense, what happened in and to Catholic parishes represents a microcosm of what happened in and to the Northeast United States overall. To understand the parish is to begin to understand America.

Valid historical understanding today requires an avoidance of the old elitism. A social institution like the parish must be examined "from the bottom up" as well as from the point of view of its clerical leadership. For that reason, this study of parish life in the Northeast will address several themes and attempt to analyze the interaction of many internal and external forces over time. Major consideration will be given to the location, size, and ethnic composition of parishes, the roles of laity and clergy, organizational complexity, popular pieties, religious socialization and education, and the relationships of Catholic parishioners with those outside the system. This may seem like an overly ambitious project within the limited scope of this work, but it is intended to be incomplete and a prod to future historians.

# CHAPTER ONE

# Organization, 1850–1880

In its original biblical context, the word "parish" denoted transience. The primitive Christian community thought of itself as a pilgrim lacking citizenship on this earth and finding its permanent homeland only in heaven. Such a vague otherworldly definition, however, fell prey to the very worldy insecurities, contests for power, and social dislocations of subsequent centuries. Despite the vigorous exertions of Church leaders and the pronouncements of conciliar documents, confusion, distortion, and abuse crept in, to the detriment of the *cura animarum*—the care of souls—of the faithful in their pilgrimage through life.

Only the cataclysm of the Protestant Reformation shocked the Church into a full-scale evaluation of what the parish was and what it should do. The Council of Trent (1545–1563) did its best to reform parish life and parochial structures, but it necessarily did so within the context of the assaults then being made on the Church. It did reassert the care of souls as the guiding principle, but in other respects it veered far away from the original understanding of the parish. It was emphasized that after the bishop, the parish priest was responsible for the spiritual well-being of his people; and that in order to carry out this obligation faithfully, he must reside among them in a territorially defined parish. The laity was relegated to a generally passive role, its main duty being unquestioning obedience to Church authority and its principal rights being the availability of the Sacraments and pastoral care. The impact of the council, praiseworthy in terms of what had preceded it, was a preoccupation with the parish as a juridico-geographical district of the apostolate and not as the people of God or as a pilgrim community in which the Church is actualized.[1]

As is evident from subsequent legislation, the mandates of the council, either through neglect, resistance, or local circumstances, were only imperfectly realized. That was true in seventeenth- and eighteenth-century Europe, and it was true when the parish first made its appearance in colonial America. When Catholicism began to take root in the British colonies, there were at first no churches, private homes serving as meeting places, and parishes were few in number and were enormous, often including several colonies. Because the parishes were large and their congregations widespread across the land, their priests, when they were available, were frequently on horseback, and there was no possibility of developing what can be called parochial consciousness. Moreover, that kind of identification was further obviated by the fact that such large territories prevented any sort of ethnic homogeneity. Catholics gathered wherever they could, were ministered to by any itinerant missionary, and worshiped together with whoever happened to be in the area at the time.[2]

But America was from the first an immigrant society, and the population was always increasing through new additions from Europe. By the mid-eighteenth century, there were already Catholic churches being built in Pennsylvania, and ethnic clusterings were beginning to form. When this occurred, Catholic laymen demanded smaller, more intimate parishes with their own resident priests, and new ethnic groups speaking languages other than English felt the need for worshiping communities based more on similarities in language and culture than on territoriality. In Philadelphia, for example, where there were only two parishes serving Pennsylvania, New Jersey, and parts of New York by the mid-eighteenth century, the considerable number of Germans who had settled there desired a parish of their own where their children could be instructed in the German language and where they could follow the customs of their own country in matters religious. In 1785, therefore, these German laymen took the initiative in purchasing a parcel of land for a church and in petitioning Bishop John Carroll for a parish of their own. Carroll, setting aside his many reservations about dividing up the faithful along ethnic lines, and considering that Trent never could have envisioned the unique circumstances of Catholic life in the American environment, finally did grant the petitioners the right to establish the German "national" parish of Holy Trinity.[3]

The Holy Trinity case is illustrative of the Catholic parish experience in the Northeast in two respects. First of all, lay initiative was crucial in the founding of many parishes. Clerical leadership was often nonexistent, distant, or transient. Second, especially in the Northeast where the peoples of many different European nations settled, ethnic identity became accentuated. The Catholic parish system in the Northeast would not have burgeoned as it did without these two elements, but they also created problems that to many clerical leaders seemed to hearken back to pre-Tridentine abuses.

By 1850, the Northeast was being inundated by large numbers of immigrants, Irish and German Catholics, who were fleeing religious and political persecution and economic hard times in their homelands. Proportionately, the greatest growth in Catholic population through immigration took place in the forty years after 1820, with the result that Catholicism had become the largest single Christian denomination in the region by 1860. By 1880, the number of Catholics in the Northeast had quadrupled, while the population at large had merely doubled. It was an amazingly rapid growth, and it meant that a region which was only 9% Catholic in 1850 had become one which was 20% Catholic just thirty years later.[4]

The massive influx of largely impoverished and poorly educated Irish, who made up nearly one-half of the immigrants in 1850, was a profound cultural shock, not only to native-born Protestants, but also to the small, better-educated, and generally Americanized group of older Catholic families with respectable connections in the non-Catholic world. Even the Germans at Holy Trinity Parish had by 1810 become so Americanized that they could no longer confess to their priests in German. The Irish could not have appeared on the American scene at a worse time for the established groups that were just then hanging on by their fingernails to the "old" America and the values that seemed to make it work. In a society already reeling from the multiple shocks of urbanization, increasing violence, the broadening of the franchise, a plethora of reformist crusades, and the variety of conflicts that would eventually culminate in the Civil War, the strangeness and threatening character of this new demographic phenomenon was accentuated.

At first glance, it would appear that rural areas were experiencing the greatest increases. In northeastern and north-central New York State, Catholics multiplied four times faster than the rest of the population. In rural New England, the increase was two and one-half times the general population increase. True, the Irish, and the Germans, one-third of whom were Catholic, were attracted by employment opportunities in railroad and canal construction, and by the fertile agricultural lands in some of those regions, but the rapid increase in Catholic population was proportional, occurring as it did in areas where there had formerly been few Catholics. Even after Maine, New Hampshire, Vermont, and western and central Massachusetts had been separated from the enormous diocese of Boston between 1853 and 1870, the remaining three counties centering on the city of Boston still held 320,000 of the 585,000 Catholics in all of northern New England. By comparison, there were, in 1880, only 35,000 Catholics in all of Vermont, and only 80,000 Catholics in the states of Maine and New Hampshire. Likewise, the counties centering on New York City contained 800,000 Catholics in 1880, compared to only 403,000 for the entire remainder of the state. The truncated diocese of Philadelphia, which lost large amounts of territory to the diocese of Harrisburg and Scranton in 1868, still held, in 1880, 300,000 of the 540,000 Catholics in the whole state of Pennsylvania.

Catholicism, then, was concentrated in the large urban centers of the Northeast, and for this peculiarity, recent Irish immigration was largely responsible. Although 80% of the Irish came from rural areas, only about 6% of them settled in the American countryside. In fact, throughout its history, American Catholicism was never to have more than 15% of its population living in rural areas. German Catholic immigrants tended to occupy a wider range of territory and moved more rapidly through the eastern cities into the interior, where they figured largely in the establishment of parishes in the dioceses of Rochester, Pittsburgh, and Erie.

Catholic population growth had two important consequences. It meant, first of all, that Catholics as a group were becoming more visible in American society.

In the countryside, their visibility was due to their relative newness; and in the cities, Catholic visibility was enhanced by their concentration and by the shortage of priests, which made large parish congregations the norm in urban areas. In both places, the foreign origins of the new Catholics was what attracted so much attention and, frequently, so much hostility. Nativism, the term given to that hostility, played a large part in shaping the structure of Catholic parishes as well as influencing its internal life. Second, population growth meant that a chief priority of Catholics, both clerical and lay, became the establishment of more and more parishes to keep up with the increase in population, and the providing of priests, and later nuns for the schools, to administer to the swelling congregations. The period from 1850 to 1880 has thus been aptly labeled the age of organization in Catholic parish life.

The statistics of the period demonstrate the organizational problems in a more tangible fashion. In 1850, we find that there were 448 priests in the Northeast to minister to 737,000 Catholics, and that these Catholics had available to them regular priestly services in 428 organized parishes, and intermittent visits by traveling clerics in about one-hundred missions or stations. Overall, that would mean that there was one priest for every 1,623 Catholics and that the average parish size was approximately 1,722. The efforts of bishops and laity in the next thirty years in establishing new parishes and recruiting from Europe largely regular order clergymen seem to have borne considerable fruit because the statistics reveal considerable improvement in numbers and proportions. By 1880, even though the Catholic population of the region had risen to nearly three million, the number of priests had climbed to 2,430 and there were now 1,827 parishes and 761 missions. That meant overall an improvement in both the priest-to-people ratio as well as in the average size of the parish. In 1880, there was one priest for every 1,164 Catholics, and parish size had been reduced to 1,549.

Subregional comparisons, however, reveal a somewhat different picture and highlight the variable organizational developments in different places. Take, for example, the most rural areas of New England. In Maine and New Hampshire, there were 5,000 Catholics, six priests, and only eight missions in 1850. The ratio of priests to people was good—one priest for every 833 people—but the mere handful of clerics there had to travel long distances every week to visit their widely scattered missions. In fact, some areas of Maine were actually cared for by priests from across the border in New Brunswick and Quebec. By 1880, the Catholic population of the area had jumped to 80,000, and even though there were now seventy-three priests available, the priest-to-people ratio had declined to only one for every 1,095.

The Catholics of rural Vermont in 1850 were concentrated mostly in the western part of the state. There, about 20,000 were cared for by only five priests, or one for every 4,000 faithful. Since there were already ten parishes established, average parish size was 2,000, but only half of those parishes had resident priests.

Thirty years later, the Catholic population had increased to only 35,000, a much slower rate of increase than in Maine and New Hampshire. Consequently, with the thirty-two priests and sixty-six parishes available to them, these Catholics were being better cared for than their northern neighbors. The slower rate of growth in Vermont allowed the parish system to keep pace with the population. That is evident in an 1880 priest-to-people ratio of 1/1,094 and an average parish size that had declined to 530.[5]

A similar variety characterized urban areas of the Northeast. The Diocese of New York, centered on Manhattan and Brooklyn, was already a heavily urbanized area, and through it traveled the bulk of foreign immigrants entering America before the Civil War. In 1850, the area held 202,000 Catholics, for which there were 109 priests and seventy parishes. Thus, the overall ratio of priests to people was 1/1,853, and average parish size was 2,886. Thirty years later, even though the whole northern portion of New Jersey had been detached from it, the dioceses of New York and Brooklyn held 800,000 people, 534 priests, and 277 parishes. That meant a priest-to-people ratio of 1/1,498, an improvement from the past, but average parish size had increased slightly to 2,888.

If one focuses on Manhattan, however, a quite different picture emerges. In 1865, the ratio of priests to Catholics in the city was 1/4,861, up from the 1840 ratio of 1/4,454. The average city parish in 1865 had 10,937 members compared to 8,500 in 1840. In 1867, Immaculate Conception Parish on East 14th Street, which averaged ten sick calls a day, had an estimated population of 25,000 people. In 1880, when it was described as not one of the larger parishes, it still had 17,000 parishioners. Taking the seating capacity of all the city's churches in 1868, and multiplying it by the number of Masses said every Sunday, it appears that Manhattan churches could accommodate comfortably only one-half of their parish populations. And this situation continued to exist despite the energetic efforts of Archbishop Hughes (1840–1864) in founding sixty-one new parishes. No wonder his successor, Cardinal McCloskey (1864–1885), felt compelled to break that record, establishing eighty-eight new parishes.[6]

On the other hand, there was the case of the Diocese of Philadelphia, which in 1850 included all of eastern Pennsylvania, the southern half of New Jersey, and the state of Delaware. In that year there were 170,000 Catholics, eighty-eight parishes, and ninety-three priests. The priest-to-people ratio was 1/1,828, about the same as for New York, but average parish size was less, at 1,932. Because of the energetic efforts of Bishop Neumann, and the fact that the Catholic population in that region did not increase as fast as in New York, Philadelphia was able to provide more effectively the essentials of parish institutional life. By 1880, the priest-to-people ratio had improved to 1/1,063, and average parish size had been reduced to 1,474.

The variety evident in these few examples should not obscure the fact that Catholic population growth placed tremendous strains on the existing parish system, and that failures to provide either sufficient priests or organized parish life were often registered in numerical losses to the religion.[7] In order to forestall that eventuality, and in the face of mounting nativist hostility, American Catholicism was forced into the bare-minimum activities of gathering the swelling hordes of people into organized parish communities in which some clerical discipline could be exerted over them. In the process, the finer points of Catholic belief often got lost in the exigencies of what has been called the "edifice complex."

In the development of the edifice complex, the foreign origins of the new immigrants were significant. The Irish came in such numbers, and so did Irish clergymen, that most parishes in the Northeast became staffed by Irish priests, most parish schools were taught by Irish-born women, and much of the upper leadership of the Church was Irish. The Irish came to dominate the Church so completely that then, and even today in some places, a parish that had no particular national association was referred to as the "Irish" church.

In response to this conquest, as well as to those terrors of assimilation so poignantly described in Oscar Handlin's *The Uprooted,* other ethnic groups sought voluntary segregation in their own "national" parishes. This often meant a demand for more parishes than could be adequately staffed by the available clergy and a financial burden for parish structures difficult to manage for all concerned. It also frequently meant that Catholic parishes in the Northeast became even more homogeneous than neighborhoods. The combination of religious with ethnic identity held the people in strong bonds to their particular church, school, and priest. And while it may have softened the culture shock of re-establishing life in a new land, that homogeneity also fostered a spirit of exclusiveness and defensiveness among parishes and between parishes and the rest of society.[8]

Of the 1,399 new parishes established in the Northeast between 1850 and 1880, about 9% were national, but in some areas the proportion was much higher. By 1880, 22% of Pittsburgh's parishes were national, and in Harrisburg the proportion was 20%. In Buffalo, Brooklyn, and New York, the proportions were 18, 17, and 12%, respectively.

As in the case of Holy Trinity in Philadelphia, foreign-language immigrants at first worshiped in the few churches that were available. There was a French priest in Boston for those immigrants as early as 1788. In 1808, at St. Peter's Parish in New York City, services in English, French, and German were conducted every Sunday. By 1834, there was a German national parish in New York, by 1839 a German church in Pittsburgh, and by 1841 there were French parishes in Boston and New York.

In many areas, this development of ethnic segregation seemed to possess a certain logic based upon overcrowding, language, and socioeconomic conflicts. In the Rochester area, for example, the number of German Catholics, attracted by the fertile soil and opportunities for craftsmen such as bakers, butchers, and brewers, increased tenfold between 1835 and 1880, making them second only to

the Irish among the immigrant groups there. St. Patrick's was the only parish in
Rochester in 1835; and the Germans, disturbed by the overcrowded conditions
and never quite reconciled to belonging to an English-language "Irish" parish
made up of canal and railroad laborers, decided to look for a church of their own.
The laity purchased an unfinished African Methodist Episcopal church in downtown Rochester, obtained the services of an Austrian Redemptorist, and opened
a parish school where a German layman taught the children both English and German, all before the church was dedicated as St. Joseph's in 1837.[9]

In the 1870s, many French Canadians immigrated to Springfield, Massachusetts, attracted there by the agents of New England mill owners who found the
French willing to work for less money, and less prone to strike, than either Yankee
or Irish workers. Upon arrival, the French found that their fellow workers were
not averse to using violence in expressing their displeasure with Canadian labor
docility. In order to preserve their ethnic and group solidarity in a locally hostile
environment, the newcomers formed a variety of French-Canadian organizations,
the most important of which was their own national parish. At first, they rented
a small, white church, formerly owned by Unitarians, which they called St. Joseph's. There, in very crowded conditions, the 1,200 Canadians of Springfield
enjoyed the services of a French priest from Quebec. In 1872, however, just a
year after the invasion of their homeland by Irish Fenians, they lost their priest
and fire destroyed their rented church. For a whole year, they were forced to worship at the "Irish" church, St. Michael's. In 1873, Father Louis Gagnier arrived
from Quebec, and, after a period of fund-raising, he and his parishioners began
digging the foundations of a new church. Within a short time, they had opened a
school in the church basement where their French language and traditions could
be maintained.[10]

Frequently, numbers or social antagonisms had little to do with the founding
of national parishes. In 1850, for example, there were only about 200 Italians in
South Philadelphia, a highly respectable and well-accepted lot whose children
were being given religious instruction at St. Paul's Church on Sunday afternoons.
Early in 1852, however, a group of Italian laity laid plans for the establishment
of its own parish. In the interim, Bishop Neumann gave these people the use of
the Cathedral chapel for Sunday Mass. By autumn, the bishop had purchased a
Protestant chapel that was converted for Catholic use, and that was soon replaced
by a new church, named St. Mary Magdalen de Pazzi. This became the first Italian national parish founded in the United States. With a similar disregard for numbers, but with an abiding concern for preventing the loss of non-English speaking
immigrants to the faith through negligence, the Archdiocese of New York established St. Stanislaus Parish in 1872 for the small number of Poles in the city at
that time.[11]

The initiative and expense of founding or enlarging parishes, both territorial
and national, were frequently carried by the laity. Archbishop Hughes of New

York once pointed out that American Catholicism was uniquely established by the laity and not the clerical missionary coming to convert a pagan population. And as Henry J. Browne has argued, "It was the vision and, more concretely, their donations from the sweaty pay envelopes of laborers digging canals and laying railroads and cutting through city streets that made our parishes possible."[12]

In the 1850s, for example, the generally Irish Catholics of Hingham, Massachusetts, had to walk miles to the nearest church in Quincy or Weymouth, or attend services by a traveling missionary in the Hingham Town Hall. Confessions were heard in private homes. A group of laymen, therefore, sponsored a course of eight weekly lectures on the history of the Roman Catholic Church, and with the proceeds purchased, in 1866, a site for a church. Over the next three years, through fairs, parties, and other social functions, they raised the money for building St. Paul's Church, which was completed in 1871. Much of the digging and construction work was performed by the men and boys of the parish. They worked hand in hand with their new resident pastor, Father Hugh P. Smyth, and by 1877 they had purchased a house to be used as a rectory.[13]

The building of new churches in those days did not always mean the immediate appointment of resident pastors. Priests were too few to permit that luxury, especially in rural or developing areas. Instead, missionary rectors were usually named to central parishes—Father Smyth had been the pastor of the central St. Francis Xavier Parish in Weymouth—and entrusted also with one or more outlying missions, i.e., congregations with churches, or mission stations like Hingham, which had no church.[14]

All of the early parishes were legally incorporated by trustees, a majority of whom were laymen. Often, it was state law that forced lay parishioners to be responsible for church property. The trustees collected money, paid the bills, provided the priest's salary, and took care of legal affairs. By the early 1800s, some trustees also began to arrogate to themselves the right to hire and fire their own priests. Since Roman Catholic custom and law gave that authority exclusively to bishops, very serious conflicts between lay trustees and bishops, often resulting in excommunication, interdict, and schism, developed throughout the Northeast. The trustees invoked old canonical notions of lay presentation and patronage previously conceded to monarchs in Europe—notions that were to have been laid to rest at the Council of Trent—but the real sources of trustee rebelliousness were probably more American-made. Usually, there was some dissident clerical personality in the parish who acted as a leader or rallying point. Close checks on the suitability of many immigrant clerics, which also had been demanded by Trent, were difficult in a region where there was a high demand by growing Catholic populations for any priest to minister to them. Also, personality and ethnic differences within parishes were frequently paramount in these often publicly scandalous battles. And, of course, one must take into account the spirit of democracy to which American conditions gave rise, and the desire of upwardly mobile and

Americanized Catholic lay leaders to imitate their Protestant neighbors in matters of church governance. They frequently sought, and nearly always received, outside assistance from non-Catholics.[15]

Earlier trustee controversies at Holy Trinity and St. Mary's in Philadelphia had been resolved in favor of the bishops but only at the price of schism. When Father Joseph Prost, pastor of St. Joseph's Parish in Rochester, New York, informed his congregation, in 1838, that he proposed to build a new and larger church for them on another site, there was an outcry among his German parishioners. They objected because the Redemptorist Fathers, rather than the congregation, would be the owners of the new property. Faced with increasing resistance, Father Prost simply took himself off to Europe, leaving the church without a resident pastor for several months. By the time he finally sent Father Simon Saenderl to succeed him in 1839, the agitation had largely subsided. Some parishioners continued to resist, however, because they wanted a German parish on another site. Bishop John Hughes granted their request on the condition that Father Saenderl also approve; but the dissident parishioners refused to ask the latter's consent and went ahead on their own with the construction of their new church. When they could find no priest to lay the cornerstone, the laymen performed the rite themselves, sealing in the stone a rancorous document that declared: "Whereas we have been deceived by the Redemptorist Fathers, we are going to build in spite of them." When the new St. Peter's was completed, Bishop Hughes visited the parish and demanded, in return for not declaring the church schismatic, that the deed to the property be handed over to him. After much stonewalling, the trustees finally relented in 1842.

The Archbishop of Albany, John McCloskey, had to fight trusteeism in Troy, Oswego, and especially Carthage where the situation became so serious that he placed the parish of St. Mary's under interdict in 1861. In Buffalo, the Germans of St. Louis Parish were a major source of lay trustee rebellion, even refusing a decision by the Papal Legate. On being excommunicated in 1854, they submitted to Bishop Timon, but only temporarily. They petitioned the state legislature to reaffirm a law passed in 1784 prohibiting church property from being invested in individual clerics, and they were assisted by the election victory of the anti-Catholic Know-Nothing Party, which was only too happy to perpetuate lay trusteeism through the Church Property Bill passed in 1855. That bill, however, was never enforced; and it was repealed in 1863 in favor of another strongly influenced by Archbishop Hughes of New York. This new bill provided that each parish be incorporated separately and have five trustees. Three of them, the Archbishop, the Vicar General, and the pastor, were to serve *ex officio;* the others were appointed by the Archbishop on the nomination of the pastor.[16]

As understandable as trusteeism was in the context of conditions in America, the frequent assistance given to lay dissidents by anti-Catholic forces made any significant participation by laymen in parish administration in the future suspect.

The relative weakness of pastors and priests to calm these disputes enhanced the power and prestige of the bishops who became less and less willing to share that power. Moreover, strong episcopal leaders were able to gain more and more support from newly arriving Irish immigrants, especially as so many episcopal leaders were being raised from the ranks of the Irish. There was not much the bishops could do to eliminate the trustees where they were already strongly established, but when parishes like St. Peter's, St. Paul's, Transfiguration, and St. James' in New York City went bankrupt, Bishop Hughes was able to buy them at sheriffs' auctions and put the properties in his name as archbishop. Of course, every new parish that was opened was vested in the bishop's name, thus avoiding the problem from the start. Lay dissidence was not eliminated, as the parochial experience with later immigrants would demonstrate, but trusteeism had been dealt a severe blow.[17]

These trustee controversies occurred in the context of a native American public opinion, which, in the 1830s, was beginning to turn hostile toward the expansion of Catholicism in the Northeast. The social turmoil of the period was a big factor. Industrialization and urbanization, which began to make remarkable strides in the region, seemed to be threatening the values of Protestant rural and village-green America. That perennial enemy of traditional society, the city, seemed to be encroaching on the countryside, which had always nurtured the best there was in America. What was even worse in the eyes of Protestant Americans was that these warehouses of dirt, congestion, crime, corruption, and every other sort of evil were apparently being taken over by odd-smelling, odd-looking, and odd-sounding immigrants, a startling percentage of whom held unswerving allegiance to that traditional enemy of individualism and democracy, the Roman Catholic Church. An inordinate proportion of these immigrants ended up in penitentiaries and workhouses, thus confirming native-American prejudices. Nor were native-American fears to be assuaged by the specter of more and more Catholic churches being built, by the publicity given to disputes between bishops and trustees—especially the ultimate victory of the clerical hierarchy over the more democratic laymen— or by the inclination of the immigrants, especially the Irish, to affiliate themselves with big-city political machines.

These accumulated fears erupted in the years before the Civil War in a series of murders, riots, church and convent burnings, and in the victory of the American, or Know-Nothing, Party in several states of the Northeast. A major focus of nativist-Catholic hostility in those years was the issue of Bible reading in the public schools. Because of the lack of Catholic parochial schools, most Catholic children either received no education or were enrolled in public schools where they were compelled to read Protestant versions of the Bible, as well as to recite Protestant prayers, sing Protestant hymns, and read textbooks containing passages ridiculing the Catholic religion. Efforts by Catholic bishops to get exemption for their children from these exercises were converted by nativist demagogues into a Catholic campaign to eliminate *all* Bible reading in the schools. Other efforts by bishops to get public funding for separate Catholic schools generally met with failure.[18]

Nativists were really lashing out at a wide range of social changes that were transforming the world to which they were accustomed. Their Bible symbolized that world. It remained a fixed star in a shifting universe. Certainly the increase in the number of Catholics in the Northeast was one of those despised changes, but it was particularly Irish Catholics that they saw as symbolizing everything that was going wrong in America. That became evident in 1844 when nativist antipathy led to massive rioting in Philadelphia in which sixteen people were killed, dozens of homes were destroyed, and the churches of St. Michael's and St. Augustine's were burned. The riots had been preceded by months of tension between nativists and Irish Catholics, and on their way to St. Michael's, nativist incendiaries passed right in front of St. Peter's Church without giving it a second look. It was a German church, and it was the Irish church they were after.

In the next ten years, the flames of hatred were fanned by all sorts of rumors. Irish servant girls in New England were supposed to be poisoning the Protestant families they served. Catholic priests were accused of abducting respectable girls to seduce them in the seclusion of convents. As a result, churches in Dorchester and Lawrence, Massachusetts, were destroyed by mobs, and one in Charlestown was barely saved by the authorities. Know-Nothings blew up a church in Manchester, New Hampshire, and set fire to another in Bath, Maine. When the pastor of St. Joseph's Parish in Eastport, Maine, supported a move to grant Catholic pupils the right to read their own Bible, he was seized by a mob in Ellsworth, tarred, feathered, and ridden out of town on a rail. In Providence, Rhode Island, where the Bishop of Hartford lived because of the larger Catholic population there and the relative lack of nativist hostility, the Know-Nothings threatened to storm the convent of the Sisters of Mercy.

Newark, New Jersey, was swept by nativist riots in 1854 during which St. Mary's Church was wrecked and Catholics were assaulted in the streets. The coroner's jury, which held an inquest on a young Irishman who died in the riot from bullet and knife wounds, brought in a verdict of death from cholera. St. Mary's Church in Elizabeth, New Jersey, was saved from destruction only by the women of the parish, who, with their babies in their arms, ringed the church and dissuaded a mob from their intention.

Nativists also rioted in Brooklyn where they shot one Catholic dead, wounded several others, and were about to set fire to a church when the police intervened. Pastor Rev. David Bacon of St. James Church in Brooklyn had to muster several of his able-bodied male parishioners to protect their church from destruction. In Manhattan, similar acts of violence were nipped in the bud by Archbishop John

Hughes' strong warning to the mayor that Catholics in his diocese would defend themselves with force if necessary and that "if a single Catholic church is burned . . . , the city will become a second Moscow."[19]

The general atmosphere of hostility and derision faced by Catholics in the 1840s and 1850s became an important part of the social milieu in which Catholic parish life evolved. It made the ordinary difficulties of immigrant assimilation into a new culture even more severe. It forced many of them to withdraw into the friendlier environment of their parishes. These became like besieged sanctuaries for them. Within these fortresses, Catholics constructed their own societies, complete with an alternate system of institutions to provide them with the services they were denied in the outside world.

Within this alternate system of institutions, the most important became the parochial school. This impetus to create their own schools was reinforced by the already felt need for such institutions caused by the extremely low level of religious knowledge found among many in the new immigrant groups. Already, in 1829, the First Provincial Council of Baltimore announced that "we judge it absolutely necessary that schools should be established in which the young may be taught the principles of faith and morality, while being instructed in letters." With the advent of organized nativist hostility, the clamor for parochial schools increased. In 1850, Bishop Hughes of New York told his people, "The time has almost come when we shall have to build the schoolhouse first and the church afterward." By 1852, the First Plenary Council of Baltimore was strident in its exhortation "through the bowels of the mercy of God" to "see that schools be established in connection with all the churches" of each diocese. The 1875 campaign of President Ulysses S. Grant for taxation of religious property, mandatory free public schools everywhere, and prohibition against the use of public money for church-affiliated schools simply added another reason for Catholics to concentrate on an educational system of their own. The Newark Synod of Bishops, in 1878, urged pastors to put the establishment of schools in their parishes before all the other duties of their office. By 1884, the Third Plenary Council of Baltimore ordered every pastor who could do so to provide a parochial school within two years, and it made failure to do so grounds for removal. As Dennis Clark has written, "The parishes and schools were a response to Catholic needs and non-Catholic pressures, and as such they formed a responsive institutional fabric in which the immigrant could find the self-assurance, familiarity and practical aid he needed."[20]

The curriculum in the parochial schools was essentially the same as that in the public schools with the major difference being that the children were taught catechism, Bible history, and the lives of the saints. The books used in the schools emphasized fidelity to Catholic tradition and patriotism for their adopted land. As might be expected in an age of anti-Catholic hostility, parochial education had strong separatist tendencies such as emphasizing the antiquity of the Roman Catholic faith over the recent Protestant off-shoot, or cautioning against mixed marriages that might lead to a loss or weakening of the true faith.[21]

Parochial schools, in addition to providing an elementary education for many poor immigrants who would otherwise have remained illiterate, became the primary vehicle for Catholic socialization. There they were introduced to not only the world of knowledge, but also to the world of moral requirements and Church obligations. There they learned of the sacramental life of the Church and their European heritage, which was inextricably bound up with their Catholic faith. The schools also provided the opportunity for Catholic marriages and vocations.

Many of the early parish schools were primitive and understaffed. St. Francis Xavier school (1842) and the Church of the Gesu school (1873) in Philadelphia were housed in the basements of their churches. When future bishop Bernard J. McQuaid became pastor of St. Vincent de Paul Parish in Madison, New Jersey, in 1849, his parish contained all of three counties and parts of two others. Although he was, therefore, a roving missionary for much of the time, he still opened a parish school in the church basement where he himself taught for six months until he could find a teacher. This was the first parochial school in New Jersey.[22]

The first teachers, however, were usually laypersons. In Philadelphia, at St. John's Parish school founded in 1853, and at St. Charles, Kellyville, the first faculty members consisted of two laywomen each. At St. Patrick's Parish school, the first teachers were six laywomen who were paid $150 a year. At St. Denis Parish in rural Delaware County, Pennsylvania, the first school was opened in the 1850s with one lay teacher. Gradually, as the population expanded, and the expenses mounted, most parish schools became staffed by religious orders of women. When St. Augustine's in Philadelphia was reopened in 1853, after its destruction by a nativist mob, its 400 boys and girls were taught by lay teachers. By 1860, however, the Brothers of the Holy Cross came to teach the boys, and the Sisters of the Holy Cross the girls. The laywomen teaching at St. Patrick's were replaced after five years by the Sisters of St. Joseph. Immaculate Conception Parish on East 14th Street, Manhattan, was unusual in still having, as late as 1880, twenty-two lay teachers alongside fourteen nuns.[23]

In terms of numbers, great progress was made during this period in expanding the parochial school system. In 1850, there were about fourteen parochial schools with an enrollment of a few hundred in the state of Pennsylvania. By 1880, there were 169 schools with 44,217 pupils. New York started out with seventeen schools with 9,120 pupils, but within thirty years there were 209 schools with 76,392 pupils. Perhaps the greatest increase occurred in New Jersey, which went from one small school in 1850, to eighty schools enrolling 22,503 pupils in 1880.

Parochial school expansion was much slower in New England. One school with 400 pupils was opened in Lowell, Massachusetts, in 1850. By 1866, however, when New York had thirty-one and Philadelphia had twenty-six schools, the city of Boston had only nine. By 1880, in all of New England, there were 103 schools with 38,010 pupils, but the Diocese of Boston, with the largest system, still ranked below the dioceses of Newark, New York, Pittsburgh, Philadelphia, Buffalo, Brooklyn, Albany, Rochester, Erie, and Hartford in the number of schools, and below New York, Newark, Philadelphia, Brooklyn, and Pittsburgh in the number of pupils.[24]

Throughout the Northeast, however, only about 30% of the parishes established by 1880 had parochial schools. The Diocese of Newark was far ahead of the average with 60%, and the dioceses of Philadelphia, New York, Brooklyn, Pittsburgh, Harrisburg had between 35 and 40%. The dioceses of Boston and Springfield, Massachusetts, were the lowest with only 12%. Moreover, only about 25% of the Catholic children in the Northeast were enrolled in parochial schools by 1880. In the dioceses of Harrisburg, Newark, Pittsburgh, Rochester, and Erie the percentages were 54, 51, 47, 45, and 40, respectively. The lowest percentages were found in Ogdensburg (9%), Springfield (13%), and Boston (14%). In Buffalo and Brooklyn, the percentage was 39%, in Philadelphia, 26%, and New York was actually below average with 20%.

High percentages of participation in the parochial school system may have been directly related to the relatively higher percentage of Germans vis-à-vis Irish in some dioceses. In addition, the low percentage in New York was probably affected by the popularity among the Irish of the local ward schools over which they had considerable control.

In general, however, even after thirty years of strenuous parochial school foundation, the majority of Catholic children were not in the system. In every area, as Catholic population grew, there were just too many children and too few schools. Also, many of the parochial schools charged tuition that many of the poorer immigrants could not, or would not, pay, especially when there was a free public school system available.[25]

As schools were added to more and more parishes, the power of the pastor was enhanced. The budget and operating funds were under his control. When a convent or a brothers' house had to be built to house the school's teaching staff, that power, and the financial responsibility, was increased again. Increasing parish populations frequently required new and bigger buildings for the pastor's assistant priests. The pastor, then, had to become a "brick and mortar" businessman in administrating his growing parochial plant.[26]

The maintenance of such conspicuous plants was difficult to achieve simply by the free-will offerings of generally poor parishioners. Consequently, seat collections, pew rentals, lotteries, bazaars, lecture series, oratorios, and fund-raising associations had to be resorted to, all of which engaged the energies of laity and clergy alike. Some pastors outdid themselves. Father Arthur J. Donnelly started St. Michael's Parish on the West Side of Manhattan in the midst of the Panic of

1857. The parish grew so fast that it was twice divided. Even though the remainder was composed almost entirely of extremely poor people, the parish built one of the largest parochial plants in New York, with a school numbering 1,600 children by the 1880s. More common, especially during the several economic depressions that rocked the country in this period, was the example of St. Peter's Parish in New York City, which had by 1840 accumulated a debt of $135,000 and was eventually sold at public auction. Few parishes, like St. John the Evangelist in the small village of Lambertville, New Jersey, were fortunate enough to receive some public funds for the maintenance of their schools. But even there, when public funds were withdrawn in 1870, tuition payments by the students were insufficient to keep the school open. Many parishes could not even pay the interest on loans to them by parishioners. Diocesan Church Debt Associations were of little help, and the failure of many boards of lay trustees to manage parish debts was a contributing factor to the demise of that system.[27]

Enormous expenses placed a premium on maintaining large groupings of people in the parish, especially in the cities. This development attracted a storm of criticism in the 1870s by a group of well-educated New York priests led by Father Edward McGlynn. They felt that the basic financial burden, that of supporting a parochial school, was what was making parishes so unwieldy in size and, therefore, impersonal. The constant round of fund-raising activities seemed to be antithetical to what they perceived as the essentially religious mission of the parish. Instead, they favored the creation of more and smaller parishes scattered throughout the residential areas of the city, and the elimination of the parochial school system altogether. Their ideas were generally regarded as impractical at the time, and probably did not take into sufficient account the importance of ethnicity, nativism, and the struggling nature of a developing parochial system swamped by newcomers.[28]

The core of parish life, of course, was the liturgy and devotions. In the average city parish in the mid-nineteenth century, there were three to five Masses in Latin on Sunday, often beginning as early as 5:30 A.M. In all but the German parishes, these Masses took place in an atmosphere of reverent silence. The Germans exhibited more of a sense of pageantry, with music and singing accompanying the liturgy. In all parishes, the last Mass, at 10 A.M., was usually a High Mass with music and singing. In the countryside, rural parishes usually had only two Sunday Masses, at 8 and 10 A.M. In some parishes, in New York at least, before 1868 some Christmas Masses were celebrated before 4 A.M. In both urban and rural areas, most parishes had sung Vespers on Sunday afternoon and devotions, often with Benediction, and always with a sermon, in the evening. After the late Mass on one Sunday a month, there was frequently the recitation of the Rosary. Many parishes also had some form of instruction and devotion each evening or several times a week, usually assigning each to a different parish society. Sunday school, taught by the older girls of the parish, was conducted on Sunday at 2 or 3 P.M.[29]

Long sermons were the rule. At Sunday High Mass, on special occasions, and often at devotions, sermons usually lasted for one hour. In all parishes, the confessional was well-attended. Many churches had confessions on Friday as well as on Saturdays. Some had them on Sunday for the benefit of those whose occupations prevented them from coming at other times. At the German parish of St. Nicholas in Brooklyn, for example, Sunday confessions went from 5 to 8 A.M. In the average city parish, a session of four to five hours was considered light duty for a confessor.[30]

Still, it has been estimated that only about 40% of Catholics attended Sunday Mass regularly, even though it was a prime requirement of the Church. This was partly due to the shortage of priests, the inadequacy of the churches, and the practice of pew rents and even entry fees. But, probably, low Mass attendance was due principally to the religious ignorance of the new immigrants, many of whom did not even know how to make the sign of the cross.

A great many Catholics received Holy Communion only once or twice a year, generally at Easter. In the mid-nineteenth century, it was unusual to begin receiving the Eucharist before the age of fourteen; and in the German parishes, the age was often after eighteen. Holy Communion was allowed at funerals, but most funerals, because of the shortage of priests and because of the peculiarities of the Irish custom of the wake, took place at home without a Mass. Baptisms were also at first generally performed in the home. Gradually, both funerals and baptisms were moved into the church, thereby shoring up the central position of the parish church in the religious life of the people. Wakes, however, continued to be celebrated outside.[31]

The devotional life of the people was encouraged in a variety of other ways. May devotions were introduced in the 1850s with evening services four times a week honoring the Blessed Virgin and always accompanied by a well-attended May Procession. Devotions to Mary, on the feasts of the Assumption and the Immaculate Conception, and by means of the Rosary and a litany of prayers to Mary, became especially popular. The feast of Corpus Christi, honoring the Sacrament of the Eucharist, became another occasion of extraordinary prayer, and Eucharistic Processions became common. The custom of preparing for the principal feasts by novenas was introduced at this time, as was the practice of retreats.

The season of Lent was taken very seriously. All the weekdays from Ash Wednesday to Easter were fast days of precept, allowing only one full meal and a collation. Meat was permitted, once daily on Monday, Tuesday, and Thursday from the First Sunday of Lent to Palm Sunday; and fish and meat were forbidden at the same meal. The services of Holy Week preceding Easter emphasized the sorrowful beauty of Christ's suffering. Everything involved in the Lenten preparation for Easter was designed to achieve spiritual catharsis at its culminating Easter Sunday Mass.[32]

In 1853, devotion of the Forty Hours' Public Adoration of the Blessed Sacrament was introduced into the United States and attracted large crowds. Within a year, it was being celebrated in the city parishes of Philadelphia, and by 1862 it had reached rural areas of the diocese. The devotion was introduced into New York in 1865 by Father Thomas Preston, a convert from the Episcopalian clergy and pastor of St. Ann's in Manhattan.[33]

Various religious communities brought with them their own special devotions. The Redemptorists introduced the novena to Our Lady of Perpetual Help, the Purgatorian Society, Holy Week adoration before the tomb of the crucified Christ, the Archconfraternity of the Holy Family, and the general Blessing of the Sick. Deceased, as well as living, parishioners could become members of the Purgatorian Society, whose purpose was, through Masses and prayers, to shorten the suffering of the souls in Purgatory. In the Archconfraternity of the Holy Family, men and women were segregated, as were the married and the single, in separate groups with their own programs of spirituality. The aim of each was to foster a more frequent reception of the Eucharist. The general Blessing of the Sick consisted of a weekly gathering at which, after a sermon and an Act of Contrition, the sick were blessed with a relic.

The Redemptorists also introduced the parish mission, a kind of revival meeting with confession and Benediction, whose function was to stimulate lukewarm Catholics to a more fervent practice of their faith. The Fathers of Mercy at the French Church of St. Vincent de Paul in Manhattan introduced the Christmas crib, the Holy Thursday Repository, and the first Rosary Society in New York.[34]

Spiritual organizations of laypersons were formed to pursue a variety of devotions and good works. These organizations were segregated by sex and they combined particular devotions with social activity. Many parishes had an Altar and Rosary Society, made up of women devoted to prayer as well as to the practical function of taking care of the altar linens and sometimes cleaning the church. For women, the Jesuit-inspired Sodalities of the Blessed Virgin Mary, and for men, Societies of the Holy Name of Jesus, had as their main purpose the renewal of the inner life of the parishioner through some spiritual exercise or devotion, but they quickly became involved in other affairs in the parish. The original purpose of the exclusively male Holy Name Society was to prevent cursing or swearing, especially by the holy name of Jesus. Its members met once or twice a month and received Holy Communion as a group four times a year. In some parishes, women organized themselves into Holy Name Auxiliaries.[35]

Temperance societies, as they formed in the 1840s under the inspiration of Father Theobald Mathew of Ireland, consisted of men and women who took a pledge before the altar to refrain from alcohol. But they were also beneficial societies, entitling members and their families to benefits for sickness (unless the sickness was due to boxing, drunkenness, or violence) and death. These societies acquired the funds to pay benefits from dues and from fines levied against members for breaking the pledge, for frequenting taverns, and even for speaking unkindly about another member. After a period of declining membership in the 1850s, the societies were reborn in the 1860s, but now in a segregated fashion. Each parish in the 1870s generally had four societies: a men's group, a women's group, a boy's (cadets) group, and a girl's group. Each of the societies within a parish had a regular meeting night once a month. By 1872, a national organization known as the Catholic Total Abstinence Union was formed.

Many city parishes built or purchased halls for temperance society members' use, where books, periodicals, newspapers, and games were furnished. Some of the societies inaugurated free public lectures, readings, recitations, singing, instrumental music series, and panoramic exhibitions. Some also instituted Emigration Committees to assist needy immigrants.[36]

Societies of St. Vincent de Paul, first organized in New York's Cathedral Parish in 1846, were organizations of laymen active in visiting welfare institutions and in youth work. They differed from the temperance societies in that they had no convivial purpose and in that they operated in confidentiality in order to maintain the privacy of the poor people they assisted.[37]

Benevolent societies, sometimes attached to sodalities, collected dues that allowed poor immigrants to borrow money from them, or to receive sickness and death benefits, at a time when such services were not provided by private industry to those considered poor risks. One such society organized on a national level was the Irish Catholic Benevolent Union, which paid benefits to widows and orphans of deceased members, and also provided sickness and death insurance for members who traveled.[38]

Like the benevolent societies, parish building and loan associations assisted low income Catholics in obtaining credit that would otherwise have been unavailable to them. In these associations, a member deposited a specific sum in his account weekly, and when the balance reached a certain amount, he became eligible for a housing loan at a relatively low rate of interest.[39]

There were even parish organizations directed toward adult education and the intellectual interests of parishioners. Reading Room Societies maintained lending libraries from which any adult Catholic could borrow one book at a time for a two-week period. Literary Institutes also maintained libraries and sponsored debating activities as well.

Almost all parishes eventually formed choirs that beautified the celebration of the liturgy. Some parishes went further in that they also organized Glee Clubs and various sorts of chamber orchestras and marching bands.[40]

In German parishes, Jaeger Companies were formed. These were initially devoted to the physical defense of church property during the period of nativist violence; but they soon became beneficial societies. Like the others, they sponsored a yearly round of fairs, excursions, and picnics, which helped to support the growing expenses of an expanding parochial plant and also provided leisure-time activities for a largely working-class population.[41]

Of course, formal devotions and parish societies did not exhaust the ways in which Catholics kept to their faith. Perhaps we will never be able to recapture on paper the richness of Catholic piety in the mid-nineteenth century. We know that they decorated their houses with religious pictures and that even the most common utilitarian items in their homes, such as towels, breadboards, bottles, buttermolds, and needlework, contained religious motifs. Many acts of popular piety were noninstitutional. Take, for example, the case of Frank Bierwirth who was chosen in 1859 to help clear the lot where St. Nicholas Church in Egg Harbor, New Jersey, was to be built. When asked by a neighbor why he worked out in the hot sun without a hat, he responded that he did so out of respect for the Blessed Sacrament that would someday be there.[42] Nevertheless, the parish system of alternate institutions did channel more and more religious ideas and practices into more formal paths.

At the head of the whole parish apparatus was the priest. Initially, when they were few and far between, priests were seen, by themselves and by their parishioners, as laborers among the poor and sick, often wasting themselves in tireless service to their people. Typhus, often called ship fever, took a heavy toll among the new immigrants and also among the clergy who attended them. Father Patrick Murphy was the pastor of the Staten Island parish of St. Peter's, which included the Quarantine Hospital for the new immigrants. In 1848, he died of fever contracted from one of the more than 800 patients there. Father John Smith, pastor of St. James Church in Manhattan, went to anoint Father Murphy, caught the fever from him, and died a few days later. Within a few months, Murphy's successor was also dead from the fever.

Take as another example of heroic leadership the case of the Carthusian monk, Father Alessandro Muppiatti, the first Italian priest to work in New York. As assistant at Transfiguration Parish in Manhattan, he was popularly regarded as a saint and had a strong influence over the people he ministered to until his death at the age of forty-three. There was nothing newsworthy about his parish labors. He simply taught himself English and, though he suffered from serious heart trouble and was never without pain, he carried on a zealous and fruitful apostolate in the confessional and in the visitation of the sick.[43] Or take again as examples the thousands of priests who spent practically their whole clerical lives as traveling missionaries among the more remote Catholic communities in backwoods New England and upstate New York. Father James A. Darragh, an Augustinian born in New York City, was only twenty-five years old and only little more than a year ordained when he was sent to St. Mary's Parish, Cambridge, in the Diocese of Albany, in the winter of 1863. He arrived to discover a residence with "no knob on the door, no knocker, no bell, 3 blind chimneys, 4 blind windows, a parlor without any carpet, and a row of shanties in the rear" and a church, as he said, that was "so dreadfully cold sometimes on Sunday I don't know whether my feet or hands are on my body or not." Lonesome, and with only six Catholic families in the town, Father Darragh mused about his fate as if talking about some other miserable wretch:

> His *Shuperior*, God forgive him, wants to make an American saint out of him, by all means, or he would never have sent him to this ungenial solitude at the foot of the wild mountains without a single companion to talk to except the bare walls. . . . It's a saint they want to make of him, and a *purty* one he will make if they leave him here alone much longer without someone to assist with all the sick calls he has, and such unreasonable distances from the house. . . . When they call him out to a place 20 or 22 miles off, it comes hard on him, the very inside of the man is rattled out of him, he drives an average 24 miles a day and the roads in such an awful state. . . .[44]

Despite the difficult conditions of the times, the record of parish priests in the Northeast is generally praiseworthy. Sometimes, clerical leadership was exercised in rather unorthodox manners. Rev. Thomas M. Killeen was the burly pastor of St. John's Parish in Newark, New Jersey, during the 1860s and 1870s. It was his custom after confessions every Saturday night to walk through the parish, making sure that certain "establishments" were closed up by midnight. On one of these nocturnal circuits, he heard the cry of "Murder!" coming from behind the pastoral residence. Investigating, he found one of his parishioners intoxicated and beating his consumptive wife. He flew at the man, wrestled with him, pummeled him severely, and finally sat on him until that chastised individual promised never to abuse drink or his wife again. From that time onward, it was reported that the man proved to be a model husband in the parish.[45]

The Civil War era provided many instances when clerical leadership had to be exercised in the parishes. Here, the priests had to move with caution, for while the cause of the Union was popular among recent immigrants in the parishes (attested to by the large number of Catholic recruits in the Northern army), abolitionism was practically anathema. Cathedral parishioners in Erie, Pennsylvania, rose up in rebellion against their Massachusetts-born pastor and bishop, Josue Young, because of his outspoken anti-slavery views. He certainly did not exercise very prudent leadership by declaring a vote for peace candidate George B. McClellan in the 1864 presidential race to be a mortal sin. Nor did he endear himself among his people by locking the church doors to prevent the congregation from walking out on his political sermons or by scolding his Irish parishioners that they must not, in their pride, consider themselves better than blacks.

Generally, however, clerical leaders adopted a noncommital stand on slavery. They saw their first priority as the building up of the Church in America, and they saw slavery as a divisive issue that was destroying many Protestant establishments. Like their parishioners, they may have also viewed abolitionism as one more of the Protestant crusades that so far had done no good for Catholics.

That strong coincidence of opinion may have been a major reason why Catholic priests were able to mitigate many of the worst excesses of the Draft Riots when they broke out in the Northeast in 1863. Catholic priests were in the streets that year preventing as much destruction and violence against blacks and Protestants as they could. Considering the accumulated grievances Catholics had against Protestants from the preceding twenty years of nativism, and considering how newly arrived Irish immigrants saw themselves singled out to do the dirty work of fighting in a civil war that would unleash millions of former slaves to compete with them for unskilled jobs, it is surprising with what authority the Catholic clergy took their parishioners to task. Some pastors demanded, as the price of admission to heaven, that the rioters return, or pay for, all stolen property, and confess their crimes. One priest told his congregation on the Sunday following the riots that even though rebellion might at times be justified, "the good Catholic need not think he will not know when this time occurs; for whenever it is right and proper the church will notify him."[46]

This extraordinary assertion of clerical authority was indicative of a new relationship between priest and people in the parish. Gone was the suffering servant image of the priest. Now clerical leadership became measured in terms of how many parish faithful he had under his control, the number of buildings he had constructed, and the number of parish organizations he had founded. This was especially true after the collapse of the lay trustee system. The income of the new brick-and-mortar priest and his business responsibilities of administering ever larger and more complex parish structures, and his position as the principal bridge between newly arrived immigrants in the parish and a bewildering hostile world outside, placed him, in his own and in his parishioners' eyes, quite above the rest.[47]

By 1880, then, the organization of the parochial system in the Northeast had been completed. That organization was both structural and attitudinal. More and more parishes were founded to accommodate the rapid increase in population. In an age of nativist hostility and defections from the faith, Catholic clergymen gave priority to the gathering of the Catholic population into the world of the parish. Often, the only way to do that was by means of rather unspiritual appeals, or concessions to ethnic exclusiveness, cultural paranoia, political antagonism, and the desire for mutual support. Once there, so the reasoning seems to have developed, clerical leadership and a proliferation of devotional practices could begin to turn a religiously lax laity into good practicing and believing Catholics. In some respects, the Catholic parish very much resembled hundreds of other utopian communities that were spreading across the northern United States in the years prior to the Civil War.

Some historians have argued that the resultant development of strong parochial consciousness, quite absent in the "old" Catholic parish before the 1830s, had many unfortunate consequences. It has been said that the homogeneous society of the parish provided Catholics with blinders, and that national parishes, in particular, merely institutionalized bigotry. The alternate system of institutions in the parish, providing not only worship, but language, education, poor relief, easy credit, marriage partners, and entertainment, has been blamed for depriving the rest of society of full Catholic participation. Moreover, the proliferation of parish structures has, it is said, corrupted the priestly function and shackeled the laity with unnecessary financial burdens harmful to economic mobility. It has been argued also that Irish influence on American Catholicism has created a sexually repressed people, that the demise of lay trusteeism has inculcated passivity in the laity, and that the concomitant rise in the power of the priest has accustomed Catholics to an authoritarianism with occasionally unfortunate political consequences.[48]

On the other hand, one can argue that without the strong leadership and example of the priest, Catholicism in America would have died off. The parish, with all of its functions, did ease the process of assimilation for many immigrants, provided very practical services to the poor, the struggling, and the uneducated, and certainly gave meaning to the ordinary rites of passage through religious ritual and community support. Finally, one must also recognize that the creation of the parish system was popular—laymen demanded them and often initiated their foundation in advance of clerical services—and it was more often than not a cooperative effort between priests and people.

## Notes

1. Rev. Paul T. O'Connell, "The Parish: An Historical Evaluation Prior to the Second Vatican Council" (J.C.L. dissertation, Catholic University of America, 1968), 41–46.

2. Msgr. James F. Connelly, *The History of Old Saint Mary's* (Phila., 1970); Rev. P. A. Jordan, S.J., *History of Old Saint Joseph's* (Phila., 1873); Leo G. Fink, *From Bally to Valley Forge* (Phila., 1953).

3. *1789–1914: A Retrospect of Holy Trinity Parish* (Phila., 1914); Vincent J. Fecher, *A Study of the Movement for German National Parishes in Philadelphia and Baltimore, 1787–1802* (Rome, 1955); Rev. Joseph E. Ciesluk, *National Parishes in the United States* (Wash., D.C., 1944), 29.

4. These and all subsequent statistics may be found in the Appendices, unless otherwise noted.

5. Francis T. Tschan, "The Catholic Church in the United States, 1852–1868: A Survey," *Records of the American Catholic Historical Society of Philadelphia* (hereafter cited

as *RACHSP*), 59 (June 1948): 90; Rev. William L. Lucey, *The Catholic Church in Maine* (Francetown, N. H., 1957), 152–155, and "The Position of Catholics in Vermont, 1853," *RACHSP,* 64 (Dec. 1953): 225.

6. Msgr. Florence D. Cohalan, *A Popular History of the Archdiocese of New York* (Yonkers, 1983), 75, 88–89.

7. Tschan, "Catholic Church," 90; Robert F. McNamara, *The Diocese of Rochester* (Rochester, 1968), 34.

8. Kathleen Gavigan, "The Rise and Fall of Parish Cohesiveness in Philadelphia," *RACHSP,* 86 (Mar.–Dec., 1975): 122–23.

9. McNamara, *Diocese of Rochester,* 36–38, 41–42, 47–48; Ciesluk, *National Parishes,* 29–30, 33.

10. Kathryne A. Burns, *Springfield's Ethnic Heritage: The French and French-Canadian Community* (Springfield, Mass., 1976), 9–11.

11. *Program, Dedication of the Newly Renovated Chapel of Saint Mary Magdalen de Pazzi* (Phila., 1967), 11; Richard Juliani, "Church Records as Social Data: The Italians of Philadelphia in the Nineteenth Century," *RACHSP,* 85 (Mar.–June 1974): 3–16; Cohalan, *Popular History,* 94.

12. Henry J. Browne, "The Changing American Parish," in *The Postconciliar Parish,* ed. by James O'Gara (N.Y., 1967), 13.

13. *St. Paul's Church Centennial, 1871–1971* (Hingham, Mass., 1971), 2, 5; *Souvenir Program, 1870–1952: 82nd Anniversary of St. Paul's Church* (Hingham, Mass., 1952), 4.

14. McNamara, *Diocese of Rochester,* 32–34, 39, 44.

15. Patrick J. Dignan, *A History of the Legal Incorporation of Catholic Church Property in the United States, 1784–1932* (N.Y., 1935); Rev. Chester J. Bartlett, "The Tenure of Parochial Property in the United States of America" (Ph.D. dissertation, Catholic University of America, 1926); Rev. Peter Guilday, "Trusteeism," United States Catholic Historical Society, *Records and Studies* (hereafter cited as *USCHRS*), 18 (March 1928): 7–73.

16. McNamara, *Diocese of Rochester,* 41–43.

17. *Ibid.;* Msgr. James F. Connelly, ed., *The History of the Archdiocese of Philadelphia* (Phila., 1976), 70–131; Francis E. Tourscher, *The Hogan Schism* (Phila., 1930); Richard Shaw, *Dagger John: The Unquiet Life and Times of Archbishop John Hughes of New York* (N.Y., 1977), 39–59, 74–76, 97, 110–111, 120–132, 177–193, 226–227, 281–283, 292–298; Cohalan, *Popular History,* 74–75, 87; Lucey, *Catholic Church in Maine,* 139–140. Bishop Francis P. Kenrick of Philadelphia complained of "how hard it is to uphold sacred rights when laymen meddle in the affairs of the Church." Francis E. Tourscher, *The Kenrick-Frenaye Correspondence* (Phila., 1920), 156. The much tougher Bishop John Hughes of New York wrote, "I will suffer no man in my diocese that I cannot control." Shaw, *Dagger John,* 227. The plea for continued and greater lay responsibility in parish affairs can be found in Daniel Callahan, *The Mind of the Catholic Layman* (N.Y., 1963), 48, and in Vincent F. Holden, "Father Hecker's Vision Vindicated," *USCHRS,* 50 (1964): 49.

18. Ray Allen Billington, *The Protestant Crusade, 1800–1860* (Chicago, 1938); James Hennessey, *American Catholics: A History of the Roman Catholic Community in the United States* (N.Y., 1981), 108–109, 118–127; Tschan, "Catholic Church in U.S.," 41,

83–91; James J. Kenneally, "The Burning of the Ursuline Convent: A Different View," *RACHSP*, 90 (1979); 15–21; Michael Feldberg, *The Philadelphia Riots of 1844: A Study of Ethnic Conflict* (Westport, Conn., 1975); Shaw, *Dagger John*, 197; Lucey, *Catholic Church in Maine*, 131–132, 155; Cohalan, *Popular History*, 115; Raymond A. Mohl, "Education as Social Control in New York City, 1784–1825," *New York History*, 51 (1970): 231; John W. Pratt, *Religion, Politics, and Diversity: The Church-State Theme in New York History* (Ithaca, N.Y., 1967), 161–190; Diane Ravitch, *The Great School Wars: New York City, 1805–1973* (N.Y., 1974), 3–84; Vincent P. Lannie, *Public Money and Parochial Education: Bishop Hughes, Governor Seward and the New York School Controversy* (Cleveland, 1968); Timothy L. Smith, "Protestant Schooling and the American Nationality, 1800–1850," *Journal of American History*, 53 (March 1967): 679–695; William Bourne, *History of the Public School Society of the City of New York* (N.Y., 1870), 168, 529; Vincent P. Lannie, "Alienation in America: The Immigrant Catholic and Public Education in Pre-Civil War America," *The Review of Politics*, 32 (Oct. 1970): 503–521.

19. Tschan, "Catholic Church in U.S.," 59:41, 83–91; Billington, *Protestant Crusade*, 68–76, 220–234; Lucey, *Catholic Church in Maine*, 131–132; Shaw, *Dagger John*, 197; Paul V. Flynn, *History of St. John's Church, Newark* (Newark, 1908), 115–116.

20. Cohalan, *Popular History*, 55–56, 106; *Concilium Plenarium totius Americae septentrionalis foederatae . . . Anno 1852* (Baltimore, 1853), 47; Harold A. Buetow, *Of Singular Benefit: The Story of Catholic Education in the United States* (N.Y., 1970), 146–147; Marie C. Klinkhamer, "The Blaine Amendment of 1875, Private Motives for Public Action," *Catholic Historical Review*, 42 (1956): 15–49; Dennis Clark, *The Irish in Philadelphia* (Phila., 1973), 99. On the relative importance of founding parochial schools for the Irish and the Germans, see Jay P. Dolan, *The Immigrant Church: New York's Irish and German Catholics, 1815–1865* (Baltimore, 1975), 102.

21. Dolan, *Immigrant Church*, 113–120.

22. *One Hundredth Anniversary, Saint Francis Xavier's Parish, 1839–1939* (Phila., 1939), 26; *Golden Jubilee, Gesu Parish, 1888–1938* (Phila., 1938), 12; Cohalan, *Popular History*, 115.

23. Gavigan, "Rise and Fall," 112–114; McNamara, *Diocese of Rochester*, 45; Cohalan, *Popular History*, 89; Joseph P. Barrett, *The Sesquicentennial History of Saint Denis Parish, 1825–1975* (Havertown, Pa., 1975), 68–69; *Historical Sketches of the Catholic Churches and Institutions of Philadelphia* (Phila., 1895), 19, 189–211; Rev. Robert T. Mulligan, "The Status and Role of the Lay Teacher in the Catholic Elementary Parochial School in the Nineteenth Century," (Ph.D. dissertation, Catholic University of America, 1967).

24. In addition to the Appendices, see Thomas J. Donaghy, *Philadelphia's Finest: A History of Education in the Catholical Archdiocese, 1692–1970* (Phila., 1972), 64–68, Tschan, "Catholic Church in U.S.," 89, Gavigan, "Rise and Fall," 114, Cohalan, *Popular History*, 56.

25. Dolan, *Immigrant Church*, 108.

26. Browne, "Changing American Parish," 5–6.

27. *Ibid.*, 6–7; Cohalan, *Popular History*, 117; Dolan, *Immigrant Church*, 47–49; *St. John the Evangelist Parish, Lambertville, New Jersey* (South Hackensack, N.J., 1968), 20.

28. Browne, "Changing American Parish," 7; Cohalan, *Popular History*, 124–125.

29. Dolan, *Immigrant Church,* 59, 79–80; Cohalan, *Popular History,* 76, 94–95; *Sesquicentennial, Saint Denis Parish,* 85, 91.

30. Cohalan, *Popular History,* 76. See also the excellent treatment of Catholic sermons in Dolan, *Immigrant Church,* 141–158.

31. Cohalan, *Popular History,* 76–77; Dolan, *Immigrant Church,* 61–62.

32. Cohalan, *Popular History,* 77, 116; *Sesquicentennial, Saint Denis Parish,* 65, 88; *Souvenir, 1852–1902, Golden Jubilee of Our Mother of Sorrows Parish* (Phila., 1901), 6.

33. Cohalan, *Popular History,* 77, 116; *Sesquicentennial, Saint Denis Parish,* 65.

34. *Manual for the Members of the Purgatorian Society and of the Archconfraternity of Our Lady of Perpetual Help and St. Alphonsus;* Cohalan, *Popular History,* 77. Jay P. Dolan, *Catholic Revivalism: The American Experience, 1830–1900* (Notre Dame, 1978), 22.

35. Gavigan, "Rise and Fall," 115; *Sesquicentennial, Saint Denis Parish,* 154; *Souvenir, Our Mother of Sorrows Parish,* 3; *Golden Jubilee, Gesu Parish,* 12; Cohalan, *Popular History,* 162.

36. *Souvenir, Our Mother of Sorrows Parish,* 5; "Papers Relating to the Church in America," *RACHSP,* 7 (1896): 348–349; James J. Green, "The Organization of the Catholic Total Abstinence Union of America, 1866–1884," *RACHSP,* 61 (1950): 80–88; Cohalan, *Popular History,* 78; Joseph C. Gibbs, *History of the Catholic Total Abstinence Union of America* (Phila., 1907), 206–208; *Historical Sketch of St. Francis Xavier's Parish* (Phila., 1939), 85; Joan Bland, *Hibernian Crusade: The Story of the Catholic Total Abstinence Union of America* (Wash., D.C., 1951); *Constitution of St. Augustine's Catholic Temperance Beneficial Society* (Phila., 1840); *Proceedings of the Twenty-Second General Convention of the C.T.A.U. of A.* (Phila., 1893), 14; *Souvenir of the Twentieth Anniversary of the Cathedral Total Abstinence Society* (Phila., 1893).

37. *Souvenir, Our Mother of Sorrows Parish,* 3; Gavigan, "Rise and Fall," 115–116; Cohalan, *Popular History,* 79.

38. *Historical Sketch, St. Francis Xavier Parish,* 81, 87; Gavigan, "Rise and Fall," 116.

39. Gavigan, "Rise and Fall," 116–117.

40. *The Constitution and Bylaws of the St. Augustine Reading Room Society of Philadelphia* (Phila., 1853); *Souvenir, Our Mother of Sorrows Parish,* 3, 5; *Historical Sketch, St. Francis Xavier Parish,* 83; *Historical Sketches,* xliv–xlviii.

41. Dolan, *Immigrant Church,* 79, 81; *Souvenir, Our Mother of Sorrows Parish,* 4; *Sesquicentennial, St. Denis Parish,* 82–83.

42. Such tangible objects of popular piety can be viewed in the Museum of Religious Americana at St. Charles Borromeo Seminary, Overbrook, Phila., Pa. On Frank Bierwirth, see Rev. James F. Betz, ed., *A History of St. Nicholas Church, Egg Harbor, N.J., 1858–1981* (1981), 5.

43. Cohalan, *Popular History,* 60, 74.

44. Quoted in Joseph L. Shannon, O.S.A., *Saint Joseph Parish, Greenwich, New York* (Granville, N.Y., 1978), 11–13.

45. Flynn, *History of St. John's Church, Newark,* 69–70.

46. On clerical influence over lay opinion regarding slavery and the Civil War, see Sister Mary Alphonsine Frawley, *Patrick Donahue* (Wash., D.C., 1946); Shaw, *Dagger John,* 344, 360–69; Hennessey, *American Catholics,* 147–151; Thomas F. Meehan,

"Archbishop Hughes and the Draft Riots," *USCHRS*, 1 (1899): 171–190; Albon P. Man, Jr., "The Church and the New York Draft Riots of 1863," *RACHSP*, 62 (Mar. 1951): 33–50; and James McCague, *The Second Rebellion: The Story of the New York City Draft Riots of 1863* (N.Y., 1968).

47. Dolan, *Immigrant Church*, 64–66.

48. Gavigan, "Rise and Fall," 129.

# CHAPTER TWO

# Expansion, 1880–1930

The parochial system that had been established in the Northeast by 1880 with such great exertions was denied a breathing space during the next fifty years. Indeed, a more hectic period ensued during these years as America experienced its largest immigration increases in all of its history, with 14,531,197 people arriving during the years 1901 to 1920 alone.

The lion's share of this immigration settled in the Northeast, with New York, Pennsylvania, Massachusetts, New Jersey, and Connecticut heading the list. Overall, Catholic population increased about 1.5 times faster than the population at large. That increase was even faster in rural New England and central Pennsylvania, where the Catholic population grew three times faster than the rest. Somewhat lower but still notable increases were registered in central New York State and in western Pennsylvania. Only the dioceses of New York and Brooklyn failed to keep pace with the great general population growth. Still, the largest numbers of Catholics in 1930 were to be found in the urban dioceses of New York, Boston, Brooklyn, Philadelphia, Newark, and Pittsburgh. Overall, the Northeast had become a region that was 29% Catholic by 1930.

It was not just the sheer numbers of newcomers that affected the parish system, but the places of origin of those immigrants. Whereas earlier Catholic immigrants had been chiefly Irish and German, the new immigrants were Polish, Hungarian, Slavic, and, particularly, southern Italians. The largest number of Italians and Poles went to New York and Pennsylvania, and the largest number of Slovaks, Croats, and Slovenians went to Pennsylvania. Massachusetts also received many Italians and Poles, but there the Irish continued to make up a large proportion of the newcomers. Thus, not only was a considerable augmentation in religious and social services required, either in the form of new parishes, schools, and organizations, or in the expansion of already existing plants, but Catholic parish life also had to adjust to the peculiar demands and needs of a bewildering array of unique immigrant groups.[1]

Between 1880 and 1930, 2,626 new parishes were opened in the Northeast, more than all the parishes founded in the region from 1730 to 1900. Thanks largely to the opening of diocesan seminaries, the supply of priests also increased. The 2,430 priests of 1880 had grown to 11,333 by 1930, with the largest increase (6,395) occurring after 1900. What this meant in terms of overall ratios was one

37

priest for every 881 people and an average parish size of 2,241. In other words, while the priest-to-people ratio had improved remarkably from the 1/1,164 of 1880, the average parish size had increased from 1,549.

As in the previous period, subregional comparisons reveal differential rates of development. Whereas there had been one priest for every 1,095 people in rural Maine, New Hampshire, and Vermont in 1880, fifty years later there was one for every 793. The average parish size had been reduced from 1,742 to 1,508. In the urban dioceses of New York and Brooklyn, the priest-to-people ratio had also improved, from 1/1,498 to 1/1,011, but average parish size had climbed from 2,888 to 3,569. In eastern Pennsylvania, the dioceses of Philadelphia, Scranton, and Harrisburg, which in 1880 had a priest-to-people ratio of 1/1,063, likewise saw an improvement to 1/729, but experienced only a moderate increase in average parish size, from 1,474 to 1,562. Boston saw a great improvement, 1/1,385 to 1/892, in the numbers of priests to people, but experienced an enormous expansion in average parish size, from 1,963 to 3,595. Of course, the abstract nature of these figures should be apparent when one considers, for example, that the city of Philadelphia in 1930 contained such widely different parishes as Holy Trinity with ninety-eight parishioners and St. Mary Magdalen de Pazzi with 15,950 parishioners. The overall trend is clear, however. Despite extraordinary efforts in the establishing of new parishes, the Catholic Church in the Northeast was not able to keep up with the increase in population. The Church was much more successful in recruiting more priests to administer to the people.[2]

In addition to the building of new churches to serve as the focal point of parish life, the building of parochial schools was a chief priority, especially after the exhortation of Baltimore in 1884. Between 1880 and 1930, 1,945 new parochial schools were opened in the Northeast, and the enrollments jumped from 181,072 pupils to 1,050,020. The largest system, with 288 schools and 124,679 pupils, was to be found in the Archdiocese of Philadelphia. By 1910, there were more children in Philadelphia's Catholic schools than in the public schools of all but a dozen cities. Other large parochial school systems developed in Pittsburgh, New York, and Brooklyn.[3]

Enormous progress had been made. The number of parishes that maintained schools jumped from 30% in 1880 to 56% in 1930, with the dioceses of Philadelphia (74%), Newark (70%), Brooklyn (69%), Harrisburg (67%), and Pittsburgh (65%) far ahead of the rest. Generally speaking, New England and north-central New York continued to lag behind. But when one looks at the percentage of Catholic children who were enrolled in parochial schools, it was in those latter areas that the greatest progress had been made. Overall in the Northeast, the percentage of Catholic children in parochial schools had risen from 25% to 42%, with Harrisburg (74%), Buffalo (69%), and Philadelphia (61%) heading the list. Still, less than half of all Catholic children were in parochial schools in the Northeast.

The growth that did occur was due principally to the ability of parishes to find sufficient teachers among the religious. By 1895, for example, ten of the ninety-eight schools in Philadelphia were staffed by brothers, and the remaining eighty-eight by six orders of religious women. Throughout the Northeast, the number of nuns increased from 6,779 in 1880 to 40,021 in 1930, and a considerable number of them found their way into parochial school teaching. The school system would never have expanded the way it did if parishes had had to staff their schools with lay teachers.[4]

Conditions in the parochial schools were not optimal by any means. The overall average student population of the schools increased from 322 in 1880 to 419 in 1930. In the Archdiocese of Boston, the average pupil density in 1930 was 647 and in Brooklyn it was 530, and large city parishes often had three times that number. Frequently, as many as a hundred boys and girls were crowded into a single classroom in the charge of a religious sister who more often than not had only a secondary school education herself. In an age of child labor, moreover, only about one-quarter of these children finished the eighth grade.[5]

Despite those conditions, supporters of the parochial school system were nearly frantic in their exhortations to Catholic parents to get their children out of the "world" and into the safe and correct environment of the parish school. One apologist in Brooklyn wrote in 1905:

> Catholic parent, do you send your child to a public school? Then you are a disobedient child to your mother the Church. . . . You are a traitor. You turn the brains and talents of your child to build up, to energize, to glorify a system of education which is truly the enemy of your child, the State, your religion and your God. . . . Let me ask you, would you allow your darling to enter the room of one dying of smallpox! "No," you say. Why not? Because of the danger of infection. Just so. You allow your child to breathe for five days of the week a moral atmosphere which if not infidel is at least un-Catholic. The public school stands for naturalism. The Catholic school stands for supernaturalism. How can you wonder if, after a short while, your child's soul and mind is filled with worldliness, the love of amusement, the thought only of this world and the almighty dollar, to the complete obliteration of spiritual ideals and heavenly thoughts.[6]

Parochial expansion in this period also meant providing new services for specific groups. In rural areas, Catholic growth led to the founding in 1905 of the Catholic Church Extension Society, which supplemented the activities of an organization begun in the 1890s, the American Catholic Missionary Union. By 1908, thirty mission bands of diocesan priests were involved in a ministry of outreach to neglected Catholic parishes as well as to others interested in Catholicism.[7]

Most attention, however, was of necessity devoted to those areas where Catholics were concentrated: in the cities. One example of the expansion of special services there was that instituted by Monsignor Luke J. Evers, pastor of St. Andrew's Parish in Manhattan. Seeing the need for a special Mass for the benefit of the printers who worked at night, he introduced a 2:30 A.M. Printers' Mass every Sunday. Rome still placed rigid limitations on the hours when Mass could be celebrated, but after four months of appeals, Evers' innovation was approved. It was an instant success, with attendance averaging about 1,400 every Sunday until the newspapers moved away from that area of the city, and it was soon copied in many other places.[8]

Of course, the largest special need to be dealt with involved the new ethnic groups from southern and eastern Europe, most of whom settled in the cities of the industrializing Northeast where there were expanding opportunities for unskilled laborers. Each group wanted its own parish where its language and customs would be preserved, even though in some cases the active part of the congregations formed were often smaller than would have justified the expense of creating entirely new parochial plants for them. Some groups introduced discordant elements into fairly well-established parochial practices, when their Old World habits of lay initiative confronted the by-now clergy-dominated system in America, or when Old World ethnic and political antagonisms prompted them to resist hierarchical—frequently seen as Irish—direction.

Whereas between 1850 and 1880 only 9% of the new parishes established in the Northeast were national parishes, between 1880 and 1930, 30% were national. Locally, the percentages could be much higher. In Manhattan, for example, 50% of the new parishes opened between 1902 and 1918 were national, and one-third of those were Italian. Similarly, in Philadelphia between 1897 and 1908, 51% of the new parishes were national, one-third of them being Polish.[9]

Poles emigrated to the Northeast bearing a long tradition of a nationalism closely identified with the Roman Catholic religion. The Catholic Church was the one institution common to all three of the eighteenth-century partitions, and it served to differentiate Poles from their mostly non-Catholic conquerors. Before 1880, Polish immigrants came principally from Prussian Poland, and the majority of them were craftsmen who were familiar with the German language spoken by many people in the United States. In their adopted country, they founded a large number of voluntary associations, like the Polish National Alliance and the Polish Roman Catholic Union, whose purposes were political, social, educational, and religious.[10]

The Poles who came to the Northeast after 1880, however, were mostly rural peasants from Russian Poland, and entered mostly unskilled jobs in American cities. They could not speak German, and, therefore, had a greater need to belong to parishes where they could hear sermons and make their confessions in Polish. Those who settled in Philadelphia, for example, had to travel between thirty-five and ninety-five miles each Sunday to attend Polish services in Trenton, New Jersey, Shenandoah, Pennsylvania, and Baltimore, Maryland. In 1882, they organized and raised money for the building of a Polish church in Philadelphia. They petitioned Archbishop Wood who sent them Rev. Julian Dutkiewicz from Brooklyn. At first, Polish language services were held in the basement of the German church of St. Boniface, but, by 1890, the Polish parishioners had raised the $75,000 needed to build their own St. Laurentius Church in the northern part of the city. Shortly, thereafter, they built a rectory and the first Polish parochial school in Philadelphia. By 1910, there were seven Polish parishes in the city of Philadelphia.[11]

Wherever one looks into the history of parish development, the Poles stand out in their enthusiasm and sacrifice as great builders of parishes and parish institutions. The Poles who immigrated to Pittsfield, Massachusetts, in the 1890s to work in the woolen mills there, at first attended the "Irish" church of St. Charles. The pastor there, Father Dower, was very popular, and the Poles in his congregation responded by enthusiastically supporting him in building a new larger church, even buying bricks for 25¢ each when their average weekly earnings in the mills were only $10. When the new church was completed in 1900, Polish Masses were said in the basement once each Sunday, and Father Dower brought in a Polish missionary for missions and confessions two or three times a year.

By 1913, the Poles at St. Charles, through their voluntary associations, had petitioned and received their own parish centered around the Immaculate Conception Chapel of the Mother of God. A Ladies' Rosary Society was formed to aid in the raising of funds for books, church items, and vestments. Both men and women of the Polish community assisted in the carpentry and plastering, made vestments, and contributed generously to paying off the debt. Masses were said in the chapel daily throughout the 1920s, but on Sundays many of the Polish parishioners still had to attend St. Charles because the chapel could not hold them all. So the Poles once again got to work, completing by 1924 a new larger church of their own, Holy Family. There, the parishioners contributed their time to teach the children their Roman Catholic religion and their Polish language and history three times a week. For the Poles of Pittsfield, as elsewhere, their religion was inseparable from their nationality.[12]

As in the case of earlier parish formation, lay initiative was significant among the Poles. Like the Germans in the 1840s, Polish laymen frequently incorporated themselves and built churches even before consulting the bishop. But the post-1880 period was a time when, at least from the episcopal point of view, the evils of lay control had been effectively laid to rest. When a new Polish parish was established, therefore, the parish committee was required to surrender title to the church property to the bishop. Only after the transfer would the bishop allow several laymen to serve on a board of trustees, in which clerics normally had the majority of votes.[13]

Lay dissidence in Polish parishes was often a combination of personality conflicts and lay desire for more control of parish affairs than was allowed in the American system. Such tensions led in 1892 to the forced resignation of two priests at St. Stanislaus Parish in Philadelphia and the withdrawal of several parishioners into a schismatic church. A similar dispute at St. Adalbert's Parish in Buffalo in 1895 also resulted in the creation of an independent church. When that schismatic parish's clerical leader deserted them the following year, Father Anthony Kozlowski—who had formed the Polish Catholic Church in America out of a schism in Chicago—arrived and attempted to install two of his priests in the parish. They were, in turn, ousted by Father Stephan Kaminski who had formed the competing Polish Catholic Independent Church in America.

Another independent Polish denomination arose in Scranton around the same time as the dissension in Buffalo. The rapid influx of Poles into upstate Pennsylvania had created an urgent need for Polish priests, which Bishop William O'Hara could not always meet to the satisfaction of some laymen who took it upon themselves to hire itinerant immigrant priests. At the Polish Parish of the Nativity in Plymouth, this practice led to the lay hiring and firing of six priests in as many years.

At Sacred Heart Parish in Scranton, the pastor, Father Richard Aust, who was generally regarded as progressive by most Poles, was denounced in 1896 by a group of his parishioners as a tyrant. Complaining of a lack of democracy at Sacred Heart, they seceded from the parish and established St. Stanislaus just a few hundred feet from their former church. They appointed as their pastor, Father Francis Hodur, who had just arrived from Nanticoke where he had led a group of dissidents in forming Holy Trinity congregation out of St. Stanislaus Parish there. Hodur's demands that the property of St. Stanislaus in Scranton be held and administered by the congregation and that the laity have a voice in clerical appointments were rejected by Bishop O'Hara as the old evils of lay trusteeism. On being excommunicated in 1898, Hodur founded the weekly Polish newspaper *Straz* through which he attacked the bishop, the Irish in general, and the bishop's "Polish-Irish" supporters.

In the midst of all this turmoil, Hodur went to Buffalo to compete for control of Father Stephan Kaminski's home parish, apparently at the request of an anti-Kaminski faction. He was unsuccessful in this attempt, and he returned to Scranton where he gradually exerted his control over five small independent congregations. These became the core of the Polish National Catholic Church, which by 1907 had absorbed all of Kozlowski's and Kaminski's parishes.[14]

Other eastern European groups proved equally unruly. Large numbers of Slovak, Hungarian, and Lithuanians immigrated to America where they took jobs in the coal mines of northeastern Pennsylvania. Greek Ruthenians began coming to the Northeast after 1879, principally to Pennsylvania. The first church of the Byzantine rite in America, St. Michael's in Shenandoah, Pennsylvania, was founded in 1885, largely at the instigation of Ruthenian laymen. Among all the eastern European groups, quarrels were frequent, especially where one ethnic group was forced to worship in a parish controlled by another ethnic group.[15]

At St. Stephen's Hungarian Parish in Plymouth, Pennsylvania, Slovak parishioners in 1889 ordered their priest, Father Joseph Kosalko, to leave the parish because he was a "Magyarone." This was a term given to Slovak clergymen who opposed all manifestations of Slovak nationalism, working instead for the assimilation of Slovaks by the Hungarians. Kosalko duly left, became rector of St. Joseph's Hungarian Parish in Hazleton for a short time, returned to St. Stephen's between 1893 and 1898, and then took up a position at St. John Nepomucene Parish in Bridgeport, Connecticut.

At St. John's, Kosalko was no more popular among his Slovak parishioners than he had been at St. Stephen's, rejecting their requests for a parochial school where their children could study Slovak. This time, however, it was the dissidents, not Kosalko, who departed, and received permission from the Bishop of Hartford, Michael Tierney, to establish their own parish, which was named Saints Cyril and Methodius.

Advertisements for a priest for the new parish brought the Slovaks Father Matthew Jankola in 1907. Very popular with his new flock, Father Jankola had not always been so. While at St. Joseph's Parish in Hazleton, Pennsylvania, he had decided to downgrade the role of the church organist merely to playing the organ and no longer teaching in the parochial school. This dual role was common in Polish parishes as well. Some of the organist's friends, however, decided to show their displeasure with the decision by bombing the rectory. Father Jankola left town as quickly as possible and was happy to take up the advertised position in Bridgeport.

Father Jankola became so well liked at Saints Cyril and Methodius that when he died in 1916, his successor, Father Gaspar Panik—selected by the Bishop of Hartford and not by the parishioners—was rejected by them. When the bishop refused to replace him, one hundred women of the parish marched on the rectory, broke down the door, and chased Father Panik and his few friends up into the attic where they barricaded themselves. After the mob had ransacked the rectory, the police intervened and arrested several of the women. Father Panik remained in the parish, but in a very subdued role.

Sometimes, as in the Polish cases, these internal parochial disputes ended in schism. In 1909, for example, Slovaks at St. Michael's Parish in Homestead, Pennsylvania, whose request for the removal of their pastor was refused by the Bishop of Pittsburgh, withdrew and formed their own St. Anne's Independent Slovak Catholic Church, which eventually became affiliated with the Polish National Catholic Church. Slovaks in Passaic, New Jersey, excommunicated because of parochial dissension, established an Independent Czechoslovak Church in 1924. Similarly, internal conflicts and quarrels with the Latin hierarchy led, by 1914, to the defection of about 43,000 Ruthenian Catholics into the Russian Orthodox Church.[16]

A somewhat different model of ethnic demand on the parochial system is presented by the French-Canadians. Although not a new immigrant group, they began pouring into the Northeast in greater numbers after 1885. When economic depression hit Canada between 1920 and 1924, 525,000 Canadians entered the region. Unlike the eastern Europeans, however, the French already had many established national parishes, and in the late nineteenth and early twentieth centuries, there was still a desire among many of the French to retain religious and cultural contacts with their past. Around 1900, for instance, the French-speaking people of North Uxbridge and Linwood, Massachusetts, expressed a desire for a parish of their own. At that time, they were members of St. Mary's in Uxbridge, or St. Patrick's in Whitinsville. A lay group, La Societe des Artisans, began to organize and plan for the future. By 1904, they were worshiping separately in an old electric power house. There, the founding pastor of what had become Good Shepherd Parish stretched a board across two barrels to serve as an altar. A choir and a small pump organ played by the pastor's sister provided the musical accompaniment, of which the French were so fond. Soon, land was given to the congregation by the Whitin Cotton Mills, where many of the parishioners worked, and a church building was completed in 1907. By 1921, a convent and a school had been added.[17]

There were some unique pressures on the French of New England. Their relations with the Irish, because of job competition, had never been very cordial. By 1893, the French, who had formerly been Democrats, shifted to the Republican Party in opposition to the Irish. On the other side, the Irish complained of the increasing religious and political influence of the French in New England, and their antipathy was in no way assuaged when Quebec nationalist, Louis La Fleche, Bishop of Trois-Rivieres, prophesied that New England would ultimately be annexed to Quebec. Also, in 1884 the French Protestant Society had been founded in Lowell, Massachusetts, to prey upon French discontents and to persuade them to leave Catholicism. Moreover, many parish mutual benefit societies founded to protect French ethnicity and religion were beginning to lose members to English-language associations.

To combat these outside influences, many French-Canadian immigrants insisted on more national parishes. In the 1890s, the French of North Brookfield, Massachusetts, began petitioning for a parish of their own. Diocesan authorities, however, felt that the Irish priest at St. Joseph's spoke French adequately enough to minister to them. In 1891, Bishop Beaven of Springfield did make the concession of appointing a French-Canadian priest at St. Joseph's, but the French parishioners remained unsatisfied. They wanted their own separate church, and in 1899 they began supporting their own choice, Father John A. Berger. This so angered diocesan authorities that, henceforth, they forbade the establishment of a French parish in North Brookfield. The French, however, unlike the Poles or the Slovaks, never thought of schism as an acceptable alternative.

By comparison, when in 1907 a mere three French-Canadians from the North End of Springfield petitioned this same Bishop Beaven for a new French parish, he readily acquiesced, and St. Thomas Aquinas Parish was established within a year. By the end of 1908, there had been erected a combination chapel-school, and in 1913 a rectory was purchased. In 1919, a separate church building was completed and by 1928, a new school.[18]

The Italians provide a third model for consideration. Before 1880, the Italians who came to the Northeast originated in northern Italy, learned the English language quickly, and intermarried with native-Americans. After 1880, when the Italians became the largest single ethnic group immigrating to America, they were mostly from southern Italy, poor, and illiterate. Three-quarters of them were men who were either unmarried or who came without their families in the hope of earning enough money to send for them. Most were unskilled workers who came under contract to work in American industry and on the railroads. Many were shamefully taken advantage of under the "padrone" system, or by employers who included some of their own compatriots.

The Italians were different from other groups. For one, a large number of them were "birds of passage." Between 1911 and 1920, for example, an astonishing 82% of them returned to Italy. Second, they were more clannish than either the French or the Poles. This was due to their traditional fondness for social life, the lack of means to enter mainstream culture, and their sensitivity to ridicule. Moreover, while an Italian would do anything for his "paesano," a person who came from the same area of Italy, he was generally antagonistic to other Italians. Northern and Southern Italian dialects were so different that Italians from these areas could scarcely converse with one another. The Italians, therefore, settled together in sharply segregated village groups, venerated their own local saints, intermarried, and belonged to the same benevolent societies.

Another special feature of the Italian immigrants was the indifference or strong hostility shown by many of them to the Catholic Church. They came from an Italy pervaded by doctrines of Materialism, Socialism, and Masonry. Anti-clericalism ran high because the clergy appeared as anti-nationalistic after Italian unification. Church attendance came to be seen as an occupation suitable for women only. Italian men might still go to church to be married, to have their children baptized, or to be buried, but the parish had very little other meaning for them. When they came to America, they found, not one priest for every 370 parishioners (the average in Italy), but two or three priests for 25,000 parishioners. In Philadelphia, for example, there was only one Italian parish, St. Mary Magdalen de Pazzi, before 1897. This parish could not handle a parochial population approaching 50,000, and it was feared that many of them would be lured away from Catholicism by rather aggressive Protestant proselytizing efforts. Therefore, Our Lady of Good Counsel Parish was formed, which took in 25,000 Italian parishioners in the western part of the city. By 1900, the parish had grown to 32,000 people, and 3,000 children attended its school.

In the thirty years following the establishment of Our Lady of Good Counsel, just about one new Italian parish was created every year in Philadelphia. It seems that in the case of the Italians, diocesan authorities did everything in their power to provide increased services to these new immigrants. A very large percentage of requests for church improvement loans by Italian pastors was granted readily.

Many of these new churches were built, decorated, and repaired by the Italian parishioners themselves, but there did not seem to be the same insistence on national parishes as there was among the eastern Europeans or the French. Although the Italians were urged to attend their own national parishes, as they expanded in numbers they began going to other churches usually begun by the Irish. Many of these parishes eventually became predominantly Italian, although not national. This often caused friction with the pastors of the national parishes who argued that, because of the poverty of the Italians, they needed as many parishioners as possible for survival.

Part of the reason for this development was that as the older immigrant groups began experiencing greater social mobility, they began moving out from the older parishes, thereby creating a parochial vacuum that was filled by the newer and poorer Italians. Another reason was that many of the older Catholics were not pleased with the Italians, whom they regarded as a burden instead of a reinforcement—much as they themselves had been regarded in the 1840s and 1850s by the more established Catholics. The Italians were looked down upon, being called a variety of derogatory names, and their appearance on a block of houses caused others to move away. This opened up new spaces to accommodate the crush of Italian immigration, but it further enhanced their clannishness. Every major city developed its Little Italy. Many of the Irish, Germans, and Poles, moreover, who had suffered so much for their religion in the Old Country, were disconcerted and scandalized by the lax Italian attitude toward the Catholic Church.[19]

The first decades of the twentieth-century also saw the beginning of an influx of Hispanic people into the northeastern United States. Their greatest impact would be felt much later, but already in 1902 there was a Spanish national parish, Our Lady of Guadalupe, in New York City. In 1912, Our Lady of the Miraculous Medal Parish opened in Philadelphia at the same time that Our Lady of Esperanza was founded in New York. As Hispanics began arriving in larger numbers in Harlem, the Milagrosa Church was opened by the Spanish Vincentians in 1926.

Another group, the Portuguese, moved mainly into southern New England. Many of them came from the Azores, and most of them established themselves as deep-sea fishermen. By 1930, there were twelve Portuguese parishes in the Diocese of Fall River and three in the Diocese of Providence.[20]

In this period another type of "national" parish developed for which language could not be used as a reason for founding, although many other factors could. This was the black parish. In Philadelphia, most blacks had settled in the southeastern corner of the city and worshiped, probably in segregated pews, at the old parishes of St. Joseph's, St. Mary's, and St. Augustine's. In 1886, Holy Trinity, the German parish, reserved a Mass on Sundays solely for blacks. There, the black parishioners organized themselves into a society called the St. Peter Claver Union, sponsored by the pastor, Father Hilterman. When Hilterman was transferred, the Union stopped meeting at the church and began meeting on Sunday evenings in the members' homes.

When the Union members petitioned for a parish of their own, the Archbishop told them he had no priest available; but Katharine Drexel, when she heard of their desire, convinced the Holy Ghost Fathers of Pittsburgh to send a priest. She also sent money to buy a school building to be staffed by the School Sisters of Notre Dame. When an Irishman, Patrick Quinn, died and left $5,000 to the "Colored Catholics of Philadelphia," the money was used to build St. Peter Claver Church in 1889.

Katharine Drexel was also instrumental in founding the second black parish in Philadelphia, Our Lady of the Blessed Sacrament, in 1909. Two years later, St. Catharine's was established in the Germantown section. As in the case of St. Peter Claver, the initiative was taken by black laymen. In a letter to Archbishop Ryan, they complained of racial prejudice in the various churches where they worshiped. In one of the churches, the Blessed Mother Sodality had voted to exclude blacks. The petitioners also pointed out that despite their earnest desire to have their children receive a Catholic education, the parochial schools in Germantown shunned them. Even though these Germantown blacks had formed a society to raise funds to build a church, each member paying 25¢ a month, Archbishop Ryan at first replied that the diocese did not have the funds to allow the creation of another black parish. Within a few months, however, a mission for the blacks in Germantown was under way. By 1930, there were a total of four black parishes in Philadelphia.

In New York, the first parish for black Catholics, St. Benedict the Moor in Greenwich Village, was established in 1883. This parish moved to West 53rd Street in 1898, but by 1925 it was no longer in the center of the black community, which had moved to Harlem. The 1920s had seen a sharp increase in the black population of most major cities of the Northeast. As in the case of the Italians, as the blacks moved in the whites moved out. The growth in Harlem by 87,417 new blacks was more than matched by the departure of 118,792 whites. To meet the demands of this shift in population, Cardinal Hayes transferred Monsignor Thomas M. O'Keefe from St. Benedict's to St. Charles Borromeo on West 141st Street in 1925. Hayes encouraged the new pastor to raise funds for St. Charles from other parishes if he could—an expedient to which the pastors of Italian parishes often had to resort—but he let it be known that he could expect no direct assistance from the Archdiocese. As in most of the black parishes established in the Northeast during this period, the poverty of the parishioners made progress difficult.[21]

In a sense, then, the conditions from 1850 to 1880 were reproduced in the

48 History of the Catholic Parish in the Northeast

following period with only the names changed. The need for new parishes was still in evidence with continued immigration. The demand for separate parishes based on ethnicity was still heavy, only now the petitioners were Poles, Italians, or blacks. Once again, lay initiative in the forming of parishes was significant, and once again lay trusteeism presented the clergy with challenges to its well-established authority.

As in the preceding period also, not all of the pressures on the parochial system originated from within. The combination of rapid socio-economic changes and the massive influx of foreign Catholics into the Northeast contrived once again to give rise to a period of nativist hostility. In the 1880s, a Committee of One Hundred was formed in Boston that flooded the country with anti-Catholic documents. Newspapers, like the *Menace,* appeared bent on exposing the errors of Popery, and one of them printed an alleged Papal Bull calling for the massacre of all Protestants in 1893. Patriotic Societies—pressure groups within each of the two major political parties—were formed, and secret fraternal organizations, designed to protect American culture from ethnic pollution, became popular. The American Protective Association, founded in 1893, had its members pledge neither to vote for nor employ Catholics. Various states in the Northeast passed laws that threatened to close off economic opportunity to Catholic immigrants by prohibiting them from working on state and local public works, by imposing literacy tests, or by deducting special taxes from their wages. New York, in 1908, required aliens to pay $20 for a hunting license that cost only $1 for American citizens. A little later, Pennsylvania entirely prohibited aliens from hunting and from possessing shotguns, rifles, or dogs. In two counties of Massachusetts, it became a crime for aliens to pick wild berries or flowers except on their own property. The Ku Klux Klan reemerged in 1915 to keep America "Native, white, and Protestant," and by 1925 its membership reached five million.

After years of individual persecutions of the newcomers, these nativist groups were eventually successful in obtaining what they considered the cure-all for urban, industrial America's ills. In 1924, they succeeded in having an act passed that established national-origins' quotas for immigration, which effectively reduced the influx into America of people from southern and eastern Europe.[22]

It was in this context of the internal needs created by immigration and assimilation and the external pressures from hostile nativism that parish life flourished and expanded. More and more parish societies were founded, and both old and new organizations took on a more social or entertaining aspect. The old temperance societies, and the new ones like the Young Men's and Young Women's Catholic Associations founded in the 1880s, flourished at least until the 1920s. But now they began to include classes in penmanship, reading, elocution, dressmaking, millinery, history, and literature. They sponsored baseball teams, and their meeting halls were often equipped with bowling alleys, gymnasiums, parlors, baths, amusement rooms, and halls for public entertainments.[23]

Catholic Clubs became popular by the first decade of the twentieth century. These were organizations providing places of relaxation and recreation for men. Some developed sports programs and presented theatrical entertainments like minstrel shows. Boy Scouts, Girl Scouts, various military battalions, athletic teams for boys and girls, and Friday night dances for the youth all became regular facets of parish life.

Most parishes still maintained beneficial and benevolent societies. Catholic Clubs were considered beneficial societies. In Polish parishes, the society usually took the name of a saint or Polish national hero, and religious and patriotic holidays were celebrated by the organization with assemblies and parades. The members were required to speak the Polish language at their meetings, and official records were kept in Polish. The Knights of St. Casimir began as a military organization that met to discuss prospects for Polish independence and to be militarily prepared to assist in the overthrow of foreign domination of the homeland. They were active in the social life of the parish, and with the establishment of an independent Poland in 1919, the military aspect of the society was discontinued. Polish Beneficial Associations, usually taking the name of a patron saint, provided sickness insurance and death benefits to members. Ruthenian parishes had a similar organization, called Provydinia (Providence).

In Italian parishes, originally religious societies like St. Peter Celestine, St. Salvatore, St. Rocco, St. Blase, Our Lady of Mount Carmel, St. Anthony, and Blessed Gerard Magella eventually became chartered beneficial societies that celebrated the annual feast day of the patron with feasting and the elaborate procession of the patron's statue through the streets.[24]

The popular education movement founded on the Chatauqua model found its way into many parishes. Reading circles and literary institutes were to be found everywhere, but by World War I, most of them had become more social than intellectual, putting on minstrel shows, "smokes and eats," and sporting events.[25]

Popular religious societies proliferated. Parish records indicate an increase in the percentage of the congregations that belonged to Altar and Rosary Societies, Sodalities, Purgatorian Societies, and the various Archconfraternities. Some new societies were also on the parish scene. The Pious Union of Our Virgin Mother of Good Counsel was a worldwide organization bound together by a spiritual tie of mutual assistance through prayer. Each member had to recite three Hail Mary's daily and had to have exposed to view in their homes a picture of Our Virgin Mother of Good Counsel. Members of the Archconfraternity of St. Augustine wore a leather cincture, or girdle, as an emblem of chastity, recited thirteen Our Father's and Hail Mary's every day, and participated in all the spiritual privileges granted to laypeople in connection with the Order of St. Augustine. Members of the Third Order of St. Francis professed themselves after a triduum, and at churches where this order was established, anyone visiting the church on a certain day could gain what was called a Portiuncula indulgence.

Parish conferences of the St. Vincent de Paul Society doubled in number between 1880 and 1900. This was a time of periodic economic depression, and the parish societies were kept busy putting on various entertainments whose proceeds aided the poor. In some parishes, the society established day nurseries during the Great Depression years after 1929. Frequently, ladies' auxiliaries, known as the Ladies' Guild, were formed and provided entertainments and amusements for members as well as making clothing for the poor.[26]

With the increase in parish populations and the increase in the number of priests in each parish, the schedule of Masses increased. For example, at the Mission Church Parish in Boston in 1906, there were 5:30, 7, 8:30, 9, 9:30, 10:30 (High), and 11 A.M. Masses on Sunday and weekday Masses at 5:30, 6, 7, and 8 A.M. Innovations included having multiple Masses at the same time, if the parish had an upper and a lower church, and the reservation of one Mass on Sunday, usually around 9 A.M., exclusively for the parochial school children. At these children's Masses, cards were punched to prove attendance. The Sunday High Mass became an elaborate affair, where in some parishes, the ushers wore morning suits and white carnations. Funeral Masses were almost always held at 9 A.M. Funerals without Masses were still conducted, usually in a basement church or chapel.

Nearly all parishes continued to conduct Sunday School or Catechism Class—after 1884 using the standardized Baltimore Catechism—on Sunday afternoon, although more frequently now it was held after the earlier children's Mass. Various combinations of Vespers, Benediction, and Rosary services were held on Sunday afternoons and evenings, and in the evenings of Holy Days of Obligation and First Fridays. Confessions were heard at a variety of times. In 1891, at Sacred Heart Parish in Worcester, Massachusetts, confessions were heard every morning before Mass. At the Mission Church Parish in the same city, they were heard on Fridays, Saturdays, the eves of Holy Days, and Thursdays before First Fridays between 3 and 6, and between 7:30 and 10 P.M., on Wednesdays between 3 and 6, and after services on Sunday evenings.

By the 1920s, the last Mass on Sunday was being moved to 12:30 or 1 P.M., High Masses were becoming less frequent, and Vespers practically disappeared. Other practices, like the "churching" of women who had borne children in lawful wedlock, were continued, but they had become voluntary.[27]

By all admissions, the most important season of the parish year continued to be Lent. In the days before Ash Wednesday, fat days were observed. It was the carnival period, especially among the new immigrants, with much dancing, gaiety, and feasting. Some immigrant groups observed empty days, just before

Lent began, during which a dance or play would be held in the parish hall, followed by a community meal.

During the somber and penitential time of Lent, when many immigrants wore dark clothing unadorned with ribbons and jewelry, and when every Catholic observed the fast and abstinence regulations, various parish groups and religious associations were entitled to gain Plenary Indulgences by receiving the Sacraments of Penance and the Eucharist, visiting the church, and praying for the intention of the Holy Father. Separate feast days for this were set aside for members of the Archconfraternity of the Holy Family and the Purgatorian Society—both of which could obtain indulgences applicable to souls in Purgatory—the League of the Sacred Heart, those engaged in regular works of charity and in teaching Christian doctrine, and those who wore the Blue Scapular of the Immaculate Conception, the Black Scapular of the Seven Dolors, and the Brown Scapular of Our Lady of Mount Carmel.

Everyone was encouraged to attend daily Mass during Lent. The parish children would often attend before going to school. At Mass they would usually receive Communion, which meant they would have nothing to eat all morning until lunchtime at school. It was seen as a form of penance to cleanse themselves of sin. Meat was not allowed on Wednesdays and Fridays, and people, young and old alike, fasted and "gave up" some food or activity they especially liked as another form of penance.

Lenten services were held on Wednesday and Friday evenings, and a special session for school children was held in the afternoons. The priest and altar boys would walk slowly around the church, stopping at each station on the wall, carrying a cross and candles. Prayers would be said at each stop with the congregation answering the priest's recitation. All would sing "At the Cross my station keeping, I stand mournful, sadly weeping" as the procession moved on to the next station. When the stations were completed, the rosary was said, or the Latin prayers and song recited—*Pange Lingua* and *Tantum Ergo*.

Halfway through the Lenten season, the statues in church would be draped with purple cloths to represent sorrow for Our Lord. This was the beginning of Passion week. The following week, starting with Palm Sunday, Holy Week began, during which people fasted by eating no meat at all. During this week, immigrant groups followed the old practice of cleaning their houses from top to bottom, and of preparing various ethnic food dishes that would be blessed by the priest on Holy Saturday. Eastern Europeans prepared elaborately decorated eggs. They were a symbol of fertility because a new and living creature emerged from a seemingly dead object. It represented for them the rock tomb out of which Christ emerged to the New Life of his Resurrection.

On Palm Sunday, everyone dressed in their best attire. Palms were distributed to the parishioners during the Mass. These palms had been purchased by the pastor and blessed. Many parishioners braided the palms and placed them over a holy picture in their houses where they would remain until the following year. Other palms were made into the form of a cross and pinned on the lapel of a coat or suit. In Europe, in medieval times, palms were believed to have power to drive away demons, lightning, diseases and the "evil eye," and were placed in every corner of the home.

Maundy Thursday services included the priest washing the feet of twelve altar boys or parishioners, symbolic of Christ washing his disciples' feet at the Last Supper. The altar was stripped, the organ stilled, the candles were extinguished, one by one, and the church grew darker. The last one, representing Christ, was carried behind the altar at the end of the services, and the congregation silently left the church. A vigil was kept by the people, meditating about Christ's Last Supper and Agony in Gethsemane. Altar boys would be dressed in their cassocks and girls in their white Holy Communion dresses and veils, standing watch, as Peter was to have done.

On Good Friday, there was the Personification Mass at which the tabernacle door was left open and the light in the sanctuary extinguished. In the afternoon there was Stations of the Cross, and in the evening a sermon and Veneration of the Cross. At this service, a large wooden crucifix was placed at the foot of the altar and people approached it, genuflected three times, and kissed its feet. The entire day was quiet, and from noon to 3 P.M., no one spoke. People prayed the Rosary or Stations of the Cross at home, or attended church services.

On Holy Saturday, people would bring their food to the church to be blessed, or, in some parishes, the priest would visit each home to do that and would usually be presented with a gift of money. In the evening, there was the blessing of the fire and water. Parishioners were given jars of holy water to take home, baptismal vows were renewed, and the Paschal Candle was prepared and lighted.

The Easter Vigil Mass was often said at midnight, but more often at 6 P.M. The fast ended at this time, but everyone waited for the Easter morning meal, following the early Resurrection Mass at 6 A.M. The purple cloths were stripped dramatically from the statues, all the candles in the church were lighted, and once again bells and organ music filled the church. It was an intensely emotional event, a catharsis after the weeks of denial and mourning, and in the glittering ornate churches that the new immigrants had built, it was a far cry from the plain and simple liturgies of the earlier period.[28]

Probably the second most important season in parish life was the month of May, a time when the mother of God was honored in a variety of ways. At some parishes, the Rosary was recited every evening of the month, children under six were enrolled in Sodalities of the Infant Jesus and of the Holy Angels, and special indulgences could be earned by visiting the parish church twelve times and praying for "Concord among Christian Princes, the Extirpation of Heresy, the Conversion of Sinners, and the Exaltation of Holy Mother Church." Every parish had a special May devotion, with the culminating event being the May Procession, at which young boys and girls, dressed in a variety of uniforms and carrying flowers, marched around the church and placed a crown on a statue of Mary.[29]

Under the encouragement of Pope Leo XIII, recitation of the Rosary became more common, with some parishes forming Confraternities of the Rosary. October became the special month of the Rosary, and all Catholics were urged to bring their beads to Mass, thus creating a practice that would later be heavily criticized.

Holy Hours of Adoration became popular. In 1903, the Nocturnal Adoration Society held its first meeting at St. Jean Baptiste Church in Manhattan, under the auspices of the Blessed Sacrament Fathers. In 1906, the first noonday devotions ever held in this country began at St. Peter's in New York City. Novenas continued to attract many, and the cult of the Eucharist was strengthened by bringing in the Reparatrice Nuns from Italy in 1910 and the Sacramentine Nuns from France in 1911. Closed retreats for laymen began in 1909 and were common by the 1920s. Devotions to St. Thérèse of Lisieux spread widely after her canonization in 1925. Shrines to Our Lady of Lourdes were begun in some parishes in the early 1900s, and the water from the Grotto became an object of demand.[30]

Many churches enshrined relics of saints. Often, it became the practice to venerate them every Sunday after the recitation of the Rosary. At the foot of the statues of saints in some churches, boxes were placed into which a parishioner could drop an intention for a Mass, plus an offering of money. Vigil lights for a variety of intentions were also available. One devotion, known as St. Anthony's Bread, consisted in praying to this saint for "favors spiritual and temporal," and, in return for any favor received, making an offering of money to buy bread for the poor. Another practice was that of St. Nicholas' Bread. Blessed loaves were distributed on the Feast of St. Nicholas of Tolentine, September 10th, and in order to make use of the bread as a remedy for sickness, one had to grate part of it into water while reciting certain prayers.[31]

Benedictions of the Blessed Sacrament became more frequent, often being given every Sunday after Vespers, at the First Friday Mass, on the eve of Holy Days, every morning during the Octave of Corpus Christi, every evening during October, and on Sunday evenings at the meetings of the League of the Sacred Heart, the Children of Mary, and the Rosary Society. Parish missions for adults and children were spread by religious orders like the Jesuits, Redemptorists, Paulists, and Vincentians. During these and the Forty Hours' Devotion, where the Blessed Sacrament was exposed for veneration, Plenary Indulgences could be obtained by making a good confession and Communion and praying for the intentions of the Holy Father.[32]

Nearly every parish in the Northeast spent considerable time and energy in attempting to manage its financial debt, often at considerable sacrifice to both priests and people. Depending upon the particular circumstances of parish age, population, ethnic composition, or the stage of physical development, these constantly rising expenses originated from a variety of sources, but they generally had to do with the construction or expansion of a church or school. At the old West Philadelphia parish of Our Mother of Sorrows (1852), the debt on church property increased from $16,400 in 1900 to $517,235 in 1930. Holy Child Parish in the Oak Lane section of Philadelphia was established in 1909, but by 1930, it too had accumulated a staggering debt, $902,400, which kept on rising.[33]

The financial and human struggles of some of these new parishes are perhaps best illustrated with one out of many examples. In 1907, Father Joseph Kirlin was appointed to establish a new parish to accommodate the growing numbers of Catholics in the north central part of Philadelphia. A plot of land for this Most Precious Blood Parish was purchased for $45,000, and the pastor had to rent a room in an office building in which to celebrate Sunday Mass. Later, he rented a garage for $70 a month and converted it into a chapel. When a real chapel was finally constructed, plans for adding two floors for a school had to be abandoned for financial reasons. There were initially 500 families in Most Precious Blood, but in 1911, people living outside its boundaries petitioned for inclusion in the new parish because they lived too far from other churches. When the boundaries were extended, parish population more than doubled. Since a school was now imperative, construction of a rectory had to be abandoned. The parish priests had to continue living in congested and unhealthy rented accommodations, which, added to the mounting financial worries, probably contributed to Father Kirlin's nervous breakdown in 1915. The following year, two ten-room houses had to be purchased and converted into a convent for the sisters teaching in the school, so completion of a rectory was delayed until 1917. It was not until 1928 that a permanent church building was opened. Along the way, and despite the expansion in parish population, the parish faced the years of the Great Depression with a debt of $219,690.[34]

A variety of methods was used by which parishes financed their growing debts: pew rents, plate collections, special collections, proceeds from funerals or loans, donations, and association dues. Each parish differed in the proportion of total receipts derived from each of these sources, and the proportions changed over time. In general, however, by 1930 the proportion of revenue derived from pew rents and funerals had gone down, while that derived from special collections had increased. This may have indicated that the increasing amounts contributed by increasing populations, which would have been reflected in pew rents, plate collections, and perhaps funerals, proved insufficient to keep up with the cost of expanding parochial plants. Consequently, more appeals in the form of special collections had to be initiated. In any case, pew rents had always been difficult to collect, and the amount in arrears proved to be a constant source of frustration to pastors.[35]

Laymen, however, were always in the forefront in organizing extraordinary fund-raising projects that took the form of Building Fund Societies, Church Improvement Societies, and Church Debt Associations, membership in which often carried some spiritual benefit.[36] In some parishes, like Holy Innocents in Philadelphia founded in 1927, collaboration between priest and people was perfect. There, every working person gave $100 to pay off the ground debt, and pledged $1.25 each week to meet interest payments and reduce the debt on the chapel as well as provide for current expenses. In return, the pastor refused any salary until the parish was financially in the black, and he agreed to live without expense to the parish during his whole tenure as pastor.[37] Such agreements, of course, were possible only in rare parishes. Ordinarily, priests and people were kept busy with a full round of card parties, picnics, fairs, and other fund-raising expedients.[38]

At one "lawn fete" at Our Lady Star of the Sea Parish in Atlantic City, New Jersey, the main fund-raising attraction was a canary bird booth. More than 250 "canaries" were sold each night for a week, even though there was some skepticism among the purchasers as to the pedigree of the birds. In answer to certain charges that the canaries were nothing more than yellow-dyed sparrows, the men in the booth, with tongue in cheek, asserted that they were special Rocky Mountain canaries. Some months after the carnival, one woman parishioner approached a member of the carnival committee with the complaint that her canary would not, or could not, sing. She was told, "Wait, my dear lady, until he grows up; your canary is too young to sing." Despite the fact that in subsequent years not one of the canaries was ever known to have sung or warbled a note, most of the purchasers good-naturedly accepted the ruse for the benefit of the parish.[39]

Italian parishes were somewhat unique in that these most recent of immigrants were not accustomed to contributing to the support of churches, schools, and other parish institutions. In Italy, these had all been endowed. Consequently, Italian priests in America were forced to beg for money in the "Irish" churches. The money that was forthcoming from these sources, and from the non-Italians in his own parish, often had the unfortunate result that the parish priest neglected to build up among his Italian parishioners the spirit and morale that would create innate support. In order to raise money, the priest also had to tolerate in his parish committees of laymen who organized numerous processions through the streets with saints' statues to which money was pinned, accompanied by fireworks and bands. These processions were extremely popular among Italians, reminding them of the villages and land they had left and serving important socially integrative functions. They did provide some revenue to the parish, but the bulk of the profits apparently went to the committees. The practice also seems to have further degraded the position of the priest in the parish and perpetuated the Old World practice of overemphasizing local and village saints, to the neglect of the more central teachings of the Church. But the same distortion of priorities was occurring in non-Italian parishes for other reasons, and it must always be remembered that in this period of massive immigration, parishes were called upon to serve more than purely spiritual needs in the doctrinal sense.[40]

In any parish, of course, the amount of time and attention the parish priest had to devote to simply paying for the bricks and mortar of his parish and to maintaining an institutional separateness from the rest of a hostile world created a situation in which only selected elements of Catholic teaching were communicated to the faithful anyway. The priest was happy if he could get the majority of the Catholics in his territory into the life of his parish at all. In 1901, for example, of the 294 families within St. Joseph's Parish in Greenwich, New York, fully forty-six families were unable or unwilling to share actively in parish life.[41] After that, the priest found himself compelled to emphasize repeatedly the most basic practices and doctrines of the Church. Minimal regulations for proper conduct in church had to be established, especially when so many of his parishioners were recent immigrants, poor and with a multiplicity of practices, therefore lacking in some of the more genteel graces. Parishioners were constantly being told "to be always on time for Mass and other services," "to take holy water upon entering the church," "to avoid whispering, laughing, and looking about," and "to leave babies at home or with a neighbor when going to church." It was improper "to make the Sign of the Cross as if fanning off flies," "to go to sleep, or read the prayer book during the sermon," "to be in an ecstatic condition of devotion when the contribution box approaches," "to make a rush for the door before the priest has even descended the altar to begin the concluding prayers," or to engage in "talking, laughing, giggling, and chewing gum" in the choir loft. Good Catholics were not "to go to a party or to a theatre the evening before approaching Holy Communion," "to laugh and talk needlessly on the way to church," "to have paint or powder on the face or eyebrows," "to wear torn or soiled apparel," "to go up to the railing before the proper time," or to wait "until everybody is already at the railing and then go marching up and try to crowd in when the railing is already full." It was also not proper "to expectorate shortly after receiving" the Eucharist. A common complaint of priests had to do with the practice of climbing over others in getting in and out of a pew. As the pastor of St. Mary's in Lawrence, Massachusetts, explained, "the effect is awkward in the extreme; but when the last comer is a large, heavy woman, it is atrocious."

Common church practices, like the use of incense at Solemn High Masses, at Vespers, and at Benediction, frequently had to be explained. Among immigrant parishioners, where nationalism was often expressed in devotion to particular saints, it had to be emphasized that "Catholics worship only God," while the saints were venerated and emulated for the holiness of their lives and prayed to for intercession with God. In the parochial system, moreover, where the number of associations had proliferated, the essentials of the religion had to be constantly reinforced. Priests told their parishioners that "the practice of receiving Holy Communion monthly or weekly because one is a member of a religious society is not as meritorious an act as a quarterly or even annual Communion made out of pure love of God and a desire to fulfill the law of the Church." Even a principal

Church doctrine like the indissolubility of marriage had to be constantly drummed into the minds of changing parish populations consisting of recent immigrants from foreign lands where such explanations were often neglected.

A strong element of Catholic exclusiveness is evident in the pastoral counseling of this period. Such emphasis on Catholic-Protestant differences was to be expected in an atmosphere of renewed nativist hostility, in light of the problems of assimilation for the new immigrants, and in the institutional context of the parish that now served as the primary sanctuary from the rigors of a secular world. Catholic parishioners were cautioned never to give "a color of plausibility to the misrepresentations which enemies of the Church are addicted to making against our faith and practice." To combat what was referred to as a "pet fabrication" that Catholics were not allowed to read the Bible, one priest urged his followers "not to show indifference to the Sacred Scriptures." Always with an ear to the expressed opinions of non-Catholics, parishioners were urged to sing well and behave in the choir because "it has been remarked that in choir conduct Catholic members, to their shame, suffer in comparison with Protestants." Even something as innocuous as a parish picnic was used as an occasion for reminding the faithful that as a separate people their every action would come under scrutiny. In 1885, Father James Blake announced from the pulpit to the people of his rural Pennsylvania parish of St. Denis:

> Pic-nic will take place tomorrow. Plenty of amusements but no disorder. Let our Protestant friends see that Catholics can enjoy themselves in a sensible manner. Keep away from the saloons.[42]

Many of the comparisons, however, seemed exceptionally ill-suited to assuage Protestant fears about the growing Catholic influence in the Northeast. Catholics were constantly reminded that there was only one true Church, that "Protestant-ism is not a religion, it is a sect," and that while "the Catholic religion is based on belief, the Protestant sects are based on unbelief." A kind of triumphalism attended assertions such as the one that pointed out:

> The Catholic churches are attended every day, and filled many times on Sundays. The existing church buildings are fast becoming insufficient to accommodate the increasing numbers who do attend church, and priests find that a great part of the time which under other circumstances would be given to spiritual work has to be devoted to the erecting of new churches. Catholicity prospers and grows stronger, spreading its branches wider and further every day. Under similar circumstances Protestantism fails to thrive. From its ranks infidelity has gained most of its victims. Catholics do go to church, but Protestants do not.[43]

Statistics were often provided to parishioners that showed startling increases in the number of Catholic churches and priests, and much lower increases in all other religions. Ironically, then, the circumstances of an increasingly immigrant Church in a hostile American environment caused many parish priests to fall into the trap of adopting quantitative assessments of religious vitality at the same time that they were bemoaning their failures to generate more qualitative religious motivations among their parishioners. Ironic, too, was the fact that the same conditions of rapid growth, which were causing increasing problems of mounting debts for parochial edifices, lay rebellions, and even schisms among new immigrants, and priestly preoccupation with dollars and cents, and bricks and mortar, were being used as an index of success in the competition for souls.

Within such a competitive environment, Catholics, of course, were forbidden to attend Protestant services, and evangelization generally meant attempting to show Protestants the errors of their ways. Conversion was one area where the laypeople of the parish were given an important role. They were told to invite their Protestant neighbors to a good Catholic sermon, and, by the example of their lives, to demonstrate the superiority of the Catholic religion. It was not considered sufficient for lay Catholics to merely hear Mass on Sundays, say their daily prayers, and occasionally receive the Sacraments. That would be enough, one priest pointed out, "in a well settled, peaceful and calm Catholic community where the Church is, as it were, in camp or on dress parade." But here in America, that was not the case. "We are," he continued, "in the midst of error, darkness, and hatred of truth, and every member of the rank and file must face the enemy from his individual position as well as the bishop or the priest in his respective sphere."[44]

The "sphere" of the layperson, then, had become defined as principally outside the parish. He was expected to be outgoing in spreading to the non-Catholic world the beliefs that had been instilled in him by his parish priest. This seems a strange assignment in light of the fact that so much of the socialization that he received in the parish was designed to have him actually withdraw from the world. It is explicable only through the metaphor of the sanctuary, the haven to which the layperson could withdraw after his daily excursions into the world. Within that otherworldly sanctuary, his real life would be safely structured for him by the dictation of his religious superior.

By this time, the image of that religious superior had become exalted. The parish priest was defined in one 1896 parish publication as "a man without whom none can enter the world or none can go out of it" and "who knows everything, who has the right to say anything, from whose hallowed lips words of divine wisdom are received by all with the authority of an oracle, and with entire submission of faith and judgment." Laymen were reminded "to rise at the entrance of a clergyman, and to remain standing until he gives the signal to be seated," and proper respect required avoiding "a loud tone when telling one's troubles to a priest" or entering the priest's parlor "with muddy shoes, wet umbrella, or lighted cigar."[45]

There were, of course, exceptions to this monarchical image of the parish priest. Rev. John J. Curran spent his entire clerical life between 1887 and 1936 in the anthracite coal regions of Pennsylvania. At the parishes of St. Mary's and Holy Saviour in Wilkes-Barre, Curran was, like most of his fellow clergymen, preoccupied with administering the Sacraments to the Irish, Slav, and Italian immigrants in his parishes. Also like the rest of the parish clergy, he spent most of his energies in building a church, a convent, a school, and a rectory. But Curran had an abiding belief that the Church could do much more to remedy the deficiencies of life in a mining community. Because for him giving greater glory to God could go hand-in-hand with beautifying lives spent largely in dark and unhealthy coal mines, Curran placed special emphasis on providing the best in architecture and music in his parish, and he was one of the principal leaders in various efforts to provide badly needed recreational facilities in the Wilkes-Barre area.

Father Curran labored in an area of the country where, even though the churches served the miners in religious matters, they were often partially dependent on the mine operators for financial support. Sometimes this took the form of direct contributions, and sometimes a worker's church dues would be deducted from his wages and paid directly to his pastor. Moreover, most of the older clergy, who were generally not local natives, retained a distrust of labor organizations ever since the days of the Molly Maguires in the 1870s. Younger clergymen like Curran were generally local men who perhaps had themselves struggled in the mines as youth, and so showed a greater sensitivity to the secular needs of their parishioners. Because he maintained good relations with both owners and miners, Curran proved to be an effective mediator in the anthracite coal strike of 1900. In the much more serious strike two years later, Curran threw himself unreservedly on the side of the miners who had been pilloried in the public press as the sole initiators of the violence that occurred. While working hard for an agreement with the owners, Curran urged the young men of his parish to go elsewhere to seek employment. He administered the total abstinence pledge to as many as possible, both to help relieve the financial burden on the families of the strikers as well as to minimize the possibility of violence. From that time on, Father Curran was prominent in the growing labor movement, and was frequently the victim of threats from rival organizations. He was influential in keeping the United Mine Workers conservative in aim and nonviolent in character, and he paid for his notoriety with the bombing deaths of three friends, the burning of his rectory, and perhaps even his own death in 1936.[46]

Even Father Curran would have admitted, however, that the priest's principal leadership role was within the parish. Clerical dominance there was reinforced by long tenures in office for pastors. Compared to the period after World War II, the average pastor remained in power two to three times longer. For example, Rev. Lawrence J. Wall was the pastor of St. Dominic's Parish in Philadelphia for fifty years from 1876 to 1926, a tenure four times longer than any of his successors.

Long tenures meant that priests could know their parishioners intimately, encourage vocations practically from the cradle, and institute long-range parish programs with strong certainty of continuity.[47]

There was no area of life for the Catholic that was off limits for the parish priest. He admonished, and frequently demanded compliance, on such matters as the relations between husbands and wives, child rearing, social drinking, modes of dress, hair styles, gambling, dating, courtship, amusements, reading matter, punctuality, financial success, attitudes, and even facial expressions.[48]

No indisputable indices exist for measuring the impact of clerical leadership on lay behavior or for proving the extent to which the whole complex of parish life, in practice and ideology, held the allegiance of Catholic parishioners. There are simply too many variables, and each individual in each parish was subjected to a different mix of influences. Some illumination is possible by focusing on two heavily emphasized obligations, the Easter Precept and the prohibition against mixed marriages.

The Easter Precept, or Duty, meant that all Catholics, under pain of mortal sin, were required to go to confession and Communion during Eastertime, even if they did not go at any other time of the year. It was thus a minimum requirement for being a Catholic in good standing. A sampling of parishes from eastern Pennsylvania finds that in 1900 Polish and German parishioners were assiduous in keeping this commandment of the Church. Only .07% of the Poles and 1% of the Germans failed their Easter Duty, compared to 3.3% for the Irish and 9.3% for the Italians. Thirty years later, there was not much change in Polish and German behavior. Although the Polish percentage had increased to 0.4% and the German percentage had barely risen to 1.1%, they were still the groups that exhibited the greatest conformity to that Church precept. At the other extreme, Italian failure of the Easter Duty had soared to 16%. The biggest change, however, occurred among the Irish, whose percentage of failures plummeted to only 0.7%. To put it rather simplistically, the Poles and the Germans continued their religious conservatism, the Irish increased it, but the Italians' regard for ecclesiastical dictation continued to decline.

Catholics were forever being cautioned by their parish priests against the mistake of marrying outside the faith. Mixed marriages were presented as leading to the possible loss of the one true faith by one of the spouses and to the neglect of a Catholic upbringing and education for the children. The incidence of mixed marriages from our sample parishes reveals a somewhat different development than does the Easter Duty. In 1900, as one might expect, the most conservative groups on the issue of marriage were the most recent immigrants. The Poles showed no mixed marriages and the Italians a low 5.2%. Among the Irish, however, 16% of all marriages were with a non-Catholic, and among the Germans, an extraordinary 29% were mixed. Thirty years later, mixed marriages among the Poles had risen, but with an incidence of only 4.4% they remained the group most loyal to priestly advice. Among the Italians, however, their former conservatism had given way to a mixed-marriage rate of 17.9%, making them second only to the Irish whose rate had risen to 29%. The Germans, on the other hand, seem to have become more conservative. Their mixed marriage percentage had fallen to 16.5%.[49]

It seems, then, that only the Poles remained consistent on both scales. The Irish matched an increasing devotion to the minimal requirements of their religion with a greater adventurousness in their social relations with non-Catholics. Certainly, the fact that the Irish had become fully accepted into American society, felt pride in their established positions in politics, the business world, and the Church hierarchy, and the absence of any language impediment, had a great deal to do with this divergence. The hold of Catholic teachings on the Italians seems to have actually weakened as time progressed, but the evidence may be biased by the constant stream of new immigrants coming in. Certainly, by 1930, many Italians had become staunch members and benefactors of the Catholic Church in America. The decline in mixed marriages among the well-established Germans presents a problem, but perhaps the adverse image of them as a result of World War I contributed to their increasing isolation in terms of marriage.

What went on in the Catholic parish, then, between 1880 and 1930, cannot be viewed in monolithic terms. Each parish population was struggling with its own rather unique problems, and the resolution of those problems was shaped by different interactions of growth, ethnicity, location, wealth, clerical leadership, and even world affairs. At the bare minimum, larger percentages of Catholics were being held to some truths of the faith, were receiving a Catholic education, and were being provided with a parochial vehicle through which to deal with some of the more threatening aspects of modern life. Moreover, with less than half of all Catholics receiving a parochial school education, the small percentage of mixed marriages and failed Easter Duties suggests that Catholic beliefs were being successfully inculcated by other aspects of the parish system. Finally, the effectiveness of Catholic teaching and example in the parish is borne out by the tremendous increase in religious vocations during this period. The number of priests increased five times and the number of nuns increased six times, the largest for any period of American history.

## Notes

1. Hennessey, *American Catholics,* 173; Nathan Glazer and Daniel P. Moynihan, *Beyond the Melting Pot* (Cambridge, Mass., 1963), 219; Gerald Shaughnessy, *Has the Immigrant Kept the Faith?* (N.Y., 1925), 190; Cohalan, *Popular History,* 154, 157, 182; *Abstracts of Reports of the Immigration Commission* (Wash., D.C., 1911), 105–109.

2. *Annual Reports, Archdiocese of Philadelphia,* 1930.

3. Connelly, *History of Archdiocese of Philadelphia*, 379.

4. *Historical Sketches*, 19, 189–211.

5. Buetow, *Of Singular Benefit*, 179–180, 213–214; Henry J. Browne, "The American Parish School in the Last Half Century," *National Catholic Education Association Bulletin*, 50 (1953): 323–334; Raymond G. Fuller, *Child Labor and the Constitution* (N.Y., 1923), 2.

6. *Monthly Calendar, Church of St. John the Baptist, Brooklyn, N.Y.* (Sept. 1905), 15–17.

7. Francis C. Kelley, *The Story of Extension* (Chicago, 1922); James P. Gaffey, *Francis Clement Kelley and the American Catholic Dream* (Bensenville, 1980), 1: 73–202; Aaron Abell, *American Catholicism and Social Action: A Search for Social Justice, 1865–1950* (Garden City, 1960), 118–119.

8. Cohalan, *Popular History*, 174.

9. *Ibid.*, 156, 159–160, 183–184; *The Catholic Directory, Archdiocese of Philadelphia*, 1946 and 1956–1957.

10. Davis and Haller, *Peoples of Philadelphia*, 206–213; William Galush, "The Polish National Catholic Church: A Survey of Its Origins, Development and Missions," *RACHSP*, 83 (1972): 131; Sister M. Theodosetta Lewandowska, "The Polish Immigrant in Philadelphia to 1914," *RACHSP*, 65 (June 1954): 82–85.

11. Lewandowska, "Polish Immigrant," 86–90. See also, *Diamond Jubilee, 1898–1973, St. Josaphat's Parish* (Phila., 1973), 10; *St. Adalbert's Diamond Jubilee Commemorative Book*, 11–12, and John B. Wendrychowicz, "History of Saint Adalbert's Roman Catholic Parish," (unpublished manuscript, 1971), 1–2.

12. Florence Clowes, *Pol-Am: Polish Americans in Pittsfield, Massachusetts* (Webster, Mass., 1981), 7–56.

13. Dignan, *History of Legal Incorporation*, 55; John P. Gallagher, *A Century of History: The Diocese of Scranton, 1868–1968* (Scranton, 1968), 157–168.

14. Galush, "Polish National Catholic Church," 133–144; Gallagher, *Century of History*, 211–263. See also Warren C. Platt, "The Polish National Catholic Church: An Inquiry into Its Origins," *Church History*, 46 (1977): 74–89; Victor Greene, "For God and Country, the Origins of Slavic Catholic Self-Consciousness in America," *Church History*, 35 (1966): 446–460; Theodore Andrews, *The Polish National Catholic Church in America and Poland* (London, 1953).

15. *Golden Jubilee, St. Andrew Lithuanian Roman Catholic Church* (Phila., 1974), 38; *Catholic Standard and Times*, 7 February 1914, 5; Ciesluk, *National Parishes*, 131–132.

16. Mark Stolarik, "Lay Initiative in American-Slovak Parishes, 1889–1930," *RACHSP*, 83 (1972): 31–32, 152–155; Bohdan P. Procko, "Soter Ortynsky: First Ruthenian Bishop in the United States, 1907–1916," *The Catholic Historical Review*, 58 (Jan. 1973): 531. See also Joseph Cada, *Czech-American Catholics, 1850–1920* (Lisle, Ill., 1964); Miroslav Labunka and Leonid Rudnytsky, eds., *Ukrainians in Philadelphia: A Contribution to the Growth of the Commonwealth* (Phila., 1976); Josef Barton, *Peasants and Strangers: Italians, Rumanians and Slovaks in an American City, 1890–1950* (Cambridge, Mass., 1975); Bohdan P. Procko, "The Establishment of the Ruthenian Church in the United States, 1884–1907," *Pennsylvania History*, 42 (1975): 137–154.

17. *Diamond Jubilee, 1904–1979, Good Shepherd Parish, Linwood, Massachusetts* (1979), 5.

18. Burns, *Springfield's Ethnic Heritage*, 11–29, 33; *Jubile D'Or, Paroisse Saint-Thomas d'Aquin* (Springfield, Mass., 1958), 82–83; Pierre Savard, "Relations between French-Canadian and American Catholics in the Last Third of the Nineteenth Century," *Culture* (1970): 24–39; Mason Wade, "The French Catholic Parish and 'Survivance' in 19th Century New England," *Catholic Historical Review*, 36 (1950): 163–189.

19. Sister M. Agnes Gertrude, "Italian Immigration into Philadelphia," *RACHSP*, 58 (June 1947): 134–142, 189–194, 198–201; *Annual Reports, Archdiocese of Philadelphia*, 1900; *Catholic Standard and Times*, 13 December 1913, 1; Cohalan, *Popular History*, 158; Richard Juliani, "The Parish as an Urban Institution: Italian Catholics in Philadelphia," (unpublished manuscript, 1975) 6, 10; Silvano M. Tomasi, *Piety and Power: The Role of Italian Parishes in the New York Metropolitan Area, 1880–1930* (Staten Island, 1975); Henry J. Browne, "The Italian Problem in the Catholic Church of the United States, 1880–1900," *USCHRS*, 35 (1946): 46–72; Virginia Yans-McLaughlin, *Italian Immigrants in Buffalo, 1880–1930* (Ithaca, 1977); *Our Lady of Angels Parish, 1907–1957, Golden Jubilee* (Phila., 1957), 3; *Sesquicentennial, St. Denis Parish*, 143.

20. Cohalan, *Popular History*, 261; Hennessey, *American Catholics*, 175.

21. Gavigan, "Rise and Fall," 123; Cohalan, *Popular History*, 94, 261; Sister Consuela Maria Duffy, *Katherine Drexel, A Biography* (Phila., 1966), 243; *A Souvenir of the Fiftieth Anniversary of St. Peter Claver's, 1886–1936* (Phila., 1936).

22. John Higham, *Strangers in the Land: Patterns of American Nativism, 1860–1925* (N.Y., 1970), 46–51, 57–69, 72–73, 89–90, 161–162, 234–330; Cohalan, *Popular History*, 243.

23. *St. Mary's Parish, Lawrence, Mass., Calendar*, June 1896, 19, 23, July 1896, 20, August 1896, 22, 27, 29, September 1896, 8, 15, October 1896, 23, December 1896, 13; *Monthly Calendar of Sacred Heart Church, Worcester, Mass.*, March 1891, 9, August 1891, 7, October 1891, 17, November 1891, 17–18; *Monthly Bulletin, St. Mary's of the Assumption, Cambridge, Mass.*, December 1916, 27; *Sesquicentennial, St. Denis Parish*, 112–113, 154; *Golden Jubilee, St. Gabriel's Church, 1895–1945* (Phila., 1945), 152; *Saint Monica's Fifty Years Old, 1895–1945* (Phila., 1945), 65.

24. *Monthly Calendar of Sacred Heart Church*, March 1891, 9, 22; *St. Mary's Parish Calendar*, December 1896, 13; *Diamond Jubilee, Most Blessed Sacrament Parish, 1901–1976* (Phila., 1976), 31; *St. Monica's Fifty Years Old*, 65, 168; *Golden Jubilee, St. Gabriel's*, 12, 64, 93, 160–161; William J. Cusick, "History of Saint Barnabas Parish, 1919–1969" (unpublished manuscript, 1969), 10; *St. Cecelia's, A History of a Parish and Its People* (Phila., 1976), 40; *Golden Jubilee, 1890–1965, Saint Francis de Sales Parish* (Phila., 1965), 28, 44; *History of Saint Callistus Parish, 1921–1946* (Phila., 1946), 22–23, 61; *Golden Jubilee, Gesu Parish*, 123; *St. Andrew's Golden Jubilee*, 38; *Monthly Messenger, Mission Church Parish, Roxbury, Mass.*, March 1894, 22; *St. Mary Magdalen de Pazzi Parish, Souvenir and Bouquet* (Phila., 1911), 39; *Annual Reports, Archdiocese of Philadelphia*, 1900 and 1930; Lewandowska, "Polish Immigrant," 135; *Seventy-Fifth Anniversary, Saint Madeline Church, Ridley Park, Pa., 1908–1983* (Devon, Pa., 1983), 22; Procko, "Soter Ortynsky," 528.

25. Gavigan, "Rise and Fall," 121–122, 131; *Historical Sketches*, xlvi–xlviii; *Golden Jubilee, Gesu Parish*, 1.

26. *Monthly Bulletin, St. Mary's of the Assumption*, December 1916, 27; *Monthly Messenger, Mission Church Parish*, May 1905, 99, 101, February 1906, 22, 39; *Diamond Jubilee, Good Shepherd Parish*, 5–6; *Monthly Calendar of Sacred Heart Church*, March 1891, 22; *Calendar of St. Thomas Church, Jamaica Plain, Mass.*, April 1899, 87; *St. Mary's Parish Calendar*, May 1896, 13–21, June 1896, 27, July 1896, 13, August 1896, 22, November 1896, 29, December 1896, 7, February 1897, 9; *Golden Jubilee, St. Gabriel's*, 95, 151; *Saint Gabriel's Church* (South Hackensack, N.J., 1970), 12, 19; *The Gesu Parish Centennial, 1868–1968* (South Hackensack, N.J., 1969), 25, 71, 82, 88, 99, 107; *Diamond Jubilee, Most Blessed Sacrament Parish*, 26–28; *Saint Barnabas' Church, Phila., Dedication* (Phila., 1941), 7; Cusick, "History of St. Barnabas," 10; *St. Monica's, Fifty Years Old*, 38, 161, 165, 175, 184; *Souvenir, St. Mary Magdalen de Pazzi*, 39; *Saint Cecilia's, History*, 15; *Golden Jubilee, St. Francis de Sales*, 43, 58; *St. Callistus, History*, 23, 36; *A Story of Holy Angels Parish, 1900–1950* (Phila., 1950), 65; *Golden Anniversary, 1924–1974, Saint Helena's Parish* (Phila., 1974), 22; *Annual Reports, Archdiocese of Philadelphia*, 1900; Abell, *American Catholics and Social Action*, passim; *Parish Annual of St. Patrick's Church, Erie, Pa., for the Year 1902* (Erie, 1903), 22.

27. *75th Anniversary, St. Madeline*, 21; *Calendar, St. Thomas*, April 1899, 87; *Monthly Calendar, Sacred Heart*, March 1891, 22; *Monthly Messenger, Mission Church*, February 1906, 22; *St. Mary's Parish Calendar*, May 1896, 13–21, January 1898, 23; *Sesquicentennial, St. Denis*, 154; *Diamond Jubilee, Good Shepherd*, 5; Cohalan, *Popular History*, 260.

28. Clowes, *Pol-Am*, 80–91; *St. Mary's Parish Calendar*, March 1898, 1; *Monthly Messenger, Mission Church*, March 1894, 9; *Monthly Calendar*, March 1891, 2.

29. *St. Mary's Parish Calendar*, May 1896, 12, 23–27, June 1897, 23–24; *Monthly Messenger, Mission Church*, May 1905, 105; *75th Anniversary, St. Madeline*, 69.

30. *St. Mary's Parish Calendar*, October 1896, 11–12, November 1896, 21; *Calendar, St. Thomas*, March 1899, 1, 43; April 1899, 87; *75th Anniversary, St. Madeline*, 30; *Jubile D'Or, Paroisse St. Thomas d'Aquin*, 95; Cohalan, *Popular History*, 210–211.

31. *Gesu Parish Centennial*, 111; *St. Callistus, History*, 31; *St. Mary's Parish Calendar*, September 1896, 11, June 1897, 5, 23, 28.

32. *Calendar, St. Thomas*, March 1899, 37, September 1899, 276–277; *St. Mary's Parish Calendar*, June 1896, 3; *Monthly Messenger, Mission Church*, August 1905, 177.

33. *Annual Reports, Archdiocese of Philadelphia*, 1900 and 1930; *Golden Jubilee, St. Francis de Sales*, 9–11, 30, 58; *100th Anniversary, St. Francis Xavier*, 63; *Annual Report, Our Mother of Sorrows Parish Church Debt Association* (Phila., 1889); *St. Monica's Fifty Years Old*, 16–45, 96, 157; *St. Helena's Parish Golden Anniversary, 1924–1974* (Phila., 1974), 11–15; *History of the Church of the Ascension, Philadelphia: Grand Souvenir $50,000 Parish Campaign, 1918*, 1; *Golden Anniversary, 1899–1949, Ascension Parish, Philadelphia*, 25–26; *Church of the Ascension of Our Lord* (Hackensack, N.J., 1974), 17–22; *Holy Innocents Parish Golden Jubilee Celebration, 1927–1977* (Phila., 1977), 14–15; *Saint Cecelia's, History*, 6–8; *Holy Child Church Golden Jubilee, 1909–1959* (Phila., 1959), 17–27; *St. Callistus, History*, 9, 19, 33, 46, 65; Cusick, "History of St. Barnabas," 7–13; *75th Anniversary, St. Madeline*, 17–21, 22–23, 59.

34. *Most Precious Blood Parish, Phila.: Souvenir Record of the $20,000 Rectory Campaign* (Phila., 1916), 21, 25–29; Anthony J. Piperno, "A History of the Most Precious Blood of Our Lord" (unpublished manuscript, 1971), 11.

35. *Annual Reports, Archdiocese of Philadelphia,* 1900 and 1930; *Sesquicentennial, St. Denis,* 84; *Monthly Calendar, Sacred Heart,* March 1891, 12; *St. Mary's Parish Calendar,* June 1896, 5, August 1896, 21.

36. *St. Mary's Parish Calendar,* May 1896, 19, June 1896, 1, August 1896, 20, November 1896, 14, December 1896, 13; *Calendar, St. Thomas,* March 1899, 41; *Monthly Messenger, Mission Church,* February 1905, 31; *St. Helena's Golden Anniversary,* 15; *St. Callistus, History,* 11, 60; *Golden Jubilee, St. Francis de Sales,* 58; *St. Barnabas, Dedication,* 7.

37. *Holy Innocents Golden Jubilee,* 16.

38. *St. Callistus, History,* 51, 62; Cusick, "History of St. Barnabas," 7; *75th Anniversary, St. Madeline,* 22–23; *Most Blessed Sacrament, Diamond Jubilee,* 26; *St. Mary's Parish Calendar,* July 1896, 11, November 1897, 1, December 1897, 1.

39. *Golden Jubilee, 1894–1944, Our Lady Star of the Sea Parish, Atlantic City, New Jersey* (1944), 99.

40. Gertrude, "Italian Immigration," 194–197.

41. Shannon, *Saint Joseph's Parish, Greenwich, N.Y.,* 68.

42. *Sesquicentennial, St. Denis,* 83.

43. *St. Mary's Parish Calendar,* July 1897, 13.

44. *Ibid.,* August 1897, 19.

45. For the commonly accepted image of the priest in the late 19th century, see *St. Mary's Parish Calendar,* December 1896, 16. A more socially active priestly model can be found in Bartholomew F. Fair, "Father Joseph Murgas," *RACHSP,* 62 (Sept. 1951): 184–187, and Robert E. Curran, "Prelude to 'Americanism': The New York Academia and Clerical Radicalism in the Late Nineteenth Century," *Church History,* 47 (1978): 48–65.

46. Catherine Ann Cline, "Priest in the Coal Fields: The Story of Father Curran," *RACHSP,* 63 (June 1952): 68–84.

47. Shannon, *Saint Joseph's Parish, Greenwich, N.Y.,* 103–104; Notes on St. Dominic's Parish, Ryan Memorial Library Archives and Historical Collections, Overbrook, Phila., Pa.

48. *St. Mary's Parish Calendar,* June 1896, 21–23, August 1896, 8–9, 15, 23, September 1896, 23–27, October 1896, 19, 22, 27, 32, November 1896, 15, 31–32, June 1897, 22, July 1897, 13, 31–32, August 1897, 19, November 1897, 23, 29, December 1897, 17, 31, February 1898, 29, 35–36, March 1898, 25, May 1899, 107; *Calendar, St. Thomas,* April 1899, 1, 75, 83, May 1899, 1, June 1899, 139, July 1899, 1, 164, 171, 203, September 1899, 235, October 1899, 267; *Monthly Calendar, Sacred Heart,* March 1891, 20.

49. *Annual Reports, Archdiocese of Philadelphia,* 1900 and 1930.

# CHAPTER THREE

# Consolidation and Transformation, 1930–1960

Parish life in the thirty years following 1930 could hardly be labeled quiescent, given the disruptive intrusions of the Great Depression and World War II, but once the great influx of southern and eastern Europeans ceased, Catholic energies previously devoted to coping with the needs of newcomers were now consumed in consolidating and stabilizing the parochial system. The Catholic Church in the Northeast was still very much in the business of establishing new parishes and building and expanding parish structures, but the pace had slowed down considerably.

Part of this slowdown was due to the fact that the Catholic population of the Northeast increased at only a slightly faster rate (1.7 times) than the population at large (1.3 times). The most rapid growth (2.6 times) was to be found in southern New Jersey, but this was the area, heretofore sparsely populated, that was also seeing the greatest general increase (1.8 times). In terms of the relationship between Catholic growth and general growth, the most notable areas were northern New Jersey and western New York State, while the lowest relative increases occurred in New England and southeastern New York. However, the largest concentrations of Catholics in 1960 were still to be found where they had been one hundred years earlier, in the heavily urbanized dioceses of Boston, New York, Philadelphia, Brooklyn, and Newark. Combined, these five dioceses accounted for nearly half of all the Catholics in the Northeast. And Catholicism was still the fastest growing religion of the region, now due more to natural increase than to immigration. Nearly 40% of the entire population was Catholic by 1960, compared to 29% in 1930.

Only 1,043 new parishes were established between 1930 and 1960, compared to 2,626 in the previous period. The number of priests doubled, but that was less than one-half the rate of increase in the 1880 to 1930 period. There was, on the average, one priest for every 827 Catholics in 1960, a slight improvement in the 1930 ratio of 1/888, but it is obvious that a larger percentage of priests was not being funneled into parish work. In 1960, there were more missions, or parishes without resident priests, than there were parishes with resident priests. By comparison, in 1930 less than one-quarter of all parishes had been without resident priests. This shift in priorities was evident in an increase in average parish size, from 2,241 to 3,151.

There were still areas of the Northeast, it must be noted, where conditions, even in the 1940s, still approached that of a frontier. In 1945, the Redemptorists were assigned a parish in eastern Vermont with the town of Bradford as its center. The parish covered 700 square miles, there was no church, and there had been no priest up to that time. Thus, while most areas were now consolidating their gains from the previous decades, some rural areas still were in the missionary stage of parochial development.[1]

A second element in shifting parish priorities was the decline in the number of national parishes established. Only 17% of all the parishes in 1960 were national, compared to 21% in 1930. Of the forty-five new parishes established in this period in Philadelphia only two—Our Lady of Loreto for the Italians and Holy Redeemer for the Chinese—were national. Likewise, in New York only one national parish, St. Ann's Italian parish in Yonkers, was founded.[2] In fact, many already established national parishes were "denationalized," merged, or suppressed during this period. Only in New England, Buffalo, Scranton, and northern New Jersey was there any increase in this regard.

This new policy has been referred to as "Americanization." For example, a solution to the "Italian Problem" was sought in the restructuring of Italian parish organization in the 1930s. In Philadelphia, Cardinal Dougherty saw that since most Italians were attending national parishes, the regular territorial parishes in the city were practically empty because non-Italians had moved out of the neighborhoods as the Italians moved in. He decided, therefore, to redraw parish boundaries in an attempt to phase out national parishes. Italian or Italo-American priests were to be assigned to the territorial parishes, which were predominantly Italian in population, but these parishes were henceforth to be conducted "along the lines of a first-class American parish." One Italian priest heavily involved in such reorganization proceedings emphasized not only the need to establish more Italian parish schools, but also to conduct in the restructured parishes only strictly liturgical services, to impress the Italian parishioners with the authority of the bishop and pastor, to teach them to be punctual, and to allow only recognized religious societies such as the Holy Name Society. In one parish, this priest reported, "Americanization" worked very well, as evidenced by an increase in Sunday Mass attendance from 250 to more than 7,000 in a few years.[3]

In some instances, however, the process was painful for all involved. When the Italian Augustinian priest at Our Lady of Good Counsel Parish, a national parish established in Philadelphia in 1897, was ordered to be transferred so that secular priests could be substituted as part of the "Americanization" process, the parishioners rebelled. Invoking the old claims of lay control and patronage, they imprisoned their priest in his rectory and refused to let any other priest enter. The whole incident was accompanied by violent words and actions and was sensationally reported in the secular press. Dougherty thereupon closed the parish in 1932, leaving many of the parishioners bitter and unreconciled.[4]

At least until the end of World War II, however, such disturbances were the exception rather than the rule. This was a time of minimal internal change in the Catholic parish. The established patterns of parish life persisted and were elaborated. Men joined the Holy Name Society in record numbers, and those parishes only recently founded quickly established such societies. In most parishes, at least before World War II depleted the male population, the Holy Name Society was usually the largest parish organization.[5]

The St. Vincent de Paul Society was vibrant, and found plenty of work in the parishes during the Great Depression. At St. Adalbert's Polish Parish in Philadelphia, for example, many of its working-class parishioners were thrown out of work in the 1930s. The pastor since the parish's founding in 1904, Father Miecislaus Monkiewicz, worked with the St. Vincent de Paul Society to alleviate the suffering of the poor. They established a parish food distribution center, and members of the society visited the homes of the unemployed. They supervised the distribution of needed clothing, provided children with essentials for school, and even helped families pay their rent.[6]

Women continued to gather in Altar and Rosary Societies, but it was the Sodalities that saw the greatest growth in this period. Parish missions flourished, and the mansions of the wealthy became retreat houses as the weekend retreat movement expanded in the 1930s. With Prohibition repealed, the temperance crusade revived. Many bishops now demanded that prospective priests pledge total abstinence from alcohol for five years after ordination, and that boys and girls receiving the Sacrament of Confirmation do the same until they were 21.[7]

Miraculous Medal novenas, which quickly became the leading Marian devotion, were begun at St. Francis de Sales Parish in Philadelphia in 1931. At Holy Cross Parish in Manhattan, where the novena was introduced in 1934, it was attended by thousands every week. The Legion of Mary was started in New York in 1935 by Father Anthony Rothaulf of St. Anthony of Padua Parish in the Bronx. Its purpose was to visit parishioners and convince the wayward to return to the Sacraments. By the 1950s, when the legion was permitted to be established in Philadelphia parishes, it had also become a force in praying for the conversion of Russia from Communism.[8]

Individual parishes occasionally instituted new devotions and practices. One parish, in 1936, added a shrine dedicated to Our Lady of the Happy Delivery, an idea sponsored by the Pious Union of Christian Mothers. At another parish, the pastor began a devotion to the Christ Child. The devotion was held each month as a "Little Christmas" until 1935 when it became weekly. In 1939, a Pieta was added to the shrine and Holy Steps were opened for prayer and meditation. At a third parish, a Guard of Honor Society was created in 1944. It consisted of men who assembled each Sunday for one hour to pray during exposition of the Blessed Sacrament.[9]

Recreational and athletic activities were nothing new to Catholic parishes, but these activities took on an added importance between 1930 and 1960. Parish leaders, both lay and clerical, were becoming more concerned with what was called "juvenile delinquency." As one member of St. Thomas Aquinas Parish in Springfield, Massachusetts, put it, "The question is no longer that of grouping young men for the mere pleasure of recreating on the baseball field," but "now the aim of sports is to combat juvenile delinquency by directing the energy of the adolescent into a channel that will be natural and beneficial to him and to society."[10]

Catholic Youth Organizations in the 1940s and 1950s were organized in many parishes. They sponsored basketball, baseball, softball, bowling, track, swimming, and football teams, as well as spelling bees, dances, and plays. Parish organizations like the Catholic Club, Boy Scouts, Girl Scouts, and League of the Sacred Heart also were instrumental in recreational activities, which always contained an element of the spiritual in them.[11]

Building and paying debts was still a chief concern for both clergy and laity. Even recently founded parishes were compelled to expand within a few years. To take Holy Innocents Parish in Philadelphia, established in 1927, as an example, we find that the parish built a school in 1938, a new parish hall in 1951, a new church in 1953, and three new structures—an additional school, a convent, and a rectory—in 1958. This scheme of things was reproduced in all growing urban parishes. What is so extraordinary about these building programs is how well most parishes were able to keep up with and even pay off some enormous debts. Holy Innocents, a parish of 1,076 people in 1932, with 225 children in its school, had a total debt on church property of $45,000. The debt grew as the parish expanded to 8,053 people and the construction proceeded, so that by 1958 the parish debt was $125,000. But within a year, that debt had been reduced to $45,000. St. Cecilia's, another urban parish, likewise reduced a debt of $247,500 in 1958 to $8,500 in 1959.

True, the Diocesan Loan Funds established in the 1930s and 1940s were enormously helpful in managing debts. New parishes could obtain loans at lower interest rates than were available at banks. While they proved to be a curtailment of pastors' autonomy, the funds ended their previous isolation and lifted from them a heavy burden. Henceforth, whenever possible, any pastor assigned to found a new parish would be given the site debt-free and a sum of money sufficient to launch the parish without an initial crippling debt. For the majority of parishes, however, the funds were not applicable, and paying off debts in a period plagued by the Great Depression and the siphoning off of many male parishioners into military service during World War II was quite an accomplishment. It required the continuation of the many fund-raising activities and special collections that were already a common feature of parish life.[12]

Money was also called for to fund a proliferation of extraparochial purposes, including the Pope, Colored People and Indians, the Holy Places in Palestine, the Catholic University in Washington, D.C., the Mission Collection, occasionally areas where natural disasters had occurred, and the Diocesan Seminary. By the 1930s, however, and despite the Great Depression, the assessment that regularly attracted the largest amount of money was the seminary. In some parishes, nearly 90% of the collections went to the seminary, which seems to be an indication of how strong parochial attachments were, since the seminary provided the priests who served in the parish. Seminaries, and convent motherhouses as well, blossomed everywhere to handle a swarm of applicants. The number of priests, nuns, and brothers entering their professions mushroomed in the 1940s and 1950s, providing a near-surplus when they emerged in the 1960s.

There was an aspect of seminary collections that enhanced an already-strong parochial attachment. Because the supply of foreign-born and foreign-educated priests was severely reduced by immigration restrictions, it became absolutely essential for the survival of the parochial system to provide new or expanded seminaries to train native clergy. Diocesan officials, therefore, became very aggressive in their seminary fund-raising campaigns. In order to maximize collections, they fostered a competitiveness among parishes, publishing in the newspapers the amounts collected in each parish in a list beginning with the largest contributor. In a sense, then, the need to provide the priests who would guarantee parochial survival led to an increased exclusiveness, not just from the outside world, but among parishes as well.[13]

A continual supply of nuns was also required, especially to keep the parochial system alive. The number of nuns increased 1.6 times between 1930 and 1960. This was a much slower increase than in the previous period when the number had increased 6x. In 1960, 60% of all parishes maintained a school, compared to 56% in 1930, but only 38% of all Catholic children were in the system. In 1930, 42% of all Catholic children had been in parochial schools, and the decline may have reflected the relative slowdown in the number of nuns entering teaching. Moreover, whereas in 1930 average parochial school size had been 419, by 1960 it had increased to 503. It was also estimated that 38% of all Catholic children received no religious instruction at all.[14]

This perennial problem led to the creation in many parishes of Confraternity of Christian Doctrine (CCD) programs. In 1952, for example, at the French parish of St. Thomas Aquinas in Springfield, Massachusetts, the curate called together a group of parishioners for this purpose. He explained to them that there was no substitute for a parochial school, but many of the parish children attended public schools, which were increasingly secular in their orientation. The priests and nuns could not possibly instruct all of the children in the parish, especially through the more difficult ages of high school, where a competent knowledge of the religion was so badly needed. With an emphasis typical of the old fortress mentality, heightened now by the new Cold War fear of atheistic Communism, he impressed upon them the importance of a CCD by remarking

> Consider what would happen if at one fell swoop, the Church, as we know it today, were to be wiped out, the priests killed, imprisoned, or driven underground, the religious orders disbanded, their properties and schools confiscated, their work banned from the land. How could the young be instructed in their religion? How could Catholicism continue? The answer lies in you, and in persons like you, lay-people who know how, and have the will to carry on, where the clergy is out of reach.[15]

Duly inspired, the laypersons at the meeting formed themselves into groups to obtain the cooperation of the rest of the parishioners. Since the CCD was some-thing new, they received only a rather passive approbation from most. Catechism classes were begun for children attending public schools, and gradually more and more children were sent on a regular basis. "Fishers" were appointed to notify parents if their child were absent on a particular class night. Discussion clubs were formed, but they initially were confronted with obstacles of timidity, lack of exact knowledge of the religion, and the language barrier among many of the parish-ioners. Eventually, however, a few clubs began functioning on a weekly basis. Toward the end of 1952, the Parent Educator section of the CCD was established, and it began to distribute medals and pamphlets in the homes of recently born children.

By 1953, several new teachers had volunteered their services. The Catechism classes had grown so much that they had to be divided: one for high school juniors and seniors, one for other high school grades, and one for the sixth grade and junior high students. The "Fishers" now began a weekly check of every single absentee, and parental cooperation increased. Teacher preparation courses were taken at a local college, and every week after the CCD class, the teachers would meet for one hour with the priest-director who would explain the lesson for the following week. Detailed report cards were eventually mailed to the parents of the students. Soon, an Apostolate of Good Will was introduced into the program. It concentrated its efforts on the catechetical instruction of possible young con-verts.[16]

Similar instances of outreach to non-Catholics began to appear during and after World War II. At St. Monica's in Philadelphia, a young ladies' missionary group, the Cenacle Society, was founded in 1944. That same year, St. Francis de Sales Parish began a lending library whose membership was ecumenical. In conjunction with this library, the pastor also conducted a Catholic Information Society. In 1948, a Convert Guild was established at St. Francis de Sales for non-Catholics seeking religious instruction.[17]

Generally, however, parishes in the 1940s were more concerned with their internal affairs, even though with the war the outside world was intruding more and more into this sanctuary. In 1940, for instance, St. Adalbert's Polish Parish in Philadelphia contained 5,200 people and 756 men were enrolled in the Holy Name Society. But then in 1941, 273 men from the parish were drafted into the armed services. In the following year, 787 men left, and in 1943, 1,377 more were sent to the fighting. By 1945, the parish population had dropped to 4,791, and only 521 men were to be found in the Holy Name Society. In a Polish parish like this, there was understandably great enthusiasm for the war, for religious and nationalistic ties pulled in the same direction. The parish joined the Catholic League in sending clerical and liturgical apparel to Nazi-occupied Poland. In the neighborhood surrounding the church, block after block was decorated in red, white, and blue colors as neighbors and parishioners gave a send-off to someone or threw a welcome-home party for a soldier on leave. Scattered here and there could be seen windows displaying banners with gold stars on them, indicating mothers who had lost a son in the war. The pastor, Father Polityka, organized a large committee of ladies in the parish to write letters and send packages to the young men from the parish who were in military service. This Ladies' Circle of Friends of Servicemen sponsored different programs in the parish to raise necessary funds. Dignitaries from the armed forces, including Generals Eisenhower and Patton, wrote to this group expressing their appreciation of what was being done by them for the American soldier.[18]

The same diminution of population was evident at the Italian parish of St. Mary Magdalen de Pazzi, even though Italy was on the opposing side during much of the war. There, the parish population dropped from 13,912 to 8,695, and membership in the Holy Name Society fell from 108 to eighty-six. A survey of nonethnic parishes during the same years, however, reveals increases in parish population. In all of these parishes, men were drafted into military service, but it seems that only in those parishes composed predominantly of the newer ethnic groups did the war have an unusual impact. Whether ethnic ties to the traditional homeland was a major factor, or whether it was the relative poverty of the newer ethnic groups—who were more likely to be drafted or to volunteer—or whether it was some other more long-term factor that made the difference is debatable. We do know, for example, that the population of St. Adalbert's bounced back after the war—to 5,150 in 1946 and to 9,875 by 1949—and that Holy Name membership nearly doubled. But the population of St. Mary Magdalen de Pazzi continued to decline—to 8,624 in 1946 and to 7,375 by 1949. The additional fact that, of the nonethnic parishes, continued population decline after 1946 occurred predominantly in older inner-city parishes while the newer parishes farther out experienced population increases suggests a tentative conclusion. With the exception of the Poles, among whom parish and neighborhood attachments remained strong, returning GI's were loathe to return to older inner-city parishes into which blacks were beginning to move in large numbers after the war. They were much more likely to relocate in an all-white parish in the city or move to the newly opening areas of the suburbs.[19]

In all parishes, the war brought novelties in association and even in popular piety. In 1943, Holy Child Parish had placed in front of the choir gallery a picture of the Sacred Heart with a wide perforated frame. In the tiny holes were placed small American flags, one each for men and women of the parish who were serving in the armed forces. Also, the parish invested $18.75 for a $25 government bond for each parishioner serving in the war. Most parishes saw the formation of parish posts of the Catholic War Veterans in the postwar period. Exposure to Europe by many veterans also had an impact on parish practices. One parish obtained a piece of marble with an inscription on it from the Catacombs in Rome. It was placed in a glass case attached to the church wall for everyone to venerate.[20]

The Catholic parishioner of the 1950s has become a subject of fascination for many writers, most of whom emphasize his optimism and conservativism in a rapidly changing postwar America.[21] Catholics contributed generously to their parishes and their seminaries, and there was a tremendous increase in vocations. Regular Mass attendance reached 70%, and the rate of Catholics leaving the faith was a low 7%.[22] They were, as Monsignor James Connelly has concluded,

> a joyous group positive of their identity, proud of their church and of their priests and of their schools. They had little or no religious confusion. There was a truly strong parish spirit; most Catholics in a parish knew one another; the school pulled the parishioners close together as the children played and competed together on various parish teams; parishioners often socialized together and in many instances their children intermarried.[23]

This sense of internal stability was reinforced by a priestly teaching that had changed little from the 1890s. There was so little innovation, in fact, that some parish publications were actually reprinting verbatim clerical pieces of advice that were sixty years old. Fundamental church practices still made up the bulk of this advice, as did admonitions regarding family relations. Husbands and fathers were still told to be firm, but fair, as the chief authority in the family. Youngsters were still told to obey their superiors and to avoid all "occasions of sin." Females were still singled out for special instruction, being reminded that they set the moral tone of society. If they would avoid social drinking, irreverence, and liberality, then men would follow their example. Courtships longer than four months were to be terminated in order to force male suitors to get serious about marriage.

These caveats seemed especially pertinent again in a half century confused by the disillusionment of the Great Depression and by the broken or transient social relationships of the World War II era. They were designed to provide a precise yardstick for thought and behavior in an increasingly relativistic world. In large measure, clerical leadership was successful, not in stemming the tide of change, but in providing familiar guideposts in a society at drift. Catholics, like others, were caught up in those storm-tossed seas, but at least they knew precisely when they were living up to the dictates of their religion. When they erred, they knew exactly whether their sin was mortal or venial. The parish was still a sanctuary, and the Catholicism enunciated there found a comfortable home in the conservatism that emerged in the 1950s.

There were, and are, critics of Catholic parish life in those years. One writer commented on Catholic preoccupation with "living rightly" and "the quest for a clean heart." This exclusive obsession, added another, tended to promote religious "privatism" and "individualism" in a professedly communitarian Church.[24] Indeed, many observers sensed a kind of individual and social isolation even in the liturgy conducted in Catholic churches. The altar faced the wall, and the priest offering the Mass in Latin, which many did not understand, faced the tabernacle throughout the service except from time to time when he turned to address the people. Down in the nave of the church, the worshipers more or less went their separate ways. Some said the Rosary beads, while others had a set number of prayers that they said during Mass. Many followed the Mass with their Missals, hurrying to keep up with the priest who seemed to fly through the Latin. Everything had become pro forma. That was one of the chief legacies of having to regiment a multiplicity of poor and uneducated ethnic groups into some sort of consensual community in the face of generations of anti-Catholic hostility.[25]

Yet something precious had been purchased at the price of having lost accurate theological knowledge of the Mass. Here in the dimly lit and incense-perfumed temples built by the immigrants, the sense of tradition and the sacred was very strong. The constant and rapid repetition of Latin prayers served as intoxicating mantras, focusing attention on one's internal state. The derived experience was personal and emotional, not communal and intellectual. The sense of individual responsibility for one's actions and salvation was very strong, and emotionalism served a definite human need, one recognized by most of the religions of the world. Here within the silent confines of the church, a part of heaven had descended to earth, shutting out the profane world. One's Creator was very close.

Another criticism of Catholic practice in this period was that, majestically isolated from each other in their holy sanctuaries, Catholics also exhibited a sense of insularity from the rest of the community. There was very little of informed lay leadership anymore, and ecumenism, except for the commemoration of the Church Unity Octave, was practically nonexistent. In the parishes, there was definitely a greater emphasis placed upon biblical and theological reading than on social activism.[26] As Thomas T. McAvoy has observed, in social and political matters, "the Catholic body was generally inert."[27] When it did stir, on issues like birth control, public immorality, aid to parochial schools, and Communism, it appeared to do so as a reactionary monolith under the leadership of ecclesiastical superiors.

Beginning in the 1930s, for example, the National Legion of Decency asked each Catholic to annually renew a pledge to abide by the ratings attached to movies by the Legion. In 1934, Cardinal Dougherty of Philadelphia declared that "the greatest menace to faith and morals in America today is the moving-picture theatre," and he called for a complete boycott of all movies by Philadelphia Catholics. The boycott was still in effect when he died in 1951. In New York, in 1950, the Legion of Decency was able to pressure the New York City Commissioner of Licenses to ban the performance of the film *The Miracle* because it was a "sacrilegious and blasphemous mockery of Christian religious truths."[28]

Catholics of the Northeast were also generally in the vanguard of support for Senator Joseph McCarthy's crusade against Communism in the United States.[29] This support should not be surprising, given the atheistic element in Communism. Also, the growing power of Communism in the postwar period was especially disturbing to a Church that still had a large percentage of its followers from the Old World. Poles, Lithuanians, Slovaks, Germans, and other eastern European American Catholics saw their homelands' political and religious freedom eliminated by Russian occupation, and many German, French, and Italian parishioners worried over socialist victories in their countries after the war. Moreover, Catholicism in America was once again under attack by organizations like Protestants and Other Americans United for Separation of Church and State and the National Council of Churches. Strident criticism of Catholic rituals and practices, of the Church's authority structure, of its Roman relationship, and of its presumed softness on church-state separation by these organizations served to harden the separation between Catholics and others. Demands from these same people that Catholics repudiate McCarthy could only serve to have the opposite effect.

But there were other factors contributing to Catholic conservatism in the 1950s that reveal cracks in the supposed monolith. Just as participation in the Civil War had created opportunities for social mobility among Irish Catholics, so too participation in two world wars, especially World War II, created similar opportunities for more recent immigrant Catholics. Between 1930 and 1960, several Polish and Italian Catholics were elected to prominent political positions in cities, states, and even in the federal government. In the postwar period, Catholics were more likely than others to move out of the cities into the suburbs and were more likely to get a college education.[30] A Church that was predominantly an immigrant Church in 1900 was becoming one increasingly middle- and upper-middle class. The price of this success, however, was "Americanization," a process that could be deeply disturbing to such a tradition-oriented group of people. Change was something that strongly affected recent immigrant groups, especially when they saw their children rejecting the old ways as they became Americanized. Such fears could be easily transferred onto the outside world in the form of an anti-Communist mania.

Evidence of the strains created within American Catholicism was apparent in surveys which showed that in 1953 only 51% of the laity considered artificial birth control and the remarriage of divorced persons as sinful, contrary to official Church teaching.[31] In parishes throughout the Northeast, even in the more conservative Polish ones, the rate of failed Easter Duties and the rate of mixed marriages increased enormously between 1945 and 1960.[32]

At Holy Family Parish in Pittsfield, Massachusetts, for example, mixed marriages began to increase in the late 1940s. Second generation Poles were leaving home looking for better jobs and generally reveling in the increased social mobility of the descendants of immigrant Catholics. Church membership dropped off sharply. Fewer and fewer of the children cared to learn the Polish language although they clung fast to certain ethnic customs. The tide was stemmed temporarily by the pastor who, along with some of the older parishioners, formed a Polish Community Club providing recreational, social, educational, and civic activities. By 1960, the neighborhood around the church was still predominantly Polish Catholic.[33]

Similar problems plagued the French Catholic parishes of New England. Beginning in the 1940s, there was a noticeable decrease in the number of parishioners in the churches of Springfield, Massachusetts. Many of the younger people moved out to the suburbs where they attended new French parishes. Despite their attendance at Catholic churches and parochial schools, whether in the city or the suburbs, third-generation Franco-Americans lost much of their French ethnic identity. At St. Aloysius Church, for example, younger members of the parish in the 1950s were requesting that Masses be said in English. They were rejected, but they would not be put off for long.[34]

Another disturbing element of change in Catholic parish life was the massive migration of southern blacks into Northeast cities, which increased sharply after World War II. Most of these new immigrants were non-Catholic and a shortage of black priests made it impossible for most dioceses to launch a major program for those who were Catholic. Diocesan leaders, such as Cardinal Spellman of New York, did their best to keep up the standards in the parochial schools where enrollments of black children increased, and lay organizations like the Interracial Councils tried to create the best possible racial climate in parishes and neighborhoods. But as with the Irish and the Italians before them, as blacks moved into an area, whites moved out.[35]

For some clergy and laity the postwar transfer of population presented insurmountable obstacles. Racial transformation in some parishes meant that income from collections dropped to nearly nothing, Mass attendance dwindled, some schools closed, and church property crumbled. Oftentimes, the minority poor looked upon the old massive parochial school building as a status symbol, even though they could not afford to support it. In some cases, clergymen deserted by their white parishioners and suffering from low morale could do nothing but watch the progressive deterioration of the edifices that had become so much, perhaps too much, a part of parish life. Even where strong clerical leadership was evident, it proved difficult to recreate the old parochial consciousness among the poor new arrivals who had not initiated, built, or financed the plant, but merely inherited it.

For others, white flight from the inner city offered new opportunities. During twelve years of service, Father William R. McCann, pastor of St. Charles Borromeo Parish in Harlem, baptized more than 6,000 black converts. When Father Edward F. Cunnie took over St. Elizabeth's Parish in Philadelphia in 1952, the number of white families in the parish had dropped from 800 to 30, but he went to work immediately on an active conversion campaign among his 400 black families. He welcomed non-Catholic black children into the parish school, adopted the national school lunch program, and formed a parents' group. The parish, under his guidance, established a credit union and even a parochial shoe store to serve the needs of the poor in the neighborhood. Founder and moderator of the Philadelphia Catholic Interracial Council, Father Cunnie also instituted a religious survey of the area and made sure that follow-up calls were made to the hundreds of people who indicated a wish to talk to a Catholic priest. It should be no diminution of the true missionary zeal shown by Fathers McCann and Cunnie to note that changing circumstances in the 1950s were forcing inner-city parishes and their clerical leaders to open breaches in the fortresslike walls that American Catholics had so painstakingly erected against the outside world.[36]

Another significant element in the population shift was that established city parishes, which were generally free and clear of debt, were left in neighborhoods rapidly turning into ghettos while their former parishioners flooded suburban areas. The Catholic Church, therefore, had to shift its resources and priorities to meet the new demands by a whole new cycle of building—new churches, new parochial schools, and now high schools as well, and, of course, new debts. New parish formation reflected the change in priorities, for nearly four-fifths of all parishes created after 1940 were in the suburbs. That the center of financial gravity for the parochial system had moved out of the city was revealed by increasing amounts contributed by "country" parishes to seminary collections, which was accompanied by substantial decreases in urban parish contributions.[37]

Small country parishes were being transformed into large suburban parishes by the white exodus from the cities. For example, the small rural parish of St. Denis in Delaware County, Pennsylvania, had seen few changes since its foundation in 1829. In 1932, the parish still contained only 207 families (1,035 people) and 368 parochial school children. But St. Denis was situated very close to the main westerly road out of Philadelphia and midway between a trolley line and a railway. When the white exodus began, therefore, St. Denis was astride the migratory path. By 1960, the parish contained 2,186 families (8,006 people) and the school population had swelled to 1,426 pupils. Moreover, the whole area within the parish boundaries was transformed from one in which Catholics were a small minority to one in which nearly half the population was Catholic.

To accommodate such an influx of newcomers, St. Denis Parish had to repeat the experience of the urban parishes founded in the late nineteenth and early twentieth century. A new church had to be built, then a new school, and then a separate chapel. The staff of the parish school had to be increased from eleven nuns and four lay teachers in 1954 to thirteen nuns and eleven lay teachers by 1960. Between 1945 and 1959, annual expenditures at St. Denis soared from $60,117.40 to $454,774.56. The two greatest elements in that increase were for construction of new buildings and lay teachers' salaries. Postwar migration had turned St. Denis from a parish that had no debt in 1945 into one that had to begin to manage one of $332,298.13 in 1959.[38]

The "suburbanization" of American Catholicism and its parochial system in the Northeast would create even more serious problems in the ensuing years. The suburban pastor would have to struggle with ever more onerous debts, just as his forebears had had to do, but now the ties of ethnicity and neighborhood would no longer be there to reinforce parochial consciousness and clerical authority. Postwar social mobility, the "Americanization" of the old immigrant Church, black migration to the cities, and the subsequent white exodus into sprawling suburban parishes had seen to that. Moreover, added financial burdens would be added to suburban woes because of the call to the more affluent to assist the struggling efforts of the urban parishes they had left behind. And out of some of those urban parishes, consumed by their own special problems, would issue pleas for greater social involvement among American Catholics, pleas that seemed to militate against all the old traditional parochial values of otherworldliness, unquestioning respect for authority, and exclusiveness.

As the 1960s dawned, there was evident a dramatic weakening among many parochial groups of the "we-they" exclusiveness of former days, which had centered on withdrawal into the system of alternate institutions provided by the parish. Among the socially mobile, the need to separate from the non-Catholic community was now becoming less strong than the need to assimilate into it. As people's lives became more bound up with the place where they worked rather than with the place where they lived, parochial cohesiveness was weakened. The old-style residential parish required that people's worship and sacramental life be rooted in the place where they lived, but as more and more Catholics spent increasing amounts of time, perhaps an hour's commuting time, away from their homes, that sort of home parish loyalty became more difficult to maintain. Occupational and geographic mobility forced individuals to learn new patterns of behavior as they left old groups, to create new interaction patterns, and to meet the demands of new social systems. Whereas the old parish had existed in a social milieu characterized by a high degree of occupational and ethnic homogeneity, "Americanization" and population shifts since the 1930s created heterogeneity. Impersonality developed in the movement from the small community with personal relationships to the mechanical structure of society that was devoid of the intimate, private, exclusive living together.[39] A priest with wide-ranging experience in different parishes in the Diocese of Worcester, Massachusetts, wrote that "the common opinion of individuals that have lived in a particular locality their entire lives reveals that the neighborhood is not like it was in past years and there is little knowledge or relationship with those who live close by."[40]

Another reflection on the social alienation becoming increasingly prevalent by the 1960s pointed out that:

> Our urban world has lead to depersonalization; we seem to be lost in numbers. The automobile has taken us out of the home (and away from the parish) while the television set has brought us back (and kept us away from parish activities). If we are able to shop quickly by using a shopping center with its familiar mass of concrete surrounding it, so too must we leave church quickly on Sunday to make room for cars coming in for the next Mass. As we drive bumper-to-bumper on our amazingly new (and overcrowded) expressways, we may sometimes be attacked by the suspicion that we are engaged in a symbolic dumb show of modern life—each of us enclosed in a small cubicle resting on our share of asphalt, crowded beyond endurance, unable to move forward. On the highway we are very close to each other and yet so far—silently imprisoned by our preoccupation, unable to communicate with each other. . . .
>
> So too with our parishes. They are large and getting larger. We stand next to strangers at Mass, wondering who they might be. People come and go, move in and out of the parish; a ten-year resident is regarded as an old-timer.[41]

That these conditions were creating a "crisis of faith" was evident to many. It was manifest, claimed Rev. James G. Sherman, pastor of St. Denis Parish, in a falling off of attendance at Mass and in the reception of the Sacraments, and in the rise in the number of separations and divorces.[42] Perhaps, as Harvy Cox wrote in *The Secular City*, such a crisis of faith originated in the tension between life in a world of advancing material and technological potential and unchanging parish structures embedded in the immigrant past. Certainly there were those who hoped to resolve the tension by "modernizing" parish life to bring it in line with the call to greater social involvement. The expectations of these parishioners could only be raised by the exhortations and example of the most successful descendant of one of those Catholic immigrant families, John F. Kennedy, in his inaugural address of 1961. But the Kennedy image could be Janus-faced. Conservative Catholics could revel triumphantly in this Massachusetts Catholic's political victory despite the dredging up of many of the old anti-Catholic diatribes during the campaign, and they could note with pleasure his strong anti-Communist stance. Many of these parishioners could, just as validly as the "modernizers," view traditional forms of parish life as necessary bulwarks against a modern world they saw moving in the wrong direction.

There were already signs on the horizon that changes in Catholic practice were inevitable. In 1951, Pope Pius XII allowed the restored Easter Vigil and some English in the administration of baptism, extreme unction, and matrimony. Three years later, English was permitted in the prayers at funerals. A major change in 1953 was the introduction of evening Masses. That would have been impossible without a drastic revision of the laws regulating the Eucharistic fast. Therefore, the fast from midnight was abolished. In its stead, it was decreed that water never broke the fast, the sick could take medicine without an indult having to come all the way from Rome, liquids except alcohol could be taken up to an hour before Communion, and alcohol and food could be taken up to three hours before Communion. Except for the drinking of water, this relaxation at first applied only to afternoon and evening Masses. These rather mild reforms were introduced slowly into churches in the Northeast. In New York, for example, evening Masses were not initiated until 1957 with one or two Holy Days that were not also legal holidays. Only in 1959 was permission given to have them on New Year's Day, but not yet on Sunday or the feast of Corpus Christi.

In 1956, changes in the Holy Week liturgy were implemented with Masses transferred to afternoon or evening, and Holy Communion distributed on Good Friday for the first time. That same year, the International Liturgical Conference at Assisi recommended, and Pius XII agreed the following year, the extension of the new Eucharistic Fast to morning Masses, a return to early Church practice. In 1958, a new instruction from Rome encouraged the Dialogue Mass in which the congregation said aloud parts assigned to altar boys plus the Gloria, Credo, Sanctus, Pater Noster, Agnus Dei, and other prayers. Furthermore, lectors could read the Epistle and Gospel in the vernacular while the priest was saying them in Latin. If the lectors were laymen, they had to stand outside the sanctuary. The instruction also encouraged Offertory and Communion processions.[43]

As the period drew to a close, parish life was still very much what it had been like for generations, but there was a definite stirring of minds and hearts in those parishes. No one wanted to throw away what was hard-won and cherished in parish life, but social change was breaking down many of the barriers that had for so long separated Catholics from the rest of the community. For some, the challenges inherent in that transformation were heartily welcomed; for others, the future held out a loss of identity as a special people.

# Notes

1. Rev. William L. Lucey, "The Position of Catholics in Vermont: 1853," *RACHSP*, 64 (Dec. 1953): 225.

2. *Catholic Directory, Archdiocese of Philadelphia, 1982*, 151–233; Cohalan, *Popular History*, 300–301.

3. John V. Tolino, "Solving the Italian Problem," *American Ecclesiastical Review* (*AER*) 99 (Sept. 1938): 246–256, "The Church in America and the Italian Problem," *AER*, 100 (Jan. 1939): 22–32, and "The Future of the Italian Problem," *AER*, 101 (Sept. 1939): 56–67.

4. Francis Letiziano, "The 1933 South Philadelphia Disturbance Over the Closing of Our Lady of Good Counsel Church," (unpublished manuscript, 1971), 1–25.

5. *Holy Innocents, Golden Jubilee*, 22; *St. Adalbert's Diamond Jubilee*, 15; *Church of the Resurrection of Our Lord, Phila., Pa., Fiftieth Anniversary, 1928–1978* (Phila., 1978), 6; *Annual Reports, Archdiocese of Philadelphia*, 1930.

6. *Annual Reports, Archdiocese of Philadelphia*, 1930 and 1932; *St. Adalbert's Diamond Jubilee*, 15.

7. *Annual Reports, Archdiocese of Philadelphia*, 1930 and 1932; Hennessey, *American Catholics*, 265.

8. *St. Francis de Sales, Golden Jubilee*, 14, 48; Cohalan, *Popular History*, 257, 260.

9. *Resurrection, 50th Anniversary*, 6; *Holy Child, Golden Jubilee*, 32, 41; *St. Gabriel's Golden Jubilee*, 155.

10. *Jubile d'Or, St. Thomas d'Aquin*, 98.

11. *Resurrection, 50th Anniversary*, 28–29; *St. Francis de Sales Golden Jubilee*, 56; *Holy Innocents Golden Jubilee*, 36; *St. Callistus, History*, 102; *Holy Child, Golden Jubilee*, 34, 46; *Sesquicentennial, St. Denis*, 142–143; *Jubile d'Or, St. Thomas d'Aquin*, 98–99.

12. *Holy Innocents Golden Jubilee*, 22, 24, 32, 42; *St. Callistus, History*, 62, 95; *St. Cecelia's, History*, 20, 32, 52; Cusick, "History of St. Barnabas," 16; *St. Francis de Sales, Golden Jubilee*, 54; *Annual Reports, Archdiocese of Philadelphia*, 1932 and 1959; Cohalan, *Popular History*, 278.

13. Gavigan, "Rise and Fall," 126–127; Hennessey, *American Catholics*, 287; *Annual Reports, Archdiocese of Philadelphia*, 1930, 1932, and 1935.

14. Cohalan, *Popular History*, 302.

15. *Jubile d'Or, St. Thomas d'Aquin*, 89.

16. *Ibid.*, 89–92; *St. Cecelia's, History*, 22, 42; *St. Callistus, History*, 76, 88; *St. Monica's 50 Years Old*, 188–191.

17. *St. Monica's 50 Years Old*, 186; *St. Francis de Sales Golden Jubilee*, 52–53.

18. *Annual Reports, Archdiocese of Philadelphia*, 1940 and 1945; *St. Adalbert's Diamond Jubilee*, 16; Wendrychowicz, "History of St. Adalbert's," 8.

19. *Annual Reports, Archdiocese of Philadelphia*, 1946 and 1949.

20. *Holy Child Golden Jubilee*, 42; *St. Callistus, History*, 59.

21. Connelly, *History of Archdiocese of Philadelphia*, 411–412.

22. Hennessey, *American Catholics*, 287; Bernard Lazerwitz, "Some Factors Associated with Variations in Church Attendance," *Social Forces*, 39 (1960): 303; Andrew M. Greeley, "Some Information on the Present Situation of American Catholics," *Social Order*, 13 (1963); 20–21, and *The American Catholic: A Social Portrait* (N.Y., 1977), 143; Mary T. Hanna, *Catholics and American Politics* (Cambridge, Mass., 1979), 105; Jackson W. Carroll, *et al.*, *Religion in America 1950 to the Present* (N.Y., 1979), 19–20, 33.

23. Connelly, *History of Archdiocese of Philadelphia*, 411–412.

24. William Clebsch, *American Religious Thought* (Chicago, 1973), 26; Hennessey, *American Catholics*, 288.

25. *Sesquicentennial, St. Denis*, 187.

26. Hennessey, *American Catholics*, 288; Connelly, *History of Archdiocese of Philadelphia*, 411; Robert T. Handy, *A History of the Churches in the United States and Canada* (N.Y., 1977), 400–401.

27. Thomas T. McAvoy, *A History of the Catholic Church in the United States* (Notre Dame, 1969), 454.

28. Connelly, *History of Archdiocese of Philadelphia*, 384–385; Cohalan, *Popular History*, 299.

29. Seymour Martin Lipset, "Three Decades of the Radical Right: Coughlinites, McCarthyites, and Birchers," in Daniel Bell, ed., *The Radical Right* (Garden City, N.Y., 1964), 395, 407; Donald F. Crosby, *God, Church, and Flag: Senator Joseph R. McCarthy and the Catholic Church, 1950–1957* (Chapel Hill, 1978), 104, 113, 174–175, 188, 196.

30. Andrew M. Greeley, "American Catholicism: 1909–1984," *America*, 150 (June 1984): 487.

31. Greeley, "Some Information," 19–21.

32. *Annual Reports, Archdiocese of Philadelphia*, 1930, 1932, 1945, 1949, and 1960; *Black Ledger of Statistics, Archdiocese of Philadelphia Archives*, 1960.

33. Clowes, *Pol-Am.* 57–129.

34. Burns, *Springfield's Ethnic Heritage*, 41–43.

35. Jesse O. McKee, "A Geographical Analysis of the Origin, Diffusion, and Spatial Diffusion of the Black American in the United States," *The Southern Quarterly*, 12 (1974): 203–216; Connelly, *History of Archdiocese of Philadelphia*, 442, 477; Cohalan, *Popular History*, 261, 296, 297; William A. Osborne, *The Segregated Covenant: Race Relations and American Catholics* (N.Y., 1967), 126–153; Hennessey, *American Catholics*, 265.

36. Connelly, *History of the Archdiocese of Philadelphia*, 441; Cohalan, *Popular History*, 261.

37. Cohalan, *Popular History*, 301; *Catholic Directory, Archdiocese of Philadelphia 1983*, 151–233; Gavigan, "Rise and Fall," 127.

38. *Annual Reports, Archdiocese of Philadelphia*, 1932, 1945, 1959, and 1960; *Sesquicentennial, St. Denis*, 136, 137, 163.

39. P. Fellin and E. Litwak, "The Neighborhood in Urban American Society," *Social Work*, 13 (1968): 74–75; Gavigan, "Rise and Fall," 127–128; Browne, "The Changing American Parish," 8–9.

40. Rev. Paul T. O'Connell, ''The Concept of the Parish in the Light of the Second Vatican Council'' (Ph.D. dissertation, Catholic University of America, 1969), 201.

41. Lyons, *Programs for Parish Councils*, viii–ix.

42. *Sesquicentennial, St. Denis*, 187.

43. Connelly, *History of the Archdiocese of Philadelphia*, 438–439, 457–458; Cohalan, *Popular History*, 311.

## CHAPTER FOUR

# Crisis and Renewal, 1960 to the Present

The Catholic parish in the Northeast had weathered successfully many storms over the years, but never before had an institution and the people in it been buffeted by so many and so rapid dislocations as occurred with the advent of the 1960s. In that respect, the parish was just one among many institutions in America suffering severe strains in a period of reform and rebellion. What had maintained stability in those institutions in the past had been, principally, confidence in the objectives of those institutions and a respect for established authority. That had been especially true in the Catholic parish, where separateness and loyalty to clerical leadership made sense in the face of non-Catholic hostility, and at a time when ethnic and neighborhood attachments were still strong. But in the 1960s, Catholics had "arrived," so to speak. Most Catholics had become Americanized, many ethnic peculiarities having blurred with the passage of time and as the result of the kind of clerical ministry that had, perforce, emphasized the common beliefs and practices of Catholics from whatever foreign land.

Respect for ecclesiastical authority and confidence in the Church's leadership had kept parishes tightly knit. Respect for secular authority and confidence in America's mission and leadership, emphasized in priestly teaching and exemplified by widespread Catholic participation in all of America's wars and crusades, had done much to remove the taint of Catholics retaining residual foreign loyalties. Ironically, however, those authoritarian aspects of Catholic socialization, which had contributed to the acceptance of Catholics into mainstream American culture, were coming under heavy attack in America just as Catholics began to enter fully into that culture.

Everywhere one looked in America in those years, it seemed that some traditional belief or practice was being questioned. A television in nearly every home, and the immediacy of response it demanded, tended to spread the sense of crisis across the land. It was a media of communication that could circumvent all the old lines of authority of parent, parish priest, and government official. After the conservatism of the 1950s, what appeared newsworthy to television in the following decade was what could be depicted in a dramatic visual way, and that often meant instances of rebellion against the establishment. Through the "miracle'' of television, what was unique at first quickly became accepted as normative.

Even prominent Catholic leaders were seen through television to be resisting traditional authority. The symbol of Catholic success in America, John F. Kennedy, was seen by millions telling a group of Protestant ministers that he did not accept the right of any ecclesiastical official to tell him what to do in the sphere of his public responsibility. Pope John XXIII was seen encouraging Catholics to move away from the authoritarianism of the past. Catholic priests and nuns were seen breaking the established law and custom by demonstrating in support of equal rights for blacks or against what had been at first promoted officially as a moral crusade against atheistic and totalitarian Communism in Southeast Asia.[1]

Catholic parishioners already faced the bewildering world of the 1960s bereft of the unifying forces of ethnicity, neighborhood, and even anti-Catholicism, and now they found the certainty of traditional authority called into question. Catholics had arrived, to be sure, as good Americans, but now they found both Americanism and Catholicism as they had come to know them undergoing painful redefinition.

With many of the old support mechanisms provided by old-style parish life gone or withering away, every new development, even the most mundane, seemed to add to the sense of crisis. St. Thomas Aquinas Parish was still, in 1960, the center for French-Canadians in Springfield, Massachusetts, and its population continued to grow until 1966. In that year, however, "progress" intervened in the form of the new Interstate Highway 91, which cut a swath through one section of the parish. Construction of this road displaced more than a hundred families, the majority of whom left the area permanently. It had become difficult enough to maintain venerable parish institutions and practices with so many young people moving out to the suburbs, but the forced removal of more than a hundred families seemed like a major catastrophe. But, as occurred in many other urban parishes during this period, this was only one among a string of developments gnawing away at traditional parish life. Four years later, St. Thomas was jolted by a second crisis—a massive influx of Puerto Ricans into the neighborhood.[2]

What created the new immigration that affected so many urban parishes in the Northeast was a 1965 revision in the old national origins' quota system established by the immigration laws of the 1920s. As a result, Hispanic immigrants from various parts of the world began flocking to the urban centers of the Northeast looking for the opportunity that had attracted earlier immigrants. The Portuguese flooded into southeastern Massachusetts. Puerto Ricans, citizens of the United States since 1917, came in even larger numbers. In 1965, there were already 700,000 Puerto Ricans in New York City. Within ten years, Hispanics accounted for nearly one-third of the total Catholic population.[3]

The Hispanics presented the parochial system of the Northeast with a new version of an old and serious problem. The "Italian Problem" now became the

"Spanish Problem." Hispanics came from areas that for cultural as well as political reasons had always suffered from a woefully inadequate number of vocations to the priesthood and religious life, and in which the standard of Catholic practice had often been very low. They were, like the Italians, generally very poorly instructed and had no awareness of the way in which parishes were organized and supported in America. Like so many who had preceded them, Hispanics suffered keenly during the sudden transition from a stable rural society to the level of urban life open to them here, and they were dismayed by the religious, cultural, and racial discrimination that they experienced for the first time.[4]

Because of their poverty, their lack of religious personnel, and the by-now well-established practice of "Americanization," no effort was made to organize Hispanics in new national parishes. If a particular parish, or group of parishes, became predominantly or wholly Spanish, all well and good. The plant or plants were already there, and since Hispanics generally moved into old urban parishes, the debts on parish buildings were by the 1970s low or nonexistent. These parishes could be staffed by Spanish-speaking priests who were recruited widely. At the Augustinian parish of St. Mary's in Lawrence, Massachusetts, which had been rapidly transformed from an Irish to a Hispanic parish, Father Joseph Grifferty was sent for to take charge. Formerly the pastor of St. Denis Parish in Delaware County, Pennsylvania, and of St. Nicholas of Tolentine in the Bronx, Father Grifferty had already seen his share of parochial change caused by a variety of factors. In both places, he had shown himself to be an able administrator, and he possessed extensive knowledge of Spanish culture and language. He had volunteered for this new assignment at the age of 67 when most priests were seeking to retire. The Redemptorists who would eventually be assigned to the former German parish of St. Peter's in Philadelphia were sent to Puerto Rico for a year or more in order to learn Spanish and to study the cultural background and pastoral practices with which their future parishioners were familiar. The Puerto Ricans were the only immigrant group for whom it was possible to provide such a service. Classes were also arranged in every diocese for other priests, brothers, sisters, and laypeople who could help in the ever-growing effort to meet the needs of the new arrivals.[5]

Spanish Catholic Action Offices, later called Spanish Apostolates, were opened in dioceses to coordinate efforts at assimilating the new immigrants. Spanish replaced Italian as the major modern language in seminaries, and in New York the custom began of sending half the ordination class away to study Spanish.

These efforts to integrate Hispanics into already-existing parishes became visible when ethnically changing parishes introduced a Spanish Mass and Sacraments with a Spanish-speaking priest. Spanish Masses were always enthusiastic affairs with much music, usually guitar music, and singing, and were always occasions for a great deal of socializing. This would often offend the sensibilities of the "Anglo" parishioners who were accustomed to a more reserved behavior in their churches. Consequently, the early years of adjustment to the Hispanics were very difficult for those non-Hispanics who were unable or unwilling to desert their homes in the changing neighborhood. Many did flee, however, because for them parish homogeneity and parochial consciousness were shattered by the newcomers. During the transition period, charges formerly leveled at Italians—that the new arrivals were uncivilized and violent, that they refused to contribute to the support of the parish, and that they resisted learning the English language and adopting "American" food and customs—were leveled at the Hispanics.[6]

At St. Thomas Aquinas Parish, the clash of cultures was more virulent. Between 1970 and 1980, the area within the parish gained 4,409 Puerto Ricans, and lost 1,418 French-Canadians. Animosity between the two groups resulted from the French perception that the newcomers resisted assimilation and that they were destroyers of property and neighborhoods rather than builders as had been the earlier immigrants. When, in 1977, the church school was burned to the ground, it was generally believed that the Puerto Ricans were responsible. Gang fights became a common occurrence in the city park two blocks from the church, and in 1982 a French boy was gunned down in daylight by Puerto Ricans just one block from the church. The pastor of the parish adopted a "bunker" mentality in the face of the critical changes going on in the area. He maintained no communication with the growing Puerto Rican community, and, in fact, he laid plans for moving the parish entirely out of the threatened area. His successor, however, did establish relations with the Puerto Ricans by concelebrating Masses in the main Hispanic churches and by watching over Puerto Rican children playing in the church parking lot. He also went to every parishioner left in the area with an appeal to remain and continue to support the church and each other. Although membership in the parish dropped from 4,500 to less than 1,000 by 1983, the leadership of this pastor did create a greater element of stability.[7]

All city parishes that underwent ethnic transformation, either black or Hispanic, developed enormous financial problems because of the poverty of the new parishioners. The old parochial consciousness that might have, to a degree, alleviated some of those problems was, ironically, further eroded by some of the very solutions proposed to remedy the deterioration of the plants. Commissions for Inter-parochial Cooperation were established in the mid-1960s, whereby solvent parishes would contribute to needy parishes in the inner city. This kind of cooperation was a far cry from the fund-raising competitiveness that had become so much a part of parochial loyalty and pride in earlier years.[8]

Parishes sharing financial responsibilities was just one example of how traditional parish exclusiveness was faltering under the increasing demand for social activism in the 1960s. This was the age of the call to involvement in the world by the first Catholic president of the United States and by leaders of the Civil Rights Movement. It was also the age of Vatican Council II.

Minor changes in Catholic parish practices had begun in the 1950s. Under

Pope Pius XII, some English in the Mass and Sacraments, evening Masses, a revised Eucharistic fast, and the involvement of laymen as lectors had been permitted. But then, in 1962, Pope John XXIII, in opening the first Vatican Council since 1869, called for a massive updating of Catholicism to bring it into the twentieth century with all its new and puzzling problems. Some of the members of the council publicly questioned many of the long accepted, but accidental, elements of Catholic life that many regarded, mistakenly, as essential to their religious identity. Others saw the council opening up a Pandora's box, for once the idea of reform was introduced, there would be no end to the instability created.

At the council, there was relatively little sustained discussion of the parish, but its major documents looked toward a revolution in parish life. Here the faithful were referred to as the People of God and the parish as the sign of the mutual unity or fellowship of all mankind through, and in its union with, God. As such, the parish was not to be turned in upon itself and its problems in perpetuating its physical structure. It was to be involved in a twofold mission: one within the Church, constantly reforming, renewing, and redefining its methods for every generation, and another, relating the Church to and for the world. Thus, through the parish, the Church was to transform the world to true values by witness.

In this missionary quest, the council emphasized, clergy and laity were equal, although they had different roles. Everyone in the parish had a *charism,* a call from God to a particular ministry in the community, and was given the ability to fulfill that ministry. The passive apostolate of merely leading a good life was not sufficient for laymen in the modern world. Laymen were called, not to withdraw from the world, but to permeate and perfect it. And anything that prevented the Church from attaining this end—authoritarianism, centralism, absolutism, triumphalism, or privatism—should be abandoned.[9]

Implementation of the ideas expressed at Vatican II came to the clergy in a series of disciplinary and, especially, liturgical changes, since liturgy was the community-forming central focus of the Church. Between 1964 and 1968, in a series of progressive revisions, the Latin of the Mass was eliminated in favor of the vernacular. The Lenten discipline of fast and abstinence was modified almost to the vanishing point, and fish on Friday, heretofore universally recognized as a sign of Catholic identity, disappeared. A Revised Calendar was released in 1969 that placed more emphasis on the seasons of the liturgical year than on the feasts of specific saints.

It was a confusing time for everyone. The single liturgical book, which the altar boys used to move from the Epistle to the Gospel side of the altar with such great solemnity, gave way to several books. In fact, at one point, there were so many books on the altar that it was suggested that they be placed on a rotisserie, which would spin to the appropriate one. Misconceptions regarding certain reforms led to a waning in devotions to Mary and the recitation of the Rosary. The tabernacle was removed from its central place and moved to a variety of positions.

Gone was the day when a Catholic could go to Mass anywhere in the world and find it to be exactly the same as the Mass he enjoyed in his own parish. Now, it seemed, every parish had its particular variation. In some churches, the people stood to receive Holy Communion, while in others they knelt at the altar rail. Some churches did away with the altar rail entirely. Some had a good deal of singing, while others had little or none. Some spent a great deal of money moving their altars forward, while others did not even bother. In some churches, bread rolls were consecrated and passed around in baskets allowing the communicants to pick a roll and eat it.[10]

Because many of the supposed reforms of parish life were presented in terms of what seemed like accidentals, which were left to clerical authorities to implement or not as they saw fit, the early post-Vatican II period actually saw a strengthening of parochial isolation. To some it appeared that whatever unity had existed in Catholicism was being destroyed, contrary to the general philosophy of the council. To others, the loss of familiarity and stability in religious practice was painful. Many missed the musical and artistic splendor, the sense of sanctuary, solemnity and awe, or the simple atmosphere of darkness and silence that had marked older forms of worship. At times, liturgical experiments turned into circuses.[11]

The stability that parish life had once seemed to guarantee was hard to find anywhere in America in the mid-1960s. The period of rising expectations in the political, social, and religious realms that had characterized the early part of the decade were thwarted or shattered by a series of traumatic events. Camelot came to an end in 1963 with the assassination of John F. Kennedy. Hopes for reform and social justice promised by the 1964 Civil Rights Act were dashed by the intransigence of entrenched groups and by the assassinations in 1968 of Martin Luther King, Jr., and Robert Kennedy. Race riots rocked several major cities. Patriotic expectations of victory over Communist totalitarianism in Southeast Asia were crushed by the way televised news interpreted the Tet Offensive in 1968. The credibility of government leaders was destroyed when news of this unexpected, yet militarily unsuccessful, attack was placed alongside months of optimistic official reports that the insurgents were near defeat. The generation gap widened to a chasm by the ''hippie'' subculture, by the youthful rejection of traditional authority in an expanding anti-Vietnam War movement, and by the perceived overreaction of the older generation to these assaults on the legitimacy of their values.

The issues raised by the Vietnam War caught a whole generation of Catholic youth in a dilemma. Upwardly mobile Catholics, like their non-Catholic counterparts, had greater access to the resources and techniques that allowed them to avoid military service if they chose to. Young working-class Catholics, also like their non-Catholic counterparts, went to Vietnam in large numbers. As one young recruit, the product of parochial schools in central New Jersey, put it, he had been indoctrinated into anti-Communism along with the Catechism. "The nuns used to beat it into us," he later reported. "We didn't know what Communism *was,* but we knew it was *bad.*"[12] Working-class South Boston was credited with having produced more priests, nuns, and servicemen than any other community of comparable size in America. As a recruit from that area explained it, so many Catholic boys from South Boston served in Vietnam because "of the discipline of the church." "If you were a Catholic," he said, "you believed in the mysteries. You accepted them on blind faith. One of those acceptances was a blind loyalty to defending the country."[13] Moreover, the Catholic Church in America had done such an effective job of proving its loyalty to the country that it was very difficult for any Catholic youth from a working-class background to prove to the local draft board that he had sincere moral objections to serving in that war. Joel Garreau, who was in 1969 the first male ever granted conscientious objector status from his heavily French-Canadian Pawtucket, Rhode Island, draft board, was initially told that, as a Catholic, he would never make C.O. because he belonged to the "War Church."[14]

What is surprising, and it is indicative of the turmoil of the times as well as the strong residual effects of Catholic education and parish life, is the remarkable number of war protesters and resisters who came from the same working-class Catholic background. One young man from a very poor Irish Catholic neighborhood in Boston commented that he was radicalized against the war in his "unique parish which unlike most in the area, was not patriotic and gung ho." "If I had been raised in a conservative, traditional parish," he said, "I quite easily could have gone to war."[15] Another youth, who had mutilated himself in order to avoid military service, argued that he had been influenced by two strains in his Catholic education and upbringing—"the crusader, warlike one and another of martyrdom." In his case, the latter strain had won out.[16]

At a time when all Catholics, but especially the young, were being forced to make such monumental decisions, the shifting sands of institutions in the process of reevaluation provided little support. For many, Vatican II had destroyed the last fixed star in this chaotic universe. Many people left the Catholic Church for other Christian churches, or Oriental religions, or simply gave up on religion altogether. A Catholic Traditionalist Manifesto was framed in 1965, rejecting the new liturgical changes and holding to the formulary approved in 1570 by Pius V. French Archbishop Marcel Lefebvre's Society of St. Pius X was one of several traditionalist groups that attracted American followers alienated by the changes. For others, the changes seemed insufficient, or were not being implemented rapidly enough by the bishops who were given the task of implementation. Some turned to variants of enthusiastic religion or to religious-type encounter groups. Others answered the call of Vatican II for greater secular involvement by joining a variety of social crusades.[17]

As the 1960s came to an end, there was hardly a seminary in the Northeast that was free of internal tension and turmoil. Seminarians and novices split into traditionalist and progressive camps. Disillusionment with authority, with the scope or pace of renewal, or with what some called the "stratified irrelevance of the established parish," led to the creation of "underground churches"—informal ad hoc gatherings of Christians who crossed over denominational lines to celebrate improvised Eucharists in each other's homes and to study Scripture or theology together. They were sharply critical of the traditional "building-centered" parish and saw themselves as recreating the small communities of the early Church coming together for "fellowship, teaching, prayer, and the breaking of bread." And they were strongly antiauthoritarian, asserting that they would "not wait for official commissions to take five or ten years for discussion" only to come up with "anachronistically irrelevant guidelines." Episcopal disapproval of the underground churches, and the suspension of some of their clerical leaders, led to an early demise for most.[18]

The turmoil over decentralization, ecumenism, community, openness, and lay involvement began to subside in the 1970s. By 1970, the major liturgical changes had been introduced and digested, and Monthly Missalettes, presenting the Mass as we know it today, began appearing in the church pews. Dissent was lessening in all areas of American life and people began adopting a fatalistic view of things. Students began to demonstrate against the Vietnam War less and less beginning with the end of the draft, and several radical leaders began to look for ways to get ahead in the world. The oil crisis and inflation focused most people's attention on economic survival. There were no great civil rights' demonstrations after the conflagrations of 1968. Dissent became politicized and, therefore, domesticated. The Great Society of Lyndon Johnson foundered on the rocks of war expenditures. American power, triumphalism, and moral crusading were blunted by the Watergate scandal, Arab oil sheiks, the fall of Saigon, and the Iran hostage crisis. The dynamism of Kennedy and Johnson was followed by the dourness of Nixon, Ford, and Carter, and the freshness of John XXIII was replaced by the modified conservatism of the first Polish pope in history, John Paul II.

The period of turmoil, however, had created many casualties. By the early 1970s, the rate of those leaving the Church had risen to 14%, double what it had been in the mid-1960s. For the first time since 1850, Catholic population growth in the Northeast did not outstrip general population growth. By the late 1970s, 16% of those who had been raised as Catholics were professing another or no religion when they reached adulthood. Regular Mass attendance dropped from 70% to 50% and the percentage of those who attended Mass "practically never" had increased from 6% to 12%.

The number of young men entering the priesthood and brotherhood was severely curtailed, leaving many centers of clerical training with huge, elaborate, expensive, but relatively empty, edifices. Perhaps even more serious for the traditional parochial system was the decline in religious sisters. Despite the decline in priestly vocations, the numbers of priests in service had, nevertheless, managed to increase by 1,517. But the number of sisters declined drastically, from 63,712 in 1960 to only 47,780 in 1980. This meant that there were fewer sisters in service in the latter year than there were in the 1930s. To replace these nuns in the parochial schools with lay teachers was simply beyond the financial capabilities of many parishes, especially in inner-city areas. By 1980, there were 711 fewer parochial schools in the Northeast than there were in 1960, and enrollments in these schools had dropped from 1,662,234 to 804,759. This meant that only 44% of all parishes maintained parochial schools in 1980, compared to 60% in 1960, and only 17% of all Catholic children were in a parochial school, compared to 38% twenty years earlier.[19]

Additional factors in the decline in the parochial school system were the spiraling inflation of the 1970s, the social and geographic mobility of Catholics, a decline in ethnic identity among younger people, and the continuing erosion in parochial loyalty. Urban schools, like those at Good Shepherd Parish in Linwood, Massachusetts, and at St. Aloysius in Springfield, were forced to close because of a decline in the old French ethnic traditions and the flight of younger people out of the city. Many more ceased operation in the cities because the rising costs of maintenance were impossible to support on the contributions of poor blacks and Hispanics. Some were only able to keep their doors open because of inter-parochial programs and by admitting non-Catholic children, who sometimes made up a majority of the enrollment, to the school.

Even in more affluent suburban parishes, like St. Denis in Delaware County, Pennsylvania, the parochial school has been maintained only through dint of great exertions on the part of clergy and laity. In 1972, the annual cost of running St. Denis school had increased to $185,080.80, $122,137.60 of which was for teachers' salaries. The only way such expenses could be met in such sprawling suburban areas, lacking the cohesiveness once created by ethnicity and neighborhood, is by the expansion of fund-raising expedients like weekly Bingo, 50-50 raffles, and an annual two-week-long fair.[20]

The laicization of the staffs in parochial schools tended to weaken further the "we-they" exclusiveness of former days. Enrollments of Catholic children in public schools increased at the same time that the ranks in parochial schools were being thinned. In the Archdiocese of Philadelphia, which was able to maintain one of the most stable parochial school systems in the Northeast, a suburban parish like St. Denis had 28% of its children in public school in 1982, whereas the figure had stood at 8% in 1960. Rapid social change and lack of cohesiveness was a factor there as it was in the urban parish of St. Veronica's, which had seen a massive influx of Hispanics in the 1960s. At St. Veronica's, the proportion of children in public schools went from 8% in 1960 to 23% in 1982. Where ethnic and neighborhood cohesiveness remained strong, however, other changes had less effect on the parochial school. At the relatively stable Polish parish of St.

Josaphat's in Philadelphia, public school enrollments remained at a low 2% in both 1960 and 1982.[21] Finally, one must take into consideration the money-mindedness of modern Americans. At a time when inflation eats away at even large increases in income, when property taxes to support public school systems are skyrocketing, and when efforts to obtain federal tax credits for parents of parochial school children are foundering, the choice of a free public education over a parochial one that costs more and more each year in tuition seems clear. Increasingly rare are examples like the Puerto Rican mother in New York who spends $1,100 out of a $6,300 annual income to send her children to parochial school. But the fact that many more parish schools have not closed is a clear indication that support for the old system remains high among many Catholics.[22]

On a more spiritual level, a 1976 study argued that a general decline in Catholic religiousness was the result of a growing nonacceptance of papal leadership and of the Church's official ethic. The reforms of Vatican II are often identified as the source of this development. But another survey taken on the upper East Side of Manhattan indicated different conclusions. It appeared that here a 33% Mass attendance record was not occasioned by a rejection of Vatican II, but by a more serious questioning of central religious beliefs like the existence of God, the divinity of Christ, and the reality of heaven and hell. These people were dissatisfied with the new liturgy, poor preaching, and the lack of clear explanations of Church beliefs, even though they did not want retrenchment to rigid rules, clerical dominance, and privatism. Another study showed that a majority of nonpracticing Catholics argued that "the churches have lost the spiritual part of religion"; but then so did nearly a majority of Catholics who attended Mass regularly. What very imperfect evidence exists, therefore, suggests a general religious confusion in the 1970s as Catholics reeled from the multiple shocks that had buffeted many of the old forms of social and religious life.[23]

That Vatican II did have a positive impact on parish life also became evident in the 1970s. Many of the inner-city parishes of the Northeast, for example, began to be revitalized after a period of lifelessness due to ethnic and economic transformations. In some, a greater sense of community based on the more essential elements of Vatican II developed. Multiple parish organizations were formed, social functions increased in number, and social services including food services and clothing sales began to be run by and for parishioners, in the conciliar spirit of greater community involvement. This revitalization usually emerged with the arrival of Parish Renewals (essentially missions without the fire and brimstone), Communal recitation of Evening Prayer, Bible Vigils (the Liturgy of the Word sometimes followed by Benediction), parish Prayer Groups, and especially Charismatic Prayer Groups.[24]

Beginning among students and faculty at Pittsburgh's Duquesne University in 1967, the Charismatic Movement quickly became a national and then an international phenomenon. To a degree representing a reaction against the seemingly excessive preoccupation with social activism that gripped many Christians in the 1960s, the movement also reflects the Vatican II argument that the Spirit is continuously active in the Church. The movement reasserts the personal and the emotional in religion, emphasizing baptism in the Spirit and charismatic gifts like speaking in tongues and prophecy. Tending to cross parish boundaries and denominational affiliations in their organization, Charismatic Prayer Groups were a rejection of traditional parish life. A presentist approach to spirituality also seemed to give short shrift to the importance of historical developments in the American parish. On the other hand, their emphasis on the personal and individual was very in tune with Catholic parish practices of the immediate past. Thus, renewal came about through the blending of new elements with old. In addition, many charismatics grew in their attachment to certain established devotional practices such as devotion to the Real Presence and the Rosary.[25]

Charismatics, however, made up only a small percentage of any territorial parish, and at times clashes with noncharismatic parishioners over the direction of parish affairs did and do occur. At Little Flower Parish in Berkeley Heights, New Jersey, one such clash threatened to become critical in 1985. Noncharismatic parishioners there charged that the People of Hope, a charismatic group existing in twenty-four northern and central New Jersey parishes, was a "counterculture" cult that had taken control of Little Flower parochial school, used its own charismatic clergymen, and arranged marriages for its members. Angry noncharismatics protested the sect outside the church and called for the ouster of Rev. Pierce Byrne, pastor of the parish since 1977. Newark archdiocesan officials, however, argued that the People of Hope were a legitimate charismatic community with no intention of taking over the parish. A harmonious solution to the split in the parish will engage all the efforts of parish lay leaders, priests, and the bishop of the diocese.[26]

Another significant new influence in parish life beginning in the 1960s was the Hispanics. They introduced two important new movements into American Catholic life. The first, the *Cursillo de Cristianidad,* originated in Spain about 1949 and made its entrance into the United States by way of Hispanic Catholics in Texas. By the 1960s, it was spreading among "Anglo" Catholics in all parts of the Northeast. An intensive and highly emotional weekend lived at close quarters, the *cursillo* brings together priests, religious, and laypeople in an experience that places strong emphasis on communitarian religion. Marriage Encounter, the second movement, was brought to the United States in 1967. Its objective, through meetings, discussions and retreats, is to help married couples, and more recently engaged couples as well, to search for, rediscover, or strengthen their love for one another.[27]

In various other ways it has become apparent that traditional elements of Catholic parish life and devotions were not destroyed, but rather transformed, in the wake of Vatican II. For example, the importance of the Sacraments was reaffirmed, but the elements of understanding and commitment were emphasized. The three Sacraments of initiation—baptism, confirmation, and Holy Eucharist—now require a period of preparation through study and reflection that includes not just the children but the parents as well. Other shifts in emphasis saw the transformation of penance into the Sacrament of Reconciliation and extreme unction into the Sacrament of the Sick. Also, whereas in the pre-Vatican II parish priestly advice had discouraged long engagements before marriage, now a six-month preparation period before matrimony was required. Thus, post-Vatican II practices retreated from the traditional preoccupation with quantitative marks of growth, and began to highlight more qualitative aspects. Despite quantitative losses since the 1960s, parishes throughout the Northeast began to experience renewed life as thousands plunged deeper into the questions of their relationship with God and with each other.

Still, renewal was not perceived as an unmixed blessing by many. As Rev. Philip J. Murnion has written, there is now a tendency to suggest that the only real members of the parish are those who have made some kind of full commitment as adults. The new requirements for baptism, confirmation, and marriage may create the impression that the Sacraments are for those already deeply involved in the life of faith and not for those who are struggling to believe. Another potential problem emanates from orientation to the present and future evident in many of the Vatican II pronouncements. As Rev. Andrew M. Greeley has noted, ties with the past have been weakened to the point that contemporary Catholic parishioners are almost totally ignorant of their traditions. This has resulted in a decline in respect for the teaching authority of clerical leadership and the advent of "do-it-yourself Catholicism." Alienation from a rich Catholic heritage, Greeley argues, has meant that the two most important movements in contemporary Catholic life, liberation theology and charismatic renewal, have been borrowed from Marxism and Protestantism, respectively.[28]

Certainly, post-Vatican II developments have tended to blur the lines of authority and responsibility in the parish. Declining parochial school enrollments have necessitated an expansion in CCD programs, and that has brought laymen and nuns, as teachers and as directors of religious education, more directly into an area that had formerly been under the domination of the pastor. In some areas of the Northeast, nonterritorial "floating" parishes have been established to cope with modern conditions, and in some areas, especially in the dioceses of Hartford, Brooklyn, and Newark, team ministries, in which nuns serve as parish assistants, have replaced the old pastor-curate relationship.[29]

Vatican II and the decline in religious vocations have also increased the parochial importance of the laity. A range of lay ministers came into being, some to assist in administering the Eucharist, others as readers or ministers of music. Married and single laymen were ordained deacons while continuing in secular occupations. Parish councils were organized in which laymen and clergy were to cooperate on a wide range of parish concerns. There was, and still is, much confusion and frustration over what the real function of the layperson in parish administration is and should be. Bishop Frank Rodimer, former Chancellor of the Diocese of Paterson, reported in 1979 that a survey of twenty-one parish councils in his diocese showed that all tended to be preoccupied with budgets, maintenance, and running the parochial plant. There was little evidence of long-range pastoral planning regarding the mission of the parish. To many laymen, this was contrary to the spirit of Vatican II and was doing nothing to renew parochial life. Moreover, in several parish councils throughout the Northeast, there was evidence of growing factionalism between liberals and conservatives, and some councils attacked the unity stressed by Vatican II by tending to view the diocesan office as a villain, or by falling into the old parochial competitive spirit by comparing the variable rates of parish council success or failure in a particular area.[30] In the Archdiocese of Philadelphia, Cardinal John Krol encouraged, but did not prescribe, the formation of parish councils, for as he had observed during the Vatican II deliberations, "from experience we know that laymen, who set up the Trustee System many years ago . . . were a great impediment in the administration of the goods of the Church and could still be even to this time."[31]

Since dioceses tended to implement the suggestions of Vatican II along lines conditioned by their historical or ethnic or economic circumstances, or by the philosophies of their bishops who were given the power to implement them, there was some variety throughout the Northeast.[32] At the parish level as well, the ideas of Vatican II were made manifest or ignored according to local situations or clerical leadership.

Even within urban centers, there is great variety evident in parish priorities. The Church of the Gesu and Most Blessed Sacrament Parish in Philadelphia were two parishes that had seen rapid racial changes in the post-World War II period as blacks moved into North and Southwest Philadelphia, respectively. At the Gesu, a Sacred Heart Center was established in the 1960s. With the active help of Lay Apostolate members, the parish created in this center a community meeting place providing all residents of the neighborhood with practical information, both secular and religious. The Gesu parish council also watches over the needs of parishioners and determines what methods should be employed in order to cope with the varying concerns of the community at large. In 1967, the parish established the Mercy Inter-Parochial Educational Center to which are sent the upper 10% of the children from four area elementary schools. The center is designed to stimulate the children's learning processes through association and competition with children of similar achievements. At Most Blessed Sacrament, a Lay Advisory Council was organized in 1973 to find ways to keep the operating expenses of this black parish at a minimum. Along with a Community Relations Committee, the council began to work for the creation of a spirit of understanding among the people of the entire community. A counseling program was begun in the school, and the committee started to collaborate with an area organization called START (Southwest Teams Alleviating Racial Tension). Youth remains a prime concern with the parish sponsoring athletic teams and scouting. In addition, a group of sixteen youth counselors assists two nuns, a priest, a deacon, and a layperson in running a summer camp for inner-city young people. The parish also provides one of its buildings for a comprehensive day-care center, and maintains a Senior Citizens' organization composed of both Catholic and non-Catholic members.[33]

The attempts of some priests and laymen to make their parishes "relevant" to the community at large were often resisted. When Rev. Henry J. Browne, pastor of St. Gregory the Great Parish on the West Side of Manhattan, began introducing liturgical celebrations linked to neighborhood concerns and fighting for opportunities for the poor in the area, regardless of race or religion, he was sent a note that read, "I feel St. Gregory is now a Political Organization and a meeting place for the liberals, hippies, antiestablishment, etc., characters."[34] It was, and is, apparent that not everyone in the modern parish has the same priorities.

Other urban parishes have concerns not related to poverty or race, but important concerns nevertheless. In most, it appears that the new spirit generated by Vatican II has helped them to shape or reshape their priorities. Resurrection of Our Lord Parish occupies an all-white working-class area in Northeast Philadelphia populated in large part by people who had fled changing inner-city parishes. In the late 1960s and early 1970s, a Home and School Association was formed, the CYO program was expanded, and a Senior Citizens' organization was established. The CCD program was enlarged to include pre-schoolers and anyone who had a learning disability or physical handicap. The children are taken on pilgrimages, have Communion breakfasts, May processions, Christmas programs, Bible Vigils, and special children's liturgies. For adults, a Lenten Lecture Program was begun in 1971, in which well-known experts addressed parishioners on subjects of theology, Scripture, adolescent psychology, communication within the family, prejudice, and marriage. A marriage enrichment program was started in 1972, and the following year classes were begun explaining the changes wrought by Vatican II, the new function of parents in preparing their children for the Sacraments, and the introduction of the New Baltimore Catechism. All of these programs involved a great deal of time and cooperation among the parish's priests, three sisters, and forty laypersons.[35]

St. Irenaeus Parish was a new parish founded in 1966 in a former marshland in West Philadelphia. It developed a very active CYO organization, and, in 1975, a Teen Discussion Group was instituted. This was a religious discussion group led by two laypersons of the parish. They took SIGN (Service in God's Name) as the motto that described the services these young people performed for members of the parish and for the community at large. In 1972, the Golden Eagles Club was formed for senior citizens. A Women's Club emerged from a Block

Rosary held in the home of one of the parishioners. Its purpose became the raising of money for the church and rectory buildings. The St. Vincent de Paul Society and the Legion of Mary remain active, devoting their time to works for the poor and to providing summer camps for underprivileged children. A parish council was established in 1969 to provide advice and assistance to the pastor as well as to render aid, where required, to the leaders of the surrounding community. But in 1971 the parish council was abolished, and parishioners' hopes for a parish school were unrealized because of a lack of money.[36]

Ethnic traditions still remain strong in some parishes. At the French parish of Good Shepherd in Linwood, Massachusetts, most of the young people have moved away, but the pastor and the remaining parishioners still maintain ties with the past. Their Sunday announcements are still printed in both French and English, and at the parish's 75th Anniversary, the pastor led his congregation in singing "O Canada." The changes of Vatican II were not resisted, but incorporated into a traditional structure. A parish council was formed in 1968, and ten years later, the confessionals were modernized into Chapels of Reconciliation. A Eucharistic Shrine was established, and the altar boys' sacristy was transformed into a weekday chapel for daily meditation and Mass. The blending of the old and new has permitted the church to retain its importance for the largely working-class population, and this has been assisted by the fact that the neighborhood is still heavily French-Canadian Catholic. The parishioners contribute very generously to church improvements, but by the mid-1970s, support for the CCD program had been declining. That may be due to the fact that there are fewer and fewer children as the parish population ages. The parochial school had closed in 1972 for that reason. The missionary spirit, however, is very apparent in that the parish places special emphasis on contributing money for the missions.[37]

By comparison, the area around Holy Family Parish in Pittsfield, Massachusetts, is only marginally Catholic in 1980. A large number of second and third generation Poles moved out of the area in the past twenty years. Those who did, attend non-Polish parishes in the outskirts, but continue to hold nominal membership at Holy Family. They pay annual dues in order to maintain something of their Polish heritage. Their activity in the parish is limited to having their funeral Masses conducted in Polish and attending Polish services once a year at Easter. Among those who remained in the neighborhood, the elderly are the ones who fill the pews during the Polish Mass, with a larger cross section of the parish population attending the English Mass. For the most part, the people at Holy Family resisted the changes of Vatican II, but the pastor, being very popular with his people, was able slowly and subtly to introduce some progressive changes. The level of experiential religion seems to be low in the parish, with many simply clinging to the past through their church and priest. The old style of parish cohesive life is apparent here. Many church functions are planned by the parishioners, but in the final analysis, the pastor conducts affairs in his own way. There is a CCD program, but it does not appear to be very effective. Yet, parish life at Holy Family very much resembles that of a very large family, retaining that element of intimacy which often seems lost in more progressive parishes.[38]

At the other end of the spectrum we find the affluent suburban parish of St. Paul's in Hingham, Massachusetts. Originally predominantly Irish, it now contains Italians, Poles, and French, as well as Irish. Where it differs from other suburban parishes is in its social cohesion. It never really existed in a "bedroom" suburb of Boston, and the town had a long-standing identity of its own that was unmarred by post-World War II population flight out of the city. The majority of people at St. Paul's were quite content with the changes of Vatican II. Both laypersons and priests praise the work of their parish council, which is made up of parishioners with considerable experience. The special vitality of the parish is also evident in its parochial school, built in 1952 under the leadership of the Knights of Columbus, and supported by every parish organization. The pupils in the school are consistently high achievers, due partly to strong parental support as well as to excellent faculty-parent communication. There is an excellent Adult Enrichment Program in the parish, which includes courses on Scripture, family life, spiritual growth through art, the Catholic faith, human relationships, and current issues such as nuclear proliferation, abortion, and world hunger. There are programs on the Vatican II era and a series of ongoing support group programs: one for bereaved parents; one for the victims, adults and children, of separation and divorce; one for widows and widowers; and one that provides opportunities for business people to integrate Christian values into their business activities.[39]

At the suburban parish of St. Denis, outside of Philadelphia, conservatism is more in evidence. It too is a fairly affluent parish, but it is also one that saw rapid social change after World War II. Many of its parishioners had fled from racial changes in the city. Few of them were overly enthusiastic about the changes of Vatican II. In 1970, the pastor introduced a new type of mission, called a Week of Spiritual Renewal, combining church services with lectures on topical problems. But the pastor soon learned that this type of activity was really not reaching out to those in the parish who never came to church in the first place. An attempt to institute an Adult Education Program met with failure because of an unenthusiastic response. Other, less innovative, programs, however, caught on readily. A Senior Citizens' Group was formed. The Holy Name Society sponsored retreats for married couples, engaged in Nocturnal Adoration, and provided adult supervision at some of the social functions of the CYO. A charismatic prayer community was formed. The CCD program has continued, but is weakening because of a shortage of volunteers and little parental cooperation.[40]

Thus, as the above examples indicate, parishes throughout the Northeast have adopted a variety of techniques to deal with the social dislocations and alienation created since the end of World War II. Some have embraced wholeheartedly the reforms of Vatican II in order to achieve a new sense of cohesion or to realize a deepening of their faith. Others have clung to traditional practices in order to achieve those aims. Most parishes have adopted only those innovations that seem to fulfill perceived needs in parish life and have attempted a synthesis of the old and the new.

The course that parishes took between the 1960s and 1980s was directly related to the ethnic and socioeconomic composition of the community in which they existed and the degree of social change that had occurred, or was occurring, in their area. Clerical leadership and example were obviously important in these revolutionary years, but so too was the willingness or ability of laypersons to cooperate. In attempting to cope with the confusing complexity of the modern world, and in attempting to adjust to the transformation of the old values and practices of traditional parish life and make the parish relevant to present and future challenges, some communities have been successful and others have not. Most are still struggling.

Especially in parishes still made up predominantly of one of the more recent ethnic groups, the old ways continue strong. In many Italian parishes throughout the Northeast, the statue of Our Lady, or of a particular saint, is still carried in procession through the streets of the neighborhood along with the accompanying festivals. Polish parishes still cling to venerable ethnic practices and, perhaps, have been encouraged in their conservatism by the example of Pope John Paul II and the continuing nationalistic struggles in their homeland.

Overall, however, there are unmistakable signs of positive change in Catholic parish life. On the one hand, there is an evident decline in the old-fashioned religiousness, and certainly there is a decline in numbers. With large-scale immigration stemmed, with a declining birthrate, and with losses to a more secular outlook, this can only mean continued financial difficulties for parishes that attempt to hold on to an edifice-oriented mode of operation. Ironically, the old-style parish of multiple buildings, the pride of impoverished immigrants, can now be maintained only in the more affluent communities. On the other hand, the weakening of the old ethnic and neighborhood homogeneity, which had for so long been a mainstay of parochial consciousness, may have been a boon, albeit accompanied by considerable pain and disillusionment. This transformation opens the door to greater involvement of Catholics in the world at large, and as such creates the potential for infusing secular affairs with some of the time-tested ethical principles espoused by Catholicism.

It has recently been observed, moreover, that Vatican II was ahead of its time. "The internal pressures that would have surely built up," writes Father Andrew Greeley, "as a result of the social and economic and educational transformation of the last half century would have made reforms like that of the Vatican Council inevitable."[41] The fact that the conciliar changes came ten or fifteen years before they were absolutely necessary has meant that damage to the American Catholic Church has been far less severe than it could have been.

The Catholic parish and parochial life, then, have not been destroyed by the events of the past twenty years. They simply have entered a new stage of their development. Priorities have had to shift to meet new demands, but that has always been the case. Whether the demand was gathering the people together in worshiping communities in a frontier society, establishing separate national parishes to ease the fears of new immigrants, or creating an alternative system of social, financial, and educational institutions as a protection from a hostile public, the Catholic parish has been, and will be, a mirror and an example to a constantly changing American society.

## Notes

1. John Cogley, *Catholic America* (N.Y., 1973), 97.

2. Burns, *Springfield's Ethnic Heritage,* 43; "Ethnographic Observations, St. Thomas Aquinas, Springfield, Mass." (Notre Dame, 1983), 1–2.

3. Bill Kovack, "Eased Laws Alter U.S. Ethnic Profile," *New York Times,* 14 June 1971; Hanna, *Catholics,* 247, Cohalan, *Popular History,* 296.

4. Cohalan, *Popular History,* 296.

5. Cohalan, *Popular History,* 297; Connelly, *History of the Archdiocese of Philadelphia,* 440; *Sesquicentennial, St. Denis,* 165.

6. Richard Green, "History of the Cathedral of Saints Peter and Paul," (unpublished manuscript, 1971), 16; *Annual Reports, Archdiocese of Philadelphia,* 1965 and 1982; *Official Catholic Directory, Diocese of Allentown,* 1965, 32, 1982, 52; *Catholic Directory, Archdiocese of Philadelphia,* 1976, 198, 1979, 190.

7. "Ethnographic Observations," 3–5.

8. *Catholic Standard and Times,* 25 November 1966; Gavigan, "Rise and Fall," 128–129.

9. Rev. Paul T. O'Connell, "The Concept of the Parish in the Light of the Second Vatican Council," (Ph.D. dissertation, Catholic University of America, 1969), 89–151.

10. *Sesquicentennial, St. Denis,* 187.

11. Hennessey, *American Catholics,* 316–17.

12. Myra MacPherson, *Long Time Passing: Vietnam and the Haunted Generation* (N.Y., 1984), 391.

13. *Ibid.,* 79.

14. *Ibid.,* 118–119.

15. *Ibid.,* 461, 466.

16. *Ibid.,* 136.

17. Hennessey, *American Catholics,* 315.

18. Connelly, *History of the Archdiocese of Philadelphia,* 516; *Catholic Standard and Times,* 25 November 1966; Malcolm Boyd, ed., *The Underground Church* (N.Y., 1968), 5, 142, and "On Being a Contemporary Christian," *Time,* 12 April 1968; *National Catholic Reporter,* 10 April 1968.

19. Greeley, *The American Catholic,* 143; Hanna, *Catholics,* 105; Carroll, *Religion in America,* 19–20, 33; Hennessey, *American Catholics,* 320, 324, 329–330; Lawrence M. Baskir and William A. Strauss, *Chance and Circumstance: The Draft, the War and the Vietnam Generation* (N.Y., 1978), 67; Sister Margaret Mary Modde, "Departures from Religious Institutes," *New Catholic Encyclopedia,* 17: 570–571; *Newsweek,* 4 October 1971.

20. *Sesquicentennial, St. Denis,* 163, 167, 189–193, 205; *Diamond Jubilee, Good Shepherd,* 5; Burns, *Springfield's Ethnic Heritage,* 43.

21. *Annual Reports, Archdiocese of Philadelphia,* 1960 and 1982; *Statistical Report of the Superintendent of Public Instruction for the School Year Ending 1963* (Harrisburg, 1965); *Statistical Report of the Secretary of Education* (Harrisburg, 1974); *Annual Report of the Vicar for Catholic Education of the Archdiocese of Philadelphia, 1981–82* (Phila., 1982). For another example of Polish parish school stability, see *St. Stanislaus Kostka, Brooklyn, Greenpoint, New York, 1896–1971* (South Hackensack, 1972), 112–120.

22. Greeley, *The American Catholic,* 167–169; Edward B. Fiske, "Catholic Schools Attain Stability in Urban Cores," *New York Times,* 9 October 1977.

23. Greeley, *Catholic Schools,* 129; Hennessey, *American Catholics,* 331; "Catholics Reflect Shifts in Belief," *New York Times,* 10 February 1977; *Catholic Standard & Times,* 26 January 1984.

24. Gavigan, "Rise and Fall," 129.

25. Hennessey, *American Catholics,* 318; *The Saint Irenaeus Story, 1966–1976* (Phila., 1976), 31; *Sesquicentennial, St. Denis,* 194–195. See also, Kevin and Dorothy Ranaghan, *Catholic Pentecostals* (N.Y., 1969).

26. *The Philadelphia Inquirer,* 21 November 1985.

27. Hennessey, *American Catholics,* 317.

28. Murnion, "Strategies for Parish Renewal," in National Conference of Catholic Bishops, *The Parish Project Reader: Selected Articles from the Parish Ministry Newsletter, 1979–1982* (Wash., D.C., 1982), 52–53; Greeley, "American Catholicism, 1909–1984," 488–490.

29. Hennessey, *American Catholics,* 315–316, 330; *Annual Report, Vicar for Catholic Education, Archdiocese of Philadelphia, 1981–1982,* 49–55.

30. William J. Rademacher, *The Practical Guide for Parish Councils* (West Mystic, Conn., 1979), 35, 67, 69. See also, *A National Pastoral Council Pro and Con* (Wash., D.C., 1971).

31. Connelly, *History of the Archdiocese of Philadelphia,* 494.

32. See, for example, the differences between the neighboring dioceses of Philadelphia and Camden on the issue of Saturday evening Mass, or between Philadelphia and Rochester on the issue of a Priests' Senate in Connelly, *History of the Archdiocese of Philadelphia,* 530, and McNamara, *The Diocese of Rochester,* 530–531.

33. *Gesu Parish Centennial,* 10, 14, 24; *Most Blessed Sacrament, Diamond Jubilee,* 58–59, 63, 65.

34. Jay Dolan, *The American Catholic Experience: A History from Colonial Times to the Present* (Garden City, N.Y., 1985), 449.

35. *Resurrection, 50th Anniversary,* 9, 26, 27, 30.

36. *The St. Irenaeus Story,* 23, 26, 30, 32.

37. *Diamond Jubilee, Good Shepherd,* 6; "Ethnographic Observations," 10; Parish Announcements, 1975–1980.
38. Clowes, *Pol-Am,* 57–129; Rev. Thomas Splain, "Impressions of Holy Family Church, Pittsfield, Mass., Oct. 1 and 2, 1983" (Notre Dame, 1983); Tom Dowdy, "Ethnographic Field Notes, Holy Family Church, Pittsfield, Mass." (Notre Dame, 1983); Holy Family Church, Parish Notes, 2 October 1983.
39. *St. Paul's Church Centennial,* 5, 7, 10, 15; "Ethnographic Observations," 1–4; Brochure, *St. Paul's Adult Enrichment Program, 1982–1983.*
40. *Sesquicentennial, St. Denis,* 142, 154, 187–191, 197, 199.
41. Greeley, "American Catholicism: 1909–1984," 487.

## For Further Reading

Cohalan, Rev. Msgr. Florence D. *A Popular History of the Archdiocese of New York.* Yonkers: United States Catholic Historical Society, 1983.

Connelly, Rev. Msgr. James F. (ed.) *The History of the Archdiocese of Philadelphia.* Philadelphia: The Archdiocese of Philadelphia, 1976.

Dillon, John J. (ed.) *Diocese of Harrisburg, 1868–1968.* Harrisburg: Diocese of Harrisburg, 1968.

Dolan, Jay P. *Catholic Revivalism: The American Experience, 1830–1900.* Notre Dame: University of Notre Dame Press, 1978.

———. *The Immigrant Church: New York's Irish and German Catholics, 1815–1865.* Baltimore: The Johns Hopkins University Press, 1975.

Gallagher, Rev. John P. *A Century of History: The Diocese of Scranton, 1868–1968.* Scranton: The Diocese of Scranton, 1968.

Hennessey, Rev. James. *American Catholics: A History of the Roman Catholic Community in the United States.* New York: Oxford University Press, 1981.

Lord, Robert H., John E. Sexton, and Edward T. Harrington. *History of the Archdiocese of Boston in the Various Stages of Its Development, 1604–1943.* 3 vols. New York: Sheed and Ward, 1944.

Lucey, Rev. William Leo. *The Catholic Church in Maine.* Francestown, N.H.: Marshall Jones Co., Publishers, 1957.

McNamara, Robert F. *The Diocese of Rochester, 1868–1968.* Rochester: The Diocese of Rochester, 1968.

O'Gara, James (ed.) *The Postconciliar Parish.* New York: P. J. Kenedy & Sons, 1967.

Purcell, William P. *Catholic Pittsburgh's One Hundred Years.* Chicago: Loyola University Press, 1943.

# Catholic Church Statistics in the Northeast Region, 1850–1980

## MAINE
### Diocese of Portland (1853)

|                          | 1850 | 1880    | 1900    | 1930    | 1950    | 1960    | 1980      |
|--------------------------|------|---------|---------|---------|---------|---------|-----------|
| Parishes                 | —    | 0       | 57      | 126     | 132     | 132     | 143       |
| Parishes without Priests |      |         |         |         |         |         |           |
| (i.e., Missions)         | —    | 71      | 57      | 57      | 174     | 159     | 167       |
| National Parishes        | —    | 0       | 0       | 4       | 3       | 3       | 3         |
| Parish Schools           | —    | 15      | 21      | 58      | 65      | 55      | 21        |
| Diocesan Priests         | —    | 73*     | 86      | 195     | 243     | 254     | 227       |
| Religious Order Priests  | —    |         | 16      | 21      | 100     | 99      | 121       |
| Women Religious          | —    | 135     | 330     | 930     | 1,399   | 1,382   | 844       |
| Catholic Population      | —    | 80,000  | 97,000  | 174,915 | 227,192 | 259,190 | 273,043   |
| Total Population         | —    | 995,927 | 694,466 | 797,423 | 913,774 | 969,265 | 1,028,000 |

## NEW HAMPSHIRE
### Diocese of Manchester (1884)

|                          | 1850 | 1880 | 1900    | 1930    | 1950    | 1960    | 1980    |
|--------------------------|------|------|---------|---------|---------|---------|---------|
| Parishes                 | —    | —    | 55      | 83      | 100     | 116     | 126     |
| Parishes without Priests |      |      |         |         |         |         |         |
| (i.e., Missions)         | —    | —    | 49      | 40      | 78      | 105     | 149     |
| National Parishes        | —    | —    | 0       | 3       | 3       | 3       | 0       |
| Parish Schools           | —    | —    | 30      | 60      | 54      | 61      | 19      |
| Diocesan Priests         | —    | —    | 88      | 166     | 209     | 277     | 289     |
| Religious Order Priests  | —    | —    | 12      | 42      | 104     | 131     | 97      |
| Women Religious          | —    | —    | 345     | 848     | 1,283   | 1,355   | 1,179   |
| Catholic Population      | —    | —    | 100,000 | 151,730 | 184,820 | 222,467 | 286,411 |
| Total Population         | —    | —    | 411,588 | 465,293 | 529,880 | 606,921 | 784,233 |

## VERMONT
### Diocese of Burlington (1853)

|                          | 1850 | 1880    | 1900    | 1930    | 1950    | 1960    | 1980    |
|--------------------------|------|---------|---------|---------|---------|---------|---------|
| Parishes                 | —    | 66      | 57      | 67      | 88      | 93      | 100     |
| Parishes without Priests |      |         |         |         |         |         |         |
| (i.e., Missions)         | —    | 0       | 34      | 30      | 107     | 112     | 75      |
| National Parishes        | —    | 3       | 6       | 0       | 0       | 0       | 0       |
| Parish Schools           | —    | 15      | 19      | 20      | 24      | 26      | 9       |
| Diocesan Priests         | —    | 32*     | 73      | 85      | 148     | 174     | 166     |
| Religious Order Priests  | —    |         | 2       | 16      | 54      | 67      | 83      |
| Women Religious          | —    | 47      | 218     | 484     | 575     | 642     | 361     |
| Catholic Population      | —    | 35,000  | 57,000  | 89,661  | 104,846 | 124,180 | 156,073 |
| Total Population         | —    | 332,286 | 343,641 | 359,611 | 375,833 | 389,881 | 511,299 |

*Religious and diocesan priests combined.

## MASSACHUSETTS
### Archdiocese of Boston (1808)

|  | 1850 | 1880 | 1900 | 1930 | 1950 | 1960 | 1980 |
|---|---|---|---|---|---|---|---|
| Parishes | 63 | 163 | 155 | 289 | 369 | 396 | 408 |
| Parishes without Priests (i.e., Missions) | 0 | 14 | 59 | 60 | 133 | 561 | 144 |
| National Parishes | 1 | 9 | 13 | 61 | 58 | 58 | 58 |
| Parish Schools | 1 | 21 | 64 | 145 | 177 | 215 | 142 |
| Diocesan Priests | 61 | 231 | 413 | 782 | 1,065 | 1,342 | 1,324 |
| Religious Order Priests |  |  | 110 | 383 | 785 | 1,025 | 1,168 |
| Women Religious | 12 | 704 | 1,369 | 3,562 | 4,672 | 5,532 | 4,719 |
| Catholic Population | 150,000 | 320,000 | 610,000 | 1,039,000 | 1,334,420 | 1,661,233 | 2,016,950 |
| Total Population | 2,085,319 | 1,120,817 | 1,799,667 | 2,774,237 | 3,035,168 | 3,335,895 | 5,728,288 |

## MASSACHUSETTS
### Diocese of Springfield (1870)

|  | 1850 | 1880 | 1900 | 1930 | 1950 | 1960 | 1980 |
|---|---|---|---|---|---|---|---|
| Parishes | — | 116 | 136 | 203 | 122 | 132 | 136 |
| Parishes without Priests (i.e., Missions) | — | 52 | 30 | 29 | 26 | 112 | 100 |
| National Parishes | — | 9 | 19 | 3 | 1 | 1 | 0 |
| Parish Schools | — | 14 | 39 | 91 | 58 | 61 | 34 |
| Diocesan Priests | — | 108 | 235 | 426 | 296 | 329 | 271 |
| Religious Order Priests | — |  | 13 | 128 | 149 | 162 | 134 |
| Women Religious | — | 47 | 671 | 1,927 | 1,057 | 1,373 | 960 |
| Catholic Population | — | 150,000 | 250,000 | 453,660 | 296,286 | 376,604 | 353,365 |
| Total Population | — | 483,304 | 718,257 | 1,069,851 | 637,507 | 729,581 | 790,725 |

## MASSACHUSETTS
### Diocese of Fall River (1904)

|  | 1850 | 1880 | 1900 | 1930 | 1950 | 1960 | 1980 |
|---|---|---|---|---|---|---|---|
| Parishes | — | — | — | 94 | 98 | 107 | 113 |
| Parishes without Priests (i.e., Missions) | — | — | — | 23 | 63 | 108 | 94 |
| National Parishes | — | — | — | 48 | 36 | 37 | 32 |
| Parish Schools | — | — | — | 39 | 42 | 53 | 21 |
| Diocesan Priests | — | — | — | 169 | 205 | 232 | 229 |
| Religious Order Priests | — | — | — | 34 | 109 | 150 | 206 |
| Women Religious | — | — | — | 490 | 981 | 984 | 740 |
| Catholic Population | — | — | — | 172,445 | 220,125 | 258,995 | 340,000 |
| Total Population | — | — | — | 405,526 | 424,104 | 493,621 | 530,000 |

## MASSACHUSETTS
### Diocese of Worcester (1950)

|  | 1850 | 1880 | 1900 | 1930 | 1950 | 1960 | 1980 |
|---|---|---|---|---|---|---|---|
| Parishes | — | — | — | — | 100 | 125 | 128 |
| Parishes without Priests | | | | | | | |
| (i.e., Missions) | — | — | — | — | 15 | 103 | 33 |
| National Parishes | — | — | — | — | 2 | 2 | 0 |
| Parish Schools | — | — | — | — | 54 | 52 | 21 |
| Diocesan Priests | — | — | — | — | 242 | 294 | 360 |
| Religious Order Priests | — | — | — | — | 155 | 206 | 187 |
| Women Religious | — | — | — | — | 1,146 | 1,047 | 750 |
| Catholic Population | — | — | — | — | 253,400 | 326,292 | 335,806 |
| Total Population | — | — | — | — | 541,247 | 580,142 | 643,968 |

## CONNECTICUT
### Archdiocese of Hartford (1843)

|  | 1850 | 1880 | 1900 | 1930 | 1950 | 1960 | 1980 |
|---|---|---|---|---|---|---|---|
| Parishes | 12 | 106 | 129 | 234 | 279 | 184 | 223 |
| Parishes without Priests | | | | | | | |
| (i.e., Missions) | 0 | 58 | 99 | 53 | 46 | 26 | 8 |
| National Parishes | 0 | 2 | 16 | 62 | 56 | 47 | 47 |
| Parish Schools | * | 22 | 53 | 100 | 116 | 87 | 91 |
| Diocesan Priests | 14 | 123 | 247 | 461 | 683 | 532 | 539 |
| Religious Order Priests | | | 26 | 76 | 164 | 125 | 153 |
| Women Religious | * | 239 | 760 | 2,197 | 2,084 | 1,827 | 791 |
| Catholic Population | 20,000 | 175,000 | 270,000 | 604,761 | 670,000 | 714,861 | 785,871 |
| Total Population | 642,797 | 622,700 | 908,420 | 1,606,903 | 1,900,000 | 1,469,726 | 1,756,790 |

## CONNECTICUT
### Diocese of Bridgeport (1953)

|  | 1850 | 1880 | 1900 | 1930 | 1950 | 1960 | 1980 |
|---|---|---|---|---|---|---|---|
| Parishes | — | — | — | — | — | 75 | 87 |
| Parishes without Priests | | | | | | | |
| (i.e., Missions) | — | — | — | — | — | 96 | 101 |
| National Parishes | — | — | — | — | — | 19 | 16 |
| Parish Schools | — | — | — | — | — | 45 | 47 |
| Diocesan Priests | — | — | — | — | — | 183 | 242 |
| Religious Order Priests | — | — | — | — | — | 139 | 106 |
| Women Religious | — | — | — | — | — | 716 | 694 |
| Catholic Population | — | — | — | — | — | 286,197 | 327,973 |
| Total Population | — | — | — | — | — | 653,589 | 801,177 |

*Statistics unavailable.

**CONNECTICUT**
**Diocese of Norwich (1953)**

|  | 1850 | 1880 | 1900 | 1930 | 1950 | 1960 | 1980 |
|---|---|---|---|---|---|---|---|
| Parishes | — | — | — | — | — | 63 | 76 |
| Parishes without Priests (i.e., Missions) | — | — | — | — | — | 71 | 52 |
| National Parishes | — | — | — | — | — | 6 | 3 |
| Parish Schools | — | — | — | — | — | 25 | 21 |
| Diocesan Priests | — | — | — | — | — | 127 | 144 |
| Religious Order Priests | — | — | — | — | — | 90 | 77 |
| Women Religious | — | — | — | — | — | 393 | 348 |
| Catholic Population | — | — | — | — | — | 158,699 | 197,027 |
| Total Population | — | — | — | — | — | 412,319 | 576,320 |

**RHODE ISLAND**
**Diocese of Providence (1872)**

|  | 1850 | 1880 | 1900 | 1930 | 1950 | 1960 | 1980 |
|---|---|---|---|---|---|---|---|
| Parishes | — | 62 | 85 | 111 | 136 | 152 | 159 |
| Parishes without Priests (i.e., Missions) | — | 12 | 50 | 20 | 132 | 187 | 179 |
| National Parishes | — | 7 | 14 | 29 | 31 | 47 | 43 |
| Parish Schools | — | 16 | 37 | 58 | 82 | 99 | 60 |
| Diocesan Priests | — | 84 | 180 | 263 | 361 | 386 | 394 |
| Religious Order Priests | — | | 9 | 84 | 173 | 209 | 210 |
| Women Religious | — | 188 | 706 | 1,355 | 1,716 | 1,689 | 1,239 |
| Catholic Population | — | 151,100 | 275,000 | 322,570 | 435,865 | 518,717 | 615,329 |
| Total Population | — | 455,495 | 715,978 | 687,497 | 791,896 | 859,488 | 947,154 |

**NEW YORK**
**Archdiocese of New York (1808)**

|  | 1850 | 1880 | 1900 | 1930 | 1950 | 1960 | 1980 |
|---|---|---|---|---|---|---|---|
| Parishes | 70 | 190 | 267 | 366 | 387 | 401 | 409 |
| Parishes without Priests (i.e., Missions) | 60 | 64 | 188 | 84 | 599 | 625 | 649 |
| National Parishes | 8 | 22 | 41 | 86 | 68 | 76 | 53 |
| Parish Schools | 11 | 76 | 190 | 216 | 220 | 291 | 259 |
| Diocesan Priests | 109 | 381 | 478 | 860 | 1,137 | 1,188 | 1,043 |
| Religious Order Priests | | | 202 | 634 | 1,068 | 1,294 | 1,564 |
| Women Religious | 197 | 1,387 | 2,407 | 6,499 | 8,047 | 8,288 | 5,700 |
| Catholic Population | 202,000 | 600,000 | 1,200,000 | 1,273,291 | 1,288,469 | 1,610,366 | 1,839,000 |
| Total Population | 1,194,342 | 1,682,882 | 2,660,220 | 4,236,478 | 4,509,023 | 4,950,000 | 5,044,800 |

## NEW YORK
### Diocese of Albany (1847)

|  | 1850 | 1880 | 1900 | 1930 | 1950 | 1960 | 1980 |
|---|---|---|---|---|---|---|---|
| Parishes | 70 | 166 | 96 | 180 | 190 | 206 | 201 |
| Parishes without Priests (i.e., Missions) | 40 | 130 | 94 | 56 | 246 | 234 | 52 |
| National Parishes | 7 | 1 | 19 | 45 | 38 | 40 | 14 |
| Parish Schools | 3 | 25 | 38 | 68 | 75 | 104 | 62 |
| Diocesan Priests | 61 | 173 | 141 | 319 | 376 | 392 | 407 |
| Religious Order Priests | | | 41 | 68 | 211 | 251 | 222 |
| Women Religious | 19 | 496 | 783 | 1,350 | 1,600 | 1,876 | 1,362 |
| Catholic Population | 80,000 | 180,000 | 145,000 | 226,500 | 292,588 | 375,512 | 408,648 |
| Total Population | 1,248,939 | 1,192,799 | 758,001 | 935,960 | 1,031,747 | 1,121,687 | 1,472,684 |

## NEW YORK
### Diocese of Buffalo (1847)

|  | 1850 | 1880 | 1900 | 1930 | 1950 | 1960 | 1980 |
|---|---|---|---|---|---|---|---|
| Parishes | 58 | 135 | 103 | 231 | 251 | 267 | 298 |
| Parishes without Priests (i.e., Missions) | 0 | 0 | 55 | 37 | 229 | 231 | 202 |
| National Parishes | 5 | 24 | 41 | 22 | 45 | 48 | 35 |
| Parish Schools | 4 | 40 | 73 | 146 | 162 | 195 | 138 |
| Diocesan Priests | 53 | 166 | 134 | 400 | 525 | 598 | 591 |
| Religious Order Priests | | | 81 | 173 | 409 | 546 | 357 |
| Women Religious | 19 | 407 | 789 | 2,010 | 2,791 | 3,243 | 2,487 |
| Catholic Population | 70,000 | 100,000 | 156,000 | 320,129 | 658,514 | 862,433 | 822,171 |
| Total Population | 840,326 | 530,856 | 799,243 | 1,250,644 | 1,466,609 | 1,699,445 | 1,660,616 |

## NEW YORK
### Diocese of Brooklyn (1853)

|  | 1850 | 1880 | 1900 | 1930 | 1950 | 1960 | 1980 |
|---|---|---|---|---|---|---|---|
| Parishes | — | 87 | 133 | 279 | 310 | 219 | 221 |
| Parishes without Priests (i.e., Missions) | — | 22 | 26 | 28 | 30 | 12 | 5 |
| National Parishes | — | 15 | 23 | 41 | 26 | 26 | 20 |
| Parish Schools | — | 39 | 65 | 193 | 213 | 187 | 173 |
| Diocesan Priests | — | 153 | 273 | 619 | 1,104 | 917 | 935 |
| Religious Order Priests | — | | 47 | 157 | 292 | 330 | 394 |
| Women Religious | — | 624 | 951 | 1,563 | 5,083 | 4,365 | 2,373 |
| Catholic Population | — | 200,000 | 500,000 | 1,020,769 | 1,294,096 | 1,489,207 | 1,351,853 |
| Total Population | — | 743,957 | 1,452,611 | 4,103,638 | 5,201,252 | 4,436,897 | 4,095,480 |

**NEW YORK**
**Diocese of Rochester (1868)**

|                           | 1850 | 1880    | 1900    | 1930    | 1950    | 1960      | 1980      |
|---------------------------|------|---------|---------|---------|---------|-----------|-----------|
| Parishes                  | —    | 79      | 79      | 131     | 173     | 151       | 161       |
| Parishes without Priests  |      |         |         |         |         |           |           |
| (i.e., Missions)          | —    | 0       | 49      | 39      | 47      | 49        | 31        |
| National Parishes         | —    | 0       | 12      | 19      | 12      | 16        | 10        |
| Parish Schools            | —    | 22      | 41      | 72      | 77      | 94        | 73        |
| Diocesan Priests          | —    | 62      | 117     | 240     | 376     | 399       | 388       |
| Religious Order Priests   | —    |         | 6       | 22      | 87      | 179       | 154       |
| Women Religious           | —    | 17      | 592     | 1,089   | 1,347   | 1,392     | 1,035     |
| Catholic Population       | —    | 65,000  | 100,000 | 209,098 | 320,700 | 362,000   | 372,340   |
| Total Population          | —    | 607,763 | 682,321 | 909,524 | 934,081 | 1,206,446 | 1,480,500 |

**NEW YORK**
**Diocese of Ogdensburg (1872)**

|                           | 1850 | 1880    | 1900    | 1930    | 1950    | 1960    | 1980    |
|---------------------------|------|---------|---------|---------|---------|---------|---------|
| Parishes                  | —    | 42      | 75      | 106     | 113     | 118     | 122     |
| Parishes without Priests  |      |         |         |         |         |         |         |
| (i.e., Missions)          | —    | 54      | 73      | 56      | 67      | 122     | 144     |
| National Parishes         | —    | 1       | 0       | 3       | 5       | 5       | 4       |
| Parish Schools            | —    | 8       | 16      | 27      | 27      | 37      | 26      |
| Diocesan Priests          | —    | 55      | 95      | 150     | 172     | 194     | 191     |
| Religious Order Priests   | —    |         | 13      | 22      | 43      | 77      | 40      |
| Women Religious           | —    | 29      | 188     | 320     | 550     | 644     | 354     |
| Catholic Population       | —    | 58,000  | 78,000  | 107,504 | 124,433 | 161,254 | 168,644 |
| Total Population          | —    | 324,614 | 342,246 | 358,288 | 344,053 | 380,675 | 398,898 |

**NEW YORK**
**Diocese of Syracuse (1886)**

|                           | 1850 | 1880 | 1900    | 1930    | 1950    | 1960      | 1980      |
|---------------------------|------|------|---------|---------|---------|-----------|-----------|
| Parishes                  | —    | —    | 65      | 124     | 183     | 157       | 171       |
| Parishes without Priests  |      |      |         |         |         |           |           |
| (i.e., Missions)          | —    | —    | 43      | 40      | 99      | 151       | 50        |
| National Parishes         | —    | —    | 7       | 38      | 27      | 29        | 23        |
| Parish Schools            | —    | —    | 16      | 43      | 48      | 74        | 63        |
| Diocesan Priests          | —    | —    | 92      | 214     | 283     | 354       | 403       |
| Religious Order Priests   | —    | —    | 9       | 23      | 66      | 91        | 125       |
| Women Religious           | —    | —    | 190     | 641     | 811     | 1,083     | 825       |
| Catholic Population       | —    | —    | 70,000  | 201,150 | 269,441 | 359,470   | 363,005   |
| Total Population          | —    | —    | 546,254 | 813,200 | 947,422 | 1,125,199 | 1,223,710 |

## NEW YORK
## Diocese of Rockville Center (1957)

|  | 1850 | 1880 | 1900 | 1930 | 1950 | 1960 | 1980 |
|---|---|---|---|---|---|---|---|
| Parishes | — | — | — | — | — | 114 | 129 |
| Parishes without Priests |  |  |  |  |  |  |  |
| (i.e., Missions) | — | — | — | — | — | 93 | 10 |
| National Parishes | — | — | — | — | — | 4 | 3 |
| Parish Schools | — | — | — | — | — | 76 | 84 |
| Diocesan Priests | — | — | — | — | — | 376 | 488 |
| Religious Order Priests | — | — | — | — | — | 43 | 152 |
| Women Religious | — | — | — | — | — | 419 | 640 |
| Catholic Population | — | — | — | — | — | 657,497 | 1,041,915 |
| Total Population | — | — | — | — | — | 1,954,126 | 2,782,114 |

## PENNSYLVANIA
## Archdiocese of Philadelphia (1808)

|  | 1850 | 1880 | 1900 | 1930 | 1950 | 1960 | 1980 |
|---|---|---|---|---|---|---|---|
| Parishes | 88 | 130 | 212 | 388 | 401 | 439 | 307 |
| Parishes without Priests |  |  |  |  |  |  |  |
| (i.e., Missions) | 0 | 88 | 111 | 0 | 70 | 608 | 442 |
| National Parishes | 4 | 2 | 41 | 124 | 110 | 121 | 52 |
| Parish Schools | 14 | 54 | 112 | 288 | 305 | 402 | 269 |
| Diocesan Priests | 93 | 242 | 348 | 782 | 1,238 | 1,227 | 997 |
| Religious Order |  |  |  |  |  |  |  |
| Priests |  |  | 106 | 360 | 672 | 712 | 650 |
| Women Religious | 34 | 981 | 1,997 | 5,120 | 6,819 | 7,201 | 5,615 |
| Catholic Population | 170,000 | 300,000 | 460,000 | 820,000 | 1,070,692 | 1,548,285 | 1,364,816 |
| Total Population | 1,915,434 | 1,502,365 | 2,165,284 | 3,423,880 | 4,025,806 | 4,521,801 | 3,616,400 |

## PENNSYLVANIA
## Diocese of Pittsburgh (1843)

|  | 1850 | 1880 | 1900 | 1930 | 1950 | 1960 | 1980 |
|---|---|---|---|---|---|---|---|
| Parishes | 67 | 130 | 195 | 366 | 416 | 307 | 321 |
| Parishes without Priests |  |  |  |  |  |  |  |
| (i.e., Missions) | 0 | 44 | 27 | 128 | 332 | 386 | 189 |
| National Parishes | 3 | 28 | 46 | 108 | 108 | 80 | 65 |
| Parish Schools | ? | 62 | 109 | 237 | 237 | 222 | 141 |
| Diocesan Priests | 57 | 184 | 232 | 518 | 768 | 560 | 659 |
| Religious Order |  |  |  |  |  |  |  |
| Priests |  |  | 130 | 212 | 262 | 224 | 318 |
| Women Religious | ? | 526 | 1,200 | 3,200 | 4,612 | 4,632 | 3,088 |
| Catholic Population | 45,000 | 125,000 | 280,000 | 581,327 | 832,745 | 866,453 | 913,957 |
| Total Population | 791,226 | 1,065,952 | 2,931,599 | 2,596,709 | 2,799,675 | 2,306,112 | 2,241,430 |

## PENNSYLVANIA
### Diocese of Erie (1853)

|                                      | 1850 | 1880    | 1900    | 1930    | 1950    | 1960    | 1980    |
|--------------------------------------|------|---------|---------|---------|---------|---------|---------|
| Parishes                             | —    | 84      | 77      | 114     | 123     | 137     | 128     |
| Parishes without Priests (i.e., Missions) | — | 42   | 65      | 49      | 58      | 66      | 90      |
| National Parishes                    | —    | 0       | 0       | 11      | 11      | 11      | 1       |
| Parish Schools                       | —    | 22      | 42      | 46      | 53      | 58      | 54      |
| Diocesan Priests                     | —    | 65      | 91      | 153     | 208     | 265     | 289     |
| Religious Order Priests              | —    |         | 25      | 53      | 96      | 90      | 58      |
| Women Religious                      | —    | 110     | 232     | 658     | 1,071   | 1,443   | 726     |
| Catholic Population                  | —    | 45,000  | 65,000  | 127,285 | 168,218 | 204,618 | 219,843 |
| Total Population                     | —    | 461,484 | 615,061 | 732,128 | 766,873 | 853,167 | 900,971 |

## PENNSYLVANIA
### Diocese of Scranton (1868)

|                                      | 1850 | 1880    | 1900    | 1930      | 1950      | 1960    | 1980    |
|--------------------------------------|------|---------|---------|-----------|-----------|---------|---------|
| Parishes                             | —    | 70      | 109     | 207       | 231       | 235     | 240     |
| Parishes without Priests (i.e., Missions) | — | 46   | 50      | 45        | 198       | 199     | 210     |
| National Parishes                    | —    | 4       | 38      | 92        | 97        | 99      | 102     |
| Parish Schools                       | —    | 12      | 38      | 66        | 85        | 97      | 64      |
| Diocesan Priests                     | —    | 60      | 160     | 311       | 465       | 488     | 475     |
| Religious Order Priests              | —    |         | 10      | 45        | 101       | 127     | 129     |
| Women Religious                      | —    | 18      | 628     | 1,130     | 1,370     | 1,460   | 1,224   |
| Catholic Population                  | —    | 50,000  | 150,000 | 326,710   | 345,037   | 359,037 | 355,683 |
| Total Population                     | —    | 581,863 | 864,218 | 1,219,452 | 1,047,290 | 916,539 | 970,771 |

## PENNSYLVANIA
### Diocese of Harrisburg (1868)

|                                      | 1850 | 1880    | 1900    | 1930      | 1950      | 1960      | 1980      |
|--------------------------------------|------|---------|---------|-----------|-----------|-----------|-----------|
| Parishes                             | —    | 51      | 54      | 81        | 86        | 93        | 112       |
| Parishes without Priests (i.e., Missions) | — | 24   | 32      | 26        | 121       | 134       | 149       |
| National Parishes                    | —    | 10      | 17      | 13        | 10        | 11        | 10        |
| Parish Schools                       | —    | 19      | 35      | 54        | 64        | 74        | 56        |
| Diocesan Priests                     | —    | 46      | 70      | 117       | 128       | 185       | 176       |
| Religious Order Priests              | —    |         | 2       | 29        | 62        | 47        | 90        |
| Women Religious                      | —    | 109     | 219     | 993       | 827       | 950       | 868       |
| Catholic Population                  | —    | 20,000  | 45,000  | 80,541    | 119,605   | 165,638   | 209,106   |
| Total Population                     | —    | 671,227 | 830,372 | 1,071,257 | 1,246,815 | 1,405,426 | 1,844,980 |

## PENNSYLVANIA
### Diocese of Altoona-Johnstown (1901)

|                                    | 1850 | 1880 | 1900 | 1930    | 1950    | 1960    | 1980    |
|------------------------------------|------|------|------|---------|---------|---------|---------|
| Parishes                           | —    | —    | —    | 111     | 112     | 114     | 120     |
| Parishes without Priests           |      |      |      |         |         |         |         |
| (i.e., Missions)                   | —    | —    | —    | 17      | 101     | 104     | 88      |
| National Parishes                  | —    | —    | —    | 29      | 23      | 29      | 26      |
| Parish Schools                     | —    | —    | —    | 51      | 55      | 59      | 31      |
| Diocesan Priests                   | —    | —    | —    | 146     | 140     | 158     | 177     |
| Religious Order Priests            | —    | —    | —    | 54      | 103     | 106     | 104     |
| Women Religious                    | —    | —    | —    | 390     | 525     | 560     | 220     |
| Catholic Population                | —    | —    | —    | 96,213  | 136,440 | 148,525 | 150,602 |
| Total Population                   | —    | —    | —    | 587,924 | 622,879 | 626,707 | 654,338 |

## PENNSYLVANIA
### Diocese of Greensburg (1951)

|                                    | 1850 | 1880 | 1900 | 1930 | 1950 | 1960    | 1980    |
|------------------------------------|------|------|------|------|------|---------|---------|
| Parishes                           | —    | —    | —    | —    | —    | 120     | 117     |
| Parishes without Priests           |      |      |      |      |      |         |         |
| (i.e., Missions)                   | —    | —    | —    | —    | —    | 93      | 87      |
| National Parishes                  | —    | —    | —    | —    | —    | 29      | 18      |
| Parish Schools                     | —    | —    | —    | —    | —    | 56      | 46      |
| Diocesan Priests                   | —    | —    | —    | —    | —    | 146     | 193     |
| Religious Order Priests            | —    | —    | —    | —    | —    | 129     | 115     |
| Women Religious                    | —    | —    | —    | —    | —    | 632     | 464     |
| Catholic Population                | —    | —    | —    | —    | —    | 211,979 | 228,793 |
| Total Population                   | —    | —    | —    | —    | —    | 676,859 | 735,127 |

## PENNSYLVANIA
### Diocese of Allentown (1961)

|                                    | 1850 | 1880 | 1900 | 1930 | 1950 | 1960 | 1980      |
|------------------------------------|------|------|------|------|------|------|-----------|
| Parishes                           | —    | —    | —    | —    | —    | —    | 152       |
| Parishes without Priests           |      |      |      |      |      |      |           |
| (i.e., Missions)                   | —    | —    | —    | —    | —    | —    | 160       |
| National Parishes                  | —    | —    | —    | —    | —    | —    | 61        |
| Parish Schools                     | —    | —    | —    | —    | —    | —    | 72        |
| Diocesan Priests                   | —    | —    | —    | —    | —    | —    | 307       |
| Religious Order Priests            | —    | —    | —    | —    | —    | —    | 107       |
| Women Religious                    | —    | —    | —    | —    | —    | —    | 920       |
| Catholic Population                | —    | —    | —    | —    | —    | —    | 259,449   |
| Total Population                   | —    | —    | —    | —    | —    | —    | 1,000,000 |

**NEW JERSEY**
**Archdiocese of Newark (1853)**

|                              | 1850 | 1880      | 1900      | 1930      | 1950      | 1960      | 1980      |
|------------------------------|------|-----------|-----------|-----------|-----------|-----------|-----------|
| Parishes                     | —    | 150       | 114       | 229       | 210       | 246       | 248       |
| Parishes without Priests     |      |           |           |           |           |           |           |
| (i.e., Missions)             | —    | 40        | 113       | 48        | 257       | 306       | 169       |
| National Parishes            | —    | 12        | 28        | 49        | 46        | 50        | 48        |
| Parish Schools               | —    | 80        | 99        | 161       | 155       | 217       | 200       |
| Diocesan Priests             | —    | 192       | 190       | 485       | 591       | 764       | 823       |
| Religious Order Priests      | —    |           | 75        | 235       | 274       | 401       | 369       |
| Women Religious              | —    | 735       | 993       | 2,165     | 2,905     | 3,317     | 2,394     |
| Catholic Population          | —    | 175,000   | 362,500   | 1,020,659 | 1,692,836 | 2,408,817 | 2,918,469 |
| Total Population             | —    | 1,131,116 | 1,883,669 | 4,041,334 | 4,907,498 | 6,060,915 | 7,513,586 |

**NEW JERSEY**
**Diocese of Trenton (1881)**

|                              | 1850 | 1880 | 1900    | 1930      | 1950      | 1960      | 1980      |
|------------------------------|------|------|---------|-----------|-----------|-----------|-----------|
| Parishes                     | —    | —    | 86      | 161       | 157       | 175       | 213       |
| Parishes without Priests     |      |      |         |           |           |           |           |
| (i.e., Missions)             | —    | —    | 30      | 58        | 227       | 203       | 217       |
| National Parishes            | —    | —    | 11      | 35        | 98        | 30        | 38        |
| Parish Schools               | —    | —    | 87      | 96        | 75        | 95        | 113       |
| Diocesan Priests             | —    | —    | 104     | 218       | 262       | 358       | 422       |
| Religious Order Priests      | —    | —    | 17      | 55        | 127       | 78        | 198       |
| Women Religious              | —    | —    | 325     | 1,100     | 1,138     | 1,490     | 1,300     |
| Catholic Population          | —    | —    | 72,500  | 272,719   | 307,755   | 474,229   | 888,533   |
| Total Population             | —    | —    | 716,282 | 1,406,501 | 1,100,000 | 1,622,762 | 2,665,599 |

**NEW JERSEY**
**Diocese of Camden (1937)**

|                              | 1850 | 1880 | 1900 | 1930 | 1950    | 1960    | 1980      |
|------------------------------|------|------|------|------|---------|---------|-----------|
| Parishes                     | —    | —    | —    | —    | 66      | 86      | 127       |
| Parishes without Priests     |      |      |      |      |         |         |           |
| (i.e., Missions)             | —    | —    | —    | —    | 98      | 118     | 18        |
| National Parishes            | —    | —    | —    | —    | 5       | 5       | 3         |
| Parish Schools               | —    | —    | —    | —    | 39      | 61      | 68        |
| Diocesan Priests             | —    | —    | —    | —    | 126     | 228     | 375       |
| Religious Order Priests      | —    | —    | —    | —    | 26      | 41      | 43        |
| Women Religious              | —    | —    | —    | —    | 508     | 690     | 583       |
| Catholic Population          | —    | —    | —    | —    | 154,844 | 246,497 | 349,906   |
| Total Population             | —    | —    | —    | —    | 699,877 | 901,871 | 1,138,628 |

## NEW JERSEY
### Diocese of Paterson (1937)

|  | 1850 | 1880 | 1900 | 1930 | 1950 | 1960 | 1980 |
|---|---|---|---|---|---|---|---|
| Parishes | — | — | — | — | 74 | 85 | 104 |
| Parishes without Priests (i.e., Missions) | — | — | — | — | 95 | 132 | 81 |
| National Parishes | — | — | — | — | 19 | 21 | 16 |
| Parish Schools | — | — | — | — | 40 | 63 | 67 |
| Diocesan Priests | — | — | — | — | 122 | 158 | 305 |
| Religious Order Priests | — | — | — | — | 138 | 174 | 260 |
| Women Religious | — | — | — | — | 1,311 | 1,366 | 1,079 |
| Catholic Population | — | — | — | — | 157,639 | 236,389 | 300,530 |
| Total Population | — | — | — | — | 536,729 | 717,493 | 958,200 |

## VARIOUS
### Eastern Rite

|  | 1850 | 1880 | 1900 | 1930 | 1950 | 1960 | 1980 |
|---|---|---|---|---|---|---|---|
| Parishes | — | — | — | 172 | 227 | 251 | 257 |
| Parishes without Priests (i.e., Missions) | — | — | — | 78 | 36 | 31 | 41 |
| National Parishes | — | — | — | — | — | — | — |
| Parish Schools | — | — | — | 172 | 61 | 61 | 34 |
| Diocesan Priests | — | — | — | 225 | 360 | 434 | 539 |
| Religious Order Priests | — | — | — | 3 | 52 | 76 | 116 |
| Women Religious | — | — | — | 0 | 336 | 434 | 490 |
| Catholic Population | — | — | — | 558,466 | 617,584 | 600,802 | 584,739 |
| Total Population | — | — | — | — | — | — | — |

**TOTAL**
**Northeast Region**

| | 1850 | 1880 | 1900 | 1930 | 1950 | 1960 | 1980 |
|---|---|---|---|---|---|---|---|
| Parishes | 428 | 1,827 | 2,339 | 4,453 | 5,134 | 5,496 | 5,857 |
| Parishes without Priests | | | | | | | |
| (i.e., Missions) | 100 | 761 | 1,334 | 1,101 | 3,684 | 5,537 | 4,186 |
| National Parishes | 28 | 148 | 392 | 925 | 876 | 953 | 804 |
| Parish Schools | 33 | 562 | 1,224 | 2,507 | 2,663 | 3,302 | 2,579 |
| Diocesan Priests | 448* | 2,430* | 3,847 | 8,304 | 11,833 | 13,519 | 14,500 |
| Religious Order Priests | | | 852 | 2,929 | 5,882 | 7,419 | 8,107 |
| Women Religious | 281 | 6,799 | 15,893 | 40,021 | 56,564 | 63,712 | 47,780 |
| Catholic Population | 737,000 | 2,829,100 | 5,270,500 | 9,978,384 | 12,958,352 | 17,317,325 | 19,260,881 |
| Total Population | 8,718,383 | 14,507,407 | 22,123,116 | 34,446,757 | 38,980,432 | 44,742,429 | 51,734,359 |

*Religious and diocesan priests combined.

116

# A Peculiar Institution: A History of Catholic Parish Life in the Southeast (1850–1980)

Michael J. McNally

*To Philip Gleason, a gifted scholar and mentor, whose penetrating intellect, charming wit, and refined humanity have enriched both my head and my heart.*

The parish is for most Catholics the single most important part of the Church. This is where for them the mission of Christ continues. This is where they publicly express their faith, joining with others to give proof of their communion with God and with one another.[1]
*(Parish Life in the United States: Final Report to the Bishops of the United States by the Parish Project* Washington: USCC, 1983, 4)

You are a people sacred to the Lord, your God; He has chosen you from all the nations on the face of the earth to be a people peculiarly his own.
(Deut., 7:6, *New American Bible* translation)

# Contents

# Abbreviations Found in the Notes

| | |
|---|---|
| AAB | Archives of the Archdiocese of Baltimore |
| AACHS | Archives of the American Catholic Historical Society, (Overbrook, Pa.) |
| AADS | Archives of the Adrian Dominican Sisters (Adrian, Mich.) |
| ADC | Archives of the Diocese of Charleston |
| ADRa | Archives of the Diocese of Raleigh |
| ADS | Archives of the Diocese of Savannah |
| ADSA | Archives of the Diocese of St. Augustine |
| AFAM | Archives and Files of the Archdiocese of Miami |
| AFDSA | Archives and Files of the Diocese of St. Petersburg |
| AJF | Archives of the Josephite Fathers (Baltimore, Md.) |
| ASHN | Archives of the Sisters of the Holy Names of Jesus and Mary (Albany, N.Y.) |
| ASSJ | Archives of the Sisters of St. Joseph of St. Augustine (St. Augustine, Fla.) |
| n.d. | no date |
| OCD | *Official Catholic Directory* |
| RACHS | *Records of the American Catholic Historical Society of Philadelphia* |
| RG | Record Group |

# Preface

When people think or write about the history of Catholics in America, bishops like John Carroll, John Hughes, James Gibbons, John Ireland, Francis Spellman come to mind; pastors like Dimitri Gallitzin, Stephen Baden, William Hogan, Edward McGlynn, Charles E. Coughlin are remembered; intellectuals like Orestes Brownson, Paul Hanley Furfey, John A. Ryan, Dorothy Day, John Courtney Murray, SJ, and John Tracy Ellis are discussed. But American Catholicism is more than the illustrious careers of bishops or pastors, or the ideas of intellectuals. Catholicism is about people as a social unit, a corporate body, a community of faith, not just outstanding individuals. This study looks at American Catholics from the perspective of peoplehood at its basic Catholic social structure—the parish.

The parish, the basic organizational, sociological, and spiritual unit of the Roman Catholic Church, is the locus of the juridical, theological, cultural, and spiritual expression of the Church Universal and the Church Particular (the diocese) in a specific place and time. The Revised Code of Canon Law (1983) defines the parish as a stable community of the faithful within a particular church (a diocese) whose pastoral care is committed to a pastor, who is under the authority of the diocesan bishop. Generally, parishes are territorial. However, personal parishes may also be established with membership based on rite, language, or national origin. The pastor, the juridical and spiritual leader of the parish, is charged by the diocesan bishop to be the latter's alter ego—to preach, teach, sanctify, and govern according to the mandates of Scripture and the Church.[1]

But parish life does not exist in a vacuum. Rather, it is embraced by a cultural, social, historical milieu from which it takes life and by which it differs from other regions of the country. There is no single American parish, nor is there one region of the country that provides the archetype of the American parish. Certainly, American parishes have similarities, but they also have marvelous differences based on their regional and cultural history. This study is about the dynamism of parish life as it developed from 1850 to 1980 in one specific region of the United States—the Southeast Coast, that is the states of Delaware, Maryland, West Virginia, Virginia, North Carolina, South Carolina, Georgia, Florida, and the District of Columbia. The story of parish life within this territory during 130 years is one of steady growth and development, more dramatic in some localities than others. In early 1850, the region was comprised of five dioceses; by 1980, there were sixteen. In 1850, ninety-six parish priests served approximately 123,000 Catholics in 119 parishes; by 1980, approximately 1,525 parish priests ministered

121

to about 2,560,577 Catholics in 1,102 parishes. In 1850, there were approximately 1,280 Catholics for every parish priest; in 1980, each parish priest had 1,679 Catholics to care for.[2] Throughout most of the period under study, and throughout most of the region, a peculiar missionary quality characterizes parish life—a lack of Catholics, a lack of priests, a lack of religious, a lack of institutions, a lack of money, a lack of political and economic power to influence the larger society. But, although this dearth of resources and personnel curtailed Southeastern Catholicism from influencing, up to now, either American Catholicism or Southern culture, as an alternative expression to both it deserves study and reflection, especially in the light of recent developments in post-Vatican II reform and post-1960 American culture.

As with any human endeavor, this study has certain limitations. Research data were difficult to locate. Secondary material on Catholicism in the Southeast is scarce, especially material on the lower states. The availability of primary sources also presented difficulties. Where diocesan archives exist, material is sometimes in a raw, unorganized state, or in a form designed to reveal more about episcopal or diocesan administrative history, rather than parish history. Besides the limitations imposed by the sources, some choices had to be made about what locales and what data to emphasize. Although material from throughout the region was used, this study will give special emphasis to the lower states of the region because parishes of that area are more typical of the character of parish life for the region as a whole than, for example, urban developments in Washington, Baltimore, or Wilmington. Finally, this study is more exploratory than definitive because of the limitations of the sources, the limits of time imposed upon the completion of the project, and the novelty of studying Catholicism from the perspective of parish life. Beyond Joseph Fichter's *Southern Parish* (1951),[3] the Southern parish has been generally omitted in scholarly study. It is hoped that this essay might serve as a catalyst for further investigations into parish life in the South, as well as for further reflection on the meaning and development of American and Southern parish life.

**Notes**

1. James H. Provost, ed., *Code, Community, Ministry & Selected Studies for the Parish Minister Introducing the Revised Code of Canon Law* (Washington, D.C.: Canon Law Society of America, 1983), 61.

2. *The Metropolitan Catholic Almanac and Laity's Directory, 1850* (Baltimore & Fielding Lucas, Jr., 1849), 88, 186, 231; *OCD,* 1980 (New York: P. J. Kennedy & Sons, 1980), 58, 62, 177, 180, 522–523, 650, 669, 749–750, 761, 797, 834, 884, 986, 992, 1001.

3. Joseph H. Fichter, *Southern Parish: Dynamics of a City Church* (Chicago: University of Chicago, 1951).

# CHAPTER ONE

# The Parish and Southern
# Society—A Peculiar Minority

Catholic parish life in the Southeast grew from a social and cultural environment that was peculiar to the region. It is important, as we begin, to briefly characterize that environment.

## A. CHARACTERISTICS OF SOUTHERN SOCIETY

Since the beginning of the desegregation movement in 1954, social scientists and historians have intensified their scholarly interest in the Southern ethos. This ethos was mythologized and idealized by both Southerners and Northerners.

> If the mythic South appeared to be "moonlight, magnolias, and mint julips," in reality, racism, the Ku Klux Klan, grinding poverty, and intellectual stagnation molded Southern culture after 1865. Being poverty-stricken in a nation of "plenty" contributed to fatalism in the Southern Spirit. Indeed, the South carried an historic "burden" of defeatism, and progress came slowly compared with other regions of the United States.[1]

This Southern ethos has been variously identified. Some have said that the culture of the soil bred the regional virtues of leisure, devotion to place and family, a sense of history and tradition, the "scorn of dollar chasers," and manners. For them, the South was the oldest and largest counterculture in the United States, an alternative to the national consensus.[2] It is the nation's oldest and most important minority.[3] Some social scientists see Southerners as an ethnic group, a reference group—a cognitive entity that people use to orient themselves—rather than as residents of a particular region. For them, Southern identity is shaped and reinforced by historical conflict, by a sense of grievance over the ill treatment at the hands of the rest of the country, and by Celtic personality traits.[4] Intellectual historians suggest that the idea of the South "has served to weld the unintegrated social reality" of Southerners, especially during the last twenty-five years of increasing urbanization, industrialization, and integration.[5]

## B. URBAN/RURAL CULTURE AND SOUTHERN CATHOLICISM

As in the North, Catholicism in the South was and is concentrated in the urban centers and made little headway in rural areas. The character of Southern Catholicism was directly influenced by the nature of Southern cities, which differed from their Northern complements by at least three distinctive features: ruralism, biracialism, and colonialism.[6]

Life in Southern cities in the nineteenth century remained tied to agricultural cycles, while the population, landscape, and architecture reflected agrarian conceptions. Even in the mid-twentieth century when Southern city populations expanded rapidly, such growth was more horizontal than vertical, characterized by low density population and single family dwellings. Moreover, the Southern city ethos continued to exhibit rural values. Family and religion (Evangelistic and Calvinistic) have consistently remained strong Southern rural bulwarks that were transferred to the Southern city. Even in 1980, nine out of ten Southerners identified themselves as Protestants and almost one-half of the churchgoers claimed to be Southern Baptists. Southern Protestantism is indistinguishable from Southern society and inseparable from urban life, so much so that Samuel Hill, Jr., describes the pervasiveness of religion in the South as "Cultural Protestantism."[7]

A second characteristic of Southern urban society is its biracialism. The region's economic and religious institutions regulated, separated, isolated, and subjugated the black race. Rather than developing single large black ghettos as in Northern cities, the concentration of postbellum blacks in Southern cities reflected the scattered nature of undesirable housing sites, with racial residential lines hardening by the 1890s. Black isolation from white urban areas increased during the twentieth century. By 1960, only 5.5% of the Southern urban population resided in integrated neighborhoods.[8]

A third characteristic of Southern urbanism is colonialism. In the nineteenth and a good part of the twentieth century, the Southern economy was controlled by Northern interests, especially from New York. Even the most recent Sunbelt economic boom is mixed with financial colonialism. By the 1970s, the region was attracting approximately half of the nation's total annual foreign investments. For example, by the end of the 1970s, 40% of South Carolina's annual industrial investments came from foreign sources. Some areas owed their Sunbelt prosperity to spin-off benefits from earlier Northern industrial progress, which put them in a most favored position when the industrial North began to decline. Ruralism, biracialism, and colonialism still persist in the Southern city and have produced the particular and distinctive blend of urbanization that persists in the region today.[9]

Whether in an urban or rural environment, Catholics in the South were a peculiar minority amidst the hegemony of "Cultural Protestantism." Catholicism was perceived by Protestant Southerners as "alien" and "foreign" to the South for several reasons. It rested outside the Calvinist, Protestant evangelical hegemony. It comprised a considerable number of outsiders, such as immigrants or transplanted Northerners. It was for the most part a small group whose religious beliefs and practices were little known and even less understood.[10]

Unlike Protestant observers, Southern Catholics like writer Flannery O'Connor characterized Southern Catholicism as "both native and alien," a status that she saw as a professional strength.

> To my way of thinking, the only thing that keeps me from being a regional writer is being Catholic and the only thing that keeps me from being a Catholic writer (in the narrow sense) is being a Southerner. . . .[11]

But "being neither fish nor fowl," Catholicism sought consensus and cooperation with the Southern social order so that it could freely cultivate its inward spiritual garden without undue molestation. Nevertheless, since "Protestantism was the imprimatur of true Southernism," a Southern Catholic, try as he or she might, could never quite measure up to societal expectations because of religious affiliation.[12] Consequently, Southern Catholicism never matched the self-confident Catholicism of the North because of its numerical paucity, its political and economic powerlessness, and its image as a "peculiar institution" out of harmony with the strains of Dixie.

## Notes

1. William E. Ellis, "Catholicism and the Southern Ethos: The Role of Patrick Henry Callahan," *Catholic Historical Review,* 69 (January, 1983), 41.
2. Willard B. Gatewood, Jr., "The Agrarians from the Perspective of Fifty Years: An Essay Review," *Florida Historical Quarterly,* 51 (January, 1983), 313–314.
3. Leonard Reisman, "Social Development and the American South," *Journal of Social Issues,* 22 (January, 1966), 115; Gatewood, "The Agrarians," 318.
4. John Shelton Reed, *Southerners: The Social Psychology of Sectionalism* (Chapel Hill, N.C.: University of North Carolina, 1983), 4, 11, 33–36, 70–89. For other references to Southern ethnicity, see: John Shelton Reed, *The Enduring South: Subcultural Persistence in Mass Society* (Chapel Hill, N.C.: University of North Carolina, 1982); George Tindall, *The Ethnic Southerners* (Baton Rouge: Louisiana State University, 1977); Lewis Killian, *White Southerners* (New York: Random House, 1970); Grady McWhiney and Perry D. Jamieson, *Attack and Die: Civil War Military Tactics and the Southern Heritage* (University, Alabama: University of Alabama, 1982).
5. Gatewood, "The Agrarians," 320–321.
6. David R. Goldfield, "The Urban South: A Regional Framework," *American Historical Review,* 89 (December, 1981), 1011. For other recent studies on the urban South, see: Blaine A. Brownell, *The Urban Ethos in the South, 1920–30* (Baton Rouge: Louisiana

State University, 1975); Blaine A. Brownell and David R. Goldfield, eds., *The City in Southern History: The Growth of Urban Civilization in the South* (Port Washington, N.Y.: Kennikat, 1977); Howard N. Rabinowitz, *Race Relations in the Urban South, 1865–1890* (New York: Oxford University, 1978); Bradley R. Rice, "Urbanization, 'Atlanta-ization,' and Suburbanization: Three Themes for the Urban History of Twentieth Century Georgia," *Georgia Historical Quarterly*, 68 (Spring, 1984), 40–59; David Goldfield, *Cottonfields and Skyscrapers: Southern City and Region, 1607–1980* (Baton Rouge: Louisiana State University, 1982).

    7. Goldfield, "The Urban South," 1011–1027; Reed, *The Enduring South*, 57, 62; Charles P. Roland, *The Improbable Era: The South Since World War II* (Lexington, Ky.: University of Kentucky, 1975), 119–136; James C. Cobb, *Industrialization and Southern Society, 1877–1984* (Lexington, Ky.: University of Kentucky, 1984), 136–164.

    8. Letter, Father Peter Hogan, S.S.J., to Author, September 14, 1983; Goldfield, "The Urban South," 1025–1027.

    9. *Ibid.*, 1029–1033; Cobb, *Industrialization and Southern Society*, 58, 137.

    10. Wilber J. Cash, *Mind of the South* (New York: Knopf, 1940, 1970), 334; Katherine Martensen, "Region, Religion, and Social Action: The Catholic Committee of the South, 1939–56," *Catholic Historical Review*, 68 (April, 1982), 253, 262.

    11. Flannery O'Connor, *The Habit of Being*, ed. by Sally Fitzgerald (New York: Farrar, Straus, Giroux, 1979), 104.

    12. Randall M. Miller, "A Church in Cultural Captivity: Some Speculations on Catholic Identity in the Old South," in *Catholics in the Old South: Essays on Church and Culture*, ed. by Randall M. Miller and Jon L. Wakelyn (Macon, Ga.: Mercer University, 1983), 52.

# CHAPTER TWO

# The Parish and Southern History—A Historical Overview, 1850–1980

Besides the social and cultural environment, a further context for the growth and development of Catholic parish life in the Southeast is the peculiar history of the region. Five historical periods, from the flowering of the Antebellum period, in 1850, to our own times, in 1980, provide the historical context that gives distinctive shape to parish life in the region.

## A. THE ANTEBELLUM SOUTH, 1850–1860

The character of the Antebellum South furnished the initial formative milieu for parish life in the Southeast and influenced its development long after the termination of that historical period.

By 1850, the Roman Catholic Church was the largest single denomination in the United States, numbering 1,334,500 followers, 70% of whom were recently arrived Irish and Germans.[1] By 1850, the South Atlantic Region had approximately 123,000 Catholics or 9% of the national total; 119 parishes or about 9% of the national total; and ninety-six parish priests, or about 8% of the total priests in the country. By 1860, the national Catholic population had grown to 1,608,600, that is by 17%. Both the number of churches and parish clergy increased nationally by 50.5%. By comparison, the Catholic population of the South Atlantic region grew by about 19%, while the number of parishes increased by 26% and the number of priests increased by 38% during the 1850–1860 decade.[2] These statistics demonstrate that, during the first decade under study, the crucial problem of parish life in the region was a lack of personnel and material resources to expand pastoral service, a trend that typifies Southeast Catholicism until very recent times. Another trend that begins in this period and continues is that, by 1860, Southeast Catholicism loses ground by virtually every statistical measurement in comparison to national averages and, especially, to Northeast and Midwest figures.

One area in which the Southeast did not lose ground was in its ruralism. Except for concentrations of Catholics in Southeastern cities, Catholics were few and far between, scattered in pockets throughout rural areas over rather expansive territories where travel was often difficult. Virtually every parish in the region had rural missions and stations attached to it. In 1850, the percentage of the Southern population living in rural agrarian areas (less than 2,500 in population) was 90.8%. In the same year, Florida, Georgia, North Carolina, and Western Virginia had rural populations of over 95% of their total residents.[3]

Since Catholics considered themselves as Southerners, the political debates of the period influenced them.[4] Although Know-Nothingism of the 1850s was a stronger force in Northern society than in the South, it did have an effect on several parishes of the region. In 1853, the Redemptorists, who were in charge of St. Mary's and Carroll Manor in Annapolis, Maryland, were falsely accused of incarcerating a prisoner in the basement of their residence. An on-site investigation conducted by civil authorities revealed that not only was there no prisoner, but that there was not even a basement.[5] In 1856, St. Patrick's in Norfolk and, in 1858, St. Paul's in Portsmouth (Virginia) were destroyed by fire; both fires were suspected to be the product of Know-Nothing arsonists.[6] Catholics were also influenced by other Antebellum developments, such as cholera and yellow fever epidemics that decimated several Southern urban centers in the 1850s. Of particular note was the work of Irish-born Francis Devlin (pastor of St. Paul's, Portsmouth, Virginia) among yellow fever victims, in 1855. The plague ravaged the "Irish Row" ghetto of Portsmouth for three months. Devlin stayed on through it all, ten to twelve hours a day, bringing food to the sick and arranging their beds, digging graves with his own hands because of the fear of others of personal contagion, begging money from other parts to sustain the survivors. His exhausted body fell sick with the fever three times. Such heroism ended in his expiration during his third attack of the plague.[7]

Another continuity in parochial life, which began in the Antebellum period and signified its missionary poverty, was that, like Francis Devlin, most of the clergy that ministered in the South were from someplace else. Native vocations were negligible. Bishops had to recruit Northerners (but were not very successful at it because of the primitive pastoral conditions and the lack of stipends) or Europeans (who were either malcontents, incompetents, or genuinely zealous missionaries)—mostly French, Italian, German, and, especially, Irish. The latter group seemed to adjust best to the Southern, rural environment not only because they spoke English, but also because their Celtic culture and agrarian homeland harmonized with Southern culture. Many of these European clergy (including a few of the Irish) had difficulty with the English language and/or adjusting to Southern culture; too many foreign-born priests stumbled over the American idiom in sermons and conversations in a Southern environment where the general absence of educational institutions and literacy put a high value on the cadence of the spoken word. Besides linguistic and cultural difficulties, Southern clergy had financial problems. Most priests were forced to live frugally because of the general poverty of the region and because of the lack of specie in the agrarian economy. Clerical indigence often made parish priests unduly dependent on certain laypersons, especially trustees and influential plantation owners. As another expression of clerical poverty, unlike many priests in the North, Southern priests were generally not in the powerful position of being arbiters or interlocutors between their parishioners and the socioeconomic environment.[8] Besides asking for priests, Southern bishops continually begged Europeans for financial aid, mostly from missionary societies in France, Bavaria, and Austria.[9]

Another Antebellum parochial characteristic, as well as one that endured, was the predominance of one-priest parishes because of a paucity of parishioners and clergy. Moreover, most parishes had a number of missions and stations attached. What this meant for parish life was the absence of the pastor; in other words, the clergy had to be circuit riders, certainly not available on demand to most Southern Catholics. Laypeople, especially those scattered throughout the expansive countryside, were most often without either priests or churches. With priestly visitation irregular, parishes were often held together by good laymen who conducted funeral services or priest-less Sunday services, and by good laywomen who preserved for the next generation Catholic values and teachings. If Catholicism was to survive at all under these conditions, parents were crucial, especially wives and mothers, for the home and the family were the church, the school, and the locus for Catholic teaching and the persuasive force of good example. Family observances at Christmas, New Year's, weddings, anniversaries, and birthdays were religious events at which domestic Catholicism expressed itself. Family prayers, devotions, home religious instructions, meatless Fridays, socialization with other Catholic families and intermarriages with them were other means the family used to keep its Catholicism intact. But without the proximity of priest and church, such efforts took faith and courage, especially given the overwhelmingly Protestant-Calvinistic religious environment. Even the most devout of Catholics had difficulty fulfilling their religious duties. Wealthy Catholics paid to bring priests to them or could travel to towns where priests resided. But most rural Catholics lacked the time, the means, or the inclination to search out priest and church. The religious ignorance and apathy of Southern rural Catholics astonished many outside observers. A low rate of regular Mass attendance was not unusual in the rural Antebellum South, although to be considered a faithful Catholic, one was expected to receive Communion at least once a year at Easter. Many Southern Catholics sought a priest only at baptism, marriage, and burial. The isolation of Catholics and the high rate of mixed marriages with Protestants encouraged many Catholics to adopt ''Cultural Protestantism.'' Most practicing Catholics (most of them immigrants) clustered around Southern cities where churches and clerical ministry were more conveniently available.[10]

While immigration defined the character of Northeastern Catholicism, being a peculiar minority defined Antebellum Southeastern Catholicism. The South did not attract immigrants because of a lack of economic opportunity and often a lack of recruitment on the part of Southern states, whose politicians and businessmen, in an effort to "preserve" and "protect" the Southern social order, expended a great deal of political, legal, and moral energy on one ethnic group already ubiquitous in the South—blacks. Those Catholic immigrants who did settle in the South resided in or near cities and most were from Nova Scotia, Haiti, Barbados, the German states, and Ireland.[11]

The most prevalent Catholic immigrant group in the Southeast was the Irish. In the 1840s, Catholic Irish began moving into the South to work as laborers for railroad construction, especially in Virginia and Georgia.[12] Although present in some coastal Southern cities as longshoremen, bargemen, and riverboat men, Irishmen surfaced as urban laborers with the expansion of Southern cities during the 1850s. Irish labor was considered more reliable and valuable than slave labor, but in other respects they were considered expendable workers, especially in the dangerous task of loading and unloading ships at port. The living conditions of the Southern urban Irish were chaotic and destructive of human dignity. As a result, they gained the reputation as the "grand movers of all disturbances," and were prone to drunkenness, gambling, larceny, the buying and selling of stolen goods, illegal voting, assault and battery, and murder. Particularly in Charleston, the influx of the Irish upon what had been a labor pool of black urban workers created tensions and pressures. Freedmen of color were successful in resisting Irish penetration into the trades (carpentry, smithery, etc.). The inability to displace black urban workers sufficiently in Charleston led to a high rate of transiency among the Irish workers. In many places in the South, Irish itinerant laborers even competed with urban black slaves or field hands. In Virginia, many farmers preferred Irish field hands to blacks. The Irish were also transient laborers in the Southern levees or roadworks.[13]

By 1860, there were 84,000 Irish-born persons in the South; some Northern states individually had more Irish-born residents than the entire South. Only Louisiana, Tennessee, Missouri, Maryland, and Virginia had more than 1% of their population Irish-born. Cities like Baltimore, Charleston, Richmond, and Savannah had Irish populations of more than 3,000, but outside of these, few identifiable concentrations of Irish existed on the South Atlantic Coast. The Irish were not numerical enough or concentrated enough to threaten or change the existing social, political, or institutional arrangements in the South (unlike the experience of the North). The Irish accepted Southern Regional culture while retaining, at the same time, their own Irish ethnic identity.[14]

Although German Catholics were not as prevalent in the South as the Irish, they resided in small concentrations in several places. Virginia became a haven for a number of German immigrants in the 1840s. In 1850, St. Mary's Church was erected for the 700 or 800 German Catholics in Richmond. By 1860, three German parishes were established in Western Virginia. As an indication of German presence, marriage announcements in the local paper in Atlanta, in the early 1850s, were in English and German. In 1850, in Atlanta, one out of every twelve heads of households was a European immigrant; at the same time in the same place one out of every twenty households was Northern-born.[15]

Perhaps the most unique and peculiar aspect of parish life in the Southeast was its pastoral response to the South's largest ethnic group—blacks. Given the nature of Southern urban housing patterns, the importance of agrarian cultural values, and the demographic concentrations of blacks in the South, as well as the perennial Southern preoccupation with the "black question," it was impossible for even a peculiar minority of small proportions like Southern Catholics to ignore the presence of blacks in their midst and to fail to respond to that presence.

During the Antebellum period, Catholic instruction of slaves was left to Catholic slaveholders, who most often did not measure up to this responsibility. However, those who did nourished the faith among their slaves by baptizing them, by bringing them to Mass, and by having a priest occasionally come to visit. Household slaves in Catholic families in the urban South were more likely to be instructed in Catholicism and practiced in the faith than rural slaves, but the same could be said about urban white Catholics versus rural whites. Just about every Antebellum Catholic Church in the South had a gallery that was used by Catholic slaves and free people of color. Although separate black churches and schools were nonexistent, several Antebellum black Catholic societies were founded for the purpose of mutual aid, burial, and religious instruction.[16]

At least two commentators suggest that black Catholics in the Antebellum period were more numerous than during the rest of the nineteenth century.[17] Just how many black Catholics lived in the Antebellum South is very difficult to determine. The best estimates place the number of Southern black Catholics, in 1860, at 100,000, which is probably a generous appraisal; 62% were in Louisiana, 16% were in Maryland, and the other black Catholics were scattered in small pockets throughout the South.[18] In 1858, the 450 black Catholics in St. Augustine, Florida, represented a tradition of black Catholicism in that city, which had its roots in the First Spanish Colonial Period (1565–1763).[19]

What is significant about the Antebellum period is that those missionary qualities that characterized it—paucity of Catholics, lack of personnel and resources, ruralism, absence of political and economic clout, clerical poverty, a preponderance of one-priest parishes with many missions and stations attached (with all of its ramifications), insignificant Catholic immigration, and a pervasive beleaguered black population—continued to shape the unique character of parish life in the Southeast for one-hundred years to come.

## B. THE WAR AND RECONSTRUCTION, 1860–1880

No section of the country was more affected by the divisiveness of Secession and the ravages of the bloodiest war in American history than the Southeast. The unique experience of Secession, war, and Reconstruction provided a peculiar atmosphere for parish life.

With the country split in two, all Southern bishops, with the exception of Bishop Richard Whelan of Wheeling, stood with their people and their government in support of the Southern cause; Bishop Augustin Verot of the Vicariate of St. Augustine and the Diocese of Savannah and Bishop Patrick Lynch of Charleston were especially known for their support. With few exceptions, the lower clergy and the laity also gave wholehearted corroboration to the Confederacy. Yet, unlike most of the other major Christian denominations, the Catholic Church in the South did not break with the Northern Catholic Church or establish a separate ecclesial organization.[20]

The operations of war severely hampered an already difficult priestly ministry in the Southeast that was dependent upon the ability to travel to scattered settlements of Catholics. Yet, bishops and priests did cross military lines throughout the conflict because within the same ecclesial jurisdiction certain areas were under Federal control while other parts were in Confederate hands.[21]

The effects of war upon the Church in the Southeast, however, went far beyond inconvenience and procedural difficulties. Few states suffered more from the marauding armies than Virginia. In Bath, St. Vincent de Paul Church was accidentally destroyed by fire while it was being used as Confederate quarters. St. Mary's of the Immaculate Conception, Norfolk, a new church built in 1859, was used as a storehouse and hospital from 1862 to 1865. St. Patrick Church, Winchester (the scene of five armed conflicts, it changed hands seventy-two times in four years), was first used as a Federal horse stable, then later destroyed. St. Joseph's Church, Martinsburg, was used as a stable and prison. At Portsmouth, a new church begun before the war remained unfinished during its duration. The church at Harper's Ferry (St. Peter's) was the only one in the whole Diocese of Richmond left undamaged at war's end.[22]

The effects of the war in Virginia were not just physical. As the hostilities protracted, Catholic congregations in the Diocese of Richmond dwindled. Bishop John McGill of Richmond wrote, in the fall of 1863, that weekday Masses had to be surpressed for a lack of wine. By the end of the war, with Richmond in ruins, the eastern part of Virginia was laid waste.[23]

At war's end, Charleston, South Carolina, was also in ruins. Bishop Patrick Lynch wrote in 1865: "The rich have become poor, and the poor have sunk into misery;" the Bishop of Charleston had no miter, no crosier, no vestments. Outside of Charleston, two churches had been burned, three others pillaged and profaned.[24] Lynch wrote to Bishop William Elder of Natchez early in 1865:

I am like Marious, amid the ruins of Carthage. There are ruins on every side of me, architectural, ecclesiastical, industrial, religious and social. But I trust in God things will come straight. But I have a very gigantic work before me. Part of it however I will have to leave to my successor. We have churches to repair . . . the Cathedral to restore.[25]

Losses of the diocese were estimated at $316,000, not counting moneys lost in savings and Confederate bonds. Bishop Augustin Verot called his own postwar pastoral circumstance in Georgia and Florida a "heap of smoking ruins."[26]

Reconstruction of Catholicism in the South Atlantic region meant both physical and spiritual rebuilding, all in the midst of a poverty of financial and personnel resources. The most serious problem facing the Church in the South was the lack of money. Southerners had given almost everything to the war effort, while at the same time some lost their property and slaves without compensation. What funds they may have held were in valueless Confederate money. Pastors could expect little help from their parishioners. More than ever, it behooved Southern bishops to seek money for reconstruction of their parishes from outside sources— from the Northern United States and from Europe. Dioceses and parishes in the Southeast were virtually dependent on aid from the French Society of the Propagation of the Faith (Lyon). Southern bishops also sought and received some financial support from two other European sources: the *Leopoldinen Stiftung* (Vienna) and the *Ludwig Missionsverein* (Munich). Southern bishops also went on begging tours of the North. Bishop William Gross of Savannah, a former Redemptorist, preached at Redemptorist churches in New York, Baltimore, Philadelphia, Buffalo, Boston, Rochester, and Pittsburgh. Bishop Verot did likewise in late 1866 and in 1867.[27] The collected funds were used for charitable purposes and to reconstruct ruined or battered churches.

Despite the extreme poverty of Florida, Bishop Verot had great success translating the funds he was able to beg from Europe and the North into building projects. He spent nearly $40,000 on erecting and repairing churches, schools, and convents, all without creating any serious long-term debts. Other bishops were only able to rebuild by creating serious indebtedness. As late as 1876, Bishop Patrick Lynch of Charleston lamented that he only got through the year by borrowing.

I doubt if I shall be able to meet interest so as to avoid foreclosure of mortgages . . . I try to keep up heart, and to do what I can and I pray for better times . . . So that I can pay off everybody. . . .[28]

In addition to trying to recover from the ravages of war, the Reconstruction period also brought with it a national depression, termed the Panic of 1873. Although its effects were much more pronounced in the industrialized Northern states, the depression did spawn breadlines, foreclosures, and unemployment in the South, which had been moving toward economic, political, and ecclesial recovery.[29]

Even more than the physical losses due to the war, the poverty, and the Panic of 1873 was a less tangible kind of depression. The Southern Cause had been lost, husbands and sons had been killed or maimed, fields had been trampled or left unattended, and the social and economic order had been overturned (or at least so it seemed for most of the Reconstruction period). The agony of defeat was terribly demoralizing, and created a spiritual depression during the postwar years. In a pastoral letter written after the war (February 2, 1866), Bishop John McGill of Richmond expressed his concern over the moral harm done by the war. Church attendance fell, people became even more indifferent to religion, error abounded, and a general moral laxity was perceived. McGill urged the increase of Christian education and the cooperation of the faithful in building up the life of the Church.[30]

One of the chief means that Southern bishops used to combat what they perceived to be moral laxity was the parish mission, the chief tool of "Spiritual Reconstruction" in the South. Parish missions in the Southeast were not a new development. John B. David, a French emigré priest, conducted the first parish missions in the United States in Maryland from 1792 to 1804.[31] What was new was their frequency and intensity during Reconstruction. Parish missions were in such demand in 1865 that the Redemptorists, who had eighteen priests working the parish missions, had to refuse twenty-five requests. In 1866 and 1867, a great many missions were given throughout the South. In 1868, Bishop Verot, Bishop of Savannah and Vicar Apostolic of Florida, scraped up enough money to finance a three month Redemptorist campaign to the major centers of the Catholic population in Georgia and Florida. The mission series ended at Immaculate Conception Church, Atlanta, where after one week 5,500 confessions were heard and twenty-three converts were brought into the faith. After a little less than three months, a total of 140 people became Catholic converts. Bishop Verot exhalted the benefits of the 1868 parish missions in a Pastoral Letter which stated that through them sinners were reconciled to God, long-standing indifferent Catholics were brought back to the practice of the faith, sacriligious confessions were repaired, many Catholics who had become Protestants were brought back to the faith, those unbaptized were baptized, and invalid or dubious marriages were rehabilitated.[32]

In 1869, parish missions were held in all of the Southern states, except North and South Carolina. Bishop Verot invited the Redemptorists back into Georgia and Florida that year. Seven Redemptorists came for eight weeks, in January and February, and preached missions at twenty-two churches. A unique aspect of this tour was that, for the first time in the South, missions were given to exclusively black audiences in Savannah, Columbus, St. Augustine, and Jacksonville. These missions met with the same success as the year before.[33]

In the 1870s, parish missions were still a vigorous part of "Spiritual Reconstruction" in the South. Bishop William Gross of Savannah (1873–1885), a former Redemptorist who had preached on the 1868 Georgia–Florida parish missions, conducted his own one-man preaching and lecturing campaign beginning in 1873, attracting large crowds of both Catholics and non-Catholics. Redemptorists conducted several missions in Georgia, Virginia, North Carolina, and Florida from 1870 to 1876. From 1877, Redemptorist missions in the South operated out of Baltimore and were given in English, German, Bohemian, and French.[34]

Catholics remained a very small minority in the South Atlantic states. One key reason for this was the lack of Catholic immigrants in the South. While Catholic immigrants swelled the ranks of the Church in the North from 1860 to 1880, the same was not true in the South. Of the 294,357 foreign passengers who landed in New York in mid-1867, only 5,333 were headed for the Southeastern United States. In 1870, there were 5,567,229 foreign-born persons in the United States. Only 161,909 of them lived in the South, 39% of whom were in Kentucky. In 1880, the number of foreign-born in the country was 6,679,943; only 160,012 or 2.4% were in the South. In 1880, the foreign-born population in North Carolina was 0.3%; 0.8% in South Carolina; 0.7% in Georgia; 1% in Virginia; West Virginia had 3%; and Florida had the highest proportion with 3.7%.

The reason for the lack of immigrant population in the Southeast during Reconstruction was that the foreign-born had no ambition to compete with cheap black labor or live in a region mangled by war, ruled by outsiders, and burdened with political strife, social disorder, bad roads, and few educational opportunities. Another factor was that many poor Catholic immigrants did not have funds to travel from the point they disembarked, and, hence, the travel South was not considered. Finally, since the Church was so weak in the postwar South, many immigrants who valued their faith preferred to stay in those areas of the country where Catholicism was more established and more available.[35]

Of those Catholic immigrants present in the Southeast from 1860 to 1880, the Irish and the Germans formed the greatest number, as was the case in the Antebellum period.[36] South Carolina, in 1880, had only 7,886 foreign-born residents; 36% were from the German Empire; 33% were from Ireland. Although Southern states sought immigrants through advertisement and recruitment, they had little success.[37]

The effort made in Florida was typical of the other states, although it was slightly more successful. From 1868, Florida had a State Bureau of Immigration, but most of the real inducement was done by local government and private groups. Henry S. Sanford, citrus developer, publicized Florida as the Italy of the South and attracted a small group of Italians in 1872 as citrus workers. The largest number of immigrants to come to Florida were the Cubans who began arriving in Key West in 1868. They came, however, not because of effective recruitment, but because of political and economic disturbances on their own island. Baltimore also became a port of disembarkment for Catholic Poles, beginning in 1868, not so much because of recruitment, but because of the collapse of the central European grain market. Most of the Catholic immigrants who came to the South during Reconstruction settled in Southern cities over 25,000 in population.[38]

The major problem of Reconstruction centered on the future of the four million freedmen in the South. Although liberated from the shackles of slavery, Southern blacks continued to live in economic, social, and political servitude. Forty-four American bishops from both the North and the South met in October of 1866, in what was termed the Second Plenary Council of Baltimore, to discuss the relationship of the Church to Southern blacks, among other issues. At the meeting, the bishops urged priests and prelates to devote themselves to work with and educate the freedmen. Paralleling the postwar explosion of black Protestant evangelical churches, the erection of separate Catholic churches and schools for blacks was encouraged by the Council Fathers.[39] In April of 1869, the Province of Baltimore, comprising virtually all of the Southeast Coastal States, met and reiterated its concern for blacks. Bishop Verot of Georgia and Florida took the lead in the discussions by proposing that each Southern bishop build schools and churches for the blacks. However, the big difficulty with such well-intentioned hierarchical pronouncements was the poverty of personnel and resources.

Despite impoverishment, bishops in the Southeast attempted to care pastorally for freedmen by means of several creative responses, among them the nation's first black Catholic parishes and schools. In the Baltimore Archdiocese, St. Francis Xavier Church was dedicated in 1864, making it the first parish for the exclusive use of black Catholics in the United States. In addition to the black church, a black free school was also established as part of the parish; thus, Catholicism expressed a religious and educational presence in the black community.[40]

A more creative expression based on a monastic model was begun in Savannah in 1871. Bishop Ignatius Persico asked for Italian Benedictines to come to his diocese to work exclusively for American blacks. In May of 1874, with William Gross now Bishop of Savannah, two Benedictines came to Savannah from Europe to work with blacks. In April of 1875, a small church and a two-story building were completed on a 150-acre tract on the Isle of Hope near Savannah. A novitiate of three blacks was established and fifty black students were in attendance at the school. All seemed to be going well, when, in 1876, yellow fever forced the experiment on the Isle of Hope to be disbanded. The remaining Benedictines on the island journeyed to Oklahoma to work with the Indians.[41] Not easily discouraged, Bishop Gross purchased another plot of 700 acres on Skidaway Island, also near Savannah, for the purpose of establishing an abbey for blacks there. In February of 1877, two Benedictines from St. Vincent's Abbey established an agricultural and trade school for black youths in the hopes that an abbey with black priests could soon be established. In October of 1877, Gross formulated a plan to conduct a national collection, the St. Peter Claver Society Collection, which he thought would fuel Catholic black projects throughout the South. Soon, eight other Southern bishops also backed the idea. Although Gross' national collection plan finally bore fruit, in 1884, with the Negro and Indian Collection (the first national collection of any kind in the United States), the Skidaway Island project fell on hard times and was abandoned. One of the biggest problems with Skidaway was that the local black population failed to patronize the institution, partly because of the latter's agricultural and trade emphasis.[42]

Although it seems that Bishop Gross was using a monastic model in his black evangelization plans, Bishop Patrick Lynch of Charleston favored a model based on Jesuit Spanish missions in the New World. Largely influenced by the Jesuit Reductions in Paraguay in the seventeenth and eighteenth centuries, Lynch, in January of 1865, bought Folley Island, a large sea island, with the purpose of planting a religious community that would form the basis of a community of 5,000 Catholic families. After being refused by several religious congregations, Lynch finally got two Capuchins from Belgium to begin the project he called "A Paraguay Village for the Negro Catholics." It failed in a year.[43]

The earliest, most original, and successful of the Catholic Reconstruction experiments was initiated by Augustin Verot, Vicar Apostolic of Florida from 1858 to 1870, Bishop of Savannah from 1862 to 1870, and first Bishop of St. Augustine from 1870 until his death in 1876. Realizing that education was one of the most pressing needs of Southern blacks during the Reconstruction period, he visited the Sisters of St. Joseph Convent in his hometown of Le Puy, France, in July of 1865, and invited them to help him serve the black youth of his jurisdictions. Verot asked for eight sisters; sixty volunteered. The eight missionaries arrived in St. Augustine in August of 1866.[44] Verot made it clear again to the sisters why he needed them:

> I want you to understand fully and clearly that it is for the Negroes and for them almost exclusively that I have arranged for the daughters of your Order to come into my diocese. I have five or six hundred thousand Negroes in Florida and Georgia without any education or religion . . . for whom I wish to do something.[45]

After an intensive course in English tutored by the bishop himself, the sisters opened their first school for blacks in February of 1867 in St. Augustine, where black Catholics had lived since Spanish Colonial times. Unlike the schools of the Freedman's Aid Society, Verot had no public funds on which to draw, and the local Catholic community had no money to give. Verot begged most of his funds from the French Society for the Propagation of the Faith and from Northern urban parishes. More sisters arrived from Le Puy in 1867 and 1868, enabling Verot to establish black schools in Savannah (1867), Jacksonville (1868), and Fernandina

(1870). Before his death in 1876, Verot also established black Catholic schools in Palatka, Mandarin, and Key West. In that same year, over 360 black students were enrolled in seven black Catholic schools.[46]

Verot's experiment emphasized the blacks' need for education. No black parishes were part of the project. Instead, whatever black Catholics there were attended white churches in the galleries or the special sections designated for them. Verot had the only successful black school system in the North or the South.[47]

Yet, despite all of the official rhetoric and some creative attempts, the Catholic mission to reach the freedmen failed. Rather than gaining black Catholics or helping the large numbers of freedmen adjust to their new social situation, the Church did neither. What went wrong?

Hardly anything went right. Ecclesial personnel available to work with the freedmen in the South were few; scarcer still were the financial resources to finance any project among the blacks. Local parishes and dioceses throughout the South simply had no money. Catholics in the Southeast hardly had the luxury of concentrating their energies on the plight of the mostly Protestant blacks, when Catholic institutions and spiritual life needed physical and spiritual reconstruction. Little success was made with the four million blacks in the South because little effort was made. Second, the initiative for postwar outreach to the American blacks came from above, from the American hierarchy, rather than from below. Bishops were the ones who improvised and implemented the plans for the blacks in the Reconstruction South. No ground swell support was forthcoming either in the white or black communities for these episcopal efforts. Third, most of the outreach to the blacks was taken on by Europeans, many of whom had only been in the country for a short time and did not have mastery of the American idiom, let alone the texture and nuance of black English. For blacks, the oral word was crucial, both because it was valued by African culture and because almost all of them were illiterate at the time. German Benedictines, French Sisters of St. Joseph, Italian pastors, and Belgian Capuchins simply could not speak the language well enough or know the culture well enough to be effective among Southern blacks. Fourth, blacks were not looking for another religion—they already had one. The organization of separate black churches had begun even before the war among the African Methodist Episcopal Church, the A.M.E. Zion Church, and the Baptist Church. By the mid-1870s, membership in these churches in the South grew by two, three, and sometimes as much as ten times, particularly because black preachers from these denominations were very successful in making converts and establishing parishes. Separate Protestant black churches served mostly by black preachers sprang up everywhere in the South after the war. Of crucial importance during the postbellum years, these black churches had pastors who had a firm hand on their congregation and resisted vigorously any attempts by Catholics (or anybody else for that matter) to "steal" their people away. Fifth, blacks' religious sensibilities sought immediate access to God and a more friendly, emotional relationship with him than what the more rational, doctrinal Catholicism could offer. Finally, Catholics had no black preachers to offer the black community because they had no black priests. Much ado was made in 1886 when Augustine Tolton, the first full-blooded black American, was ordained in Rome. The ordination of black Catholics at the time was almost impossible because of so many formidable obstacles. First, the black candidate would have to learn how to read and write English. Next, he would have to learn Latin so as to study philosophy and theology. He would have to endure the cultural and social pressures of living in an all-white seminary, where prejudice was bound to surface. He would have to be ordained in Europe or some clandestine place in the United States because of the climate of opinion against blacks on both sides of the Mason-Dixon Line. Even after ordination, racial prejudice made the assignment of a black priest to a white rectory and parish highly problematic. For these reasons, blacks did not seek the priesthood, and white clergy and laity did not encourage Black youths to do so. Consequently, American Catholicism had the awful disadvantage of not being able to send black priests into the black community, while evangelical Protestant churches had a multitude of black ministers. Therefore, because of a paucity of personnel, financial resources, grass-roots support, native American vocations, and black priests, coupled with an apparent black disinterest in Catholicism, even the best efforts at evangelization of blacks during Reconstruction had little chance of success. In the long run, even Verot's vigorous educational efforts failed.[48]

## C. THE EMERGING SOUTH, 1880–1920

Jay P. Dolan has called the last quarter of the nineteenth century a watershed for American Catholicism—a time when the old order passed away and the new order appeared on the scene. It was the time of the rise of big business, organized labor, modernized industrialization, and the Darwinian revolution. These social and intellectual changes had a decisive influence upon American Catholicism, says Dolan.[49] Yet, what was true in the Northeast and the Midwest, where 70% of the American Catholic population lived by 1890, was not as reflective of the peculiar minority of the Catholics in the Southeast.

Certainly, aspects of the Southeast were changing in the 1880s, with more industry in the region than ever before—railroads, iron furnaces, cigarette-making machines, and the cotton textile mills. Yet, the more things seemed to change, the more they remained the same. In the 1880s, the most highly respected and most powerful member of Southern society was still the planter. Urban centers grew moderately; older towns showed almost no sign of growth. The atmosphere was bucolic—the influence of the farm and the plantation was everywhere. Political and social Reconstruction of the South dreamed of by the victors of the War Between the States did not take place. On the contrary, the political, economic, and social arrangements that existed before the war were more or less intact, and in some cases became even more entrenched (e.g., Jim Crowism).[50]

Several elements characterized Southeastern Catholicism from 1880 to 1920. If immigration continued to define the character of Northern and Midwestern Catholicism, then being a peculiar minority continued to define Southern Catholicism. Mainly because of a lack of Catholic immigrants, the growth rate of Southern Catholicism was considerably less than that of the North and Midwest. From 1880 to 1900, the United States Catholic population grew by approximately 92.4%. In the South Atlantic states the Catholic growth rate for the same period was 22.8%, while parish priests increased by 30.1% and parishes by 16.6%, all far below national averages.[51]

Immigration did not affect the South for reasons similar to previous historical periods, but with one important shift in attitude—now the South did not want any immigrants. The mostly ineffectual State Bureaus of Immigration either disbanded operations in the 1890s, or were only token agencies, or were extremely selective in whom they recruited. For example, Florida, although it had one of the highest percentages of immigrants in the Southeast from 1880 to 1920, did not actively recruit immigrants from Europe or new arrivals in the North. First, the religion of the immigrants worried Floridians. Italians, Poles, Spaniards, Lithuanians, and Cubans were Roman Catholics. In a time of rising nativism, fears were excited over Papal influence and foreign domination of the United States. If the immigrants persisted in preserving their un-American religion, assimilation would be retarded. Second, the political radicalism of some of the immigrants, such as the increase in the Socialist vote, strikes in the cigar industries of Key West and Tampa, and railroad work stopages after 1900, raised apprehensions about the destruction of the American social fabric. Third was the issue of racism and eugenics. The South appeared to many to be the last distinctly American region of the country that had to be kept untainted from the infusion of "inferior" foreign blood. Fourth, allied to the eugenics issue was the rise during the 1890s of Jim Crowism, which legalized racial segregation with more rigidity than had been the case before. Fifth, a boll weevil infestation in 1907 (the same year as a national economic panic) bankrupted many black farmers and caused them to enter the labor market, thus creating a labor glut. In short, Floridians, like many other Southerners at the time, believed that their region could preserve its unique character and protect its cherished institutions only by omitting foreigners.[52]

A second characteristic of parish life of the period was the continued predominance of one-priest parishes with a number of missions and stations attached. The clergy continued to be circuit riders. The kind of clerical culture and clerical dominance that developed in the urban North did not exist in most of the Southeast because of the necessity of clerical mobility and the paucity of priests. Also, because, as in the two previous historical periods, clergy only were available once a week, once a fortnight, once a month, or once every few months, the laity was often on its own to preserve the faith without the benefit of clerical supervision, but also without possibility of clerical dominance.[53]

A third characteristic of the 1880 to 1920 period, one which also showed a continuity with the past, was the general poverty of the Church in personnel and resources. Native vocations were relatively rare. Bishops had to recruit Northerners or Europeans, especially Irishmen. Moreover, since most parishes in the Southeast had difficulty financially supporting themselves, bishops went on begging tours in the North and Midwest, and sent begging-letters to European missionary aid societies, whose help was abruptly curtailed with the Vatican declaration of 1908, which no longer classified the United States as a missionary country. In spite of this, Southeastern bishops had to continually seek outside sources for money to support parochial services. The Southeast remained missionary long after the Vatican said it wasn't and long after other Catholics in the country were self-supporting in finances and personnel.

A fourth characteristic of the period was that diocesan and parochial structures in the missionary South, unlike the North, were decidedly unbureaucratic. For the most part, bishops and pastors of the region conducted pastoral business in an informal, personal way. Nevertheless, the one section of the region that was an exception was the Archdiocese of Baltimore, or more accurately the urban parts of the Archdiocese. Gradually, from 1880 on, the cities of Baltimore and Washington became more and more like Northern and Midwestern urban centers. Hence, the Church in those areas reflected more Northern than Southern characteristics.[54]

A fifth characteristic of the period was the development, from 1910 on, of widespread anti-Catholicism in the Southeast, a phenomenon theretofore unknown. Tom Watson, the 1890s Populist leader, published in his August of 1910 edition of *Watson's Jeffersonian Magazine* an article entitled, ''The Roman Catholic Hierarchy: Deadliest Menace to Our Liberties and Our Civilization.'' That article continued for twenty-seven installments. In 1911, Watson began another series in the magazine, ''The History of the Papacy and the Popes.'' By 1914, the rural populations in the Southeast were sensitized to the ''dangers of Catholicism'' through the broad circulation of both *Watson's Jeffersonian Magazine* and *The Menace* (started in 1911). This anti-Catholic rhetoric took political form in the Veazey Bill of the Georgia state legislature of 1915–1916, the Sidney J. Catts gubernatorial campaign of 1915 in Florida, and the 1916 trial in St. Augustine, Florida, of Sister Thomasine, SSJ, who was charged with unlawfully teaching black children, since she was white and her pupils were black (an illegal combination according to a Florida law of 1895).[55]

In a twofold response to this pre-World War I anti-Catholicism, which was particularly surprising given the paucity of Catholics in the Southeast, Catholic lay groups organized to defend Catholicism and then wholeheartedly supported America's involvement in World War I. Knights of Columbus Councils in the Southeast were founded to combat anti-Catholicism and stress Catholic patriotism, in addition to providing social benefits to members and service to the Church. As a result, one Council of Knights from Augusta, Georgia, founded the Georgia Catholic Laymen's Association in 1916, not only to combat anti-Catholicism, but also to promote good will for Catholics among Protestants and Jews. When the United States entered World War I, Southern Catholics were anxious to show, after some recent years of anti-Catholicism, that they were as American, if not more American, than any of their Protestant or Jewish neighbors. Knights of Columbus Councils and parish Women's Guilds assisted the Red Cross, sponsored socials for soldiers and sailors, helped with Masses at military camps, and sold war bonds. Southern bishops were especially visible patriots during the war. Bishop Michael J. Curley of St. Augustine, who had been a particularly strong opponent of anti-Catholicism before the war, was a vigorous proponent of the American war effort and of Americanism. He spoke at war bond rallies and even went so far as to give permission for the military to install an antiaircraft battery on Church property in Jacksonville![56]

Although the economic, social, and political situation of blacks in the South degenerated from 1890 on, by 1900 they were better served by the Roman Catholic Church than ever before. By 1900, ten black parishes and sixteen black parish schools were located in the eight dioceses or vicariates of the South Atlantic region.[57] Although the milieu of Jim Crow segregationism encouraged the establishment of separate black parishes and schools, these institutions also served a very positive function. Catholic blacks did not have to sit in the back of the church or in the galleries, or receive Communion last, or be excluded from Catholic organizations in their black parishes and schools. In addition, black schools were the most widespread, effective means of Catholic evangelization and presence among non-Catholic blacks because they existed in the black community and their enrollments were comprised of mostly non-Catholics. Moreover, black parishes and schools functioned as ethnic parishes (personal, nonterritorial parishes) and ethnic schools, except for three big differences. Unlike the black Protestant churches, rarely, if ever, were black Catholic congregations preached to or led by their fellow blacks. Also, the expressed purpose of these black parochial institutions was not to preserve or enhance ethnicity (i.e., the Afro-American cultural heritage), as in the case of German or Polish parishes and schools, for example. Finally, the far majority of those attending black parochial schools were not Catholics, unlike other ethnic Catholic parish schools.

## D. BETWEEN THE WARS, 1920–1940

For American Catholics, the end of World War I was the beginning of a new sense of self-confidence. Nevertheless, Catholics continued to be isolated from the mainstream of American life culturally, intellectually, and religiously. Nowhere was this more true than in the South, where Catholics were traditionally seen as a peculiar minority.[58] The trends of nativism, racism, and anti-Catholicism present before the war coalesced after it in the form of the Ku Klux Klan, whose growth and organization extended beyond the South, even into Northern urban areas. Yet, despite the atmosphere of intolerance created by these hooded hooligans, apparently no major confrontations occurred between Catholics and the Ku Klux Klan along the Southeast Coast. Although Catholic teachers in public schools, some individual families, and a few priests were occasionally harassed, no churches, schools, or rectories were burned, as had been the case earlier in the 1830s and 1840s in some parts of the country. It seems that such Catholic organizations as the Knights of Columbus and the Georgia Catholic Laymen's Association were active enough in the Southeast to deter any thoughts of violence against Catholics. In addition, Catholics were such a small minority in most of the Southeast states that they were hardly worth the Ku Klux Klan's bother, especially when their clandestine activities could be readily focused on a more numerous and more easily identifiable group—the American black.[59]

As early as 1925, the bubble of postwar prosperity began to burst, first in South Florida where the real estate speculation boom collapsed. Florida land fraud, overspeculation, and bank failures, beginning in the fall of 1925, received national attention and were portents of things to come throughout the United States.[60] The Great Depression brought hardships upon many in the country, especially those in the South. For example, in 1928, the net income for Florida residents was 74% of the national average. As money became harder to come by, less found its way into the collection plate on Sunday. Most Florida parishes were not able to make ends meet, and things became so bad that at one point the whole financial structure of the Diocese of St. Augustine tottered on the brink of collapse. As a result of the widespread poverty of Catholics along the Southeast Coast, institutions of charity shifted from the more local, parochial structures of the pre-Depression years, to a more centralized and bureaucratized system of social service in order to respond to the volume of requests for assistance. Parochial resources needed to be pooled, specialists to be trained in social service, agencies to be established rather than relying on the more personal methods of charity designed to deal with almsgiving on a smaller scale. The development of Catholic Social Service Agencies, however, did not eliminate parochial charity. During the 1930s, parishes in the Southeast conducted rummage sales, bazaars, and minstrel shows to supplement meagre collections. Parish St. Vincent de Paul Societies were active, supplemented by donations for the needy in the parish.[61]

Another development that resulted from the Great Depression was heightened sensitivity on the part of Church members to the plight of Southern blacks. Catholic-sponsored black recreation centers, schools of religious education, elementary schools, and more churches appeared in Southeastern black communities as a result of this heightened consciousness. By 1930, twenty-five black Catholic parishes and thirty-five black Catholic parochial schools were opened throughout the Southeast, an increase since 1900 of 150% and 113%, respectively.

Catholic women, both lay and religious, were particularly responsive to the need to serve and evangelize the black community during the interwar period. The following is just one example of female leadership in this area. Mrs. F. Agnes Dillon, a white parishioner of St. Ann's Church, West Palm Beach, Florida, along with Mrs. Victoria Huyler, a black Catholic Bahamian, recognized the need for an outreach to the black community, and, in response to requests from some interested blacks, established in the fall of 1927 a Catechism class for twelve adults and children, along with a Sacred Heart Club for adult black Catholics. But in 1934, as a result of Mrs. Huyler moving to New York and Mrs. Dillon becoming seriously ill, both the classes and the club were suspended. Soon, however, another parishioner, Miss Edna Kyle, took up the project with only four students. By late 1937, Miss Kyle had built up the class to fifteen students, with five members in the Sacred Heart Club, at which time the Dominican Sisters of Adrian, Michigan, stationed at St. Ann's Parochial School and Academy, took over the work. In December of 1937, two Adrian Dominicans opened Blessed Martin Mission, where the classes and club met and where Mass was said weekly on Sunday by a Jesuit from St. Ann's. Soon, the sisters had thirty-one children and sixteen adults attending classes.[62]

As was the case in the previous periods, the majority of those attending black Catholic schools were Protestants, although the number of Southeastern black Catholics was increasing somewhat, as is indicated by the growth in the number of black parishes. The amount of black priests increased during the period. Up to 1926, only ten American blacks were ordained priests; from 1930 to 1960, 113 were ordained, eighty-three of whom were associated with religious communities.

From 1900, the parishes and schools of older ethnic groups such as Germans, Poles, and Lithuanians declined slightly. By 1930, one begins to observe new ethnic groups expressing themselves by means of their own parishes and schools—Italians, Slovaks, and Syrian Maronites. One parish in the Western panhandle of Florida (St. Joseph's, Pensacola) was even designated as "Creole and Colored."[63]

Parish life, from 1920 to 1940, in the Southeast was still characterized by a number of stations and missions attached to each parish. By 1930, however, the number of parish priests had increased slightly so that the coverage of these missions was at least statistically better, although the ramifications for a parish that had several missions were the same as before—clerical absences and brief visits to missions and stations. The number of priests in the region increased in the thirty-year period by 49.3% (44.7%, excluding Baltimore), whereas parishes increased by 51.3%, missions by 57.0%, and stations by 58.8%. The average priest per parish remained almost exactly the same in 1930 (1.7) as it had been in 1900 (1.6); hence, priestly availability in parishes remained the same as thirty years before along the Southeast Coast.[64]

By 1940, the South Atlantic region had approximately 648,104 Catholics or about 3.0% of the nation's total, 929 parishes or about 4.0% of the national total, and 543 parish priests or about 4.0% of the total parish priests in the country. Southeast Catholicism continued to lose ground statistically by 1850 levels of comparison to the rest of the country.[65]

## E. THE POSTWAR BOOM, 1940–1980

World War II and its aftermath provided some dramatic demographic, economic, and social changes for the Southeast Coast. With the outbreak of World War II, the United States created military bases throughout the South because its salubrious climate permitted troop training year-round. As a result, thousands of servicemen experienced the Southeast for the first time. Many liked what they saw and after the war moved into the area. By 1980, more military installations (sixty-five) existed in the Southeast region than in any other region of the country. This migration of servicemen and ex-servicemen brought new Catholics, who demanded parochial presence and parochial schools. No state has shown the dramatic effects of demographic change more than Florida, the leader in the region for population growth. According to the 1980 Census, of the top ten most rapidly growing Standard Metropolitan Statistical Areas (SMSA's) in the country, six out of the top seven are in Florida.[66]

This remarkable demographic growth is reflected in the region's ecclesial statistics for the period, the most dramatic of any previous period, as indicated by the following chart:

**Catholic Statistics for the Southeast**

|  | Parishes | Missions | Stations | Catholic Population |
|---|---|---|---|---|
| 1930 | 478 | 388 | 532 | 531,009 |
| 1950 | 592 | 308 | 218 | 881,697 |
| 1980 | 1,253 | 272 | 101 | 2,973,898 |

In fifty years, parishes in the region grew by 262%, while Catholic population grew by approximately 560%. In just thirty years, from 1950 to 1980, parishes grew by 212%, and Catholic population by 337%. As another indicator of rapid development, in 1930, there were ten dioceses in the region; in 1950, eleven; in 1980, sixteen. In 1930, the Archdiocese of Baltimore contained 57.5% of the number of Catholics for the region and 35.6% of the parishes; in 1950, Baltimore was still the regional center of Catholicism with 38.1% of the number of Catholics and 17.3% of the number of parishes. But all that changed dramatically in the thirty years from 1950 to 1980; Florida became the center of Catholicism in the Southeast, with five dioceses that had 28.4% of the region's parishes and 45.5% of the Catholic population. By 1980, the Archdiocese of Miami (founded in 1958) had the single largest Catholic diocesan population with 10.4% of the parishes and 28.0% of the total Catholic population of the region, whereas Baltimore had 12.1% and 13.9%, respectively.[67]

These demographic shifts were also stimulated by improving economic conditions. Textile plants expanded in North Carolina, South Carolina, and Georgia; the Atomic Energy Commission and E. I. DuPont built the Savannah River Nuclear Plant. Other factories moved into the area to take advantage of raw materials, hungry markets, and favorable tax laws, along with cheap and plentiful labor. Although the Congress of Industrial Organizations (the CIO) made efforts to unionize the newly founded Southern industries in the 1940s and 1950s, it was not very successful, since one of the commercial appeals of the South was non-unionized labor. Southern agriculture flourished through mechanization and crop diversification. Atlanta became the commercial and transportation hub of the Southeast. Politicians, trade commissioners, and Chamber of Commerce officials worked zealously to attract industry, especially by means of the industrial park, the most famous of which is the Research Triangle near Raleigh, North Carolina. Florida's sunshine and low corporation taxes made it the second fastest growing state in the nation, bolstered by the aircraft, citrus, and tourist industries. Florida is the tourist mecca of the South, with a 3.6 billion state economy based on tourism in 1970. Besides sunshine, the Southeast also has something else to offer its visitors—namely, history and culture, as evidenced by the commercially successful historical renovations of Williamsburg (Virginia), Charleston, Savannah, and St. Augustine.

Yet with all the prosperity, the Southeast lagged behind other parts of the nation in industrial and agricultural production, as well as in general wealth. Ironically, it still contains pockets of the nation's most serious cases of poverty. Florida, the most affluent of the Southeast states, had a net personal income from its residents of 80% of the national average income in 1960 and 95% in 1970, but this is deceptive since a privileged 15% of the Florida population have most of the wealth of the state. Fifty percent of Florida's work force are employed in the three lowest paying industries—retailing, services, and agriculture. In 1960, CBS reporter Edward R. Murrow presented a television program, *Harvest of Shame,* a documentary about migrant farm labor in Belle Glade, Florida; it shocked the consciousness of Americans throughout the country. One Belle Glade farmer described the labor situation in this way: "We used to own our own slaves, now we just rent them." Labor peonage exists in one of the most prosperous states in the Union. All that glitters is not gold.[68]

Another significant shift in the life of the region was race relations. The immediate postwar economic boom in the South did not make Southern blacks beneficiaries of the prosperity. In 1949, the median income for Southern blacks was 49% of Southern white income. In agriculture, black sharecroppers and farmhands were often no better off than their slave ancestors. In industry, blacks were only hired as menials. During the 1940s, the South lost about 2 million blacks to Northern urban centers. The political and social situation of blacks began to shift in the late 1940s. North Carolina, South Carolina, Georgia, and Florida no longer required a poll tax. In October of 1947, President Truman's Committee on Civil Rights repudiated the "separate but equal" institutions and services based on *Plessy vs. Ferguson* (1896). In July of 1948, by Presidential order, racial segregation was banned in all Federal agencies, including the armed services.

But it was the issue of public education that turned the tide in race relations and gave birth to the Civil Rights Movement. Black schools in the South were separate, but never equal. *Oliver Brown, et. al. vs. the Board of Education of Topika, Kansas* (May of 1954) addressed the question of public education by saying that *Plessy vs. Ferguson* (1896) was no longer valid because separate education facilities were "inherently unequal," and were against the Fourteenth Amendment. In May of 1955, the Supreme Court issued a desegregation plan based on its 1954 decision, which was to be implemented, "with all deliberate speed." It was, in fact, implemented with all deliberate delay. What was speedy was the rapid rise of activity that represented the least savory side of the Southern temperament. The Ku Klux Klan had an upsurge in membership. The Citizen's Councils of America were founded to appeal to the more respectable elements of Southern society (bankers, lawyers, businessmen) to abort the Supreme Court's decision by "peaceful and lawful means." Senator Harry Byrd of Virginia, along with nineteen Senators and eighty-one Representatives signed a Manifesto against the Brown Decision in 1956. A number of militantly anti-integration governors were elected throughout the South in the mid-1950s. With the Montgomery bus boycott of 1955–1956 and the Greensboro "sit in" of the early 1960s, desegregation proceeded slowly in the border states, but little progress was made in the lower South. By 1959, fewer than 350 black pupils attended public school with whites in the entire Southeast. Heat was applied to the cauldron of change when "freedom riders" came to Alabama and Mississippi in 1962 and 1963, with violent results. In the summer of 1963, blacks enrolled at the University of Alabama, the last state to yield to desegregation. The long hot summer of 1967, which saw racial violence in seventy-five communities throughout the country, demonstrated that the racial discrimination and the hostility that it bred was not the sole possession of the South. The Civil Rights Act of 1964 and the Voting Rights Act of 1965 legalized the political, economic, and social rights of all Americans, black or white.[69]

The drive for integration and equal rights for blacks had a curious effect on Southern Catholicism and black Catholicism. It was an example where the American dictum of the separation of church and state did not hold true. What was going on in the secular society was interpreted literally by Catholic Southern bishops with a twofold effect. On the one hand, blacks were now on an equal footing in every Catholic Church in the South. On the other hand, the drive to integrate all but destroyed important black institutions—the black parish and the black school. Although black Catholics supported the move to integrate in the public arena, they did not wish to abolish or "consolidate" what they considered to be their parishes and schools. The move to close black parishes, influenced as it was from events in secular society, did not come from the grass roots, but from the hierarchy, which was concerned not only with cooperation with the political climate of civil rights of the times, but also with teaching the white Catholic community a lesson in social justice. The only problem was that nobody asked what the black Catholic might have preferred. Some Catholic blacks resisted the closing of their parochial institutions and the subsequent integration, usually into formerly all-white institutions. Some drifted away from the Church entirely.[70] Nevertheless, the social and political tide of integration was so strong, by the 1960s, that it was viewed by ecclesial leaders as an unquestioned principle, a good applicable to all circumstances. Consequently, many Catholic black parishes and schools were closed in the 1960s. In 1930, twenty-five black Catholic churches and thirty-five schools operated in the region; by 1950, fifty-six and forty-four, respectively; there were forty-four and thirty-three, respectively, in 1960. By 1960, black parishes were not even labeled as such in the *Official Catholic Directory,* although other ethnic parishes (German, Polish, etc.) were clearly designated.[71]

While national parishes declined in importance from World War II (most of the ethnic parishes in the period were found in the Archdiocese of Baltimore and the Diocese of Wheeling), other ethnic groups were making their way into the South Atlantic region. Puerto Ricans and Mexicans came, even though often in a transitory fashion, as migrant farm workers, especially in Florida after 1950. Although small, a Hispanic community resided in Miami before 1960. By 1980, the Archdiocese of Miami alone had a Hispanic population of 670,667; the state of Florida had 857,898 Hispanics, 8.8% of the state population. According to the 1980 Census, 1,193,823 Hispanics lived in the South Atlantic Region, 3.2% of the region's total population. Haitians were another major group of immigrants who came to America in the postwar period. Starting around 1972, they began coming to South Florida in numbers.[72]

## Notes

1. Jay P. Dolan, "American Catholicism and Modernity," *Cross Currents,* 31 (Summer, 1981), 155; *Metropolitan Catholic Almanac, 1851* (Baltimore: Fielding Lucas, 1851), 224.
2. *Metropolitan Catholic Almanac, 1850; 1851; 1860; 1861.*
3. Donald B. Dodd and Wynelle S. Dodd, *Historical Statistics of the South, 1790–1970* (University, Alabama: University of Alabama, 1973), 10–11, 14–15, 18–19, 30–31, 38–39, 46–47, 58–59, 62–63.
4. For a fine presentation of the political events leading to Secession, see: David Potter, *The Impending Crisis, 1848–1861* (New York: Harper and Row, 1976).
5. *St. Mary's Church, Annapolis, Maryland—125th Anniversary, 1978.*
6. James Henry Bailey, *A History of the Diocese of Richmond: The Formative Years* (Richmond: Diocese of Richmond, 1956), 114–122.
7. Rev. Francis Joseph Magri, *The Catholic Church in the City and Diocese of Richmond* (Richmond: Whittet and Shepperson, 1906), 80; Bailey, *History of the Diocese of Richmond,* 109–113.
8. Randall M. Miller, "A Church in Cultural Captivity: Some Speculations on Catholic Identity in the Old South," in *Catholics in the Old South: Essays on Church and Culture,* ed. by Randall M. Miller and Jon L. Wakelyn (Macon, Ga.: Mercer University Press, 1983), 47–51.
9. Michael J. McNally, *Catholicism in South Florida, 1868–1968* (Gainesville, Fla.: University Presses of Florida, 1984), 7–8, 11–16, 22–23, 29, 35, 39, 53–54, 66–68, 84, 89–91, 97–98, 210–211, 226–229.
10. Miller, "A Church in Cultural Captivity," 46–47.
11. Notwithstanding Baltimore and Wilmington (Delaware), the area in the Southeast with the highest foreign-born population was Florida with 2.4%. ADC, Folder 600.37; Jay P. Dolan, *Catholic Revivalism: The American Experience, 1830–1900* (Notre Dame, Ind.: University of Notre Dame, 1978), 26. The Catholic Irish were in the South before the 1840s. In the colonial South they came as convicts to Georgia, as Irish settlers in the Carolinas, and as Irish traders to the Indians. Charleston had an active Irish community before the Revolution. Irish indentured-servant fugitives (both Protestant and Catholic) fled into the Appalachian Mountains, giving that area Celtic cultural characteristics. With the rise of canal building in the 1820s, Irish laborers worked in Maryland and Virginia, constructing most of the 500 miles of canals up to 1860. Dennis Clark, "The South's Irish Catholics: A Case of Cultural Confinement" in *Catholics in the Old South: Essays on Church and Culture,* ed. by Randall M. Miller and Jon L. Wakelyn (Macon, Ga.: Mercer University, 1983), 197–198; Vincent de Paul McMurry, "The Catholic Church During Reconstruction, 1865–77" (M.A. thesis, Catholic University of America, 1950), 72, fn #123.

12. Bailey, *History of the Diocese of Richmond,* 136–139; Van Buren Colley, *History of the Diocesan Shrine of the Immaculate Conception* (Atlanta: The Diocesan Shrine of the Immaculate Conception, 1955), 3–13; Stephen Ray Henson, "Industrial Workers in the Mid-Nineteenth Century South: Atlanta Railway Men, 1840–1870" (Ph.D. dissertation, Emory University, 1982), 114–118.

13. Clark, "The South's Irish Catholics," 197–201. See also: Christopher Silver, "A New Look at Old South Urbanization: The Irish Worker in Charleston, S.C., 1840–1860," in *South Atlantic Urban Studies,* Vol. 3, ed. by Samuel M. Hines and George W. Hopkins (Columbia, S.C.: University of South Carolina, 1979), 141–171; Ira Berlin and Herbert G. Gutman, "Natives and Immigrants, Free Men and Slaves: Urban Workingmen in the Antebellum South," *American Historical Review,* 88 (December, 1983), 1175–1200.

14. Clark, "The South's Irish Catholics," 201–209. See also: Ella Lonn, *Foreigners in the Confederacy* (Chapel Hill, N.C.: University of North Carolina, 1940).

15. Emmet H. Rothan, "The German Immigrant in the U.S., 1830–1860" (Ph.D. dissertation, Catholic University of America, 1946), 26–27; Henson, "Industrial Workers in the South," 4–5.

16. In 1835 Bishop John England of Charleston opened a school for blacks, but he was soon forced to close because of public opinion. After 1835 most Southern states had legally banned the education of blacks, free or slave. *U.S. Catholic Miscellany,* August 1, 1835; John Thomas Gillard, *The Catholic Church and the American Negro* (Baltimore: St. Joseph's Society, 1929), 206; Augustin Verot, *A Tract for the Times: Slavery and Abolitionism* (Baltimore: John Murphy, 1861); Miller, "A Church in Cultural Captivity," 51; Benedict Roth, *A Brief History of the Churches in the Diocese of St. Augustine, Florida* (St. Leo, Fla.: Abbey Press 1922–1940), 28–30.

17. *Ibid.,* 25; Randall M. Miller, "The Failed Mission: The Catholic Church and Black Catholics in the Old South," in *Catholics in the Old South: Essays on Church and Culture,* ed. by Randall M. Miller and Jon L. Wakelyn (Macon: Mercer University, 1983), 164–170.

18. *Ibid.,* 151; Gillard, *The Church and the Negro,* 91–95.

19. Michael V. Gannon, *Cross in the Sand: The Early History of the Catholic Church in Florida, 1513–1870* (Gainesville, Fla.: University of Florida Press, 1967), 41, fn #22; 81, " 'Jeffereys' Map of 1762." In Spanish colonial times, St. Augustine harbored runaway slaves from the English colonies. Black Catholicity in colonial St. Augustine was composed of former English slaves, Spanish colonial soldiers, as well as free blacks. Gillard, *The Church and the Negro,* 22.

20. McMurry, "The Church During Reconstruction," 31.

21. Roth, *History of the Diocese of St. Augustine,* 32–33; *Georgia Bulletin,* May 28, 1955. Michael V. Gannon, *Rebel Bishop: The Life and Era of Augustin Verot* (Milwaukee: Bruce, 1964), 89–114.

22. *Mother of Churches: A History of St. Mary's Church, Hagerstown, Maryland;* McMurry, "The Church During Reconstruction," 67; Bailey, *History of the Diocese of Richmond,* 152–161.

23. McMurry, "The Church During Reconstruction," 81–82; Bailey, *History of the Diocese of Richmond,* 151–152; Magri, *The Church of Richmond,* 84–95; Thomas Joseph Peterman, *The Cutting Edge: The Life of Thomas Andrew Becker, 1831–1899* (Denon, Pa.: W. J. Cooke, 1982), 56–57.

24. McMurry, "The Church During Reconstruction," 35–36, 65.

25. Quoted in: *Ibid.*, 36–37.

26. Richard C. Madden, "The Story of Catholicism in South Carolina," *Our Sunday Visitor—The Catholic Banner Edition,* January 4, 1959; Gannon, *Cross in the Sand,* 177, 180–181; Michael V. Gannon, "History of the Parishes of North and Central Florida" (unpublished manuscript, 1966, courtesy of the author).

27. McMurry, "The Church During Reconstruction," 77–78, 117–118; Gannon, *Rebel Bishop,* 149.

28. AACHS, John Gilmary Shea Papers, Box L, Y, Z, Lynch to Sadlier, n.d.; McMurry, "The Church During Reconstruction," 126.

29. Andrew Skeabeck, "Most Rev. William Gross: Missionary Bishop of the South," Part VI, *RACHS,* 66 (June, 1955), 84.

30. Magri, *The Church of Richmond,* 89–95.

31. Dolan, *Catholic Revivalism,* 16–17. See also: John M. David, *A Spiritual Retreat in Eight Days,* ed. by Martin J. Spalding (Louisville: Webb and Levering, 1864).

32. Michael J. Curley, *The Provincial Story: A History of the Baltimore Province of the Congregation of the Most Holy Redeemer* (New York: Redemptorist Fathers, 1963), 171, fn #136; John F. Byrne, *The Redemptorist Centenaries* (Philadelphia: Dolphin, 1932), 268–275; Gannon, *Rebel Bishop,* 153–157; McMurry, "The Catholic Church During Reconstruction," 104–105.

33. Gannon, *Rebel Bishop,* 127, 157; McMurry, "The Church During Reconstruction," 106–107. In Maryland in the 1880s, Jesuits conducted both interracial and segregated parish missions for blacks and whites. Dolan, *Catholic Revivalism,* 115.

34. McMurry, "The Church During Reconstruction," 144–145; *Georgia Bulletin,* August 6, 1955; Skeabeck, "Gross: Missionary Bishop," Part VI, 84–85; ADSA, Verot Papers, 1-A-2, LaRoque to Verot, March 29, 1875; Andrew Skeabeck, "Most Rev. William Gross: Missionary Bishop of the South," Part VII, *RACHS,* 66 (September, 1955), 132–133; Curley, *The Provincial Story,* 21.

35. McMurry, "The Church During Reconstruction," 71–72.

36. Bailey, *History of the Diocese of Richmond,* 145–148.

37. Charles H. Bowman, Jr., "Dr. John Carr Monk: Sampson County's Latter Day 'Cornelius,' " *North Carolina Historical Review,* 50 (January, 1973), 10; McMurry, "The Church During Reconstruction," 72–73.

38. *Ibid.,* 72–77; George E. Pozetta, "Foreigners in Florida: A Study of Immigration Promotion, 1865–1910," *Florida Historical Quarterly,* 53 (October, 1974), 167–171; Gerald E. Poyo, "Cuban Revolutionaries and Monroe County, Reconstruction Politics, 1868–76," *Florida Historical Quarterly,* 55 (April, 1977), 407–422; Gerald E. Poyo, "Key West and the Cuban Ten Years War," *Florida Historical Quarterly,* 57 (January, 1979), 289–307; AAB, Thomas L. Hollowak, "The Emergence of a Baltimore Polonia" (unpublished paper, University of Maryland, December 20, 1982), 162.

39. *Concilii Plenarii Baltimorensis II . . . Acti et Decreta,* Titulus X, Caput IV, #484, #485, #488 (Baltimore: John Murphy, 1868), 243–246; Gannon, *Rebel Bishop,* 138.

40. McMurry, "The Church During Reconstruction," 202, 220–221. See also: John Philip Kirrane, "The Establishment of Negro Parishes and the Coming of the Josephites, 1863–1871" (M.A. thesis, Catholic University of America, 1932).

41. McMurry, "The Church During Reconstruction," 212–213; Jerome Oetgen, "Origins of the Benedictines in Georgia," *Georgia Historical Quarterly,* 53 (June, 1969), 165–183; *Georgia Bulletin,* August 6, 1955.

42. McMurry, "The Church During Reconstruction," 213–217; Oetgen, "Benedictines in Georgia," 165–183.

43. McMurry, "The Church During Reconstruction," 209; Interview, Msgr. Richard Madden, Summerville, S.C., June 4, 1983.

44. McMurry, "The Church During Reconstruction," 230–233; Gannon, *Rebel Bishop,* 131–133.

45. Quoted in: *Ibid.,* 132.

46. *Ibid.,* 133–134; McMurry, "The Church During Reconstruction," 197–198; Michael V. Gannon, "Bishop Verot and the Slavery Question," in *Catholics in America,* ed. by Robert Trisco (Washington: NCCB, 1976), 69; ASHN, *Key West Chronicles* (translation), March 7, 1870; September 30, 1875; September 4, 1876.

47. McMurry, "The Church During Reconstruction," 230–231; Gannon, *Rebel Bishop,* 138.

48. Some of these ideas were borrowed from: John Hope Franklin, *Reconstruction: After the Civil War* (Chicago: University of Chicago, 1961), 191; Howard N. Rabinowitz, *Race Relations in the Urban South, 1865–90* (New York: Oxford, 1978), 223; McMurry, "The Church During Reconstruction," 186–196; Gannon, *Rebel Bishop,* 138–144; Albert J. Raboteau, "Black Catholics: A Capsule History," *Catholic Digest* (June, 1983), 35.

49. Dolan, "Catholicism and Modernity," 156–159.

50. Franklin, *Reconstruction,* 220–226; Comer Vann Woodward, *The Strange Career of Jim Crow* (3rd revised ed.; New York: Oxford University, 1974), 67–109; Comer Vann Woodward, *Origins of the New South, 1877–1913* (Baton Rouge: Louisiana State University, 1964); Lawrence Goodwyn, *The Populist Movement: A Short History of the Agrarian Revolt in America* (New York: Oxford, 1978); Dolan, *Catholic Revivalism,* 27.

51. James Hennessey, S. J., *American Catholics: A History of the Roman Catholic Community in the United States* (New York: Oxford, 1981) 173; John Tracy Ellis, *American Catholicism* (2nd ed., revised; Chicago: University of Chicago, 1972), 125; *Sadlier's Catholic Directory,* 1880; *OCD,* 1900.

52. Interview, Msgr. Richard Madden; Pozetta, "Foreigners in Florida," 167–169; 172–180; Del Marth and Martha J. Marth, eds., *The Florida Almanac, 1980–81* (St. Petersburg, Fla.: A. S. Barnes, 1981), 104.

53. *OCD,* 1900.

54. McNally, *Catholicism in South Florida,* 11–12, 16–18; Lawrence Cardinal Shehan, *A Blessing of Years: The Memoirs of Lawrence Cardinal Shehan* (Notre Dame: University of Notre Dame, 1982), 1–29; Robert H. Wiebbe, *The Search for Order, 1877–1920* (New York: Hillard Wang, 1967); Jay P. Dolan, *The Immigrant Church: New York's Irish and German Catholics, 1815–1865* (Baltimore: Johns Hopkins University, 1977), 163; *OCD,* 1900; 1930.

55. Mary Jane Mulherin, R.S.M., "The First Years of the Catholic Laymen's Association of Georgia, 1916–1921," (M.A. thesis, Catholic University of America, 1954), 5–26, 32–44; John Higham, *Strangers in the Land: Patterns of American Nativism, 1860–1925* (New Brunswick, N.J.: Rutgers University, 1955), 81, 178–179; David Page,

"Bishop Michael J. Curley and Anti-Catholic Nativism in Florida," *Florida Historical Quarterly*, 45 (October, 1966), 107–117.

56. *History of the Parish of Sacred Heart of Jesus, Atlanta, 1897–1947;* Roth, *History of the Diocese of St. Augustine*, 135; Mulherin, "Catholic Laymen's Association of Georgia"; Christopher J. Kauffman, *Faith and Fraternalism: The History of the Knights of Columbus, 1882–1982* (New York: Harper & Row, 1982); ADSA, Curley Papers, F. P. Fleming to Curley, September 21, 1918; J. M. Braxton to Curley, October 2, 1918.

57. *OCD*, 1900.

58. William Halsey, *The Survival of American Innocence: Catholicism in an Era of Disillusionment, 1920–1940* (Notre Dame: University of Notre Dame, 1980), 8–10, 37–39.

59. Shehan, *A Blessing of Years*, 84; Mulherin, "Catholic Laymen's Association of Georgia," 20–25; Interview, Msgr. Richard Maddon. More needs to be studied on the relationship of the Ku Klux Klan and Roman Catholicism in the South. For more on the Klan, see: David M. Chambers, *Hooded Americanism: The First Century of the Ku Klux Klan, 1865–1965* (Garden City, N.Y.: Doubleday, 1965); Kenneth T. Jackson, *The Ku Klux Klan in the City, 1915–1930* (New York: Oxford University, 1967). A 1931 article tells of the increase of lynchings in the U.S. and the kidnapping of a priest in Norfolk, Va. John T. Gillard, "Norfolk Acquits a Negro," *Colored Harvest*, 19 (April–May, 1931), 4–5.

60. Carlton W. Tebeau, *A History of Florida* (Coral Gables, Fla.: University of Miami, 1975), 385–387; Gene Burnett, "The 'Binder Boys' Helped Burst the Great Real Estate Bubble," *Florida Trend* (October, 1981), 155–159.

61. Neal R. Pierce, *The Deep South States of America: People, Politics, Power in the Seven Deep South States* (New York: W. W. Norton, 1974), 461; McNally, *Catholicism in South Florida*, 53–59; Shehan, *A Blessing of Years*, 86–91; Interview, Msgr. Richard Madden; "Sacred Heart of Jesus, Atlanta." For more on Catholic social thought in the 1930s, see: David O'Brien, *American Catholics and Social Reform: The New Deal Years* (New York: Oxford University, 1968).

62. AADS, Annals and Mission Files, Blessed Martin Mission, Mrs. F. Agnes Dillon to Sister Mary, June 8, 1940; AADS, Photo Album, Blessed Martin Mission; *Voice*, October 16, 1959; *OCD*, 1900; 1930. Blessed Martin Mission in West Palm Beach was closed in 1952 when the Adrian Dominicans withdrew from the work. AADS, Annals of Blessed Martin Mission, 1937–1952.

63. McNally, *Catholicism in South Florida*, 63–66; *OCD*, 1900; 1930; Felician A. Foy, ed., *1977 Catholic Almanac* (Huntington, Ind.: Our Sunday Visitor, 1977) 119.

64. *OCD*, 1900; 1930.

65. *OCD*, 1940.

66. William J. Easton, Jr., ed., *Rand McNally 1983 Commercial Atlas and Marketing Guide* (Chicago: Rand McNally, 1983), 67, 100; Interview, Msgr. Daniel J. Burke, Savannah, Ga., May 24, 1983.

67. *OCD*, 1930; 1950; 1980.

68. ADC, Folder 600.37; "St. Mary's Church, Annapolis"; Charles P. Roland, *The Improbable Era: The South Since World War II* (Lexington, Ky.: University of Kentucky, 1975), 11–26; Interview, Msgr. Richard Madden; Pierce, *The Deep South States*, 461.

69. Roland, *The Improbable Era*, 30–58.

70. Some of these ideas were inspired by: ADR, Wesley A. Hotchkiss, General Secretary, The American Missionary Association, "Why a Black College in an Integrating Society"; Roland, *The Improbable Era*, 135; Nessa Theresa Baskerville Johnson, *A Special Pilgrimage: A History of Black Catholics in Richmond* (Richmond: Diocese of Richmond, 1978), 51–77; "St. Mary's Church, Annapolis."

71. *OCD*, 1930; 1950; 1960; 1980; Foy, *1977 Catholic Almanac*, 119. By 1980, unless one made a personal inquiry of each diocese, it is impossible to measure how many parishes and schools are *de facto* black. We do know that as of 1980 an estimated 132,904 black Catholics reside in the Southeast, 2.1% of the total blacks of the region. *Ibid.*

72. McNally, *Catholicism in South Florida*, 94–97, 224–245; "Hispanic Demography by Diocese," Southeast Regional Office for Hispanic Affairs, n.d. [c. 1981].

CHAPTER THREE

# The Parish, 1850–1960

With the preceeding historical overview as background, we will now proceed to concentrate on thematic and topical aspects of Southeastern parish life from 1850 to 1960. Five perspectives on parish life will be investigated: locale and size; organization and priorities; clergy and people; communal life; and ethnic expressions.

## A. PARISH LOCALE AND SIZE

The vast majority of the Southeast Coast was rural (2,500 or less people) from 1850 to 1960. In 1850, some 90.8% of the population of the region lived in rural areas; 75.8% did in 1900. From 1870 to 1880, the farm population increased at a rate unequaled before or since—30.7%. Up to 1930, at least 62.3% of the residents of the region lived in rural areas. By 1950, the region had become more urban (any settlement more than 2,500 in population) than rural for the first time—with 50.1% of the residents living in nonrural environments. In 1960, the figure for the nonrural population was 55.3%.

Up to 1950, in terms of general population, Maryland, South Carolina, and West Virginia were similar in size; North Carolina and Virginia were a little larger than the previous three and were both similar in population size. Florida was in a class by itself from 1850 to 1950. In 1850, Florida had a smaller population than any of the other Southeast states, but, by 1950, its population put it in the same category as Maryland, South Carolina, and West Virginia. In terms of persons per square mile up to 1950, Delaware and Maryland were similar with the greatest population density for the region; South Carolina, Virginia, and West Virginia were similar in population density. North Carolina and Georgia had the next lowest density. Florida was once again in a class by itself, with the lowest number of persons per square mile up to 1950. Demographic shifts that began to show up in 1960 changed these one-hundred year trends.[1]

These population statistics had implications for the style of pastoral ministry in the region. Catholics were a small scattered minority. Traveling to missions and stations typified the pastoral style of priests, while Catholic people, whether in the rural areas or nonrural areas, did not have the convenient or regular accessibility of priests until around 1950. This fact had its ramifications for the faithful.[2]

As with other regions of the country, Catholics of the Southeast were located predominantly in the cities where work, Catholic churches, and priests could be found. But the number and the size of Southeastern cities were smaller than those in the Midwest or Northeast. In 1900, the Southeast had only one large city (one with a population of over 250,000), which was Baltimore; at the same time, fourteen other cities existed (population from 10,000 to 250,000). By 1950, Baltimore and Atlanta were the only large cities in the region, while twenty-six other smaller cities were present. By 1960, the region's demography was beginning to shift. In ten years, Baltimore lost over 10,000 of its residents, although it still remained the region's largest city. But, by then, four other large cities (excluding the District of Columbia) existed—Norfolk, Atlanta, Tampa, and Miami—as well as twenty-four smaller cities. Although most Southeastern Catholics lived in the cities, the majority of parishes were scattered in rural districts up to 1960. City parishes ranged from 38.8% of the total parishes in the region, in 1900, to 32.6% in 1960.[3]

Both Baltimore and Wilmington, Delaware, were atypical of the region, with Catholics being between 10 to 20% of the general population of their respective states. More typical of Catholicism in the Southeastern states from 1850 to 1960 was its insignificant minority status, with Catholics making up a Southeast state average of 6.2% of the general population. The following chart gives the two states with the highest and lowest percentage of Catholics to the general population for several selected years.[4]

|      | Two Highest | | Two Lowest | |
|------|----------|---------|----------------|--------|
| 1850 | Maryland | (17.2%) | North Carolina | (0.3%) |
|      | Florida  | (5.4%)  | South Carolina | (0.3%) |
|      |          |         | Georgia        | (0.3%) |
| 1880 | Maryland | (21.4%) | North Carolina | (0.1%) |
|      | Delaware | (9.5%)  | South Carolina | (0.9%) |
| 1900 | Maryland | (20.6%) | North Carolina | (0.2%) |
|      | Delaware | (17.7%) | South Carolina | (0.6%) |
| 1930 | Maryland | (18.7%) | North Carolina | (0.3%) |
|      | Delaware | (14.7%) | South Carolina | (0.6%) |
| 1950 | Maryland | (14.3%) | North Carolina | (0.5%) |
|      | Delaware | (11.6%) | South Carolina | (0.8%) |
| 1960 | Delaware | (19.4%) | North Carolina | (0.8%) |
|      | Maryland | (13.2%) | South Carolina | (1.3%) |

In order to get some idea of the size of parishes in the region, from 1850 to 1960, a diocese in Georgia will be used below as a representative example. When the Diocese of Savannah was created in 1850, Georgia had five parishes—one in Savannah, Augusta, Macon, Columbus, and Locust Grove. Four out of five were situated in small cities (population of 10,000 to 50,000). By 1900, Georgia contained thirteen parishes—three of them were in small cities, six of them in average size cities (50,000 to 250,000). By 1930, the twenty-three parishes of Georgia were located in twenty cities (population over 10,000). By 1960, of the forty-nine parishes in Georgia, thirty-five of them were located in cities. Two points have to be kept in mind regarding the size of parishes along the Southeast Coast: (1) parishes, even in Southern cities tended to be smaller than parishes in cities of comparable size in the North, because of the lower ratio of Catholics to the general population; (2) many parishes had missions and stations attached to them, which meant that Southeast Catholicism was predominantly rural in pastoral style, at least up to 1960.[5]

Up to 1960, the growth of parishes in the region was slow. In the Savannah Deanery, for example, new parishes were founded in the following years: 1850, 1863, 1874, 1880, 1907, 1909, 1920, 1940, 1942, 1946, and 1956. Exceptions to this slow, deliberate pattern of parish growth can be found in Atlanta and in South Florida after World War II, especially after 1960. The founding of Most Blessed Sacrament Parish, in 1920, was typical of the pattern of parish size and growth in the Southeast. Established in a new residential section of Savannah, where 100 Catholics resided, a small wood-frame church seating 200 was dedicated in 1921. By 1938, the parish had 871 adults and 406 children. Up to 1960, a parish with 700 to 800 families was considered a large parish in the Diocese of Savannah and in most dioceses along the South Atlantic Coast. Prior to 1960, parishes in the region were regularly started with between 50 and 200 heads of households.[6]

A demographic continuity pervades in Southeast Catholicism in parish locale and size, from 1850 to 1960. Catholics represent a small minority within the region as a whole (about 6%) during the 110 year period; parishes were smaller in membership than those in the Northeast; the character of Southeastern parishes during the period was rural because of the rural nature of Southern cities (see Chapter One) and because virtually all parishes had missions and stations attached, thereby giving priestly ministrations a rural and missionary flavor and expression.

## B. PARISH ORGANIZATIONAL COMPLEXITY AND PRIORITIES

Up to 1960, the organizational structure of Southeast parishes was fairly simple, especially given their relatively small size. The pastor was the spiritual and temporal authority of the parish. All decisions, especially financial ones, rested on his shoulders. The pastor, however, did not make decisions in a vacuum, but always had to consider his congregation. Pastors who did not, and they were few, found themselves in deep water. Being an effective pastor has always meant the proper exercise of the *cura animarum* (the care of souls)—the promotion of communal values and singular gifts for the common good, the discernment of the Holy Spirit as expressed in individual parishioners and the parish as a whole, and the exercise of moral persuasion through dialogue and diplomacy. For example, St. Patrick's (Baltimore) pastor, James F. Donohue, came up with the idea, in 1892, to build a new church, since the existing edifice was almost ninety years old and in need of extensive repairs. After some planning, Donohue presented his case at a number of parish meetings in 1895. Despite the apparent need, the pastor's ideas for a new church did not sit well with a great many parishioners who had fond memories of the old church. Only after a good deal of discussion and persuasion was the pastor's plan implemented in 1898.[7]

Some pastors were not as successful in dealing with their parishioners as Father Donohue. Particularly after World War I, Southeastern parishioners wrote letters of complaint against their pastors to the bishop. Some of their complaints were justified. Rev. Michael F. Mullaly created a stir in 1924 in Seabreeze, Florida, with his overbearing manner. Consequently, parishioners refused to pledge money for a new church. Mullaly was transferred to St. Anthony, Ft. Lauderdale, Florida, where his pastoral style again disturbed parishioners. St. Anthony's Men's Club members wrote the bishop saying that they had asked their pastor to replace the second collection with a pew-rent offering at the door, because most of the people of the parish had been adversely affected by the recent hurricane (1926) and economic hard times. Parishioners felt hurt having the collection plate before them a second time and not being able to put anything in it. Mullaly was transferred to St. Helen's, Vero Beach, in 1929, where, after an initial flurry of complaint and protest against him, both he and his parishioners settled down to an amicable relationship that lasted over twenty years.[8]

Another factor in the organization of a parish, besides the office of pastor, was the role of lay trustees, which had become the official system of the ownership of Church property in the Baltimore Diocesan Synod of 1791. After a series of unpleasant incidents in Philadelphia, New York, Charleston, and Norfolk from 1790 to 1831, American bishops worked to establish the legal concept of corporation sole, so that they and their successors, not lay trustees, might be the sole possessors of Church property. By 1850, most of the severe aberrations of lay trusteeism had run their course, and the system of parish vestries was in rapid decline, remaining only in those older parishes in which they were a long-standing tradition.

Nevertheless, it should be pointed out that in the far majority of cases where lay trusteeism was in place, both before and after 1850, the system of a corporation board of parishioners owning and administering Church property and revenue worked without incident. Especially in the Southeast, where priests were in short supply, vestrymen (another name for lay trustees) bought land, built churches and schools, and petitioned the local bishop to have a priest come. This was the case with St. Anthony's, Florence, South Carolina, in 1873. Nevertheless, in all but a very few cases, the vestry ceased to exist as an organization by 1900.[9]

Another aspect of parish organization was the various parochial lay groups. Up to 1960, these groups were either social, service oriented, spiritual, or mutual aid societies; unlike the lay trustees, they were never a constituent part of the decision-making process of the parish. Many of these lay organizations did not require the attendance of a priest, although occasional visits by the pastor, especially when fund-raising was involved, helped direct the energies of the group. Ethnic parishes were apt to have more lay organizations than parishes that were more acculturated to the American scene, since parish-based groups in ethnic parishes helped support, adjust, and stabilize immigrants to their new environment.

One of the oldest and most prevalent parish societies was the Women's Altar Society. Women not only played a crucial role in passing on the practice of the faith within the context of their families, but they were also collectively involved in service to the parish through altar societies and similar organizations. Whether it was through the altar society or another women's group, the women of the parish, up to 1960, were a supportive and willing force allied with the pastor for the betterment of parish life.[10]

Except in ethnic parishes, men's parish organizations, before 1960, were not as numerous or as populous as women's organizations. This fact defies a simple explanation. Perhaps it was because, before 1960, men had the local tavern, or political club, in which they could express themselves collectively and socialize with other men. Or perhaps men were just not as formally religious as women, did not attend church with the same regularity, and, therefore, were less inclined to get involved in parish organizations. On the other hand, women were more inclined to join parish groups. Before 1960, women's parish organizations often provided the only social and collective outlet for many married or single women in Southern society. Another factor in the universality of women's parish groups was their concern for, and involvement with, the welfare of children (especially their own) in parish Sunday School and parochial school. For whatever reasons, women's parish organizations were more numerous and better attended than men's groups. Needless to say, virtually all of these parish organizations of the period were segregated according to sex.

From 1850 to 1920, parish lay organizations provided a sub-community of association that helped clarify an individual's identity within the community of the parish and within the larger secular community. Parish lay groups were almost always parish oriented, with no organizational links to other parishes or dioceses, a factor that complemented the Southern penchant for localism. A typically Southern expression of parish lay organizations was that black and white parishioners had separate societies. In one instance, at Key West, Florida, when St. Mary's, Star of the Sea Church was burned down in 1901, Catholic parish organizations spent five years trying to raise enough money through raffles, dances, fairs, dinners, etc., to build a new church. All of the parish organizations were involved, both black and white, although their fund-raising activities were held separately.[11]

From 1920 to 1960, parish organizations became more defined in their purposes, more bureaucratized in their organization, and more linked with extra-parochial structures in their self-conception. In the 1920s and 1930s, adult education and social service grew in popularity in urban parishes—parish study groups were organized and social workers became associated with parish work in the more affluent parishes. After World War I, Holy Name Societies became the staple men's parish organization, with clearly defined purposes and links to diocesan and national structures. By the end of the 1930s, women's and men's parish clubs were associated with larger diocesan and national organizations. In the late 1940s, the Catholic Youth Organization was established in many parishes; it, too, was a group with diocesan and national networks. In general, after 1920, parish organizations were tied to diocesan and national organizations, a trend that moved away from the parochialism and localism of the earlier period. Between 1920 and 1960, a growth occurred in the number of extra-parochial organizations, such as the Georgia Laymen's Association and the Knights of Columbus.[12]

By far the most important parish organization, from 1850 to 1960, was an ad hoc one—the "parish building committee." This organization was extremely important in making the plans and raising the money to build new churches, convents, schools, and rectories, an activity that was by far the most time consuming and resource consuming of any from 1850 to 1960. Pastors relied on experienced laymen (and sometimes laywomen) for help and advice in supplying the finances necessary to establish a physical presence of the Church in the Southeast. Fund-raising and parish building were the most important tasks that consumed the energies of pastors and laity in the Southeast from 1850 to 1960.

The top parochial priority of the Church in the Southeast, from 1850 to 1960, was the building of structures to house the liturgy, educational endeavors, social functions, priests, and religious. Much of parochial energy was spent collecting money for structures and then paying off the parish debt. No sooner was one structure completed and mostly paid off than another was needed or in need of repair. In many ways, parishes during the period were perpetual construction sites and pastors had to be brick and mortar men. Yet, this physical construction of church buildings was not without certain spiritual benefits. Through the process, both pastors and people experienced the less tactile reality of building Christian community. Through it, both pastors and people made sacrifices for one another and learned to grow in appreciation for one another, thus deepening the bonds between them.[13]

The importance and the priority of church building among the Catholic community were symbolized in the dignity that surrounded the dedication of churches, especially before 1920. On Sunday, July 1, 1894, the cornerstone of St. Joseph's Church, Petersburg, Virginia, was laid by Bishop Augustine Van De Vyver. From Norfolk, 325 visitors came and five parish organizations dressed in full regalia. From Richmond, twelve train coaches came along with ten different parish organizations. At the dedication of St. Mary's Church in Wilmington, Delaware, in 1858, tickets were sold for both the morning (at 50¢) and the afternoon (at 25¢). The ceremony, attended by Catholics and non-Catholics, began at 6 A.M., and continued until 2 P.M., with Mass and a sermon by Bishop George A. Carrell of Covington, Kentucky. Vespers followed at 4 P.M. with another sermon by Bishop James F. Wood, Coadjutor of Philadelphia. Sixteen-hundred people were crowded into a church whose seating capacity was 800.[14]

Allied with this parochial preoccupation with construction of church buildings was the importance of finances. Besides the extraordinary help from benefactors, missionary aid societies, or bishops' begging tours, parishes got their money from the voluntary offerings of their people, either from pew rents or from the collection(s) taken at the Sunday Mass. After 1920, the Sunday collection was the principal source of parish income, since pew rents were being phased-out.

Up to 1920, Southeast parishes were reluctant to take on too much debt. In fact, it was the earmark of a good pastor either not to incur debt or not to sustain an inherited debt. One reason for this was that parish income was too modest to carry heavy indebtedness. Another was that parish buildings, whether churches or rectories or schools, were usually modest wood-frame constructions with relatively small seating capacities. However, after 1920, it became more acceptable to have sizable parish debts where the interest was paid and the principal was whittled away with a long-term mortgage. (In 1950, for example, all forty-three of the parishes of the Diocese of Atlanta–Savannah were in debt.) The Great Depression not only reinforced this notion of parochial deficit spending, but also caused particularly debilitating effects upon Southeast parishes. Many parishes could not even pay the interest on their mortgages themselves, and had to be aided by their diocese. At least one diocese (St. Augustine) almost financially collapsed under the weight of indebtedness.

Parish debts, capital expenditures, and subsidies to parochial schools took up most of the annual parochial income. With their operations almost always running in the red, whether it was 1880 or 1950, parish schools were a perennial heavy drain on the parish budget. Yet, both priests and laity saw the value of Catholic education (even more so after 1920) and were willing to support the luxury of Catholic parochial schools independent of public schools and public funds.[15]

Another priority of parish life, the most obvious yet the most illusive to demonstrate, was the parochial concern for spirituality. The whole purpose for the church buildings, debts, and collections was to provide a material base for the spiritual works of the parish, as expressed in prayer and action (charity). The Catholic people were especially desirous of having their own church because it was the physical sign of their presence as a peculiar minority in the larger Southern community. It also was a house of prayer, a sacred space, where people expressed and shared their faith and communicated their deepest thoughts, sufferings, and longings to their God. Because people valued the spiritual atmosphere created by the sacred space of the church building, up to about 1920 a surprising amount of discretionary income was spent on a church organ and the choir. Parishioners understood the value of church music and as soon as they could afford it, they sought to buy an organ and even hire a church organist. St. Patrick's in Baltimore, founded in 1837 (an Irish parish), had a church organ by 1850, had installed a new one in 1868, and another model in 1891. In 1912, St. John the Baptist Cathedral in Charleston spent $1,200 to repair its organ, hire an organist, and purchase music. The parish income for that year was $1,300. St. Peter's in Columbia, South Carolina, with 600 parishioners, prized church music so much that, in 1902, the parish spent $200 on it, even though the parish had an annual income of $125.45![16]

A final spiritual priority of parish life, up to 1960, was the continuing concern for vocations to priestly and religious life. As an example of this concern, over 3,000 people gathered in September of 1873, in the newly built Immaculate Conception Church (Atlanta) for the ordination of a German-born priest, Henry Schlenke. Parish histories of the region, written before 1960, invariably have a section with the names and the religious communities or dioceses of their native sons and daughters who entered leadership roles in the church in orders or in vows.[17]

## C. THE CLERGY AND PEOPLE OF THE PARISH

Those who gave life to parish organization and priorities were people. Although any parish is comprised of many individuals and groups, the pastor and parishioners, as a whole, give form and direction to it.

Most priests in the Southeast, up to 1960, were outsiders to the region, either raised and ordained in other parts of the country or in Europe. Irish-born Bishop John England of Charleston (1820–1842) was the first Southeastern bishop to recruit Irish seminarians for his diocese. As Bishop of St. Augustine (1876–1901), Irishman John Moore initiated a policy of recruiting Irish seminarians to serve in Florida. From the 1850s, Irish-born priests began to replace French priests as the most numerous sacerdotal group on the Southeast Coast.[18] The Irish were naturals as clergy-recruits for the region. They could relate to the Irish-born bishops who shepherded many of the dioceses of the Southeast. They spoke English and were used to both poverty and rural ministry. Moreover, they had a desire to do foreign missionary work, a strong Irish tradition going back to the Irish monks of the sixth century.

Except for Maryland and Washington, D.C., vocations were scarce in the region. Before 1920, the first priest ordained in Savannah was an Irishman, Michael Cullinane (1853). The first native Floridians to be ordained, Dominic Pellicer and Dominic Manucy, were ordained together, in 1850, and were consecrated bishops together, in 1874, for San Antonio and Brownsville, respectively. North Carolina had its first native priest in 1885. Georgia's first priest was a black, James A. Healy, who was ordained in 1854 in Paris and became Bishop of Portland, Maine, in 1875.[19] Except for Maryland, Delaware, and Savannah, native priests did not really appear in the Southeast until after World War II, and then not in very significant numbers up to 1960. The colonial nature of Southern cities, which was mentioned at the beginning of this section, was ecclesially reflected in the non-Southern character of the presbyterate of the Southeast up to 1960.

Priestly life was characterized in the Southeast, especially up to 1920, by instability. One reason for this, especially in the nineteenth century, was disease. In 1862, the pastor at Key West, Florida, died of yellow fever two years after his ordination. From 1875 to 1876, three priests in the missions of Southwest Georgia died of yellow fever. In Key West, in 1877, Bishop John Moore lost to yellow fever a diocesan priest and two Jesuits; in 1878, he lost four diocesan priests in Tampa and Key West to the same disease. At the time, Moore had only fourteen diocesan priests, so to lose five in two years was something short of a disaster.[20]

Another source of instability in priestly life was the rapidity with which pastors moved from one parish to another. In Key West, St. Mary's, Star of the Sea Church (1852) had an average tenure for pastors of five years, up to 1900. St. Mary's, Annapolis, a Redemptorist parish, had an average tenure for pastors of 2.6 years, from 1853 to 1898, although it should be noted that religious priests-pastors have a higher incidence of transfers than diocesan priests. St. Mary's, Hagerstown, Maryland, saw pastors, from 1845 to 1900, an average of 4.4 years. From 1850 to 1884, Holy Family Catholic Church, Columbus, Georgia, called SS. Philip and James during most of that period, saw its pastors an average of 2.75 years.[21] After 1900, the average tenure of pastors lengthened so as to create more stability in parochial leadership. Some examples of this shift would include: an eighteen year pastorate, from 1945 to 1963, at Blessed Sacrament, Savannah; a twenty-two year pastorate, from 1944 to 1966, at Blessed Sacrament, Charleston; a twenty-two year pastorate, from 1901 to 1922, and a twenty-nine year pastorate, from 1931 to 1960, at St. Mary's, Charleston. However, in South Florida, where tremendous ecclesial institutional growth took place after World War II, priests were moved often.[22]

A third factor in the instability of priestly life was the missionary character of the region. To be a pastor throughout most of the Southeast from 1850 to 1960 meant, usually, to be a missionary. Although most Catholics were concentrated in the cities, almost 70% of the parishes of the region were scattered throughout the rural areas. Since most Southeast parishes were rural and widely scattered with several missions and stations attached, a pastor was a man who had to live out of a suitcase, which in the nineteenth century was strapped to a horse, carried on a steamboat, sailboat, or train, or, by 1920, put in the trunk of a car. In 1900, seven out of the total of nine parishes in South Carolina had missions and stations attached to them. The one priest in Aiken had a six county area to cover with six missions and numerous stations. The priest stationed at Florence (who lived at the Cathedral in Charleston) covered a ten county area. In St. Augustine Diocese, eleven out of the fifteen parishes had missions and stations attached. The Jesuits in Tampa were assigned to all the parishes (four), missions (eight), and stations (forty-seven) in the Southern one-third of Florida. As late as 1950, the Diocese of St. Augustine had seventy-eight parishes, fifty-three missions, and six stations. The Diocese of Charleston had forty-two parishes, twenty-six missions, and fifty-six stations. The missionary character of the priesthood was still very much alive in the mid-twentieth century in many places in the Southeast.[23]

Concomitant with the missionary quality of the priesthood was its spiritual and material poverty. The rural character of the region also influenced the cities and produced an economy short in specie and long on debt. Moreover, the prevalent religious/cultural values reinforced a simple no-frills life. Since most parishioners had little discretionary income to give to the Church, most pastors of the region led a simple life. Priests of the region surely did not starve, but most had little opportunity for either gluttony or avarice. Beyond the material simplicity was also the spiritual poverty. With frequent transfers, constant travel, numerous missions and stations, single-man parishes, and usually no housekeeper, cook, or secretary, the Southeastern priest often led a solitary life and a physically demanding one.

Priests of the period saw themselves as teachers of the people, hence the encouragement by pastors of Catholic education (Sunday School and parochial school) and the importance of sermonizing on Sunday, not so much on the Scriptures (most priests had little training in Scripture or homiletics), but on the systematic preaching of dogmatic truths of the faith. A few priests of the region were known as great orators, but generally content took precedence over style.[24] Priestly work stressed a ritual routine. In Hagerstown, Maryland, about 1900, Sunday was the biggest day of the week for the pastor. He said the 7 and 10 A.M. Masses. At the latter, he delivered a sermon and sung High Mass with a choir and a paid organist. At 3 P.M. Sunday School began, at which the pastor taught, followed at 4 P.M. with Vespers and Benediction. During the week, he said 7 A.M. Mass daily, oversaw the parochial school with 113 children taught by six School Sisters of Notre Dame, and visited the parish's two missions, where Masses were

said on alternate Sundays. Another priest of the region, Lawrence Cardinal Shehan, reflected on his life in the urban setting of Washington, at St. Patrick's from
1923 to 1941. His living quarters were uncommonly good, containing both a bedroom and a study. The rectory had a common room with a pool table for the four
priests stationed there. Shehan's weekly pastoral duties included: early daily
Mass; Confessions on Saturday afternoon and evening, and on Wednesday afternoon; two Sunday Masses with a sermon; the spiritual direction of the St. Vincent
de Paul Society; and religious instruction of the boys at a local orphanage. Shehan
felt that the administration of the Sacrament of Penance was the single most important and taxing priestly duty, although he admitted that this responsibility did
not keep him from having ample leisure time for reading in his study. Both of
these examples represent two styles (rural and urban) of priestly ministry that existed in the region from 1850 to 1960.[25] In both examples, the ritual routine of
priestly ministry, though filled with duty, responsibility, and some activity, does
not give the impression of being bereft of creative solitude, leisure, or unharried
time. Their lives seem anything but frenetic.

From 1850 to 1960, priestly fraternity was seen as a value, especially given
the fact that most priests in pastoral ministry in the Southeast had relatively few
opportunities to see other priests. Confirmations, Forty-Hours' Devotions, clergy
conferences, church dedications, and yearly priestly retreats were all opportunities for priests not only to receive spiritual nourishment, but also to gather with
their fellow priests to share stories, a meal, a few drinks, and fraternal solidarity.[26]

The priesthood in the Southeast had its share of notable men from 1850 to
1960. Among them was Patrick N. Lynch, a native of Ireland, ordained for
Charleston in 1840, Bishop of Charleston from 1858 to 1882, and Diplomatic
Representative for the Confederate States of America. Bishop Francis X. Gart-
land of Savannah (1850–1854) died in 1854 when he refused to leave the city of
Savannah during a yellow fever epidemic, after going from house to house la-
boring among the sick.[27] Irish-born Thomas O'Reilly was appointed pastor of
Immaculate Conception Church, Atlanta, in 1861. During the War Between the
States he assisted soldiers on both sides of the conflict. In the autumn of 1864,
Union General William Sherman ordered Atlanta burned. The Federal Army
sought to commandeer O'Reilly's rectory, but he refused and informed a Sherman
aide that if the church was burned, all Catholics in Sherman's Army in the South
would leave the ranks (the majority of Sherman's Army were Irish Catholic immigrants). Of the 3,800 buildings in Atlanta, only 400 escaped being torched;
among them was not only Immaculate Conception Church and Rectory, but also
the Atlanta City Hall and Court House, plus four other Protestant churches, all
saved from destruction through O'Reilly's intercession.[28]

Of course, not all priests of the region during the period were heroes. Most of them just did their jobs quietly, without fanfare. A few found themselves in trouble with their people and with Church authorities. In 1874, Bishop James Gibbons had to remove three of his priests in North Carolina for insubordination and misconduct. Given the fact that Gibbons had no more than eight priests in the Vicariate of North Carolina, it was a particularly bold action on his part. This episode also reveals that sometimes the priests who were attracted to serving the Southern missions were not always of the highest caliber. Bishop John Moore of the Diocese of St. Augustine lamented, in 1885, about the difficulty in finding "good priests willing to work for God and not for money." In 1925, Bishop Patrick Barry expressed some reticence about the quality of priests from Northern dioceses petitioning him to serve in Florida. He observed, with a bit of Irish exaggeration, "All the cripples and undesirables in the American continent want to help us out in Florida."[29]

The missionary character of the priesthood also meant that there was a missionary character to the life of the laity. Michael J. Curley (later Bishop of St. Augustine and Archbishop of Baltimore) was appointed pastor of St. Peter Church, Deland, Florida, in 1906. There, he celebrated Mass every Sunday except the second Sunday of the month, when he traveled to say Mass at the mission and stations of the parish. Curley had a territory forty miles wide and one-hundred miles long, which he covered either by bicycle or by train. The people who went to St. Peter's had a priest-less Sunday once a month, and those in the missions and stations saw the priest only once a month. Each of the missions of St. Peter's had a weekly Sunday School conducted by a layperson. Catholic family life, the Rosary, and Catechism were the lifeline for Catholics in the Southeast.[30]

The missionary character of the Church throughout much of the region, from 1850 to 1960, created a spirit of initiative on the part of the laity, especially in regard to parish building. Up to about 1920, parishes were founded, churches were built, and parish schools were erected on the basis of this initiative. In some places, Catholics banded together in a legal and formal way as a Board of Trustees to buy land and begin church construction, and then apply to the bishop for a priest. Such was the case of St. Peter's Parish, Columbia, South Carolina. Only in 1899 did the trustees transfer the property to the diocese.[31]

Parish building and lay initiative were not the exclusive domains of men. In Atlanta, by the turn of the century, people were settling in the city's West End. In June of 1902, the Catholic Ladies' Society was founded by ten women. At the end of the month, the group established a Sunday School Guild for the purpose of teaching the children of the West End their Catechism, since the nearest Catholic church was across town. Later in 1902, the Catholic Ladies' Society formed a Committee of West End Catholics and met with Bishop Benjamin J. Keiley, in Atlanta, to discuss the founding of a new parish in the West End. As a result of the meeting, the bishop created St. Anthony's Parish in the West End, in 1903, and appointed a residential pastor. When the priest arrived, the Ladies' Society changed its name to the St. Anthony's Guild and purchased a lot for the church for $3,250; the St. Anthony's Guild assumed payment for a $2,000 loan from the bishop. The pastor had to pay off the other $1,250. On the purchased lot was a cottage that was remodeled through the efforts of the St. Anthony's Guild. After St. Anthony's Chapel was dedicated in September of 1903, the needs of the chapel and the rectory became the main objects of the St. Anthony's Guild charity until a new church was dedicated in 1911.[32]

Until around 1920, trustees and lay groups were instrumental in establishing parishes in the Southeast. From 1920 to 1940, because of economic hard times, individual benefactors were key to the establishment of parishes, most particularly in small towns or rural areas. Once again, these philanthropists and benefactors to parish building were composed of both men and women.[33]

Lay initiative by both men and women of the Southeast was not limited to petitioning for parishes and priests, raising and donating money, and physically putting together church buildings. The laity was active in the building-up of parish community in quiet ways. Mary L. Brosman (1874–1946) was an instructor for fifty years at Albany Public High School, Georgia, attended daily Mass most of her life, and taught for many years at St. Teresa's Sunday School. In 1927, in West Palm Beach, Florida, at their own volition, Mrs. Agnes F. Dillon (a white) and Mrs. Victoria Huyler (a Black Bahamian) started a Catechism class for black children and the Sacred Heart Club for Adult Negroes. When Mrs. Huyler and Mrs. Dillon were no longer able to keep up the classes, Mrs. Edna Kyle (a white) continued the program until 1938, when the Dominican Sisters of Adrian, Michigan, took up the task. In Miami, Florida, the lay members of Gesu Parish, along with their pastor, formed Associated Catholic Charities in 1931 as a liaison between the Community Chest and the St. Vincent de Paul Society. In 1939, the agency changed its name to the Catholic Welfare Bureau and became the basis for the Catholic Charities organization in the seven dioceses of Florida.[34]

By 1940, throughout the Southeast parish building, whether the physical plant or the faith community, became more centralized. Influenced by the bishops' establishment of the NCWC, the governmental bureaucratization necessary to deal with the immensity of the Great Depression, and the rapid demographic influx associated with World War II, more centralized planning was necessary both on a diocesan and parish level. Lay initiative ebbed, and often only came into play as a result of the bishop or pastor, unlike previous periods. The climate of opinion was perhaps best symbolized in a flier dated 1958 and given to the parishioners of Immaculate Conception Parish, Hialeah, Florida, by their pastor. Its purpose was to muster up financial support for an addition to the school and a new parish hall. The privileges of the parishioner were outlined, including the right to use the parish church, school, and portions of the rectory. Obligations of the parishioner were also delineated: the parishioner (layperson) "must contribute according to his means to his parish." During the 1940 to 1960 period, the role of lay initiative seemed to be limited to "paying and praying."[35]

Parish lay organizations began to show signs of centralization and affiliation with diocesan and national bodies beginning in the 1920s. Before the organizational revolution created by the necessities of U.S. involvement in World War I, parish organizations were parochial in the full sense of the word (i.e., localized). Beginning in the 1920s, the National Council of Catholic Women and the National Council of Catholic Men began to affiliate local parish men's and women's organizations. In the 1930s, the Catholic Youth Organizations were organized on a national, diocesan, and parish level. By the 1950s, just about every parish organization in the Southeast had some connection with a larger diocesan or national umbrella organization.[36]

## D. PARISH COMMUNAL LIFE

One of the most important tasks of the parish and one essential to its continued growth and development was the socialization of its members. People needed to be initiated into the faith, taught about its meaning, and kept within the parameters of its expression. This socialization activity at the parish level was the most immediate, personal contact that individual believers had with the Roman Catholic Church. The process took place in different ways: through the family, through educational institutions, through parish missions, through ecumenism, through the practice of Catholic piety, and through the exercise of charity.

Given the isolated nature of rural Catholics throughout most of the period from 1850 to 1960 in the Southeast, the family was the most important agent of socialization because it was by means of the family that a young person was formed in Catholicism. Women, in particular, were instrumental in maintaining a sense of Catholicity by preparing meatless meals on Fridays, overseeing the important religious and cultural feasts of Christmas and Easter, and giving children their first religious instruction by word and deed.[37]

The next most important institution for Catholic socialization was Sunday School. Except for the large urbanized parishes, Sunday Schools were more numerous and better attended than parochial schools in the Southeast. Sometimes even before a parish was founded, a Sunday School was in operation. Atlanta's West End had a Sunday School in 1902; the parish was founded in 1903 and the church was dedicated in 1911. Sunday School met, as the name implies, on Sunday morning or afternoon. Sometimes classes were led by the pastor, but most often they were conducted by the laypeople of the parish, especially women. The teaching method used was the memorization of the doctrinal formulas of the *Baltimore Catechism*.[38]

Beginning in the 1920s, the Confraternity of Christian Doctrine (CCD) began to replace Sunday School throughout the Southeast. The CCD was not necessarily taught on Sunday and had some connection with a diocesan office, but the teaching method was the same as Sunday School. A variation of the CCD formula was the Summer Catechetical Camp, such as the one begun in Savannah in 1923, in Inverness, Florida, in 1948, and in Charleston in the early 1950s. All of these Sunday School and CCD efforts were an attempt to supplement the religious instruction that children received in the homes. Catechism methodology emphasized memorized intellectual doctrinal content; other nondoctrinal parts of the faith, other pedagogy, other broader and deeper formative aspects of modeling, as in the family environment, were not implemented in the Sunday School or CCD format up to 1960.[39]

In 1852, in 1866, and again in 1884, the American bishops meeting in plenary session in Baltimore urged all American pastors to build parochial schools in order to do away with the dangers to which Catholic children would be exposed in public schools (which at the time were *de facto* Protestant schools). The bishops recommended the employment of religious women as teachers in these schools.

It should be noted, however, that the origin of the American Catholic school system was not simply the result of synodal decrees. Rather, it grew out of a need expressed on the parochial level, as, for example, by the German Catholics of Baltimore. In response to German immigrant parents, John Neumann, CSSR, German-born vice-gerent (vice-provincial) for the Redemptorists in the United States from 1847 to 1849, brought over from Germany the School Sisters of Notre Dame to teach in the Redemptorist German parishes in Baltimore—St. Alphonsus, St. James, and St. Michael's. When Neumann became the Bishop of Philadelphia in 1852, he brought with him the idea of the Catholic parochial school and applied it not only to German parishes, but to all of the parishes of Philadelphia. In the Southeast, Baltimore was the first place where the nascent parochial school system began through the efforts of German parents, Neumann, and the School Sisters of Notre Dame.[40]

Catholic schools were seen as a value and a priority by both the hierarchy and Catholic laity. In small, rural Newton Grove, North Carolina, John C. Monk, M.D., made his profession of faith in 1871 and began interesting his relatives and neighbors in Catholicism. In 1875, the 100 Catholics there built a Catholic school and hired a Catholic woman from Baltimore as a teacher. By 1899, they had a church and their first resident pastor; in 1900, the parish operated two Catholic schools, one for blacks and one for whites. It was only in 1928 that religious women finally staffed the schools.[41]

Although they were seen as a value, Catholic schools were generally not founded concomitantly with the parish before 1940 in the Southeast.[42] There were several reasons for this lag between the establishment of a parish with a resident pastor and the establishment of a parish school in the Southeast. One problem was finances. The people simply did not have the money to afford the luxury of private Catholic education. Some parishes tried, but failed because of finances. Parochial schools have always been expensive to run, and have almost always been in the red. Education, like the fine arts, has to be subsidized. It was not unusual for the school to take from one-third to one-half of the parish budget, from 1850 to 1960, because of teachers' salaries, convent expenses, school repairs, and upkeep.[43]

Another reason for the lag in establishing parochial schools went beyond finances to personnel. Religious women teachers were scarce in the Southeast. It was very common to have two or three sisters teaching six or eight grades in most of the Southeast before 1940. Sometimes parochial schools were started without the benefit of the favored religious women teachers. The difficulty with lay faculties was their instability. Bishops, pastors, and people favored religious women (even though they were hard to get), not only because they felt they were more dedicated teachers, but because their commitment to a parish was not just a personal, individual one, but rather an institutional commitment by their religious community. This institutional commitment to a parish school provided a necessary stability for parochial education.[44]

Another reason that parochial schools were slower in coming in some places was that women's religious communities owned and operated academies (boarding schools) throughout the Southeast. The academy was established to provide room and board for students who lived too far away to commute every day, to provide a formative Catholic environment for the education of youth, and to provide a source of income for the religious community itself. The Sisters of the Holy Name of Jesus came to Key West in 1868 and opened up an academy for girls. In 1881, they also opened an academy in Tampa. By 1880, Florida had six academies (and no strictly independent parish schools), North Carolina had two academies (and five parochial schools), Georgia had six academies (and three parochial schools), West Virginia had seven academies (and twelve parish schools), Delaware had three academies (and five parochial schools), and Virginia had seven academies (and seventeen parochial schools). Sometimes the religious community that operated the academy also ran a day school or even a parochial school for local children, as was the case in Key West. During the interwar period (1920–1940), academies as boarding schools began to be phased out where they existed. Economics was a key factor in their demise. Rather than own and operate a boarding school, it was much cheaper for the religious community to work in a parochial school where salary and room and board would be paid by the parish. With the demise of the academies, religious communities moved from being educational entrepreneurs to hired professionals.[45]

Beginning around 1900, as a natural outgrowth of the parochial grammar school, a few places began establishing parish high schools. Beginning in the late 1930s, the concept of consolidating parochial high schools into central high schools began to be implemented. A diocesan school "system" was organized, and a Superintendent of Schools was appointed in the Diocese of Savannah–Atlanta in 1938. Superintendents of Education and Catholic school "systems" were developed throughout the Southeast after World War II, which indicated a shift in the control of Catholic secondary education from the local parish level to the diocesan level.[46]

After World War II, another shift in parochial school policy took place. By order of local bishops, new parishes were now to establish parochial schools concomitantly with the erection of the church. Catholic parochial education was now seen as integral to the whole concept of a Catholic parish. This mandate complemented rising school enrollments and the rising demand voiced by Catholic parents for parochial education. It also dovetailed with the increase in religious vocations, especially among women, which reached a crescendo in the decade from 1958 to 1968. More religious women than ever before were available to teach in parochial schools. Often, the school was built before the parish church, so intimately was the perceived connection between the life of the parish and the life of the school.[47]

Catholic parochial education in the Southeast developed along several unique lines. Foremost among these innovations was the development of government-sponsored Catholic/public schools in Georgia and Florida. Soon after his appointment as Bishop of Savannah (while he remained the Vicar Apostolic of Florida from 1858), French-born Augustin Verot made his first appeal in March of 1862 to Chatham County and the City of Savannah to have Savannah Catholic Schools be supported by the city and county government. After the war, public school systems for free public education were established for the first time throughout the South. After eight years, Verot signed an agreement with the Savannah Board of Education, in 1870, to enable Catholic parochial schools to be part of the public school system of the city. The ten point agreement put Catholic parochial schools under the supervision of the Savannah Board of Education, which had the control of the school buildings, as well as discipline, instruction, appointment of teachers, and general management. Forty-six percent of the elementary school students of Savannah were in Catholic schools. The arrangement seemed to work to the satisfaction of all parties.[48] As the Superintendent of the Savannah Public School system wrote in 1872; "The system by which the Catholic schools were placed under the supervision and charge of the Board has proved most satisfactory to all concerned, and has not been jarred by the slightest discord." In 1873, of the seven Catholic schools in Savannah, and the five others in the rest of the state, five were part of county public schools.[49] Savannah and Chatham County were not the only places in Georgia where the public school system included Catholic schools. In 1873, Bibb County organized its public school system, which included three Catholic parish schools. These arrangements lasted from 1878 to 1903 in Augusta, from 1873 to 1902 in Macon, and from 1871 to 1916 (forty-five years) in Savannah.[50]

Although the Georgia experience was one of the longest-running government-sponsored Catholic/public school systems in American history, it was not the only such arrangement in the Southeast. Bishop Augustin Verot, the architect of the Georgia Catholic/public school system, sought to duplicate his educational plan when, in 1870, he became the Bishop of St. Augustine. However, the Florida legislature refused to act on his 1875 petition. In 1878, Bishop John Moore, who succeeded Verot, wrote to St. John's County Board of Public Instruction (St. Augustine) and proposed basically the same plan as implemented by Verot in Savannah. St. Joseph's Academy became Public School #12 and a black Catholic school became Public School #13 (the only black Catholic school in the country ever to be supported by government funds). Both were taught by a total of five Sisters of St. Joseph of St. Augustine. Catholic/public schools also existed in Mandarin and Fernandinia Beach. Given the climate of anti-Catholicism and nativism, which had been growing in the lower Southeast from 1910, it was not surprising that by 1914 the Catholic/public school was no longer a reality in Florida.[51]

The Catholic/public schools in Georgia and Florida (which taught both Catholics and Protestants) were products of the creative imagination of Bishop Verot, who was more than likely influenced by his knowledge of Canadian and Prussian school systems. He was successful in implementation because he had something to offer the nascent Southern school systems in his diocese; he was a patient bargainer and not afraid to enter the public arena; he was a well-known patriotic figure during the War Between the States. What caused the demise of the agreement between county public school systems and Catholic schools was not just the rising tide of anti-Catholicism after 1910, but also a shift to a more narrow Constitutional interpretation of the First Amendment and similar provisions in State Constitutions, along with a centralization of education policy. Until 1910, education was seen as pretty much the business of the local community. Beginning about 1910, public education and public funds for education had become the business of state governments. Hence, state politics became mixed with local politics to form a volatile political mixture, which influenced local public education in a way that had not been formerly the case. Also by 1910, the public school system no longer needed Catholic teachers and school buildings as it did at its impoverished beginnings. All of these factors coalesced to ring the death knell for the Catholic/public school system.

Another unique feature of Catholic parochial schools in most of the Southeast was that they were patronized and supported by Protestants. In Miami, Florida, St. Catherine's Academy (under the direction of the Sisters of St. Joseph), which also served as the parochial school of Holy Name Parish, opened in 1905 with ninety children. Fifty-eight percent of the white student body were non-Catholic. In 1912, Mary Star of the Sea Parochial School had a 63% non-Catholic, white population. Protestants patronized Catholic schools with strong percentages up to the interwar period from 1920 to 1940.[52]

Although Catholic parochial schools were a means of socialization for Catholics and a force for evangelization among non-Catholics, the parish mission was the primary tool for the renewal of the faith-life of the parish itself, as has been previously mentioned. As part of the "Spiritual Reconstruction" of the Southeast during the late 1860s, the 1870s, and the 1880s, parish missions reached most of the significant Southern urban parishes with their brand of Catholic revivalism. Even after the turn of the century, the parish mission continued as an effective tool of parish renewal, although with decreasing effectiveness.[53] One unique expression of the parish mission technique was a fifteen year attempt to reach the Protestant majority in the rural areas of the South. Although the first Redemptorist mission to non-Catholics in the United States took place in 1856 in Norfolk, Virginia, the first concerted effort at reaching non-Catholics with the message of Catholicism began in the 1890s. In 1904, Walter Elliott, a Paulist priest, opened the Apostolic Mission House on the campus of the Catholic University of America in Washington, D.C. Of the six diocesan home missionaries working in the South, two were working in the Southeast—Patrick J. Bresnahan in Florida and J. F. Maloney in South Carolina. Irish-born Bresnahan, from November of 1904 to June of 1910, conducted missions in forty-five different locations. However, these efforts ceased by 1915 because of growing anti-Catholicism, and because dioceses in the Southeast could ill afford the luxury of training and sending their few priests away from parochial work in order to evangelize non-Catholics. In addition, the rigors of this kind of missionary activity were not very appealing to many diocesan priests, and the results of their efforts were less than encouraging.[54]

Besides the important task of socialization of its members, parish communal life also involved ecumenical relationships between Catholics and Protestants. Yet, except for those brief periods of anti-Catholic agitation in the 1850s, the 1910s, and the 1920s, relations between Southern Catholics and Protestants were generally cordial throughout most of the Southeast from 1850 to 1960.[55] Although it was never expressed this way, at the time, the relationship between Protestants and Catholics in the Southeast can be termed "practical ecumenism." Never on a theoretical level and never a matter of theological dialogue or sharing of liturgical services, the Catholic minority did not just passively co-exist with the Protestant majority, but for the most part had positive, practical, day-to-day relations with their neighbors. For one thing, Catholics married Protestants throughout most of the period at much higher rates than their fellow Catholics in the North because of the paucity of Catholics and of immigrant conclaves. Generally, the

more Americanized (acculturated) a parish became in the Southeast, the higher
the percentage of mixed marriages (a Catholic and a non-Catholic) as is indicated
in the chart below of two Charleston parishes:

| Year | Number of Mixed Marriages | | Percentages of Total Marriages | |
|------|------------|------------|------------|------------|
|      | St. John's | St. Mary's | St. John's | St. Mary's |
| 1850 | 0  | 0 | 0     | 0     |
| 1880 | 1  | 2 | 5.3%  | 25.0% |
| 1900 | 3  | 2 | 12.5% | 28.6% |
| 1930 | 9  | 0 | 56.2% | 0     |
| 1950 | 15 | 4 | 55.6% | 44.4% |
| 1960 | 8  | 3 | 40.0% | 50.0% |

In 1850, both Charleston parishes had considerable numbers of Irish and French/
Haitian immigrants. As these groups became more acculturated, the rates of
mixed marriages increased, especially in the post-World War II period. Diocesan-
wide parish statistics bear this out. From 1949 to 1953 in the Diocese of Charleston, 46.6% of its total marriages were mixed. From 1950 to 1954, the dioceses
of Charleston and St. Augustine had 47.9% and 48.5% mixed marriages, respectively. Cordial relations with Protestants began within Catholic family structures.[56]

Many concrete examples indicate the practical cooperation of Protestants contributing property and money for the building of Catholic churches throughout the
region.[57] This kind of monetary cooperation between Protestants and Catholics
occasionally took place until World War II, when it became much rarer. Mention
has already been made about the large percentage of non-Catholics enrolled in
Catholic parochial schools in the Southeast right up to 1940. Protestants also donated to the building of Catholic schools, such as St. Catherine's in Miami (1905)
and St. Joseph's School for blacks in Ybor City, Florida (1921). Practical ecumenism also took on other forms. At St. Mary's Church, Hagerstown, Maryland,
the Catholic pastor and the pastor of the Zion Reformed Church had a warm
friendship from 1870 to 1915. In Clewiston, Florida, in 1930, the Community
Church allowed the Catholic pastor to say Sunday Mass at its church until St.
Margaret Mary Church was dedicated in 1932.[58]

Besides "practical ecumenism," another aspect of parish communal life from
1850 to 1960 was the pietistic practices of parishioners. These expressions were
done in the home in the context of the family, in the church building in the context
of a communal service, and in the hearts of individuals faithful in the context of
private personal devotions. Unlike almost any other aspect of parish life, Catholic
pietistic practices changed little from 1850 to 1960.

Often, without the availability of clergy or church buildings, the family played a crucial role in the transmission of Catholicism. In the family, mothers and grandmothers were the transmitters of Catholic piety and prayers, of attitudes toward others, of values, and of dietary practices. On priest-less Sundays, so widespread in the Southeast, the Rosary and prayer books were important means of individual, familial, and communal prayer. Catholic religious expression in the Southeast was largely privatized, a fact that could only be reinforced by the style of individualized Protestant Christianity that formed their sociocultural environment.[59]

From 1850 to 1960, the piety of Catholics (especially in urban areas) was also formed weekly in the church building by the priest's catechetical preaching, based on doctrine and Catholic moral teachings, and sometimes presented weekly in a thematic way following the Roman Catechism. Scriptural homilies were almost nonexistent. In the 1940s and 1950s, bishops began issuing diocesan preaching syllabi for each parish priest. Before 1920, Catholic preaching at times outside of Mass could be found in the context of parish missions or at Sunday Vespers services, where it was not unusual to have a sermon of over an hour in length. Favorite themes of sermons at Mass, parish missions, or at Sunday Vespers were: heaven, hell, sin, the last judgment, the bloody sufferings and sacrifice of Christ, and the Sacraments.

However, this kind of intellectual Catholic piety, which stressed having the right answers on questions of faith and morals, and the fear of punishment due to sin nourished by the doctrinal preaching in the church, was also balanced by another type of piety generated within the church building—an overpowering sense of the mystery of God. From 1850 to 1960, the liturgy was in Latin and this ancient language provided a sense of the sacred to those who did not understand it, which was just about everybody. Mass attendance was an exercise in private piety, where the congregation might have an English–Latin missal to follow what was going on, or a rosary to pray, or might simply meditate as it heard the familiar sacred sounds and priestly actions. Sung by a special choir and not by the congregation, music for Mass was seen as a value (as was the organ), and was much appreciated by the congregation members since it added to their sense of mystery and oneness with God.[60]

Personal devotions could be done by an individual at home or in church or just about anyplace else without the assistance of a priest. Directed toward a special sacred object, such as a saint, devotions played an essential role in Catholic piety up to 1960. One of the most popular devotions among American Catholics in the later part of the nineteenth century was to the Sacred Heart of Jesus. It was a good, affective counterpoint to some of the harshness of Catholic doctrinal preaching and the intellectualized approach to the passing on of the faith. So popular was this devotion during Reconstruction that the dioceses of Savannah (1872), Baltimore (1873), Richmond (1873), and the Vicariate of North Carolina (1873) dedicated their dioceses to the Sacred Heart of Jesus. The League of the Sacred Heart, a parish-based organization that was purely spiritual (with no meetings or projects), was popular in the Southeast throughout the period. Members dedicated their Morning Offering (a prayer) for the intention of the Holy Father, promoted the devotion to the Sacred Heart, and attended, if possible, a day-long adoration of the Blessed Sacrament each Friday. Another extremely popular devotion throughout the period was to the Blessed Virgin Mary, especially through the instrumentality of the Rosary. The Rosary was said at Mass, in family groups, and alone, almost anyplace. It was a prayer that was uniquely Catholic, which was simple enough for anyone to say no matter what their age or intellectual abilities. Another extremely important devotion of the period was Forty Hours, that is, the exposition of the Blessed Sacrament in the church for forty consecutive hours, followed by solemn Benediction. This practice, which was held in almost every parish once a year, encouraged devotion to the Blessed Sacrament (even when frequent reception of Communion was not the rule in many places, at least before 1920) and the nourishment of a personal prayer to Jesus in the Sacrament of the Eucharist.[61]

By the 1950s, the more astute Catholics were beginning to perceive the aridity of some Catholic devotionality. Flannery O'Connor wrote the following about novenas in 1956:

> Having grown up with them, I think of novenas the same way I think of the hideous Catholic churches you all too frequently find yourself in, that is, after a time I cease to see them even though I'm in them. The virtue of novenas is that they keep you at it for nine consecutive days and the human attention being what it is, this is a long time. I hate to say most of these prayers were written by saints-in-an-emotional state. You feel you are wearing somebody's finery and I can never describe my heart as "burning" to the Lord (who knows better) without snickering.

A few years later she said this about devotional exaggerations:

> The IBM business would look better to you if you had ever seen a little atrocity called "A Check on the Bank of Heaven." Some Sisters in Canada send me these: "Pay to the order of *Flannery O'Connor* 300 Hail Marys." At one corner is a picture of the Christ Child & under this, the word *President*. On the other side is the Virgin—*Vice President!* It takes a strong faith & a stronger stomach. . . .[62]

A final area of investigation about parish communal life, from 1850 to 1960, centers on the parochial concern for charity. Whether it was responding to yellow fever epidemics, the ravages of war, the aftermath of defeat, the effects of the Great Depression, or the needs of widows and orphans, the Catholic parish community in the Southeast always used its often meagre resources for works of charity. Pastors were the chief dispensers of the Church's charitable care, which was immediate, personal, albeit limited in scope. Some urban Southern parishes ran orphanages that were usually under the care of women religious, and were supported by frequent parish collections and much begging. Many parishes had parish-centered St. Vincent de Paul Societies (started in the United States in 1845 and in Baltimore in 1864), which were composed of laymen who assisted the pastor in collecting and dispensing alms for the poor, especially indigent families.

But, the focus of Catholic charity began to shift from the parish to diocesan structures around 1920. The St. Vincent de Paul Society and personal help from priests continued on the parish level, but the large activities, such as orphanages, were managed by centralized Diocesan Catholic Charities.[63]

## E. ETHNIC EXPRESSIONS OF PARISH

Parish life in the Southeast exhibited special characteristics among the Irish, Germans, Poles, blacks, and other Catholic ethnic groups. Although proportionately small in number in comparison to other parts of the country, the presence of Catholic ethnic groups in the Southeast from 1850 to 1960 was hardly insignificant, especially given the paucity of Catholics in the region.

The Irish-born were the largest, most widespread, and most significant Catholic ethnic group in the Southeast from 1850 to about 1890. Coming to the Southeast as railroad workers and as shipyard laborers, they settled in substantial numbers in many of the urban centers along the coast. Unlike most other Catholic immigrants, the majority of the Irish had the advantage of speaking English. Hence, regular territorial, not national, parishes were established for them, parishes that were staffed for the most part by Irish-born priests. Because of the poverty and squalor of their urban living conditions, the Irish earned a reputation for being pugnacious and alcoholic. Although not as powerful or pervasive as their counterparts in the North, Irish pastors were occasionally arbiters between their Irish parishioners and Southern society. Such was the case in Staunton, Virginia, in 1853 when Irish railroad laborers demanded a wage increase. When the workers threatened violence, the Governor of Virginia sent in a company of light infantry, but the pastor, Irish-born Daniel Downey, was able to defuse the situation. Yet, the Irish did not stay in their shantytowns for very long, and soon gained political and economic influence, acclimating themselves to their surroundings while still holding on to their Catholicism, at least in the cities.[64]

German Catholics were especially concentrated in Baltimore, coming there in sizable numbers about the same time as the Irish in the 1830s and 1840s. The German Redemptorists from Austria arrived in Baltimore in 1832, invited by Archbishop Samuel Eccleston, to care for arriving Catholic German immigrants. The Redemptorists brought over, in 1847, five School Sisters of Notre Dame, who established a mother-house and school at the German parish of St. James, Baltimore. In the fall of the same year, the sisters also began German parochial schools at St. Michael's and St. Alphonsus. Eleven more sisters arrived in 1848.

The purpose of these German parochial schools was well articulated by Mother Theresa Gerhardinger, foundress of the SSND's in Germany and America, in a letter to King Ludwig in 1848:

> Unforgettable are the words of your Majesty added in your own handwriting; to the effect that this generous donation belonged exclusively to the School Sisters in the German Schools, in order that the Germans and their descendents in North America might remain German. May God grant this! For our part, we shall do all that is possible, for piety and a solid character will prevail so long as the Germans in this country do not lay aside the national characteristics with their language.[65]

So, with a heady mixture of the preservation of Catholicism, German nationalism, culture, and language, the three German national parishes and schools of Baltimore were designed as agents of socialization for German Catholicism, but not primarily for American Catholicism. As an example of the parochial school's importance in the mind of the Germans, St. Michael's Parish School for girls was begun in 1847, five years before the parish church was opened. St. Michael's School attendance reached an all-time high in 1897 with 1,600 pupils. In 1927, it had 825 pupils. As an indication of the size of the parish, St. Michael's Church baptized over 425 children each year from 1866 to 1898. Unlike most parishes in the Southeast, the number of intermarriages with Protestants at St. Michael's was extremely low as the following table indicates:[66]

| Year | Marriages | Mixed Marriages | Percent Mixed |
|------|-----------|-----------------|---------------|
| 1852 | 103       | 5               | 4.9%          |
| 1880 | 83        | 8               | 9.6%          |
| 1900 | 39        | 8               | 20.5%         |
| 1930 | 30        | 13              | 43.3%         |
| 1950 | 34        | 9               | 26.5%         |

The intermarriage rate rises with the rate of American acculturation, but still never reaches the proportions of many other Southeastern parishes.[67]

The Germans, like the Irish, were regular contributors to their parishes, even if individual offerings were small. Besides the commodious church and school, St. Michael's parishioners also indicated their priorities with the money they spent on a lyceum for young men (1888), a choir gallery (1889), a bell tower and clock (1891), stained glass windows (1893), and a new parish hall (1901), which included a stage/auditorium that could fit 1,000 for the meetings of the various parish societies, and a gymnasium. The Germans were willing to support a large parish plant, which served the needs of a complex parish organization. In German parishes, lay church groups were particularly prolific, more than any other Catholic ethnic group, and included several social clubs, beneficial societies (which were all consolidated into one German Baltimore beneficial society in 1887), drama societies, and choral societies. In 1894, St. Michael's had its highest population: 9,500 parishioners or 2,150 families. The parish reached its zenith of organizational activity and growth in 1900. Another priority of German parishes was the care of the sick and orphans. St. Alphonsus, St. James, and St. Michael's parishes, of Baltimore, founded St. Joseph's German Catholic Hospital in 1872, a cooperative effort rarely accomplished by other ethnic groups of the American Church in the nineteenth century. Finally, another priority of the German parish was the fostering of vocations, a task that has always been nurtured in the home. From 1852 to 1927, St. Michael's produced an abundance of vocations: fifty-one priests, sixty-seven brothers, and 160 women religious.

The German parishes of Baltimore were heavily influenced by the piety of the Redemptorists, which stressed the devotion to the Infant Savior and the Blessed Sacrament (Benediction and Forty Hours). Marian feasts and May devotions had a special place in the devotional life of the Germans of Baltimore. The image of Our Lady of Perpetual Help was enshrined at St. Michael's in 1871. A rosary chapel was dedicated in St. Michael's Church in 1888. Heard for many hours weekly and on days before special liturgical celebrations, confession (the Sacrament of Penance) was another fulcrum on which piety rested. Beginning in 1888, confessionals were designated at St. Michael's for "Men Only" or "Women Only," a rather unusual practice, but one which reflected the separation of the sexes in parish societies. Statues also played an important part of the prayer life of people. From 1872 to 1906, twenty statues were placed inside the church, plus Stations of the Cross and thirteen paintings. All of these statues demonstrate how much popular piety was dominated by the cult of the saints, and also show the value placed on saintly veneration by those who had enough money to donate the statues.

Even though the German parishes of Baltimore sought preservation of their culture and language, they could not help but be gradually influenced by the urban American culture that surrounded them. In 1890, the children's Mass was preached in English instead of German for the first time. In 1894, priests were required not to preach more than thirty-five minutes. In 1905, the parish mission held that year was preached partially in English and partially in German. In 1918, St. Michael's School was closed on Mondays as part of the American war effort to conserve coal. In 1928, English confessions outnumbered German five to one. In 1942, all German sermons were canceled in the parish. During World War II, the Ladies of Charity offered meals for servicemen at USO clubs, and the parish wholeheartedly supported the war bond effort.[68]

Not all German Catholics in the Southeast lived in urban parishes, such as St. Michael's in Baltimore. Like their Irish counterparts, they settled throughout the Southeast. Though not as numerous as the Irish, their parishes reflected their distinctive German qualities longer than those of the Irish. German Catholics were also found in the nineteenth and early twentieth century in the places already mentioned, as well as in Wilmington, Richmond, Charleston, Atlanta, and Savannah, and in such small towns as Fitzgerald, Georgia and San Antonio, Florida.[69]

Other ethnic groups were also represented in the Southeast, although in proportionately smaller numbers than in the North or Midwest, and concentrated mostly in urban centers of Baltimore, Wilmington, Washington, and Wheeling. Bohemians (Czechs) settled in Baltimore after the War Between the States and formed St. Wenceslaus Parish in 1870. Bismarck's *Kulturkampf,* implemented in the Polish Prussian provinces from 1871, forced many Poles to leave their native land and settle in Baltimore, where a Polish community existed from 1832. Like the Germans, the Poles took the initiative in establishing their parishes and schools, which were the center of their religious and social life. The St. Stanislaus Kostka Beneficial Society was organized in 1875 to provide, among other things, a financial and organizational basis for the establishment of a Polish Parish in Baltimore. In 1878, Polish-born Piotr Koncz, fluent in both Polish and Czech, was named pastor of St. Wenceslaus, which both Czechs and Poles attended. In 1879, Father Koncz said that he could no longer serve the Bohemians as pastor. St. Stanislaus Beneficial Society withdrew from the parish and the St. Stanislaus Congregation heard Mass in Father Koncz's rented house. In 1880, a Polish school was founded, staffed first by laymen, then by Felician Sisters. In 1880, Archbishop James Gibbons bought property for a Polish parish, which was dedicated St. Stanislaus Church in 1881. In the meantime, Father Koncz had been given a Polish assistant with whom he quarreled. The clash centered on money and personalities, factors that contributed to a series of disturbances within the Baltimore Catholic Polish Community from 1881 to 1886. Troubles among Catholic Baltimore Poles continued, even after Koncz died in 1886, after which other Polish parishes were established in Baltimore. This incident at St. Stanislaus illustrates not only the difficulties of establishing a parish community among immigrant Poles, and the difficulties with foreign clerical leadership, but also the importance that the parish had for immigrant Poles. People don't fight with such intensity about something they don't care about. By 1955, St. Stanislaus, though still considered a Polish parish, had a structure and organizations that reflected a typical American parish of the day.[70]

Two other Catholic immigrant groups, Italians and Cubans, smaller in number than the Irish, Germans, or Poles, reflected a more Latin expression of Catholicism. Small Italian colonies existed in the Southeast in Baltimore, Charleston, St. Helena (North Carolina), Wheeling, Wilmington, Washington, and Tampa. St. Leo's, Baltimore, was organized as an Italian parish in 1880. From the beginning, English was used in some of the services, since the Italians spoke different dialects and some of them spoke only English (the first stream of Italians came to Baltimore in the 1850s). With the dedication of the church in 1881, about 900 Italians comprised St. Leo's Parish, which also had 1,500 non-Italian parishioners (another important factor for having English services). Although Italians were not as strong supporters of national parish schools as the Germans or Poles, St. Leo's had an Italian parish school in 1882, taught the first year by lay teachers. With the flow of new Italian immigrants into the area, the parish grew in the 1890s. Popular piety expressed itself by means of festivals and processions in honor of patronal saints, a custom carried over to America from the towns and villages of Italian immigrants. As a means of organizing such *feste* for the benefit of St. Leo's, the St. Anthony Society was founded in 1904 to sponsor two annual *feste*—Our Lady of Mount Carmel in July and St. Gabriel's in August. Through these processions and festivals, which lasted from three to ten days, popular piety was channeled into an official parish activity, the unchurched were made to feel part of the parish through their participation in these *feste,* and the parish benefited from income that might not otherwise be made accessible. Women played an important role at St. Leo's. They prepared the food and goods for the various church festivals and benefits; they were prominent in most of the parish organizations; they were the chief participants in parish novenas and Masses, in activities related to the school, and in the general parish projects and pursuits.[71]

Women also played a significant role among Italian and Cuban families as transmitters of the faith, even more than the institutions of church and school. Cuban Catholicism, especially popular piety, was primarily transmitted in the family through the mother. In Ybor City (Tampa, Florida) from 1885 onward, Cubans and Sicilians of the area lived in the same neighborhood, worked in the same cigar factories, and went to the same church, although they had separate beneficial and social societies, most of which were separate from the parish structures. Both had a poor experience of Catholicism in their homeland and, therefore, did not identify with the Church or with the practice of the faith, as did the Germans or Poles. In both cultures the family structure was key. Individualism was denigrated in favor of the greater family good. Sicilian women were significant in preserving culture, in inculcating family values of frugality and hard work. As a Sicilian proverb stated: "If the father should die, the family would suffer; if the mother should die, the family ceased to exist."[72]

Another group of Catholic immigrants not only did not come from northern Europe or from Latin cultures, but did not even belong to the Latin Rite. Lebanese Catholics in the Southeast had the usual immigrant problems of adjustment to American culture and language, and also the additional distinction of having a different liturgical rite that set them apart from their fellow Roman Catholics. Small groups of Lebanese, or Syrians as they were often referred to, began coming to the Southeastern United States at the turn of the century for religious, political, and economic reasons. Many became peddlers of household goods, especially along the coast from North Carolina to Florida. A few Lebanese/Syrian churches were established: St. Peter's, Greenville, North Carolina, 1917; St. Ann's, Kingstree, South Carolina, a mission from 1896 and a parish in 1947; and

St. Joseph's, Atlanta, in 1917. Most Lebanese/Syrian Catholics in the Southeast, however, did not have their own parish.[73] What happened in Jacksonville, Florida, is a good case in point. In 1880, a small number of Syrian and Lebanese families settled in Jacksonville. Other waves came after 1900 and after World War I. Syrian priests arrived at Jacksonville in 1906, 1916, and 1928 to solicit funds for the homeland, but left immediately. In 1923, a Melkite priest came to organize the Lebanese community there, but failed because there were at least five different rites among them: Maronite, Melkite, Syrian, Antiochene, Chaldean and Byzantine. Finally, in 1935, Shamoun Yazigie began saying Mass in the Antiochene Rite at Holy Rosary Roman Catholic Church. Up to that point, Syrians and Lebanese had attended Latin Rite Masses and schools. Although there were about 700 people in the Syrian/Lebanese community at the time, not many attended Mass with Yazigie, who was replaced in 1950 by Andrew Shashy. By 1950, Jacksonville had the largest Arab-speaking community in the United States, but Shashy was able to get only about 100 to his liturgies.[74] The Lebanese/Syrians were known for their generosity to the Church, yet unlike many other Catholic ethnic groups in the Southeast, they had few priests to say Mass in their rites, they had few churches, and they had no schools that were uniquely theirs.[75]

In summary, religion played an important role in the adjustment of immigrants to their new environment in the Southeast. Each Catholic ethnic group used its relationship to the Church in a slightly different way to filter its experience. The world of meaning offered by their religion in the Old World gave them a ground on which to build a new structure of meaning in the New World.

Blacks were the largest ethnic group in the Southeast, although few were Catholics. During the time of slavery, little was done by the institutional Church as far as ministerial outreach to the blacks in the Southeast. The onus fell upon Catholic slaveholders, as Bishop Verot's *Tract for the Times* (1861) indicated. Although many Catholic slaveholders were delinquent in their responsibilities to nourish the faith among the slaves, others showed concern by baptizing their slaves, bringing them to Mass, and having a priest occasionally come to visit. Household slaves in Catholic families in the urban South were more likely to be instructed in Catholicism and practiced in the Faith. The Second Plenary Council of Baltimore (1866) encouraged the erection of separate churches and schools for black Catholics.

Black Catholic schools were of much more significance than black parishes, as is illustrated by the following example. In Charleston, the black Catholic St. John's Burial Association donated a lot to the Diocese of Charleston in order to build a church, which was dedicated in 1880. However, from 1904, the church was used as a school. In 1923, a new church building was erected, and it too was used as a school until 1928, when the building was dedicated as a church, Immaculate Conception.[76] One reason for their higher valuation in the Southeast was that black schools were the most widespread means of service and evangelization within the black community. Although both were located on property within local black communities, black Catholic churches reached only the small numbers of black Catholics in the region, whereas schools, whose student body was mostly Protestant, reached a broader spectrum of the black population. Even though their enrollments were never large, by 1900 a total of sixteen black Catholic schools was located in every diocese in the Southeast, except Wilmington; by 1930, thirty-five; by 1950, forty-four; and by 1960, thirty-three.[77]

Black Catholic schools in the Southeast had some unique features, which separated them from other Catholic ethnic schools. Unlike the German or Irish parish schools, the teachers in black Catholic schools were often not from the same ethnic background as their students, that is, not black. Unlike the student population of the European ethnic schools, most students in the African Catholic schools were Protestant. Unlike the other Catholic ethnic schools, which were designed to preserve language, culture, and ethnic pride, black Catholic schools exposed their pupils to the prevailing white American Catholic culture and tradition, including, sadly, racism. As the head of St. Joseph's School in New Bern, North Carolina, expressed it in 1942:

> We try to train their character primarily, to help make them responsible citizens, a help to society, instead of a hindrance. We teach them hygiene and sanitation as well as reading and arithmetic. We train them for jobs for which we think they are suited and fitted. Above all, we teach them to be honest and dependable.[78]

If this negative tone toward the moral character of the black student and the limited curricular concerns expressed above are both representative of Catholic teachers and schools serving the blacks in the Southeast, then we can safely say that, unlike Polish, German, or Bohemian Catholic ethnic schools, the black Catholic schools did not communicate to their students a very positive self-image, or a strong sense of self-worth, or a pride in one's ethnic heritage, all of which are so necessary in the fulfillment of one's human potential.

Yet, despite all of these limitations, the black Catholic school did serve the black community in a positive way. Black Catholic and Protestant parents sent their children to these schools because they felt the discipline and the education were better there than in the segregated public schools. Given the state of segregated public schooling in the South prior to 1960, they were probably right. Black parents also saw the value of these black Catholic schools because they were operated locally right within their own community. As with most Catholic schools everywhere, the black parochial school did engender in the student a certain elitism, a certain esprit de corps flowing from the fact that the school was both private and Catholic, a rather exotic plate to partake of for blacks in an environment where choices were limited to rather plain fare. Moreover, concerned white Catholics felt these schools were paramount as a service and presence in the black community. As a Josephite pastor of St. Francis Xavier Parish of Baltimore expressed it in 1878:

> We need schools more than churches; it is the opinion of the fathers who are here, and it was the opinion of the fathers who worked here, that we must first build schools, then churches.[79]

Black parishes were founded as personal, nonterritorial parishes, often from a mission which had formerly been attended by a nearby white parish. Before 1960, the pastoral care of black parishes was generally put in the hands of religious communities, such as the Mill Hill Fathers (Josephites), the Fathers of the Holy Ghost, the Society of Divine Word, the Society of African Missioners, each of which originally came from Europe to serve the black race. In 1900, the Southeast had ten black parishes and missions; in 1930, twenty-five; in 1950, fifty-six; and in 1960, forty-four. Both black parishes and schools were distributed throughout the dioceses, with concentrations in the dioceses of Baltimore, Washington, Charleston, Raleigh, Savannah, Atlanta, and St. Augustine.

This Southern parochial mission to blacks was not easy, regardless of what side of the racial fence one stood or was placed. Besides financial and personnel limitations, white Southern Catholics in their ministrations to blacks exposed themselves to heavy social pressure and prejudice from other whites, as well as resistance from many blacks, who had a strong attachment to their own black Protestant churches. In addition, the black Protestant pastor held a prominent place in Southern black culture and was particularly solicitous about not letting any of the flock stray from the Evangelical fold.[80] One Sister of St. Joseph of St. Augustine expressed her own frustration with the difficulties of the missionary enterprise among blacks when she wrote in 1872:

> Their ministers preach assiduously to them. They have their Bishop too. From time to time missions, in their customary ware, are given them; they have extraordinary prayer time. They spend the whole Sunday long almost entirely in Church. . . . We haven't any hope to win them; they are held too firmly.[81]

Because many Southern blacks already had a religious affiliation and expression that seemed to serve their needs well, the black Catholic harvest was minute, even during the height of the black Catholic mission from 1930 to 1960. In 1954, the following dioceses reported the number of black Catholics in their region to be: Charleston—2,102; Raleigh—2,811; Richmond—3,834; St. Augustine—2,558; Savannah/Atlanta—2,576—considerably less than 1% of each of the respective diocese's total black population, and less than 10% of each diocese's total Catholics. The year 1954 witnessed the peak of the black Catholic apostolate with the highest numbers of black schools and churches ever. As of that year, the Diocese of Raleigh led dioceses of the region in the black apostolate with the most number of parishes and missions (twenty-four) and the most number of black Catholic schools (fifteen). The North Carolina black apostolate was also unique since it operated mostly out of small cities and towns.[82]

Being both black and Catholic in the Southeast was never easy. Most white Southerners were of the opinion that people of the black race were inferior economically, morally, intellectually, and socially. This attitude was fostered during the days of slavery and nourished by the political and social recovery of the South from the 1890s on, as typified by legal disenfranchisement and social segregation. However, it should be noted that racism against blacks was not found only in the South. Northern institutions were never threatened by black political or social supremacy; therefore, many careers available to blacks in the North were not available in the South. But Northerners had a feeling of repugnance toward blacks. Southerners were more fearful of the change in their institutions and society that could take place with the introduction of blacks into social, economic, and political seats of power, especially when blacks often accounted for 40 or 50% of the population, or more. On the other hand, repugnance toward blacks was never expressed very much in the South, since both blacks and whites were in close proximity at the workplace, on the farm, in the house, or in the streets of the neighborhood. The impersonal hostility of Northern big city racism rarely occurred in the South because the big city didn't exist there.[83]

Be that as it may, racism was still racism no matter in what modality it was expressed. Being a black Catholic categorized a person as part of a minority of a minority in Southern society, a peculiar specimen within a peculiar Southern religious institution. Being black and Catholic did not insulate one from the chill and barbs of prejudice, both from within and without the Church; black Catholics suffered double discrimination from white Americans, in general, and from their co-religionists, in particular. Southern white Catholics pushed black Catholics into basement chapels, escorted them to galleries, forced them to sit in back pews or side coves, segregated them into separate parishes and schools, and discouraged them from seeking the priesthood. Historian Albert Raboteau tells of one incident from his childhood that captures something of the experience of being black and Catholic in the South.

> One summer, when I was eight years old and lived in the Midwest, my family took a trip South to a small town on the Gulf Coast. I was born there and most of my relatives had been settled there for generations. I had three encounters with racism on that trip, the first when I wanted to drink from a water fountain meant for whites only and the second when I tried to play on a beach off limits to blacks.
>
> The third incident in this summer of my education took place on a Sunday, in a Catholic church. For some reason we had missed Mass at the black church and went instead to the white church, which my grandfather, a carpenter, had helped build years before. We crowded into a half pew in the back with the only other black

worshipers. The pew was too small to seat us all, so during Mass we had to take turns kneeling and sitting.

In front of us two white men had a whole pew to themselves. The message was obvious: they belonged there; we didn't. Hot, tired, and angry I couldn't understand how something so unfair could happen in a church.

Then we went to Communion. Since we were seated in the back, we brought up the rear of the line to the altar rail. But as we knelt, there were still some white communicants waiting to receive the Host. To my amazement, the priest passed me by, not once, but twice, until he had distributed Communion to all the whites. Then he returned to me. That Mass, my mother commented afterward, hadn't done her a bit of good since all she felt during the service was hate. I didn't say anything. I just felt humiliated and betrayed.[84]

At times powerless but never passive, black Catholics often initiated the establishment of their own parishes and schools, especially after 1900, although some were founded as a result of a decision by the local bishop or by members of a religious community. Such black Catholic enterprise resulted in the foundation of St. Benedict the Moor, St. Augustine (1911); St. Pius, Jacksonville (1921); St. Francis Xavier, Miami (1938); and St. Mary's, Annapolis (1946). Another expression of the autonomy, the initiative, and the independence of black Catholics was the establishment of black parish organizations, many of which existed even before the black parish or school itself.[85]

## Notes

1. Donald B. Dodd and Wynelle S. Dodd, *Historical Statistics of the South, 1790–1970* (University, Alabama: University of Alabama, 1973), 14–41.

2. ASSJ, Sister Marie Sidone to Father Superior, December 18, 1872; ADSA, Kenny Papers, Rev. Anthony B. Friend to Bishop William Kenny, September 1, 1906; Vincent de Paul McMurry, ''The Catholic Church During Reconstruction, 1865–77'' (M.A. thesis, Catholic University of America, 1950), 110.

3. Dodd and Dodd, *Historical Statistics of the South*, 24–76; *OCD*, 1900; 1950; 1960.

4. Dodd and Dodd, *Historical Statistics of the South*, 14–41; *OCD*, 1850; 1880; 1900; 1930; 1950; 1960.

5. Interview, Msgr. Daniel Burke, Savannah, Ga., May 24, 1983; *OCD*, 1850; 1880; 1900; 1930; 1950; 1960; *Georgia Bulletin*, November 12, 1955; Dodd and Dodd, *Historical Statistics of the South*, 74–76.

6. ''Church of the Most Blessed Sacrament, 1920–1980 (Savannah)''; Interview, Msgr. Daniel Burke; ADC, Folder 705.19, Quinquennial Report, 1950–54; *OCD*, 1950; ADSA, Quinquennial Report, 1940–44; 1950–54. Georgia had two missionary territories by the turn of the century, both based in one parish each. The Brunswick Missions and the North Georgia Missions centered in Atlanta. Florence, S.C. (St. Anthony's) was a center for a four-county territory of 9,283 square miles, four chapels, and numerous stations

where Mass was said in the homes. ADC, Folder 604.7; *Georgia Bulletin*, May 26, 1956; "Sacred Heart of Jesus, Atlanta."

7. "St. Patrick's Parish, 1797–1942 (Baltimore)."

8. ADSA, Barry Papers, 18-P-4, Parishioners of Seabreeze to Mullaly, December 15, 1924; AAB, Curley Papers, M-2093, Curley to Mullaly, March 14, 1927; ADSA, Barry Papers, 5-T-9, St. Anthony's Men's Club to Barry, March 28, 1927; 14-0-21, Members of St. Helen's to Mullaly, December 4, 1929.

9. John Quenten Feller, Jr., *Statutes of the Baltimore Diocesan Synods* (Baltimore: Catholic Century, 1965), 8–9; "St. Patrick's Parish, 1792–1942 (Baltimore)"; ADC, Folder 604.7; *The Catholic Banner*, October 28, 1962; "St. Mary's Church, Hagerstown, Md." For more on lay trustee problems, see: Francis E. Tourscher, *The Hogan Schism and Trustee Troubles in St. Mary's Church, Philadelphia, 1820–1829* (Philadelphia: Peter Reilly, 1930); Peter Guilday, *The Catholic Church in Virginia, 1815–1822* (New York: U.S. Catholic Historical Society, 1924); Patrick Carey, "The Laity's Understanding of the Trustee System," *Catholic Historical Review*, 64 (July, 1978), 357–376. Interestingly enough, St. Mary's in Charleston faced fierce trustee problems from 1793 to 1824, but had a vestry until 1897, when the congregation voted to turn the property over to the bishop. ADC, Folder 601.40, "A Brief History of St. Mary's Roman Catholic Church, Charleston (1961)." For the mode of tenure of diocesan property in the Southeastern states, see: *Mode of Tenure: Roman Catholic Church Property in the United States* (Washington, D.C.: N.C.W.C., 1941), 27–31, 33–40, 69–70, 121–123, 147–149; 169–171.

10. ADC, Folder 602.1, "A Chronological History of St. Patrick's Church, Charleston, S.C., 1837–1937"; "St. Theresa's School, Albany, Georgia (1952)."

11. ADSA, Moore Papers, 2(y)-D- 2, *notitiae*, Immaculate Conception, Jacksonville, January 1, 1880; 2(y)-B-15, *notitiae*, St. Mary, Star of the Sea, Key West, January 1, 1880; *OCD*, 1880; Benedict Roth, *A Brief History of the Churches in the Diocese of St. Augustine, Florida* (St. Leo, Fla.: Abbey Press, 1922–40), 31; ADSA, Kenny Papers, 3 (z)-N-23, "Monthly Collections and Pew Rents of Catholics of Key West from October 1, 1901 to July 16, 1905"; 3(z)-N-25, Friend to Kenny, January 8, 1906.

12. St. Theresa's School, Albany, Georgia (1952)"; "St. Patrick's Patrician Club, 1931–81"; "Msgr. William Barry, P.A.-Golden Jubilee of Priesthood, 1910–60."

13. ADC, Folder 601.1; 601.6; Michael V. Gannon, "History of the Parishes of North and Central Florida" (unpublished manuscript, 1966, courtesy of the author); Thomas Joseph Peterman, *The Cutting Edge: The Life of Thomas Andrew Becker, 1831–1899* (Denon, Pa.: W. J. Cooke, 1982), 182; Interview, Mr. James Kindelan, Miami Shores, Fla., September 16, 1981; Interview, Msgr. Thomas O'Donovan, Pompano Beach, Fla., September 19, 1981.

14. ADC, Folder 602.1, "History of St. Patrick's, Charleston"; "The Church of St. Mary of the Immaculate Conception, 1858–1958"; Rev. Francis Joseph Magri, *The Catholic Church in the City and Diocese of Richmond* (Richmond: Whittet & Shepperson, 1906), 130–131.

15. ADC, Folder 301, Annual Parish Reports-1902; 1930; 1950; 1960; Folder 601.40, St. Mary's, Charleston; 600.25, St. Joseph's, Andersonville; AFDSP, Report of Msgr. John Moore, Bishop of St. Augustine, to the Sacred Congregation of the Propaganda, February, 1885; ADSA, 2(y)-N-10; 2(y)-E-3; 2(y)-K-18; 2(y)-D-2; 2(y)-K-21; 2(y)-B-15;

2(y)-C-25, selected *notitiae,* 1880 and 1900; AAB, Parish Statistics, St. Patrick's, Mount Savage, 1924–1960; ADS, FB-1, Bishop's Building Fund, 1948–55.

16. ADC, Folder 301, St. Mary's, Charleston, St. John the Baptist Cathedral, Charleston—Annual Parish Reports; 601.40; 602.1; "St. Patrick's Parish, Baltimore, 1792–1942"; *The Georgia Bulletin,* May 7, 1932; "St. Mary's Church, Hagerstown, Md."; "Sacred Heart of Jesus, Atlanta."

17. St. Mary's on the Hill, Augusta, Georgia (1961); "St. Mary's Church, Annapolis"; "St. Mary's Church, Hagerstown, Md."; "St. Patrick's, Mt. Savage, Md., 1873–1973"; *Georgia Bulletin,* April 12, 1955; Van Buren Colley, *History of The Diocesan Shrine of the Immaculate Conception* (Atlanta: The Diocesan Shrine of the Immaculate Conception, 1955), 34, 55–56; Sister Ann Parker, "History of Our Lady of Perpetual Help Parish, Rocky Mount, N.C." (M.S. thesis, Marywood College, July, 1975), 11–12.

18. ADC, Folder 601.6; David Page, ed., *Peregrini Pro Christo* (Orlando, Fla.: *Florida Catholic,* 1967); *Georgia Bulletin,* February 19, 1955; April 2, 1955; ADC, Folder 603.1, St. Peter's, Columbia.

19. Michael V. Gannon, *Cross in the Sand: The Early History of the Catholic Church in Florida, 1513–1870* (Gainesville, Fla.: University of Florida Press, 1967), 157; Albert Foley, *Bishop Healy: Beloved Outcaste* (New York: Farrar and Straus, 1955), 13–22; "Commemorative Booklet of the 25th Anniversary of the Death of Edward A. Pace—1963."

20. "St. Theresa's School, Albany Ga. (1952)"; *Georgia Bulletin,* April 2, 1955; May 7, 1932; Vincent de Paul McMurry, "The Catholic Church During Reconstruction, 1865–77" (M.A. thesis, Catholic University of America, 1950), 130–138; Michael J. McNally, *Catholicism in South Florida, 1868–1968* (Gainesville, Fla.: University Presses of Florida, 1984), 15.

21. *Georgia Bulletin,* May 7, 1932; "Sacred Heart of Jesus, Atlanta"; Gannon, "History of the Parishes of Florida"; "St. Mary's Church, Annapolis"; "St. Mary's Church, Hagerstown, Md."; "Holy Family Catholic Church, Columbus, Ga. 1880–1980."

22. "Blessed Sacrament (Savannah)"; "St. Theresa's School, Albany, Ga."; ADC, Folder 601.1, Blessed Sacrament, Charleston; Folder 601.40, "St. Mary's, Charleston"; McNally, *Catholicism in South Florida,* 86.

23. *Georgia Bulletin,* April 2, 1955; *OCD,* 1900; 1950.

24. Parker, "O.L.P.H., Rocky Mount, N.C.," 23; Interview, Father Francis R. Moeslein, Wake Forest, N.C., June 7, 1983; Interview, Msgr. Daniel J. Burke, Savannah, Ga., May 24, 1983; Peterman *The Cutting Edge,* 297–306; Magri, *The Church of Richmond,* 117–130; Robert F. McNamara, *Catholic Sunday Preaching: The American Guidelines, 1791–1975* (Washington, D.C.: Word of God Institute, 1975).

25. "St. Mary's Church, Hagerstown, Md."; Lawrence Cardinal Shehan, *A Blessing of Years: The Memoirs of Lawrence Cardinal Shehan* (Notre Dame, Ind.: University of Notre Dame, 1982), 75–77. For a fascinating, thorough, comparative study of priestly ministry in New York in 1920 and 1970, see: Philip J. Murnion, *The Catholic Priest and the Changing Structure of Pastoral Ministry: New York, 1920–1970* (New York: Arno, 1978).

26. James Henry Bailey, *A History of the Diocese of Richmond: The Formative Years* (Richmond: Diocese of Richmond, 1956), 141; Roth, *History of the Diocese of St. Augustine,* 138, 142–143; McNally, *Catholicism in South Florida,* 87.

27. *Georgia Bulletin*, February 19, March 5, April 2, 1955; Bailey, *History of the Diocese of Richmond*, 112–113.

28. *Georgia Bulletin*, July 9, 1955; Colley, *History of Immaculate Conception* (Atlanta), 16–22.

29. McMurry, "The Church During Reconstruction," 120–121; AFDSP, "Report of Moore, 1885"; AAB, Curley Papers, B-348, Barry to Archbishop Michael J. Curley, November 26, 1925.

30. Roth, *History of the Diocese of St. Augustine*, 218–222; Parker, "O.L.P.H., Rocky Mount, N.C."; "St. Theresa's School, Albany, Ga."

31. Bailey, *History of the Diocese of Richmond*, 136–137; ADC, 602.44, St. Peter's, Columbia, S.C.; "St. Theresa's School, Albany, Ga."

32. ADS, RG-St. Anthony's Church, Atlanta, Ga.; *Georgia Bulletin*, January 7, 1956; Roth, *History of the Diocese of St. Augustine*, 132–133.

33. *Atlanta Herald*, September 23, 1942; ADC, Folder 600.66, Our Lady of Perpetual Help, Camden, S.C.; Folder 600.57, St. Andrew, Bluffton, S.C.; McNally, *Catholicism in South Florida*, 53; *Georgia Bulletin*, May 7, 1932.

34. "St. Theresa's School, Albany, Ga."; AADS, Annals and Mission Files, Blessed Martin Mission, Mrs. Agnes Dillon to Sister Mary, June 8, 1940; *Catholic Service Bureau Golden Anniversary, 1931–81*.

35. *Immaculate Conception Anniversary, 1954–1979.*

36. The Knights of Columbus, Ancient Order of Hibernians, St. Vincent de Paul Society were extra-parochial organizations founded before 1920. The Holy Name Societies in the Archdiocese of Baltimore had an Archdiocesan organization from 1911. Magri, *The Church of Richmond*, 140–141; "Golden Jubilee Convention-Baltimore Archdiocesan Holy Name Union, April 16, 1961." For information on parish organizations in the Southeast, see: ADC, Folder 602.1, "A Chronological History of St. Patrick's Church, Charleston, S.C., 1837–1937"; Roth, *History of the Diocese of St. Augustine*, 132–135; "Blessed Sacrament, Savannah"; Gannon, "History of the Parishes of Florida"; "Church of St. Mary of the Immaculate Conception, 1858–1958 (Wilmington)"; "St. Mary's Church, Hagerstown, Md."; Magri, *The Church of Richmond*, 98–102; "St. Mary's on-the-Hill, Augusta, Ga."; "Sacred Heart of Jesus, Atlanta."

37. Peter Guilday, ed., *National Pastorals of the American Hierarchy, 1792–1919* (Westminster, Md.; Newman, 1954), 247–253.

38. ADS, RG-St. Anthony's Church, Atlanta, Ga.; *Georgia Bulletin*, January 7, 1956; "Church of St. Mary of the Immaculate Conception, 1858–1958 (Wilmington)"; ADSA, Barry Papers, 5-W-22, Father James J. McLaughlin, S.J., to Father James Nunnan, April 27, 1927; Moore Papers, *notitiae*, 2(y)-B-15; 2(y)-C-25; 2(y)-D-2; 2(y)-E-3; 2(y)-K-18; 2(y)-K-21; 2(y)-N-10; ADC, Folder 301, Annual Parish Reports, 1902–1960.

39. Sister Mary Felicitas Powers, "A History of Catholic Education in Georgia, 1845–1952" (M.A. thesis, Catholic University of America, 1956), 114; ADC, Folder 600.23; 600.46; 705.19.

40. McMurry, "The Church During Reconstruction," 154; Guilday, *National Pastorals of the American Hierarchy*, 189–191, 215–216; 243–247; James Hennesey, S.J., *American Catholics: A History of the Roman Catholic Community in the United States* (New York: Oxford, 1981), 186; *OCD*, 1880; Interview, Rev. William Burn, Charleston, S.C., May 30, 1983; Michael J. Curley, *The Provincial Story: A History of the Baltimore*

*Province of the Congregation of the Most Holy Redeemer* (New York: Redemptorist Fathers, 1963), 103–104, 169. For more information on Neumann and Catholic parochial schools, see: Michael J. Curley, CSSR, *Venerable John Neumann, CSSR: Fourth Bishop of Philadelphia* (Washington, D.C.: Catholic University of America, 1952); Harold A. Buetow, *Of Singular Benefit: The Story of Catholic Education in the United States* (New York: Macmillan, 1970).

41. ADRa, Parish Histories, PR2.200.4.

42. "St. Theresa's School, Albany, Ga."; "Blessed Sacrament, Savannah."

43. "St. Mary's Church, Hagerstown, Md."; Patrick J. Bresnahan, *Seeing Florida with a Priest* (Zepherhills, Fla.: Economy Print Shop, 1938), 18; Roth, *History of the Diocese of St. Augustine*, 257–263; ADC, Folder 301, Annual Parish Reports, 1902–1960; Folder 601.24, St. John's, Charleston, S.C.; *Georgia Bulletin*, June 11, 1955; ADS, "Data for Report to Vatican-1945."

44. ADC, Folder 601.40; 601.6; Peterman, *The Cutting Edge*, 121–122.

45. Gannon, "History of the Parishes of Florida"; "Holy Family Catholic Church, Columbus, Ga."; ADC, Folder 604.54, St. Mary, Greenville, S.C.; *OCD*, 1880; 1930.

46. "St. Mary's Church, Annapolis"; Roth, *History of the Diocese of St. Augustine*, 262–263; "St. Mary's Church, Hagerstown, Md."; "Sacred Heart of Jesus, Atlanta"; ADC, Folder 604.54, St. Mary's, Greenville, S.C.; Powers, "Catholic Education in Georgia," 115; ADS, FB1, "Report to the American Board of Missions, 1937–38."

47. McNally, *Catholicism in South Florida*, 83; "Immaculate Conception (Hialeah)."

48. Michael V. Gannon, *Rebel Bishop: The Life and Era of Augustin Verot* (Milwaukee: Bruce, 1964), 170–184; ADS, *Rules and Regulations for the Public Schools for the City of Savannah and Chatham County* (Savannah: *Morning News*, 1870); Powers, "Catholic Education in Georgia," 13–15.

49. *Ibid.*, 13–14. See also another contemporary description of the Savannah Plan: *Boston Pilot*, June 2, 1873; Andrew Skeabeck, "Most Rev. William Gross: Missionary Bishop of the South," Part VI, *RACHS*, 66 (June, 1955), 80–90; McMurry, "The Church During Reconstruction," 176–178.

50. Powers, "Catholic Education in Georgia," 15–20, 54–61; Gannon, *Rebel Bishop*, 190–191. Georgia was not the only place where there were Catholic–public schools, although it was the first and most widespread. The Poughkeepsie Plan involved St. Peter's Parochial School in Poughkeepsie, N.Y. It lasted from 1873–99. St. Paul, Minnesota, had a similar arrangement (Faribauilt Plan) that lasted from 1891–93. There was no connection between the Georgia and New York or Minnesota plans. Daniel F. Reilly, *The School Controversy* (Washington, D.C.: Catholic University of America, 1943), 67–106.

51. Gannon, *Rebel Bishop*, 187; McMurry, "The Church During Reconstruction," 179–181; ASSJ, Bishop John Moore to St. John's County Board of Public Instruction, July 1, 1878; Petition, Committee for American Education to Governor Park Trammell, July 14, 1913; Sister M. Dominic, S.S.J., to Mr. E. A. Hathaway, Supervisor of Public Education, Duval County, July 21, 1914; Hathaway to Sister M. Dominic, n.d.; *St. Augustine Evening Record*, August 22, 1913; *Living Waters-Centennial Booklet, 1866–1966* (Jacksonville, Fla.: Ambrose the Printer, 1966), 15.

52. ADC, Folder 603.1, St. Peter's, Columbia, S.C.; *Georgia Bulletin*, August 20, 1955; ADC, Folder 604.7, St. Anthony's, Florence, S.C.; ADSA, Kenny Papers, 3-G-7, Sister M. Euphemia to Bishop Kenny, September 13, 1905; 3-G-8, Father Patrick J. Ken-

nedy to Kenny, September 14, 1905; St. Mary, Star of the Sea, Key West, *notitiae*, 1888–1912; ASHN, School Reports, Key West.

53. Bailey, *History of the Diocese of Richmond*, 131; "St. Mary's Church, Hagerstown, Md."; "St. Theresa's School, Albany, Ga."; *Georgia Bulletin*, April 2, 1955; Roth, *History of the Diocese of St. Augustine*, 32; Jay P. Dolan, *Catholic Revivalism: The American Experience, 1830–1900* (Notre Dame, Ind.: University of Notre Dame, 1978), xvii.

54. John F. Byrne, *The Redemptorist Centenaries* (Philadelphia: Dolphin, 1932), 265; Dolan, *Catholic Revivalism*, 50–52; ADSA, Kenny Papers, 3-M-22, Father Alexander Doyle, C.P., to Kenny, May 13, 1908; Patrick J. Bresnahan, *Seeing Florida with a Priest* (Zepherhills, Fla.: Economy Print Shop, 1938); H. W. Santen, *Father Bishop, Founder of Glenmary Home Missionaries* (Milwaukee: Bruce, 1961).

55. *Georgia Bulletin*, April 2, 1955; Parker, "O.L.P.H., Rocky Mount, N.C.," 23–24; Roth, *History of the Diocese of St. Augustine*, 154–156; AFDSP, "Report of Moore, 1885."

56. Baptism, Marriage, and Burial Registers, St. John the Baptist Cathedral and St. Mary Church, Charleston, S.C., 1850–1960; ADC, Folder 705.19, Marriage Statistics 1949–53; Quinquennial, 1950–54; Diocese of St. Augustine, Office of the Chancellor, Quinquennial, 1950–54.

57. "St. Mary's Church, Annapolis"; Skeabeck, "Gross: Missionary Bishop," 83; Parker, "O.L.P.H., Rocky Mount, N.C.," 23–32; "St. Theresa's School, Albany, Ga."; Roth, *History of the Diocese of St. Augustine*, 261–269; ADSA, Moore Papers, 2(a)-P-8, *Lake Worth News*, March 26, 1896; Barry Papers, 12-D-21, Barry to Merrick, April 22, 1924.

58. ADSA, Kenny Papers; 3-G-8, P. J. Kennedy, S.J., to Kenny, September 14, 1905; Jane Quinn, "Nuns in Ybor City: The Sisters of St. Joseph and the Immigrant Community," *Tampa Bay History*, 5 (Spring-Summer, 1983), 39; "St. Theresa's School, Albany, Georgia"; "St. Mary's Church, Hagerstown, Md."; Roth, *History of the Diocese of St. Augustine*, 202–203; Interview, Msgr. Daniel Burke.

59. ASJ, Sister M. Sidonie to Father Superior (LePuy, France), December 18, 1872; *The Jesuits in Florida: Fifty Golden Years, 1889–1939* (Tampa: Salesman, 1939), 35; Interview, Sister Kathleen Reilly, SSND, Baltimore, July 20, 1981; Ann Taves, " 'External' Devotions and the Interior Life: Popular Devotional Theologies in Mid-Nineteenth Century America," *Working Paper Series-Center for the Study of American Catholicism* (Spring, 1983), 56.

60. Robert F. McNamara, *Catholic Sunday Preaching: The American Guidelines, 1791–1975* (Washington, D.C.: Word of God Institute, 1975), 17–42; "St. Theresa's School, Albany, Ga."; Dolan, *Catholic Revivalism*, 91–112; Shehan, *A Blessing of Years*, 81.

61. Taves, "Devotions," 15, 54–56; McMurry, "The Church During Reconstruction," 143–144; "St. Theresa's School, Albany, Ga."; "Sacred Heart Church, 1888–1913 (St. Joseph, Florida)"; Interview, Msgr. Daniel Burke; Magri, *The Church of Richmond;* Byrne, *Redemptorist Centenaries*, 473–475; Shehan, *A Blessing of Years*, 77.

62. Flannery O'Connor, *The Habit of Being*, ed. by Sally Fitzgerald (New York: Farrar-Straus, Giroux, 1979), 145, 569.

63. "St. Patrick's Church, Baltimore, 1792–1942"; Gannon, "History of the Parishes

of Florida''; *Georgia Bulletin,* April 2, 1955; "Sacred Heart of Jesus, Atlanta''; Shehan, *A Blessing of Years,* 85–92; ADC, Folder 301, Annual Parish Reports, 1902–1960.

64. Cathedral of St. John the Baptist, Savannah, Baptismal and Marriage Registers; ADS, RG, Immaculate Conception, Atlanta; ADC, Folder 601.31, St. Joseph's, Charleston; St. John the Baptist Cathedral, Charleston, Baptismal, Marriage, and Death Registers; "St. Patrick's Church, Baltimore''; Bailey, *History of the Diocese of Richmond,* 134.

65. Letter of Mother Theresa to King Ludwig I, March 30, 1848, quoted in: Sister M. Hester Valentine, ed., *The North American Foundations: Letters of Mother M. Theresa Gerhardinger* (Winona, Minn.: St. Mary's College, 1977), 79. For material on the coming of the School Sisters of Notre Dame, see M. T. Flynn, *Mother Caroline and the School Sisters of North America,* Vol. 1 (St. Louis: Woodward and Tiernan, 1928), 24–32.

66. "St. Michael's Church, Baltimore—Diamond Jubilee, 1852–1927''; "St. Michael's Parish Centenary Celebration, 1852–1952.''

67. "St. Michael's Church''; "St. Michael the Archangel Church, 1852–1977.''

68. *Ibid.,* "St. Michael's Church.''

69. Gannon, "History of the Parishes of Florida;'' Magri, *The Church of Richmond,* 76–85; Bailey, *History of the Diocese of Richmond,* 108, 125–126; Ignatius Remke, OSB, *Historical Sketch of St. Mary's Church, Richmond, Virginia, 1842–1935* (Richmond: Privately Published 1935); ADC, Folder 601.31, St. Paul's, Charleston; 42-G-4, Francis Sadler to Lynch, January 27, 1868; 43-S-6, Shadler to Lynch, June 1, 1868; 45-G-1, Shadler to Lynch, October 8, 1868; 46-W-6, "Statement of Money Collected and Expended, January 1, 1866–September 1, 1869''; Peterman, *The Cutting Edge,* 122–123; ADS, RG, "Immaculate Conception, Atlanta''; *Georgia Bulletin,* April 14, 1956; Marriage and Baptism Register, St. John the Baptist Cathedral, Savannah; ADSA, Kenny Papers, 3-H-2, Bresnahan to Kenny, January 12, 1906.

70. Thomas L. Hollowak, "The Emergence of a Baltimore Polonia'' (Unpublished paper, University of Maryland, December 20, 1982). Other Bohemian parishes of the Southeast include: Sacred Heart, Richmond (1906); St. Mary's, Masarytown, Fla. (1931). Magri, *The Church of Richmond,* 138; Gannon, "History of Parishes of Florida.''

71. *OCD,* 1930; ADC, 49-P-4, Luigi A. Folchi, S.J., to the Bishop of Charleston, February 2, 1871; AAB, Parish Statistics, *notitiae,* St. Leo's, January 1, 1882; "Diamond Jubilee of St. Joseph's Church, Burgan, N.C., 1908–1983''; "Church of St. Leo the Great, 1881–1981.'' For more on Italian-American parish life see: Silvano M. Tomasi and Edward C. Stibili, *Italian-Americans and Religion: An Annotated Bibliography* (New York: Center for Migration Studies, 1978); Silvano M. Tomasi, *Piety and Power: The Role of the Italian Parishes in the New York Metropolitan Area, 1880–1930* (Staten Island, N.Y.: Center for Migration Studies, 1975); Rudolph J. Vecoli, "Prelates and Peasants: Italian Immigrants and the Catholic Church,'' in Keith P. Dyrud, Michael Novak, and Rudolph J. Vecoli, compilers, *The Other Catholics* (New York: Arno, 1978), 217–268.

72. Gary R. Mormino and George Pozetta, "Immigrant Women in Tampa: The Italian Experience, 1890–1930,'' *Florida Historical Quarterly,* 61 (January, 1983), 296–312; Jane Quinn, "Nuns in Ybor City,'' 24–41; Gerald E. Poyo, "Key West and the Cuban Ten Years' War,'' *Florida Historical Quarterly,* 57 (January, 1979), 289–307; McNally, *Catholicism in South Florida,* 30–34. The quote is taken from Mormino and Pozetta, "Immigrant Women in Tampa,'' 299.

73. ADRa, Parish Histories, PR 2.200.4; Interview, Msgr. Richard Madden, Summerville, S.C., June 4, 1983; ADC, Folder 605.49, St. Ann's, Kingston, S.C.; *Georgia Bulletin,* January 21, 1956; ADS, FB1, "Apostolic Delegation, 1950–54;" RG, St. Joseph's of Lebanon Church, Atlanta, Ga.; "St. Theresa's School, Albany, Ga."

74. ADSA, Barry Papers, 27-B-7, Barry to Yazigie, July 1, 1935; Interview, Msgr. Andrew Shashy, Jacksonville, June 30, 1983; Interview, Rev. Anthony Sebra, Jacksonville, June 28, 1983; Gannon, "History of the Parishes of Florida."

75. Interview, Msgr. Shashy; ADRa, Parish Histories, PR 2.200.3.

76. ADC, Folder 601.22, Immaculate Conception, Charleston.

77. Sister Mary De Sales Harris, "A History of Catholic Elementary Schools for the Negro in North Carolina, 1924–60" (M.A. thesis, Catholic University of America, 1965), 4–22; *Georgia Bulletin,* May 7, 1932; *OCD,* 1900; 1930; 1950; 1960; AJF, Tampa, Fla.-St. Peter Claver File; ADRa, Parish Histories, PR 2.200.4; *Concilii Plenarii Baltimorensis II . . . Acta et Decreta,* Titulus X, Caput IV, #484, #485, #488 (Baltimore: John Murphy, 1868), 243–246.

78. *The News and Observer,* November 29, 1942.

79. AAB, Parish Statistics, *notitiae,* St. Francis Xavier Church, January 1, 1878.

80. *The 1951 National Catholic Almanac* (Paterson, N.J.: St. Anthony Guild, 1951), 345–346; ADC, 46-Y-3, Rev. Luigi Folgi, S.J., to Bishop Patrick Lynch, September 11, 1869; Magri, *The Church of Richmond,* 119–120.

81. ASSJ, Sister Marie Sidonie to Father Superior (Le Puy), December 18, 1872.

82. Gannon, "History of the Parishes of Florida"; ADC, Folder 602.44; Letter, Rev. Peter Hogan, S.S.J., to Author, Baltimore, Md., September 14, 1983; Harris, "Catholic Elementary Schools, N.C.," 9–17; ADS, FB-17, "Religion in the Southeast-Report," n.d. [c. Spring, 1955].

83. These ideas were influenced by English Bishop Herbert Vaughn's (founder of the Mill Hill Fathers) comments during his 1872 tour of America. McMurry, "The Church During Reconstruction," 222.

84. Albert J. Raboteau, "Black Catholics: A Capsule History," *Catholic Digest* (June, 1983), 32–33.

85. Roth, *History of the Diocese of St. Augustine,* 5–28; "St. Mary's Church, Annapolis"; McNally, *Catholicism in South Florida,* 64–66; Letter, Hogan to Author, September 14, 1983; ADC, Folder 601.22, Immaculate Conception, Charleston; ASSJ, Sister Marie Sidonie to Father Superior (Le Puy), December 18, 1872; McMurry, "The Church During Reconstruction," 230–231; "St. Francis Xavier Church Centennial, 1863–1963."

CHAPTER FOUR

# The Parish, 1955–1980

## A. A SPIRITUAL EARTHQUAKE

Beginning around 1960, some dramatic shifts took place in America and Southeast Catholicism. When the Russians launched Sputnik in 1957, Americans questioned their national strength and resolve. In the midst of these national anxieties, as the first Catholic President, the youthful John F. Kennedy's rhetoric of the "New Frontier" raised the expectations and hopes of all Americans. Meanwhile, the Civil Rights Movement was becoming the single most important domestic political issue of the 1960s. But the assassination of Kennedy in 1963, the shift of the black movement from civil disobedience to civil disorder and black power, and the increasing involvement of United States troops in Viet Nam produced, by 1968, a feeling of disenchantment among many Americans. Authority, morality, institutions, personal freedom, and relationships, in short the whole fabric of American society was being questioned in a way it never had been before. In the midst of this American cultural upheaval of the 1960s, American Catholics were also being shaken by events within their own Church. In 1955, John Tracy Ellis produced his influential essay "American Catholics and the Intellectual Life," which critiqued the absence of Catholic contributors to American intellectual life. In early 1959, the newly elected Pope John XXIII announced his intention to call an ecumenical council of the Church. From 1962 to 1965, Vatican Council II convened and wrought changes in every area of Church life, from law to liturgy, changes that are still working themselves out twenty years later. In addition, after 1960, many places in the Southeast (especially Florida) showed demographic shifts from migration and immigration that raised the Catholic population of the region. These rapid and dramatic cultural, ecclesial, and demographic shifts in the intellectual, attitudinal, and social terrain in the Southeast, after 1960, created a "spiritual earthquake" by 1968, one that has shaken and shifted Catholic parish life in the Southeast in an unprecedented manner.[1]

## B. PARISH LOCALE AND SIZE

From 1960 to 1980, the Southeast Coast showed a continued decline in the ratio of rural to urban areas. In 1960, the region was 55.3% urban; in 1980, the figure

194

was 62.7%. West Virginia was the region's most rural state (63.8%); Florida was the most urban (84.3%). By 1980, Florida had the largest population of any state in the Southeast (9,746,342), followed by North Carolina (5,881,766). From 1970 to 1980, Florida was the fastest growing state of the region (43.5%), followed by South Carolina (20.5%). The average growth rate for the United States from 1970 to 1980 was 11.4%. Maryland and Delaware were the slowest growing states of the region with 7.4% and 8.4% growth rate, respectively, from 1970 to 1980. According to the 1980 Census, Florida (7th), North Carolina (10th), Georgia (13th), and Virginia (14th) were among the top fifteen populous states in the country.[2] What these demographic statistics demonstrate is a shift of demographic importance from Maryland and Delaware from 1850 to 1950, to Florida, Georgia, and North Carolina from 1960 to 1980.

As in the previous period, Catholics in the Southeast lived predominantly in towns and cities, yet continued to be influenced by the Southern character of these urban areas, as recent studies indicate.[3] In 1960, Baltimore was the largest city in the region with 939,024 residents, although it had been losing population since 1950. Norfolk, Atlanta, Miami, and Tampa trailed in population in that order. By 1980, the largest city in the region was Baltimore with a population of 786,775, followed by Jacksonville, Atlanta, Miami, Charlotte, Norfolk, and Virginia Beach (in order of size). The number of city parishes (population over 50,000) in the region increased from 273 in 1960 to 343 in 1980; however, the percentage of urban parishes in the region decreased from 32.6% in 1960 to 27.1% in 1980, owing to the growth of satellite suburban areas around the cities. Catholics were still concentrated in and around Southern cities in 1980.[4]

The following chart gives the two states with the highest and lowest percentage of Catholics in the general population in two decades:

| Year | Highest Percentage | | Lowest Percentage | |
|------|--------------------|--------------------|--------------------|--------------------|
| 1960 | Delaware | (19.4%) | North Carolina | (0.8%) |
|      | Maryland | (13.2%) | South Carolina | (1.3%) |
| 1980 | Delaware | (20.3%) | North Carolina | (1.6%) |
|      | Florida | (13.9%) | South Carolina | (1.9%) |

The average state ratio of Catholics to non-Catholics in the Southeast (excluding the District of Columbia) in 1960 was 6.2%, while in 1980 it was 7.6%. Catholics made slight gains throughout the Southeast in the two decades, but significant gains were made in Florida, where in 1960 the Catholic population was 3.2%, while in 1980 it was 13.9%, with concentrations as high as 24.4% in South Florida.[5]

Between 1960 and 1980, just over 400 parishes were founded in the Southeast, an increase of 49.5% in two decades. On the other hand, missions attached to parishes decreased from 339 to 255 in the twenty-year period, or by 24.8%. Although the rural missionary character had not disappeared from the Southeast, certainly fewer priests and people proportionately experienced this kind of ministry than ever before. Most of the growth of Catholicism from 1960 to 1980 was in the cities and small cities of the region. Parish size grew slightly in some places over the period. In the Diocese of Savannah in 1960, the largest parish had about 700 families. By 1980, five or six parishes of the diocese had 1,000 families. In general, a parish of 600 families in 1980 was considered substantial. The average rural parish (about 40% of the parishes of the diocese) had about 100 families. By 1980, parishes in the dioceses of Baltimore, Washington, Wilmington, and Miami were larger in size and much less rural in content, but these were still exceptions to the region. In the Archdiocese of Miami, by 1980, it was rare that a parish be less than 1,000 families. The few rural parishes were mainly devoted to migrant ministry. In 1960, the Diocese of Miami had perhaps five parishes that exceeded 2,500 families; by 1980, there were at least twenty.[6]

## C. PARISH ORGANIZATIONAL COMPLEXITY AND PRIORITIES

The year 1960 is a watershed for Southeastern Catholicism, as well as for American Catholicism in general, since it was about that time that many Catholics "arrived" socially and economically. Symbolized by the election of this country's first Catholic President, John F. Kennedy, in 1960, Catholics were viewed as socially more acceptable by Protestant and Jewish Americans. In addition, the post-World War II economic boom brought more Catholics into the Southeast and raised their standard of living, so much so that many were becoming solidly middle class. Consequently, around 1960, Catholics in the Southeast were able to be more generous in their offerings to the Church. Collections rose and the institutional Church had more income, reflecting its more affluent membership, and making available more financial resources, which meant the possibility for more construction of ecclesial institutions—churches, schools, rectories, social halls, and social service institutions. The Diocese of Miami was an extreme example, but from 1958 to 1968 the following ecclesial institutions were constructed there: two seminaries, fifty-eight new churches, eight new mission churches, nine new high schools, seventeen new parish schools, twenty-seven new convents, four diocesan office buildings, sixteen new facilities for dependent persons, and four high school faculty residences.[7]

All of the construction activity also encouraged something relatively new in parochial and diocesan management—large-scale deficit spending. Before 1960, parishes sometimes had debts, but the general policy was to avoid indebtedness.

After World War II, with the amount of ecclesial construction that was undertaken, many parishes were getting used to having a perpetual debt.

One example of the implications of this kind of deficit spending is Corpus Christi Parish in Miami. With its $330,000 church dedicated in 1959, it was one of the larger parishes in Miami, with a membership composed of mostly middle-class whites. But in less than two years after the church was built, the rosy financial picture of the parish darkened. Many of the most loyal members of the parish (founded in 1941) were moving because two interstate highways had cut wide swaths through the area, and because blacks and Cubans were rapidly settling into the neighborhood. The school's yearly deficit was rising as a result of the inability of Hispanic parents to pay tuition. In 1961, the parish had 3,300 families and a parish debt of $432,600. By 1971, the parish had a total debt of $586,000 and a yearly deficit of $45,000; in 1976, the church needed a new $50,000 roof, but could not afford it. The pastor sought an Archdiocesan subsidy for the parish, but the subsidy was refused.[8] This example of Corpus Christi Parish shows what happens when the expected income is not available; how deficit spending can become a financial quagmire, especially when population shifts occur in a parish; how financial difficulties can compound through deficit spending; and how important the chancery became in directing and financing parishes.

By 1960, most Southeast dioceses had a yearly diocesan-wide collection that helped, among other things, to bankroll parish and diocesan building projects. By 1960, social services, secondary Catholic education, some parish organizations, and parish finances became fused to a more centralized, bureaucratized diocesan chancery; this development encouraged the efficient orchestration of coordinated parochial diocesan-wide efforts, but it also reduced the autonomy and local decision-making of an individual parish.

An additional boost in the post-1960 trend toward diocesan centralization and bureaucratization came from another kind of construction that was going on, the call for the renewal of the Church through the implementation of Vatican Council II. Lawrence Cardinal Shehan developed a two year plan (1966–1967) to visit parishes in his Archdiocese of Baltimore in order to introduce and implement the decrees of the council, especially liturgical changes. Shehan was rare among the bishops of the Southeast in his solicitude for informed implementation of the council. Most bishops, as well as most pastors, simply imposed liturgical changes with little or no preparation for people or priests. What most people knew about the post-Vatican II changes they read in the newspaper or heard over the media.[9]

The council and its implementation created shifts in the organizational complexity of the parish and priorities that parishes sought. The spiritual renewal called for by Vatican Council II pointed out the need for education in the broad sense, especially regarding the new liturgical changes and the new changes in ecclesial perspectives. As a result of the council, parishes began offering Scripture courses, prayer groups, and family ministry. In the late 1970s, the Rite of Christian Initiation for Adults (RCIA) was introduced in many churches, as well as parish renewal programs. The newly revised sacramental rites were supplemented with parish-based programs for education of the recipients as to the meaning of these Sacraments. Another priority of the post-Vatican II period has been the remodeling of parish churches to accommodate the new liturgical changes. Virtually every parish has undergone some face-lifting as a result, both in sanctuaries and confessionals.

Other shifts in parochial organization and priorities were based on socioeconomic considerations. Vatican II, together with the aftermath of the civil rights movement, created a renewal in social concern for the poor and minorities. Parish and diocesan structures were developed and money channeled into helping the poor and disadvantaged of the region. In addition, demographic shifts in the urban areas, including "white flight," changed the complexion of many once-thriving inner city parishes over the last twenty years. The disparity between wealthier parishes and poorer parishes became more pronounced. Finally, although the fostering of vocations continued to be a rhetorical concern from 1960 to 1980, religious and diocesan vocations declined dramatically during that period, especially among religious. Parishes were no longer producing the numbers of vocations they once had. Yet, vocations were no longer a *de facto* priority, despite all the rhetoric. Swift shifts in the nature of family life, religious life, priestly life, and American cultural values all contributed to the devaluation of priestly and religious vocations.[10]

The most significant organizational shift in the post-1960 period has been the move toward collaborative effort on the parish and diocesan level, with its resultant meetings, committees, and reports—in short, bureaucracy. New parish organizations sprang up alongside already extant ones from the pre-1960 period. Before 1960, Holy Family Parish, Columbus, Georgia, had five or six major parish organizations. By 1980, it had fifteen, including such newcomers as the Parish Council, the Worship Committee, lectors, the Religious Education Committee, and the Christian Service Committee.[11]

The crystallization of the new parish organization, the new collaborative effort, the new shift in priorities, is found in the most significant parochial development in recent times—the parish council. A product of Vatican II, the parish council is an administrative aide in the identification of parish needs, priorities, and objectives, as well as a collaborative aide for the ordinary operation of the parish. It also reflects the American penchant for participatory government and finds a home in American political traditions. Parish council members are either elected, appointed *ex officio,* appointed by the pastor, or a combination thereof. They are for the most part advisory, although some make provisions for overriding the pastor's veto (St. Gabriel's, Greenville, North Carolina) or not allowing the pastor to veto at all (St. Katherine of Sienna, Baltimore). Each parish council has committees that address the spiritual and temporal needs of the parish. For example, St. Gabriel's Parish Council, Greenville, North Carolina, has the following committees: Family Life and Social; Social Action; Liturgy; Education; Publicity; Finance; and Maintenance and Planning.

This new type of parish collaborative administration by means of the parish council was received with mixed reactions by pastors and bishops. For this reason, not every parish in the Southeast has a parish council. In 1971, the Archdiocese of Miami, which comprised 111 parishes, had only fourteen parish councils (12.5%). In 1980, forty-three of the 130 parishes of the Archdiocese of Miami (33.1%) had them. On the other hand, the Diocese of Savannah mandated that in 1970 every parish have a parish council; by 1976, this mandate was realized. It should be noted that just because a particular parish does not have a parish council does not mean that parishioners do not have a say or are not involved in parish decision-making. On the other hand, having a parish council does not assure that it is functioning or effective. A parish council is only a tool for parishioner involvement and responsibility; it cannot work unless properly applied, and it might not be the answer to every parochial situation.[12]

On the one hand, the collaborative effort approach to parish organization and priorities is more efficient, more democratic, more collegial, and recognizes the importance of trying to solve problems from a social-structural point of view. On the other hand, it is less personal and more bureaucratic. Often, a great deal of time is spent maintaining the institutional structures in meetings, in procedures, in referring to proper committees, and in writing up reports and evaluations. Not only is the parish council a triumph of American democratic traditions, but it is also a triumph of American bureaucracy, which was growing larger from 1960 to 1980 not only on the parish level, but also on the national and diocesan level.

## D. THE CLERGY AND PEOPLE OF THE PARISH

The changes in pastoral ministry induced by Vatican II and American culture in the 1960s created a qualitative shift in the way the priest perceived himself and the way he was perceived by his people. Up to that time, priests had been theologically trained in the antimodernist mode of neoscholastic manuals written in Latin, had been sequestered in seminaries with little pastoral experience before ordination, and had been taught that they were the sacred, separated, and sole authority of the parish after ordination. Trained to say Mass in Latin with his back toward the people, the priest was now required with the Revised Liturgy of Pope Paul VI to say Mass in vernacular facing the people. This change in liturgical language and posture symbolized the radical change that was now expected of the parish priest. Both in the liturgy and outside it, he was now to face the people, speak to the people, work *with* the people as servant-leader, a role for which he was ill prepared in the pre-conciliar seminary. With Vatican II came not only the change in the liturgy, but also the multiplication of ministries. Deacons, extraordinary ministers, pastoral assistants, lectors, directors of religious education, leaders of lay groups, all aware of the priesthood of the baptized, sought a ministerial role within the parish community. No longer was the priest the sole minister of the parish. In addition, parishioners were making demands on the parish priest, some of which had not heretofore been made. They sought good preaching, a celebrative style, an approachable personality. If they did not find it in one parish, they could go to another or drop out from parish life altogether. All of these new expectations could be a source of new joy in the priesthood through collaboration with the faithful in building up the Body of Christ. They could also be a threatening source of stressful anxiety.[13]

Priestly response in the Southeast to the revision of priestly identity brought on by the changes induced by Vatican II and American culture after 1960 was varied. In many urban and suburban parishes, personal pastoral visitation became impossible because of the larger size of parishes and the new bureaucratic complexus of priestly demands. Beginning around 1967 in the Southeast, some priests responded to the questioning of priestly identity by leaving the priesthood altogether. Most dioceses in the Southeast lost an average of at least one priest a year from 1967 to 1980, a rate unheard of in the region before. Both the departure of priests from the priesthood and the general questioning of priestly identity hurt priestly morale and made young men reluctant to enter a profession that seemed so unsure about its own identity. The number of young men in diocesan seminaries peaked in the mid-1960s, and then by 1980 dropped to figures similar to the pre-1960 period, as is indicated by the following statistics for the region:

|                        | 1950 | 1960 | 1965  | 1968  | 1970  | 1980 |
|------------------------|------|------|-------|-------|-------|------|
| Diocesan Seminarians:  | 384  | 994  | 1,557 | 1,310 | 1,034 | 489  |

In interpreting these statistics, one must keep in mind that the early 1960s has generally been regarded as a unique period in American Catholic history for vocations. Also, beginning in the late 1960s and early 1970s, most high school seminaries ceased operations. The 1950 and 1960 figures represent seminarians in high school, college, and theologate, whereas the 1980 figure reflects mostly seminarians in theologate. Actually, more seminarians were studying theology in 1980 than in 1950.[14]

Another new expression of priesthood, which was a response to the shift in the ground of ecclesial life, was the rise of collaborative priestly efforts. Although social activism in political or social questions was not very common among Southeastern priests (except for those in Baltimore and Washington), tensions rose between the local bishop as an authority figure and priest groups and individuals. These local incidents did not attain the notoriety of Archbishop O'Boyle's confrontation with his priests in Washington over the *Humanae Vitae* document (1968), whereby the Archbishop suspended thirty-nine priests, but episcopal authority was being challenged by priests. One such local incident took place in Miami in the summer of 1971. After a series of transfers, which involved 78% of the pastors being moved from 1969 to 1971, the Archbishop was confronted about his practices by several priests at a clergy conference in September of 1971. The tense meeting had to be abruptly adjourned. Post-1960 priestly collaboration took other forms also with the creation in every diocese of a priests' senate, which was an advisory council for the bishop and a representative priests' forum for collective pastoral action. Another more recent development of priestly collective action has been the formation of small priest support groups and prayer groups among the clergy. On a broader diocesan scale, Ministry to Priests and the Emmaus Program were also instituted to foster priestly fraternity, prayer, and support.[15]

In general, the people of the Southeast were better served by the Church from 1960 because of more parishes and fewer missions and stations than in the pre-1960 period. Yet, the ratio of diocesan priests per Catholic declined from the 1970 figure, as the following figures indicate:

|                                | 1950 | 1960  | 1965  | 1968  | 1970  | 1980  |
| ------------------------------ | ---- | ----- | ----- | ----- | ----- | ----- |
| Number of Catholics per priest: | 856  | 1,217 | 1,226 | 1,172 | 1,138 | 1,353 |

Lay initiative, so characteristic of the faithful up to 1940, returned once again in a slightly different form in the post-1960 period. The laity continued to be interested in parish building, but not just from a material-financial perspective. With the withdrawal of religious men and women from parochial schools because of personnel shortages and personal preference, more laypersons taught in parochial schools than ever before. Although laypersons, especially women, taught religious education to public school children as before, a new position opened up in the field that allowed for more lay leadership—the Director of Religious Education, a concept developed first in Miami in 1968. Other avenues open for lay involvement from 1960 to 1980 were lectors, Eucharistic ministers, lay ministers, and parish council members.[16]

Some lay parochial organizations began to fade around 1960, while others blossomed fresh from the new terrain of the post-Vatican II Church. One casualty of the post-1960 period was the Holy Name Society. Yet, besides parish councils, which were initiated from the top down, other lay movements of the period were begun from the grass roots. A number of movements in the Southeast developed from 1960, all designed to renew the faith of individuals, of couples, of families, and of parishes. Among these groups were: *Cursillo,* Christian Family Movement, Marriage Encounter, *Encuentro Familiar,* Engaged Encounter, and Search. Although these movements sometimes were based in a parish, they often saw themselves as extra-parochial. The Charismatic Renewal Movement also spread throughout the Southeast, and it too had both a parochial and extra-parochial character. Two small, autonomous charismatic communities developed in Augusta, Georgia, and Americas, Georgia. Sometimes, the Charismatic Movement has been a great benefit for a parish, since it helped deepen the spiritual life of parishioners and empowered them to make important contributions to the life of their parishes. In other instances, Charismatic Renewal has created tensions and divisions within a parish. Such was the case at St. Mary of the Assumption Church, Pylesville, Maryland, when several charismatic parishioners decided to abandon their parish and Roman Catholicism to join a fundamentalist church. The effect and extent of the Charismatic Movement in the Southeast has yet to be studied and is, perhaps, still too young to be clearly assessed at this time. A new form of the parish mission did develop in programs like Parish Renewal; the devotionally and sacramentally oriented parish mission, so successful in the pre-Vatican II parish, proved unsuccessful as a format for parochial renewal in the post-Vatican II era. Those involved with the various lay movements often demanded corporate or individual spiritual direction—another expectation for which most priests were inadequately trained. One of the older organizations that continued to have strong leadership and support on the parish and diocesan level was the Council of Catholic Women. Parish life continued to receive the strong support of women, who also were active in the larger issues in society, such as abortion.[17]

Even more important than the organizations of laypeople in the parish were the attitudes of the laity that were emerging during the post-1960 period. From 1945 to 1960, about 80% of the Catholics in the Southeast were regular churchgoers. They saw their attendance at Mass as a legal obligation and their nonattendance as a mortal sin. People were quite familiar with the contents of the *Baltimore Catechism,* since they had memorized its dictums as children and heard reverberations of its contents in the dogmatic sermons delivered on most Sundays. People were generally subservient to their bishops and pastors, and were somewhat in awe of them since they were distant figures, somehow above and beyond the rest of humanity. This mentality was all but shattered by the "spiritual earthquake" of Vatican II and the cultural whirlwind of America in the 1960s. Authority and freedom were key issues of the period, both in ecclesial and secular society. The laity began to see its pastors with all the faults and failings of the human condition. In the past, priestly faults were often overlooked or excused by parishioners; now, the imperfection of leaders was not easily tolerated, and no longer was the pastor's authority unquestioned as it had been in the 1950s.[18]

Other shifts in lay attitudes in the post-Vatican II period were more theological in nature. Perhaps 50% of Southeast Catholics were going to church in the mid-1970s. For many, no longer was church attendance seen as an obligation or sin.

Ironically, at the very time when the Rite of Penance was being thoroughly revised, fewer and fewer Catholics were going to confession frequently or even regularly. This was once the hallmark of a good Catholic. On the other hand, more Catholics were receiving Communion than ever before. In an environment where ecumenism was stressed, Catholics were being more and more influenced by Protestant fundamentalism, which was experiencing a resurgence. While family movements proliferated in parishes, more Catholics than ever before experienced divorce, following a national trend. The Church's teaching on birth control did not receive the full support of Catholics, but why and to what extent in the Southeast needs further study. On the other hand, virtually every parish in the region had people active in the pro-life movement. Most remarkable, in a region known for social conservatism, no anti-Vatican II lay movements of any consequence developed.[19] Generally, laity in the Southeast took to the liturgical and attitudinal changes of the post-Vatican II Church with flexibility and alacrity. Usually, the laity found it easier to adapt to the post-Vatican II age than did ecclesial professionals, such as priests and religious, perhaps because the laity had less, personally, at stake than the professionals.

Another attitudinal shift that reflected lay involvement was the expression of more demands to pastors and bishops by some laypeople. Many laity felt a greater sense of ownership of their parish than they had felt in the recent past. Yet, experienced pastors seemed to feel that the number of people intensely involved in parish life has really not changed much from the 1950s—they give a figure of about 10%. Those who have been involved with parish councils, ministries, or movements have been changed attitudinally by them, but these currently represent a small proportion of parishioners.[20]

## E. PARISH COMMUNAL LIFE

The socialization of members into the Church after 1960 became more problematic than ever before. Unlike the times past, it was not so much the lack of material resources or personnel that hindered the socialization process, but rather a shift in the cultural and ecclesial climate that made older techniques less effective.

The family continued to be the core instrument of the transmission of the beliefs and practices of Catholicism, yet the American Catholic family was being stretched and twisted by the same social and cultural forces that were affecting American families in general. Catholic divorce and remarriage rose to rates proportional to the rest of the country. The effects of the abortion issue, contraception, working mothers, feminism, and divorce upon Catholic families in the Southeast have yet to be studied, but these social forces must have contributed to a change in the role of the Catholic family in religious socialization.[21] As another indicator of change in family life, the number of marriage cases (annulments) processed by diocesan marriage tribunals increased dramatically in the last several years, as is suggested by the following chart:[22]

|                           | 1973 Cases | 1978 Cases | 1977 Cases | 1982 Cases |
|---------------------------|:----------:|:----------:|:----------:|:----------:|
| Diocese of St. Augustine  | —          | 44         | —          | 242        |
| Diocese of Raleigh        | —          | 58         | —          | 149        |
| Archdiocese of Miami      | 17         | —          | 153        | —          |
| Diocese of Savannah       | 2          | —          | 49         | —          |

The number of mixed marriages in 1980 (a little over 50%) seems to be consistent with general trends that existed before 1960 in the Southeast, except in those areas where Catholic ethnic groups predominate, such as Miami (where mixed marriages are at 25%). In areas such as North Carolina, where Catholics are about 1.5% of the population, mixed marriages in 1980 were about 75%.[23] Given the importance of the family in the past as the key socializer in the faith, some sociological study should be undertaken to determine the state of the Catholic family in the Southeast as a force of socialization.

By 1960, the Confraternity of Christian Doctrine (CCD) did not seem as powerful a force for socialization as the older Sunday School, even though it became more organized and professionalized. After 1960, the CCD reached proportionately fewer young people than it had before 1960. Also, a tremendous shift occurred in the content and the manner of teaching religion. No longer was the Baltimore Catechism the universal text for the CCD; new texts were coming out all the time after 1965, influenced by both the results of Vatican II and by new educational theories that emphasized methodology more than content. Moreover, the volunteer religion teachers of the parish who taught the CCD were ill prepared to teach the new method and content presented in the new texts. In addition, parents seemed less cooperative than before in bringing their children to CCD classes; thus, enrollments were reduced in proportion to the number of public school children in the parish. In general, the CCD became involved with the preparation of children for penance, First Communion, and Confirmation. On the other hand, adult education, such as Bible study groups, adult prayer groups, the Rite of Christian Initiation for Adults (RCIA), as well as sacramental programs for the parents of children to be baptized, receive First Communion, be Confirmed, proliferated in most Southeast parishes. But, except for those sacramental programs where parental attendance was required, nonsacramentally oriented adult education programs produced mixed results and unspectacular attendance. In spite of the new CCD texts, the new CCD organization, the new pedagogy, and the new adult education programs, these efforts at socialization did not seem to produce the desired effects quantitatively or qualitatively.[24] Perhaps a strictly intellectual, rational, formal approach (more classes, more programs, more structure) to post-Vatican II education was not the answer.

In the 1950s, it was generally assumed that a parish in the Southeast also would have a school. During the period from 1960 to 1980, Catholics continued to believe in the concept of Catholic education, which, it was felt, provided religious education, discipline, and better academic training. In this period, some parents sent their children to Catholic parochial school for other reasons—namely, to avoid integration and bussing.[25] Although, theoretically, Catholic parochial education was supported, statistics indicate that the number of parochial schools and students dropped from 1960 to 1980, as the next chart indicates. Although the number of parochial schools in the Southeast decreased by only 4.8%, the number of parochial school students dropped by 30.4%. Even in Florida, the general population grew by 96.8% from 1960 to 1980, while the Catholic population grew by 190.2%, whereas the Catholic school population grew by only 7.3%.[26]

**Parochial Schools and Students by State 1960–1980**

| State | Parochial Schools 1960 | Students 1960 | Parochial Schools 1980 | Students 1980 | (1960–1980) Loss/Gain Schools | Loss/Gain Students |
|---|---|---|---|---|---|---|
| Delaware | 32 | 14,630 | 25 | 9,856 | − 21.9% | − 32.6% |
| District of Columbia | 68 | 41,032 | 76 | 24,196 | + 11.8% | − 41.0% |
| Florida | 104 | 47,671 | 136 | 51,165 | + 30.8% | + 7.3% |
| Georgia | 36 | 9,966 | 29 | 8,947 | − 19.4% | − 10.2% |
| Maryland | 101 | 56,970 | 83 | 25,632 | − 17.8% | − 55.0% |
| North Carolina | 54 | 8,932 | 36 | 8,527 | − 33.3% | − 4.5% |
| South Carolina | 31 | 4,082 | 32 | 6,361 | − 3.2% | + 55.8% |
| Virginia | 52 | 30,216 | 50 | 16,258 | − 3.8% | − 46.2% |
| West Virginia | 48 | 11,858 | 34 | 5,846 | − 29.2% | − 50.7% |

One can only speculate at this point as to why many Catholics, theoretically, posited the value of Catholic education, yet, in fact, attendance in both CCD classes and, particularly, Catholic schools was on the decline. An obvious explanation for the waning of attendance was the smaller number of school-aged children because of a decline in the birth rate in the 1960s. Yet, this is only a partial explanation. Catholic parochial schools that had reinforced and preserved the immigrant culture no longer filled this function. The new Hispanic immigrants of the 1960s, the 1970s, and the 1980s did not have their own Hispanic schools, but were integrated into existing parochial schools. After 1960, black schools were mostly either closed or integrated with white schools. One example of the effect of the closing of black parochial schools can be seen with Our Lady of Lourdes School, Baltimore, Maryland. The black parish was at its height with 850 parishioners in 1973. With the closing of the parish school in that year, families of the parish left, reducing parish membership to 250. In addition, like almost everything else sacred or profane, the general purpose and reason for parochial schools was called into question in the 1960s. Part of that questioning provoked many religious women, who had been teaching in parochial schools, to move into other kinds of ministry in the Church. Thus, the dedicated cadre of women religious teachers in parochial schools declined because of personnel shortages or personal choice. As a result, some parochial schools closed; others continued with lay staffs. Moreover, the costs of parochial education rose after 1960, not only because the parish had to hire more lay teachers for the schools, but also because education costs in general skyrocketed as a result of demands placed on the schools by new educational standards and accrediting agencies. Some parishes simply had to get out of the business of education because they could not afford to subsidize the schools. In the past, a parish elementary school could be run on small salaries, few capital expenditures, and a limited number of educational materials (sometimes just chalk, a blackboard, and desks with pen, ink, paper, and a few standard texts). Now, by means of law and accrediting associations, government agencies and public education institutions were dictating the rules about education policies and standards, which could only be met with the resources of a broad tax base and private endowments. Furthermore, some Catholic parents were no longer interested in supporting Catholic schools because they themselves were indifferent about their faith, or could no longer afford the tuition, or felt that the specifically Catholic dimension of parochial education was being co-opted. The Diocese of Savannah noted recently that in a test given to all eighth grade students in parochial schools, their weakest area was religion.[27]

One additional change occurred in parochial education after 1960. Whereas many parish schools were characterized especially before 1940 with having a considerable Protestant population, after 1960 this phenomenon began to disappear with few exceptions. North Carolina had the highest Protestant population in its parochial schools in the Southeast region. In 1960, 23.9% of its parochial students were Protestants or Jews; in 1980, 36% were of other religions. North Carolina had the lowest percentage of Catholics to the general population than any state in the region. In the Diocese of Savannah in 1980, 22% of the parochial school students were Protestants and Jews. About 2.9% of the general population were Catholic in the Savannah Diocese. In Maryland and South Florida, percentages of people of other religious faiths in the parochial schools are much lower (less than 5%) and the ratio of Catholics to those of other faiths is much higher (10% and 25%, respectively).[28]

The Catholic family, CCD programs, and the parochial schools did not seem to be doing the job of socialization they once had done. One indication of the decline in the traditional sources of parochial socialization can be seen in convert statistics. From 1960 to 1980, the number of converts in the Southeast dropped by 2.9%, while the overall general population increased by 37.8%. In North Carolina, the general population increased by 29.1%, while converts decreased by 9.6%. The District of Columbia showed the greatest convert decrease by 37.5%, although the general population there (mostly black) increased by 35.1%. Florida showed the greatest increase in converts, 65.1%, with a general population increase of 96.8% from 1960 to 1980. Nevertheless, new forms of parish life seemed to be more successful at the task of socialization. Through parish sacramental programs, *Cursillos,* Marriage Encounters, charismatic prayer groups, and other such movements, the faith was renewed and revitalized—a task formerly achieved by the parish mission. Although the purpose of these movements was to revive the faith of individuals and get them involved in the life of the parish, in particular instances the movements became ends unto themselves, whereby people's loyalties were attached more to the movement than to the parish. Some pastors were unwilling to utilize the newly revived faith of the laity, consequently frustrating people toward the movements with parish life and encouraging them to turn and seek other support groups for spiritual sustenance and Christian activity.[29]

The relations between Catholics and those of other faiths, before 1960, were described earlier as generally cordial and ecumenical on the practical level. The gradual trend of increased numbers of mixed marriages in the region continued to grow slightly during the 1960 to 1980 period. In 1960, about 56% of the number of marriages in the South Atlantic region were mixed; by 1980, about 60% of the total Catholic marriages were mixed.[30]

The general atmosphere favoring ecumenism improved after 1960 because of the more liberal attitude in society created by the American cultural events of the 1960s, and the official endorsement of ecumenical gestures on the part of Vatican II. Bishops, for the first time, encouraged ecumenical dialogue with Protestants and also tried to encourage activities of mutual interest between Catholics and other Christian denominations. This meant, in some cases, pulpit exchanges, ecumenical Thanksgiving and Easter services, and mutual charitable projects. One Catholic parish in Virginia (Holy Apostles, Norfolk—beginning in 1977) even shares its chapel with an Episcopal parish, a joint effort called the Anglican-Roman Catholic Congregation of Tidewater.[31]

Nevertheless, the entire ecumenical picture in the Southeast was not positive. Beginning around 1970, fundamentalist churches, including some Southern Baptists, began to articulate a militancy by a skillful use of the media, and by means of blatant proselytization and even anti-Catholicism, especially directed to youth and immigrants. Given the spiritual and cultural upheaval experienced by many Catholics from 1960 and the religious disorientation that resulted, aggressive fundamentalism has been viewed by some, especially those working among recent

Hispanic and Haitian immigrants in South Florida, as a particular pastoral problem for Catholics. As a result, ecumenical efforts have been weakened. Some fundamentalist Protestant churches have set themselves up in Hispanic and Haitian enclaves, purposely giving themselves such misleading titles as "The Orthodox Catholic Church of St. Barbara," "The Church of St. Lazarus," and "The National Catholic Church." Evangelical storefront churches have cropped up throughout Miami, catering to unchurched Hispanic and Haitian immigrants. From 1967 to 1980 in Miami, Baptist baptisms increased by 225%. As of 1978, Miami had the largest number of Baptist baptisms of any city in the world.[32]

Popular piety is another area of parish communal life that has experienced the tremors and shifts associated with the spiritual earthquake of Vatican II, and the cultural upheaval of the post-1960 era. Liturgical and devotional transformations occurred, which have no counterpart in the history of American Catholicism.

Alterations in the structure of the liturgy took place as a result of mandates from Vatican Council II, from the U.S. Bishops' Conference, and from local ordinances. The shift in emphasis from devotional to liturgical piety that resulted took place relatively rapidly. In about four years, the structural requirements of the new liturgy were in place—priest and altar facing the people, liturgy in the vernacular, a restoration of the more ancient order of Mass and liturgical functions shared by different ministers, and an increased participation of the people in the liturgy through various liturgical roles, through liturgical dialogue, and through liturgical congregational music.

Although they had little preparation for the seismic shift in which they had little say, the laity seemed to adapt to the liturgical changes with equanimity—weekly Communions and daily Mass attendance increased, while more laity exercised more liturgical roles. The faithful took a renewed interest in the sermon, with its new liturgical emphasis on a homily based on the Scriptural texts of the day. Besides the renewal of the Mass, other liturgical revisions made significant differences in the expressions of popular piety. All of the sacramental rites of the Church were revised by 1978 by means of a unified set of liturgical principles. In addition to these changes in the sacramental rites, communal penitential rites and Bible vigils were added to the liturgical repertoire. Yet, in spite of all of this liturgical variety, Mass was said more frequently in the parish than ever before. More Masses were added on the weekend for the convenience of parishioners, including Saturday Vigil Masses. Mass was also celebrated in parishioners' homes on weekdays, after retreats or at parish renewals, for a myriad of parish groups and organizations, and in conjunction with the different lay renewal movements, such as *Cursillo* and Marriage Encounter.[33]

Yet, despite all of the positive aspects of the liturgical reforms, certain signs indicate that this dramatic shift in the style and content of Catholic piety has not been as smooth as might have appeared at first. The pre-Vatican II model of spirituality characterized by a variety of private devotions was replaced in some instances with nothing. In many parishes, devotional statues were removed by individual parish priests, often with little or no explanation or consultation. Many of the trappings of the privatized pre-1960 devotional life of the faithful (novenas, patronal statues, the Rosary, First Friday, Forty Hours, Stations of the Cross, Benediction) were removed or ceased with little put in their places, besides more Masses and sacramental rites.[34]

Although the new liturgical piety provided an enriched spiritual environment, ironically at the very time implementation of the new liturgy was being completed (*Missale Romanum*, 1970), Mass attendance and participation in the Sacrament of Penance declined. The quality of the spiritual life of some Catholics was being deepened by the new liturgical piety, while the number of Catholics participating in these rites seemed to be declining, at least from 1950 levels. Mass attendance at most parishes averaged about 50% in 1980. Changes in the new liturgy, changes in the formerly legalistic view about Mass attendance, and changes in the social and moral climate in American society have all contributed to a decline of attendance since the 1950s. Perhaps this fact can be relativized if one considers that, up to about 1940, parish life throughout most of the Southeast had a missionary quality about it, and many Catholics scattered about the coastal countryside did not have the opportunity for weekly Mass. Perhaps weekly attendance for Catholics, up to 1940, was about 50% of the total number of Catholics, even though the reasons for nonattendance before 1940 might have been due to the unavailability of a priest. There seems to be enough evidence for the lukewarm character of Southeastern Catholics to suggest that lack of availability was not the only factor.[35] More study needs to be done on statistics and attitudes of Catholics in the Southeast, regarding Mass attendance and the new liturgy.

Pastors throughout the Southeast point to the decline in the number of confessions in the parish, a phenomenon that follows a national trend. Recall that Cardinal Shehan as a young priest in Washington in the 1920s viewed hearing confessions as one of the primary tasks of the priest. This decline in the reception of Penance was observed even before the new rite of Penance was implemented in 1977. In an unscientific readers' poll conducted by *U.S. Catholic Magazine* in 1982, while 68% of the respondents rated the Sacrament of Penance important in their lives and preferred the new rite, and 91% felt the need for a sacrament of forgiveness, only 24% received Penance more than a few times in the year.

Why are people staying away from the Sacrament of Reconciliation, even with the new rite? Indications seem to point to cultural and post-conciliar attitudinal shifts regarding people's view of sin, the new rite itself, and their perception of the priesthood. Some Catholics don't consider sin as prevalent in their lives as before, since they feel that serious sin is difficult for ordinary people to commit. Influenced by the new morality of American culture, some do not feel that the

Church's moral teaching has any relevance for them. For some, the new rite demands a moral sensitivity and a willingness to dialogue to a degree that they have not developed or have little interest in developing. In the past, some Catholics went to confession as a devotional act, as they said the Rosary or lit a candle. With the shift from devotionalism, so came the shift away from regular confession. For others, the main problem is the priest. Some feel that they can receive forgiveness from God and do not need a priest. Some extreme feminists are affronted at confessing to a man (priest). Others have had bad experiences in the past with tactless, insensitive confessors, whose impatience found their sins trivial. Certainly, the revised rite of Penance, like the new liturgy, has put new demands on priests, demands which many of them were unprepared to meet. Before 1960, the priest in the confessional was more of a judge of attitudes and intentions. It was not unusual to hear thirty confessions in one hour. With the new rite of Penance, hearing confessions is more akin to spiritual direction and discernment of spirits. The personality and spirituality of a priest shines forth in his pastoral solicitude for the penitent, especially with the face to face option. Today, a priest might only be able to hear three confessions in an hour. Many priests were simply not trained for, or personally inclined toward, the new demands of their penitential role. In any case, the phenomenon of the decline in the reception of Penance also needs to be studied more carefully.[36]

Some new forms of popular piety have arisen from the ashes of the old devotionalism. Those active in the movements, for example *Cursillistas,* have developed a Eucharistic and prayerful spirituality as a result of their initial experience and continued attendance at support groups (*ultreyas*). People from some of the movements, especially *Cursillistas,* have asked for priests to be their spiritual directors. Charismatic prayer groups have been another source of new piety for some in the Southeast, as elsewhere in the country. For many laity, their new-found liturgical roles have been a source of piety.[37] Although for some the quality of their spiritual life has deepened as a result of the new liturgical piety, the number of people experiencing this new piety may indeed by quantitatively less than those affected by the older devotionalism. Of course, piety and its effects are elusive to measure. The phenomenon of the "spiritual earthquake" and different expressions of piety are only twenty years old, and as one experienced pastor has put it, "It will take a long time for us to know what has happened to us."[38]

## F. ETHNIC EXPRESSIONS OF PARISH

With the rise of the Civil Rights Movement in the early 1960s, the consciousness of all ethnic groups was raised, including Catholic ethnics. One example is the Italians of St. Leo's. In the 1960s, when families and businesses began leaving downtown Baltimore to flee to the suburbs, the residents of Little Italy and St. Leo's Italian Parish didn't budge. Italian parochial pride bristled over the issues of the possible closing of the parochial school, and the proposed path of an interstate highway that was to lop off a corner of Little Italy. Several Italian–American community organizations were formed to address both of the issues. Even though the parish school was eventually closed (1980), the vitality of the neighborhood quickened and the parish flourished. In 1967, St. Leo's Italian Festival began and a weekly Italian Mass was resumed, a sign of renewed ethnic pride.[39]

Another ethnic group that seemed to rediscover its roots as a result of political and cultural events of the 1960s was the Lebanese. Even though they had begun coming to the Southeast in appreciable numbers since the turn of the century, most were never able to establish parishes in their own rites, but attended Latin Rite churches. Unlike most ethnic groups that came to the United States, the Lebanese did not have their own priests to follow them. The new ethnic consciousness, as well as impetus from Vatican II, inspired the founding of several Eastern Rite Lebanese parishes, from 1960, in the Southeast, including: Our Lady of Lebanon—Maronite (Miami); St. Jude Melkite Catholic—Melkite (Miami); St. Michael's—Maronite (Fayetteville, North Carolina); Epiphany of Our Lord—Maronite (Annandale, Virginia); Holy Transfiguration—Melkite (McLean, Virginia).[40]

Many older ethnic parishes and groups of the region were assimilated into American culture to a great extent by 1960, as is demonstrated by the closing of national parish schools indicated in the following chart:[41]

**Selected Catholic Parishes in the Southeast**

| Year | German | | Polish | |
| --- | --- | --- | --- | --- |
|  | **Churches** | **Schools** | **Churches** | **Schools** |
| 1900 | 10 | 13 | 3 | 3 |
| 1930 | 8 | 3 | 8 | 8 |
| 1950 | 3 | 3 | 8 | 6 |
| 1960 | 3 | 3 | 8 | 6 |
| 1980 | 0 | 0 | 5 | 4 |

Most national parish groups from 1960 to 1980 went the way of the Irish before them, and became more Americanized as their parishioners became more assimilated.

Beginning around 1960, a new wave of Catholic immigrants found their way to the Southeast, namely Hispanics, and to a lesser extent Haitians and Vietnamese. Puerto Ricans, Mexicans, and Mexican-Americans began moving into the lower Southeast, especially into Florida, as seasonal farmworkers in the 1950s.

They presented a particular pastoral challenge because they were migrants, mostly unchurched, and victims of social injustice. A mobile ministry to migrant farmworkers, composed of Sisters of St. Joseph of St. Augustine and priests, was established as early as 1954 in South Florida. In the 1960s, a series of migrant missions, which were the equivalent of extra-territorial national parishes, was established in the Diocese of Miami.[42] By the 1970s, Georgia Catholicism was beginning to see the need for a Hispanic ministry to migrants. By far, the most significant Hispanic immigrant group of the post-1960 era was the Cubans. For social, political, and economic reasons, about 10% of the Cuban population left its island after 1959, as a result of the Marxist revolution of Fidel Castro. In 1960, 24,000 Cubans resided in Dade County (which includes Miami), a figure that represented 32.4% of the total Hispanics of the area. In 1970, just over 200,000 Cubans lived in Dade County, 42.1% of the total Hispanics there.

This sudden immigration of Cubans and other Hispanics into South Florida had some dramatic effects on parish life. In the space of a few years, parishes that were Anglo-American became thoroughly Hispanic. It was decided by Bishop (later Archbishop) Coleman F. Carroll that national parishes or schools would not be established as had been the case with German or Polish immigrants in the past. Instead, newcomers (both priests and people) were integrated into existing and new parishes.

Nonetheless, certain Miami parishes did turn out to be, in effect, Cuban national parishes, though not specifically designated as such. St. John Bosco Parish, Miami, is the archetype of the Cuban exile parish in Miami. Founded in 1963 as an urban mission of a nearby parish and named for a famous Havana parish, St. John Bosco took physical form from a remodeled downtown three-storied automobile dealership. By January of 1964, St. John Bosco had six Masses on Sunday, five of which were said in Spanish. Besides the Cuban-born pastor, the parish was staffed by an assistant pastor, three Cuban Christian Brothers, and several Mexican Guadalupanas Sisters. The religious brothers and sisters taught the CCD to the public school children of the parish, since a traditional parochial school did not exist. Continued renovation of the parochial structure took place under the direction of the pastor, Emilio Vallina. Since the pastor's parishioners, which numbered over 5,000 families, were of lower- and lower-middle income, unaccustomed to making weekly contributions through the envelope system, and since most of his parishioners did not attend Mass regularly, Vallina had to devise other means of raising the necessary funds to fuel his renovation projects. One of the most successful was a semiannual parish festival, the *tombola,* which, because it was held in the open in an area densely populated by Cubans, was well supported by both the churched and unchurched members of the parish.

From its inception, St. John Bosco was a unique place. Although technically a territorial parish, it drew people from different parts of Miami because either they preferred its Cuban style of operation, or they were former parishioners who, although now living outside of the parish boundaries, kept emotional ties with the parish. At a time when devotional piety was declining in most American parishes, St. John Bosco parishioners were openly expressive of their devotions to the saints, even while Sunday Mass was going on. In the rectory section of the parish edifice, phones rang constantly from 7 A.M. to 11:30 P.M., yet people rarely called for an appointment to see a priest. Instead, they simply showed up at the parish and waited in the reception room until a priest (preferably the pastor himself) saw them. Lay involvement was considerable and parish lay organizations (mostly involving some aspect of family life) proliferated, necessitating meetings at the church until late into the evening. Yet, with all of the lay activity, the pastor remained the ultimate director of the spiritual and physical destiny of the parish, although a great deal of diplomatic skill was exercised by him in order to balance the sometimes conflicting demands of different individuals and groups. Instead of a parochial school, St. John Bosco *Escuela Cívico-Religiosa* opened in 1967. Since it was not a parochial school subject to diocesan regulations (including the demand that classes be taught in English), St. John Bosco parents had the opportunity of having their children attend class conducted in Spanish on Cuban Catholicism and culture on Saturdays, and after their public school classes on weekdays. St. John Bosco was at the peak of its numerical strength and parochial activity in 1968.

Unlike many other Catholic immigrants who preceded them, Cubans and Hispanics were not primarily churchgoers; their lives did not revolve around the parish. Although some Cuban and Hispanic laity showed immense zeal and energy in initiating various support groups and evangelical groups based in the parish, such as *Cursillos, Encuentro Familiar,* and *Moviemiento Familiar Christiano,* the vast majority of Hispanics in South Florida were not touched by parish life, except through the Catholic schools, the Sacraments, or through a unique evangelical enterprise, the *Ermita* (the shrine to Our Lady of Charity, national patroness of Cuba), created by the energetic Reverend (now Bishop) Agustín Román.[43]

From April to June of 1980, another wave of Cuban immigrants came to the shores of South Florida, 120,000 so-called Mariel Cubans. About 1,300 Cubans arrived every day during those months, thus creating tremendous strains on the civic and ecclesial structures. The arrival of so many Hispanics on the South Florida peninsula from 1960 to 1980 created tensions and challenges for parochial life in the area—both for the arriving Hispanic immigrants and for the host peoples.

It should be noted that although South Florida was the focus of Hispanic immigration from 1960 to 1980, the Southeastern states in general saw considerable increases in their respective Hispanic populations. For example, from 1976 to 1980 the states of the Southeast saw the following percent of growth in Hispanics: Florida, 28%; Georgia, 166%; North Carolina, 5,561%; South Carolina, 457%.

As of 1980, Hispanics in the Southeast represented the total percentage of population as follows:[44]

**Percentage of Hispanics in the South Atlantic Region (1980)**

| State | Hispanics per Total Population | Per Catholic Population* |
|-------|-------------------------------|--------------------------|
| Delaware | 1.6% | 8.1% |
| District of Columbia | 2.8% | — |
| Florida | 8.8% | 63.4% |
| Georgia | 1.1% | 41.0% |
| Maryland | 1.5% | 15.7% |
| North Carolina | 1.0% | 59.9% |
| South Carolina | 1.0% | 56.6% |
| Virginia | 1.5% | 28.0% |
| West Virginia | 0.7% | 12.4% |

*It is highly probable that the percentages registered under "Per Catholic Population" are actually somewhat lower and don't reflect the true ratio of Hispanic to total Catholic population since Hispanic surnames may show up in the United States Censuses, but not in parish censuses; thus, Hispanics might not be fully incorporated into the total Catholic population figures.

Given the rapid increase of Spanish-speaking peoples in the region and their generally unchurched character (hence, the need for evangelization), the number of Hispanic priests in the Southeast is certainly not sufficient for the needs of the community. By 1980, in the Archdiocese of Miami, where Hispanic populations are the highest in the Southeast, thirty-three parishes (25.4%) were predominantly Hispanic; only seventy-two of the total of 508 priests (14.2%) were Hispanic. Miami represents the best ratio of Hispanic priests to Hispanic people (one to 9,314 Hispanic Catholics) in the Southeast region as of 1980.[45]

Two other new immigrant groups of lesser significance for the entire region moved into the Southeast during the 1970s: several hundred Vietnamese Catholics and thousands of Haitian Catholics. The Pierre Toussaint Center (Notre Dame d'Haiti Mission) for Haitians was opened in Miami in 1979. By 1982, eight missions, five stations, five priests, and two sisters worked in the Haitian apostolate in South Florida, where virtually all of the recent Haitian immigrants (since 1972) have been located. Both groups present a linguistic and cultural challenge for the Church since both have only a very few of their own priests to serve them.[46]

Continuities and discontinuities existed in ministry to American blacks of the Southeast from 1960 to 1980. Catholic parochial education for blacks continued to serve a predominantly Protestant constituency. Yet, at the same time, the number of black Catholic parishes and schools declined, as the following chart suggests:[47]

**Black Parishes and Schools in the Southeast**

| Year | Black Parishes | Black Parochial Schools |
|------|----------------|-------------------------|
| 1950 | 56 | 44 |
| 1960 | 44 | 33 |
| 1980 | * | * |

*Impossible to determine by the *Official Catholic Directory* since black parishes are not indicated as such.

In 1960, South Florida had five black parishes and eight black schools; by 1980, there were three black parishes and three predominantly black schools.

Continuities and discontinuities existed in the way the Church was responding to cultural trends. Bishops gradually moved to integrate parishes and schools in the Southeast, beginning with Bishop Vincent Waters at Newton Grove, North Carolina, in 1953. In the 1960s, by order of the diocesan bishop, most black schools and parishes were closed and integrated with white congregations, in response to the cultural, social, and legal climate of the time. In the Diocese of Savannah, every black parish and school was integrated.[48] On the other hand, little response was given on the part of the Southeastern hierarchy to the movement of black pride and black consciousness in the late 1960s.

These episcopal actions had ramifications not foreseen by the decision to integrate Catholic schools and parishes. First, integration almost always meant the closing of a black Catholic institution, either a parish or a school. Whites were not going to integrate a black parish, so blacks had to integrate the white parishes; consequently, black Catholic institutions were closed to facilitate this integration. What in fact was happening was that blacks were being forced to go to what had been and really remained white parishes and schools. Integration was not an option for blacks. If they wanted to remain Catholics, they had to go to somebody else's parish because theirs was closed.

Second, this integration came from the top down rather than from the bottom up. Blacks were rarely, if ever, consulted about what they preferred, regarding the closing of their Catholic institutions. At the very time when blacks were becoming more conscious of their African heritage, their black Catholic religious institutions were being closed.

Third, many black Catholics resented the closing of their parishes and schools because they took pride in institutions that they considered their own. Many still remembered the struggles they endured to establish their parishes and schools. Moreover, a considerable number of black middle income, professional, and community leaders in the Southeast received their elementary educations in black Catholic schools, and felt the loss of these institutions for the black community.

The majority of black Catholics preferred their own churches in their own neighborhoods. Some black Catholics, after their church was closed, so resented that action and having to go to another church, that they just dropped out of the Catholic Church altogether.[49]

Fourth, as a result of integration and the closing of black Catholic institutions, the Church lost an important presence in the black community where these institutions were located, especially keeping in mind the evangelical character of black Catholic schools that taught predominantly Protestants. It might be argued that some of these black churches and schools were used by their dioceses as centers for social welfare programs, such as Head Start or Neighborhood Youth Corps, sponsored by the Federal Government and the "War on Poverty." Nevertheless, everybody knew that these programs were of the government, bereft of any specifically defined Catholic religious dimension and diluted by a myriad of governmental regulations. Also, since government programs depend on government money, when "poverty program" funds dried up in the 1970s, Church involvement in the black community was blown away by a lack of funding or a lack of interest. The upshot of integration was a lack of Catholic presence in the black community in the Southeast.[50]

A concrete example of all of this is St. Joseph Parish in Richmond, Virginia. In the late 1860s, three white women began teaching Catechism to black children in Richmond. St. Francis School was begun in September of 1885 with four Sisters of St. Francis. St. Joseph's Church, staffed by the Josephite Fathers, was dedicated in November of 1885. In 1887, an industrial school was started; in 1893, an orphanage began; and in 1910, Van De Vyver Grammar and High School opened. A great vitality and pride exuded from the parish; three other black parishes were formed from St. Joseph's. Then, in 1952, the Bishop of Richmond decided to integrate Cathedral High School and close Van De Vyver High. Since only blacks with high achievement in academics or athletics were accepted into Cathedral High School, most former Van De Vyver students had to go to public school. The next assault on the parish came from the Housing Authority and later the Turnpike Authority. The black community of the parish became a victim of urban renewal, removal, and nonchalance. Many black families moved out of the area. In 1969, St. Joseph's was closed by order of the bishop. The parish complex became a community center. St. Joseph's Church was torn down and Van De Vyver High School burned in 1973. In 1977, Richmond's only remaining black Catholic church, Holy Rosary, had 300 members while an estimated 25,000 black Catholics lived in the city. Integration, urban demographic shifts, and upper level ecclesial decisions all conspired to truncate the history of St. Joseph's Parish.[51] There is a sadness to this story that goes beyond the facts of the case. A number of former parishioners felt hurt and betrayed by it all. As one parishioner wrote: "The tears of the people soaked the earth. They cried, 'Many will be lost.' And it was true."[52]

In all fairness, bishops who made the decision to close black schools and parishes did so in good faith and for good reasons. When public institutions were being integrated, the Church in the Southeast could ill afford to appear segregationist. Also, the financial crunch of urban parishes was a reality that could not be overlooked. Some blacks had moved up and out of their former neighborhoods, crime rates rose in the inner city, neighborhoods became delapidated, urban renewal and expressways displaced many, education costs escalated, and socioeconomic changes transformed formerly all-white parishes or schools into *de facto* black parishes and schools. Such was the case at St. Patrick's Church and School, Charleston, South Carolina; St. Katherine's Church and School, Baltimore; St. Mary's Cathedral and School, Miami; and St. John the Baptist Cathedral School, Charleston, South Carolina.[53]

Although the decision to close black parishes and schools was usually made with the conviction that such a move represented the values of the Gospel and racial justice, entwined with these more principled motivations were economic and social pressures that tended to obfuscate the responsibility of pastoral care. Church leaders need to be circumspect in following cultural trends or economic exigencies, as well as consultative in their decision-making. Black parishes and schools were not established in the Southeast primarily as a means of emulating Southern culture and racial segregation, but as a means of reaching the black community on the local level. Black Catholics appreciated these institutions, preferred them over being treated like second class citizens in white churches, and appropriated them as their own. Historically, black Catholic parishes and schools in the Southeast provided a specifically Catholic presence within the local black community; that presence in many cases is now lost.

## CONCLUSION

The marrow of Catholicism is concentrated at its most localized and accessible level—the parish—which continues to be the most significant, most vital structure in Roman Catholicism, as the Committee on the Parish of the National Conference of Catholic Bishops has recently indicated:

> The parish is for most Catholics the single most important part of the Church. This is where for them the mission of Christ continues. This is where they publicly express their faith, joining with others to give proof of their communion with God and with one another.[1]

The vitality of the parish has endured, although this is not to say that parish life in the Southeast remained the same over the last 130 years. For the first ninety years, the locale, size, organizational complexity, and priorities of the parish in the Southeast remained more or less static, while parish communal life and ethnic expressions did move with the permutations of American culture, with the exception of Catholic piety (devotionalism). With the cultural upheavals of the 1960s and the "spiritual earthquake" created by Vatican Council II, the pastoral terrain shifted dramatically. The most outstanding shift occurred with the emphasis on liturgical piety over devotional piety, the increase of lay involvement in parish decision-making and ministry, the new vision of the priesthood and the Church, the arrival of new Catholic ethnic groups, and the shift in the apostolate to black Americans. Without question, the last twenty years have created a very new situation for Southeast Catholics as a result of dramatic theological, demographic, economic, and cultural changes. The signs of change seem to flash conflicting signals. On the one hand, the laity is more deeply involved in parish life and more critical of it than ever before, yet, on the other hand, the majority of Catholics either are not involved intimately in parish life beyond Sunday Mass or have stopped going to Mass altogether. Moreover, the Church has taken a much more benign view toward American culture, though it finds itself in conflict with that culture in its stands on marriage, abortion, contraception, capital punishment, and nuclear war. One could go through a litany of contradictory signs in the post-Vatican II age. Historically, it is much too early to be able to read these signals clearly.

And yet, in spite of all of these rapid alterations, other aspects of Southeastern parish life demonstrate continuities with the past, continuities that give a sense of stability and identity (that is, something that perdures through change).[2] To see these links with the past, one must go beyond comparing our present situation with only the 1950s or the early 1960s (as is often done when people bemoan the "vocation crisis" or the declension in Church attendance). When we look over the last 130 years of the history of Catholicism, we can see a number of important continuities: the centrality of the parish itself in Catholic life; the formative influence of the family and of women, in particular, in the quality and texture of parish life; and the significance of leadership (episcopal, sacerdotal, religious, and lay) in the development and vital expression of parish communal life. Parochial life in the Southeast has some specific characteristics that also provide an anchor of continuity in the midst of a sea of change: its missionary character (a poverty of resources, population, and personnel, yet a flexible, even creative response to pastoral challenges); an evangelical, Protestant cultural milieu; a historical consciousness and a Southeastern cultural heritage; the prevailing presence of black Americans whose poverty and unjust treatment constantly call forth a pastoral response; the rural values of people over things that have permeated Southern culture; and the constant need for institutional building. At a time when political and social trends, as well as official ecclesial documents, call for a renewed interest in the uniqueness of the local community, bishops, priests, religious, and laypeople need to be more aware of the historical tradition from which they have come. This understanding of their connections with the past will give them hope for the present and future, will enable them to see their peculiar place in South-eastern society and in American Catholicism as a gift they have to give to both that society and that religious tradition, and will empower them to articulate a vision of the human community for their time, one in which:

> Every valley shall be filled in,
>   every mountain and hill shall be made low;
> The rugged land shall be made a plain,
>   the rough country, a broad valley.
> Then the glory of the Lord shall be revealed,
>   and all mankind shall see it together.
>
> (*Isaiah* 40:4–5, *New American Bible* translation)

## Notes

1. Ideas for this summary were taken from several sources, among them: William E. Leuchtenburg, *A Troubled Feast: America Since 1945* (Boston: Little Brown, 1973); William O'Neill, *Coming Apart: An Informal History of America in the 1960's* (Chicago: Quadrangle Press, 1971); Theodore H. White "Summing Up," *New York Times Magazine,* April 25, 1982, 32ff; John Tracy Ellis, "American Catholics and the Intellectual Life," *Thought* (Autumn, 1955), 355–388; Andrew M. Greeley, *The American Catholic: A Social Portrait* (New York: Basic Books, 1977); Philip Gleason, "Catholicism and Cultural Change in the 1960's," *Review of Politics,* 33 (1972), 91–107; Donald B. Dodd and Wynelle S. Dodd, *Historical Statistics of the South, 1790–1970* (University, Alabama: University of Alabama, 1973), 14–76.

2. John L. Androit, comp. and ed., *Population Abstract of the United States,* Vol. 2 (McLean, Va.: Androit Press, 1983), 243; John L. Androit, comp. and ed., *Population Abstract of the United States,* Vol. 1 (McLean, Va.: Androit Press, 1983), 108, 115, 120, 139, 346, 566, 708, 820, 854; William J. Easton, Jr., ed., *Rand McNally 1983 Commercial Atlas and Marketing Guide* (Chicago: Rand McNally, 1983), 94.

3. John Shelton Reed, *The Enduring South: Subcultural Persistence in Mass Society* (Chapel Hill, N.C.: University of North Carolina, 1982); David R. Goldfield, "The Urban South: A Regional Framework," *American Historical Review,* 86 (December, 1981), 1009–1034; James C. Cobb, *The Selling of the South: The Southern Crusade for Industrial Development, 1936–1980* (Baton Rouge: Louisiana State University, 1982). See also: Numan V. Bartley, "Writing about the Post-World War II South," *Georgia Historical Quarterly,* 68 (Spring, 1984), 1–18; James C. Cobb, "Cracklin's and Caviar: The Enigma of Sunbelt Georgia," *Georgia Historical Quarterly,* 68 (Spring, 1984), 19–39; Bradley R. Rice, "Urbanization, 'Atlantaization,' and Suburbanization: Three Themes for the Urban History of Twentieth Century Georgia," *Georgia Historical Quarterly,* 68 (Spring, 1984), 40–59; James C. Cobb, *Industrialization and Southern Society, 1877–1984* (Lexington: University Press of Kentucky, 1984).

4. Dodd and Dodd, *Historical Statistics of the South,* 14–76, 854; Androit, *Popu-*

*lation Abstract,* Vol. 2, 94, 108, 115, 120, 139, 243, 346, 360–387, 566, 708, 820; *OCD,* 1900; 1950; 1960; 1980.

5. Dodd and Dodd, *Historical Statistics of the South,* 14–76; Androit, *Population Abstract,* Vol. 2, 243; *OCD,* 1960; 1980.

6. ADS, FB1, "Apostolic Delegation, 1959–60"; Diocese of Savannah, Office of Chancellor, Quinquennial, 1978–82; Interview, Rev. Kevin Boland, V.G., Savannah, May 26, 1983; Interview, Rev. Herbert Wellmeier, Savannah, May 27, 1983; Archdiocese of Miami, Office of Chancellor, Official Catholic Directory, 1980, File; "Parish Profiles"; Interview, Rev. Michael Smith, Savannah, May 24, 1983; Interview, Rev. David Russell, Boynton Beach, Fla., December 5, 1983.

7. Interview, Msgr. Patrick Madden, Jacksonville, Fla., June 30, 1983; Interview, Msgr. Daniel Burke, Savannah, May 24, 1983; *Voice,* January 12, March 16, December 28, 1962; AFAM, Office of Archivist, "Five Year Report, 1964–68."

8. "Corpus Christi School-Silver Jubilee, 1973"; AFAM, Office of Chancellor, Corpus Christi File; Diocese of Savannah, Office of Chancellor, Quinquennial Report, 1957–62; AFAM, Office of Chancellor, "Parish Profiles."

9. Lawrence Cardinal Shehan, *A Blessing of Years: The Memoirs of Lawrence Cardinal Shehan* (Notre Dame, Ind.: University of Notre Dame, 1982), 207, 224–233; Michael J. McNally, *Catholicism in South Florida, 1868–1968* (Gainesville, Fla.: University Presses of Florida, 1984), 170–76, 197–212.

10. Interview, Rev. Daniel Cody, Mandarin, Fla., June 30, 1983; Diocese of Savannah, Office of the Chancellor, Rev. Frederick Nijem to Sister Mary Laurent, November 18, 1982; Quinquennial, 1978–82; Interview, Rev. Boland; "Golden Jubilee-St. Mary's-on-the-Hill, 1919–1969"; *A People of Faith: A Brief History* (Savannah: Southern Cross, 1978), 41–42; AFAM, Office of Chancellor, "Parish Profiles"; Diocese of Raleigh, Office of Chancellor, Quinquennial Report, 1969–73.

11. "Holy Family Church, Columbus, Ga."

12. "Constitution and By-Laws of the Administrative Council of St. Gabriel's Parish, Greenville, N.C. (April 10, 1983)"; "St. Katherine Parish Evaluation Report, July 21, 1976"; AFAM, Chancellor's Office, Parish Council File; "Parish Profiles"; ADS, "Diocesan Policies and Guidelines," n.d., 104–105; *OCD,* 1971; M. Jennifer Glenn, "Ethnographic Impressions—St. Mary of the Assumption Church, Pylesville, Md.," November 6, 1983; Kimberly Baldt Numan, "Ethnographic Sketch—Holy Infant Church, Elkton, Va.," October 27, 1983.

13. McNally, *Catholicism in South Florida,* 200–201; Interview, Rev. Francis R. Moeslein, Wake Forest, N.C., June 7, 1983; Interview, Msgr. Daniel Burke; Rev. Boland; Rev. Wellmeier; Msgr. Patrick Madden; Rev. Cody; Diocese of Savannah, Office of Chancellor, Quinquennial, 1978–82. See also: Philip J. Murnion, *The Catholic Priest and the Changing Structure of Pastoral Ministry, New York, 1920–1970* (New York: Arno, 1978); Joseph M. White, "American Diocesan Seminaries, 1791 to the 1980's," *American Catholic Studies Newsletter,* 10 (Fall, 1984), 12–16.

14. Interview, Msgr. Dominic Barry, Pompano Beach, Fla., September 25, 1981; Rev. Moeslein; Rev. Wellmeier; Msgr. Burke; Diocese of St. Augustine, Office of the Chancellor, Quinquennial, 1974–77; Diocese of Raleigh, Office of Chancellor, Quinquennial (draft) 1980–84; Diocese of Savannah, Office of Chancellor, Quinquennial,

1978–82; Archdiocese of Miami, Office of Chancellor, Quinquennial, 1964–68; 1968–74; "Statistics"; *OCD*, 1950; 1960; 1965; 1968; 1970; 1980.

15. *Boston Pilot*, November 9, 1968; Diocese of Savannah, Office of Chancellor, Quinquennial; 1968–73; Interview, Rev. James Fetcher, Kendall, Fla., September 8, 1983; Rev. Wellmeier; Diocese of Savannah, Office of the Chancellor, Rev. Nijem to Sister Laurent, November 18, 1982; Diocese St. Augustine, Office of Chancellor, Quinquennial, 1978–82.

16. ADC, Folder 600.32, St. Andrew's Parish; McNally, *Catholicism in South Florida*, 176–81; "Immaculate Conception (Hialeah)"; *OCD*, 1950; 1960; 1965; 1968; 1970; 1980.

17. "Immaculate Conception (Hialeah)"; "St. Mary's Church, Hagerstown, Md."; Diocese of St. Augustine, Office of Chancellor, Quinquennial, 1974–77; Diocese of Savannah, Office of Chancellor, Quinquennial, 1978–82; McNally, *Catholicism in South Florida*, 205–207; M. Jennifer Glenn, "Ethnographic Impressions—St. Mary of the Assumption Church, Pylesville, Md.," November 6, 1983.

18. Diocese of Savannah, Office of Chancellor, Quinquennial, 1978–82; Diocese of St. Augustine, Office of Chancellor, Quinquennial, 1974–77; Interview, Rev. Cody.

19. For example, the St. Pius X Society, although small and widely scattered in the Southeast, was transplanted from the North and supported by mostly recent arrivals to the area. Diocese of Savannah, Office of Chancellor, Rev. William A. Smith, to Sister Mary Laurent, December 5, 1982; Diocese of St. Augustine, Office of Chancellor, Quinquennial, 1974–77; AJF, Wilmington, Del., St. Joseph Church; Greely, *The American Catholic*, 126–151; Interview, Rev. Wellmeier; Rev. Cody.

20. Interview, Rev. Wellmeier; Msgr. Patrick Madden; Rev. Moeslein; Rev. Cody; Rev. Boland; Msgr. Daniel Burke; Diocese of Savannah, Office of Chancellor, Quinquennial, 1974–77; Diocese of Raleigh, Office of Chancellor, Quinquennial, 1980–84.

21. Diocese of Savannah, Office of Chancellor, Rev. John Marquardt to Sister Mary Laurent, December 5, 1982; Quinquennial, 1974–77; 1978–82; Diocese of St. Augustine, Office of Chancellor, Quinquennial, 1974–77; Greely, *The American Catholic*, 186–212.

22. Diocese of St. Augustine, Office of Chancellor, Quinquennial, 1978–82; Diocese of Savannah, Office of Chancellor, Quinquennial, 1974–77; Diocese of Raleigh, Office of Chancellor, 1980–84 (draft); AFAM, Marriage Tribunal, Tribunal Staff to Rev. Andrew Anderson (memo), October 5, 1981.

23. Diocese of Raleigh, Office of Chancellor, Quinquennial, 1980–84 (draft); *OCD*, 1980.

24. Diocese of St. Augustine, Office of Chancellor, Quinquennial, 1974–77; Diocese of Savannah, Office of Chancellor, Quinquennial, 1974–77; 1978–82; ADC, Folder 600.46; St. Peter's, Beaufort; "St. Mary's Church, Annapolis."

25. Interview, Rev. Moeslein; Rev. Cody; Rev. Wellmeier.

26. *OCD*, 1960; 1980; Dodd and Dodd, *Historical Statistics of the South*, 14–63; Androit, *Population Abstract*, Vol. 2, 243.

27. AFAM, Office of Chancellor, Official Catholic Directory, 1980, File; Corpus Christi Parish File; Holy Name Parish File; "Parish Profiles"; "Corpus Christi School-Silver Jubilee, 1973"; ADC, Folder 600.25; 601.1; 601.24; 601.47; 603.1; 605.25; 606.35; Diocese of Savannah, Office of Chancellor, Statistics of Elementary Schools,

1967–83; Quinquennial, 1978–82; AJF, St. Joseph's Mission File, Norfolk, Va. See also: William E. Brown and Andrew M. Greeley, *Can Catholic Schools Survive?* (New York: Sheed and Ward 1970); Greely, *The American Catholic*, 164–186; Kimberly Baldt Numan, "Ethnographic Sketch—Our Lady of Lourdes, Baltimore, Md.," November 15, 1983.

28. ADRa, Quinquennial, 1959–63; Diocese of Raleigh, Office of Chancellor, Quinquennial, 1980–84; "Long Range Study of the Apostolic Missions of the Sisters of St. Francis of Philadelphia, 1981–1991," April 22, 1983; AFAM, Chancellor's Office, Corpus Christi Parish File; Diocese of Savannah, Office of Chancellor, Catholic School Statistics, 1968–82.

29. *OCD*, 1960; 1980; Interview, Bishop Agustín Román, Miami, September 11, October 17, 1981; Interview, Rev. Russell.

30. Southeast Regional Office for Hispanic Affairs, "Hispanic Demography by Diocese, 1980"; *OCD*, 1960; 1980.

31. Interview, Rev. Boland; Msgr. Richard Madden; Rev. Moeslein; Diocese of Savannah, Chancellor's Office, Quinquennial, 1978–82; Diocese of Savannah, Office of Chancellor, Quinquennial, 1968–73; 1974–77; Diocese of Raleigh, Office of Chancellor, Quinquennial, 1980–84.

32. Diocese of Savannah, Office of Chancellor, Quinquennial, 1974–77; 1978–82; Diocese of St. Augustine, Office of Chancellor, Quinquennial, 1978–82; AFAM, Office of Chancellor, Corpus Christi Parish File; Spanish Apostolate-Popular Piety File; Interview, Msgr. Patrick Madden; Rev. Cody; *Miami Herald*, October 24, 1978; *National Catholic Reporter*, March 21, 1980; *Origins*, September 11, 1980.

33. Diocese of Savannah, Office of Chancellor, Quinquennial, 1974–77; "Blessed Sacrament, Savannah"; Diocese of St. Augustine, Office of Chancellor, Quinquennial, 1974–77; 1978–82; Interview, Msgr. Richard Madden; McNally, *Catholicism in South Florida*, 172–74, 207.

34. Interview, Msgr. Patrick Madden; Interview, Bishop John Nevins, Miami, September 30, 1981; Interview, Msgr. John O'Dowd, South Miami, October 10, 1981; Interview, Rev. Russell; Diocese of Savannah, Office of Chancellor, Quinquennial, 1978–82.

35. "Gallup Study Says Catholics Have 47% Not Going to Mass," *Our Sunday Visitor*, November 30, 1975, 3; Interview, Rev. Russell; Diocese of Savannah, Office of Chancellor, 1978–82.

36. James P. Brieg, "What U.S. Catholic Readers Think About Confession," *U.S. Catholic*, October, 1982, 6–9; Thomas Frisbie, "The New Confession: Who's Sorry Now?"; *U.S. Catholic*, January, 1981, 18–21; David Sutor, "10 Reasons Why Catholics Have Stopped Going to Confession," *U.S. Catholic*, May, 1981, 6–9; Interview, Rev. Russell.

37. Diocese of Raleigh, Office of Chancellor, Quinquennial, 1969–73; Diocese of Savannah, Office of Chancellor, Quinquennial, 1974–77; *A People of Faith-A Brief History*, 43; "St. Mary's Church, Annapolis"; Interview, Rev. Moeslein; Rev. Boland.

38. Interview, Msgr. Patrick Madden.

39. "The Church of St. Leo The Great, 1881–1981."

40. *OCD*, 1980; Diocese of Savannah, Office of Chancellor, Quinquennial, 1960–65; Diocese of Raleigh, Office of Chancellor, Quinquennial, 1969–73.

41. *OCD*, 1900; 1930; 1950; 1960; 1980. For more on the Lebanese-Syrians, see: Philip M. Kayal, *The Arab Christians of America* (Boston: Twayne, 1974); Salom Rizk, *Syrian Yankee* (New York: Doubleday, 1943).

42. McNally, *Catholicism in South Florida*, 94–97; 195–96; Diocese of Savannah, Office of Chancellor, Quinquennial, 1978–82; Interview, Rev. Wellmeier.

43. McNally, *Catholicism in South Florida*, 94, 139–166; AFAM, Office of Chancellor, Immaculate Conception Parish File; "Hispanic Demography By Diocese."

44. G. J. Church and R. Woodbury, "Welcome Wears Thin," *Time*, September 1, 1980, 8–10; H. Burkholz, "Latinization of Miami," *N. Y. Times Magazine*, September 2, 1980, 44–47; "Hispanic Demography by Diocese"; *OCD*, 1980. See also: Raymond Mohl, "Cubans in Miami: A Preliminary Bibliography," *Immigration History Newsletter*, 16 (May, 1984), 1–10; Clyde McCoy, "Florida's Foreign-Born Population: A Growing Influence on Our Economy," *Business and Economic Dimensions*, 18, No. 3 (1982), 25–36; Juan M. Clark, Jose Lasaga, and Rose S. Reque, *The 1980 Mariel Exodus: An Assessment and Prospect* (Washington, D.C.: Council for Inter-American Security, 1981); Brian O. Walsh, "Boat People of South Florida," *America*, 142 (May 17, 1980), 420–421; Helga Silva, *The Children of Mariel from Shock to Integration: Cuban Refugee Children in South Florida Schools* (Washington, D.C.: Cuban American National Foundation, 1985).

45. "Hispanic Demography by Diocese"; *OCD*, 1980.

46. Interview, Rev. Thomas Wenski, Singer Island, Florida, September 22, 1983; Rev. Wellmeier; Rev. Boland; AFAM, Office of Chancellor, Notre Dame d'Haiti Mission.

47. *OCD*, 1950; 1960; 1980.

48. ADRa, Mark E. Lawson, "Fire and Brimstone in Newton Grove" (Unpublished paper, University of North Carolina, December 9, 1977), 1–26; ADRa, Scrapbook, "Ban on Segregation," Vol. I and II, 1953; Bishop Vincent Waters, *Pastoral Letter on Desegregation*, June 12, 1953; *North Carolina Catholic*, June 19, 1953; McNally, *Catholicism in South Florida*, 92–94, 191–195; AFAM, Office of Chancellor, Holy Redeemer Parish; Interview, Rev. Boland.

49. "St. Mary's Church, Annapolis"; Rev. Peter E. Hogan, S.S.J., to Author, September 14, 1983; ADC, Folder 705.20, Quinquennial, 1962–64; Interview, Rev. Moeslein; Rev. Wellmeier; Rev. Boland.

50. McNally, *Catholicism in South Florida*, 221, 224; *A People of Faith—A Brief History*, 43; Interview, Rev. Boland; Rev. Moeslein.

51. Nessa Theresa Baskerville Johnson, *A Special Pilgrimage: A History of Black Catholics in Richmond* (Richmond: Diocese of Richmond, 1978), 26–36, 40–54.

52. *Ibid.*, 56.

53. ADC, Folder 602.1; "Long Range Study," St. Katherine's of Sienna, Baltimore, April 22, 1983.

## Conclusion

1. *Parish Life in the United States: Final Report to the Bishops of the United States by the Parish Project* (Washington: USCC, 1983), 4.

2. For a detailed analysis on the meaning of identity, see: Philip Gleason, "Identi-

fying Identity: A Semantic History,'' *Journal of American History,* 69 (March, 1983), 910–931.

## For Further Reading

Bailey, James Henry. *A History of the Diocese of Richmond: The Formative Years.* Richmond, Va.: Diocese of Richmond, 1956.

Brownell, Blaine A., and Goldfield, David R., eds. *The City in Southern History. The Growth of Urban Civilization in the South.* Port Washington, N.Y.: Kennikat, 1977.

Dolan, Jay P. *The American Catholic Experience: A History of Colonial Times to the Present.* Garden City, N.Y.: Doubleday, 1985.

Ellis, John Tracy. *The Life of James Cardinal Gibbons: Archbishop of Baltimore, 1834–1921,* Vol. I & II. Milwaukee: Bruce, 1952.

Fichter, Joseph H. *Southern Parish: Dynamics of a City Church.* Chicago: University of Chicago, 1951.

Gannon, Michael V. *Cross in the Sand: The Early History of the Catholic Church in Florida, 1513–1870.* Gainesville, Fla.: University of Florida Press, 1967; 1984.

Gillard, John Thomas. *The Catholic Church and the American Negro.* Baltimore: St. Joseph's Society, 1929.

Hennesey, James, S. J. *American Catholics: A History of the Roman Catholic Community in the United States.* New York: Oxford, 1981.

Johnson, Nessa Theresa Baskerville. *A Special Pilgrimage: A History of Black Catholics in Richmond.* Richmond: Diocese of Richmond, 1978.

McNally, Michael J. *Catholicism in South Florida, 1868–1968.* Gainesville, Fla.: University Presses of Florida, 1984.

Madden, Richard C. *Catholics in South Carolina: A Record.* Lanham, Md.: University Press of America, 1985.

Miller, Randall M. and Wakelyn, Jon L., eds. *Catholics in the Old South: Essays on Church and Culture.* Macon, Ga.: Mercer University Press, 1983.

O'Connell, Jeremiah J. *Catholicity in the Carolinas and Georgia, 1820–1878.* New York: D. and J. Sadlier, 1879. Facsimile reprint. Spartanburg, S.C.: Reprint Co., 1972.

*Parish Life in the United States: Final Report to the Bishops of the United States by the Parish Project.* Washington, D.C.: USCC, 1983.

# Catholic Church Statistics in the South Atlantic Region, 1850–1980: Alphabetically by States and Dioceses as of 1980

## DELAWARE
### Diocese of Wilmington (1868)

|                              | 1850ᶜ | 1880ᶜ | 1900ᶜ | 1930ᶜ | 1950ᶜ | 1960ᶜ | 1980ᶜ |
|------------------------------|-------|-------|-------|-------|-------|-------|-------|
| Parishes                     | 4     | 8     | 14    | 23    | 30    | 34    | 41    |
| Parishes without Priests     |       |       |       |       |       |       |       |
| (i.e., Missions)             | 1     | 4     | 3     | 6     | 5     | 7     | 5     |
| National Parishes            | 0     | 1     | 2     | 3     | 3     | 3     | 3     |
| Parish Schools               | —ᵇ    | 5     | 9     | 14    | 16    | 28    | 21    |
| Diocesan Priests             | 4     | 8     | 16    | 37    | 44    | 69    | 74    |
| Religious Order Priests      | 0     | 1     | 2     | 21    | 15    | 70    | 82    |
| Women Religious              | 10    | —ᵇ    | —ᵇ    | 208   | 151   | 414   | 370   |
| Catholic Population          | —ᵇ    | —ᵇ    | —ᵇ    | —ᵇ    | —ᵇ    | —ᵇ    | —ᵇ    |
| Total Population             | —ᵇ    | —ᵇ    | —ᵇ    | —ᵇ    | —ᵇ    | —ᵇ    | —ᵇ    |

ᵇInsufficient data.
ᶜDoes not include Maryland's Eastern Shore and Virginia's Eastern Shore.


## FLORIDA
### Archdiocese of Miami (1958)

|                              | 1850 | 1880 | 1900 | 1930 | 1950 | 1960 | 1980      |
|------------------------------|------|------|------|------|------|------|-----------|
| Parishes                     | 1    | 1    | 2    | 10   | 23   | 58   | 130       |
| Parishes without Priests     |      |      |      |      |      |      |           |
| (i.e., Missions)             | 0    | 0    | 0    | 2    | 16   | 13   | 3         |
| National Parishes            | 0    | 1    | 0    | 0    | 0    | 0    | 0         |
| Parish Schools               | 0    | 1    | 1    | 7    | 15   | 42   | 56        |
| Diocesan Priests             | 1    | 1    | 0    | 9    | 37   | 66   | 260       |
| Religious Order Priests      | 0    | 1    | 3    | 9    | 16   | 36   | 197       |
| Women Religious              | 0    | —ᵇ   | 16   | 61   | 215  | 513  | 662       |
| Catholic Population          | —ᵇ   | —ᵇ   | —ᵇ   | —ᵇ   | —ᵇ   | —ᵇ   | 830,700   |
| Total Population             | —ᵇ   | —ᵇ   | —ᵇ   | —ᵇ   | —ᵇ   | —ᵇ   | 3,406,900 |

ᵇInsufficient data.

## FLORIDA
### Diocese of Orlando (1968)

|  | 1850 | 1880 | 1900 | 1930 | 1950 | 1960 | 1980 |
|---|---|---|---|---|---|---|---|
| Parishes | 0 | 0 | 4 | 16 | 16 | 25 | 61 |
| Parishes without Priests |  |  |  |  |  |  |  |
| (i.e., Missions) | 0 | 0 | 3 | 8 | 9 | 14 | 4 |
| National Parishes | 0 | 0 | 0 | 0 | 0 | 0 | 0 |
| Parish Schools | 0 | 0 | 1 | 4 | 6 | 27 | 27 |
| Diocesan Priests | 0 | 0 | 3 | 17 | 18 | 34 | 97 |
| Religious Order Priests | 0 | 0 | 0 | 4 | 8 | 13 | 33 |
| Women Religious | 0 | 0 | 5 | 15 | 41 | 90 | 195 |
| Catholic Population | —[b] | —[b] | —[b] | —[b] | —[b] | —[b] | 163,043 |
| Total Population | —[b] | —[b] | —[b] | —[b] | —[b] | —[b] | 1,785,500 |

[b]Insufficient data.

## FLORIDA
### Diocese of Pensacola–Tallahassee (1975)

|  | 1850 | 1880 | 1900 | 1930 | 1950 | 1960 | 1980 |
|---|---|---|---|---|---|---|---|
| Parishes | 2 | 3 | 5 | 11 | 18 | 21 | 38 |
| Parishes without Priests |  |  |  |  |  |  |  |
| (i.e., Missions) | 2 | 9 | 5 | 6 | 13 | 15 | 11 |
| National Parishes | 0 | 0 | 0 | 0 | 0 | 0 | 0 |
| Parish Schools | 1 | 1 | 6 | 8 | 9 | 12 | 8 |
| Diocesan Priests | 2 | 3 | 6 | 12 | 20 | 37 | 43 |
| Religious Order Priests | 0 | 0 | 0 | 0 | 7 | 5 | 13 |
| Women Religious | 0 | —[b] | 26 | 28 | 39 | 71 | 65 |
| Catholic Population | 1,500 | —[b] | —[b] | —[b] | —[b] | —[b] | 40,823 |
| Total Population | —[b] | —[b] | —[b] | —[b] | —[b] | —[b] | 819,811 |

[b]Insufficient data.

**FLORIDA**
**Diocese of St. Augustine (1870)**

|                                      | 1850 | 1880           | 1900           | 1930 | 1950           | 1960           | 1980      |
|--------------------------------------|------|----------------|----------------|------|----------------|----------------|-----------|
| Parishes                             | 2    | 5              | 7              | 14   | 19             | 27             | 44        |
| Parishes without Priests (i.e., Missions) | 1    | 2              | 8              | 9    | 5              | 7              | 14        |
| National Parishes                    | 0    | 0              | 0              | 0    | 0              | 0              | 0         |
| Parish Schools                       | 0    | 5              | 5              | 9    | 12             | 15             | 15        |
| Diocesan Priests                     | 1    | 7              | 9              | 12   | 24             | 37             | 46        |
| Religious Order Priests              | 1    | 0              | 0              | 1    | 5              | 5              | 20        |
| Women Religious                      | 0    | —[b]           | —[b]           | 79   | —[b]           | 116            | 117       |
| Catholic Population                  | —[b] | —[b]           | —[b]           | —[b] | —[b]           | —[b]           | 65,416    |
| Total Population                     | —[b] | —[b]           | —[b]           | —[b] | —[b]           | —[b]           | 1,047,000 |

[b]Insufficient data.


**FLORIDA**
**Diocese of St. Petersburg (1968)**

|                                      | 1850 | 1880 | 1900 | 1930 | 1950 | 1960 | 1980      |
|--------------------------------------|------|------|------|------|------|------|-----------|
| Parishes                             | 0    | 1    | 5    | 15   | 22   | 45   | 83        |
| Parishes without Priests (i.e., Missions) | 0    | 0    | 9    | 11   | 14   | 19   | 6         |
| National Parishes                    | 0    | 0    | 1    | 2    | 1    | 1    | 0         |
| Parish Schools                       | 0    | 0    | 2    | 9    | 12   | 23   | 30        |
| Diocesan Priests                     | 0    | 1    | 0    | 8    | 17   | 36   | 93        |
| Religious Order Priests              | 0    | 0    | 18   | 43   | 50   | 52   | 125       |
| Women Religious                      | 0    | 0    | —[b] | 59   | 149  | 224  | 355       |
| Catholic Population                  | —[b] | —[b] | —[b] | —[b] | —[b] | —[b] | 252,316   |
| Total Population                     | —[b] | —[b] | —[b] | —[b] | —[b] | —[b] | 2,254,959 |

[b]Insufficient data.

## GEORGIA
### Archdiocese of Atlanta (1956)

|  | 1850 | 1880 | 1900 | 1930 | 1950 | 1960 | 1980 |
|---|---|---|---|---|---|---|---|
| Parishes | 0 | 2 | 4 | 10 | 14 | 26 | 52 |
| Parishes without Priests (i.e., Missions) | 1 | 1 | 4 | 15 | 7 | 14 | 20 |
| National Parishes | 0 | 0 | 0 | 1 | 1 | 0 | 0 |
| Parish Schools | 0 | 0 | 3 | 5 | 9 | 16 | 13 |
| Diocesan Priests | 0 | 3 | 4 | 9 | 15 | 29 | 73 |
| Religious Order Priests | 0 | 0 | 0 | 9 | 11 | 84 | 89 |
| Women Religious | 0 | 0 | 44 | 51 | 61 | 175 | 191 |
| Catholic Population | —[b] | —[b] | —[b] | —[b] | —[b] | 30,840 | 99,742 |
| Total Population | —[b] | —[b] | —[b] | —[b] | —[b] | 1,808,208 | 3,246,250 |

[b]Insufficient data.

## GEORGIA
### Diocese of Savannah (1850)

|  | 1850 | 1880 | 1900 | 1930 | 1950 | 1960 | 1980 |
|---|---|---|---|---|---|---|---|
| Parishes | 5 | 12 | 9 | 14 | 27 | 33 | 45 |
| Parishes without Priests (i.e., Missions) | 2 | —[b] | 13 | 11 | 23 | 20 | 29 |
| National Parishes | 0 | 0 | 0 | 0 | 0 | 0 | 0 |
| Parish Schools | 2 | 3 | 5 | 14 | 16 | 20 | 16 |
| Diocesan Priests | 11 | 17 | 10 | 17 | 28 | 28 | 54 |
| Religious Order Priests | 1 | 6 | 23 | 27 | 83 | 46 | 34 |
| Women Religious | 8 | —[b] | 107 | 154 | 217 | 235 | 210 |
| Catholic Population | —[b] | —[b] | —[b] | —[b] | —[b] | 28,812 | 49,546 |
| Total Population | —[b] | —[b] | —[b] | —[b] | —[b] | 1,636,370 | 1,631,172 |

[b]Insufficient data.

230

## MARYLAND AND THE DISTRICT OF COLUMBIA
### Archdiocese of Washington (1947)

|                                    | 1850[c] | 1880[c] | 1900[c] | 1930[c] | 1950[c] | 1960[c] | 1980[c] |
|------------------------------------|---------|---------|---------|---------|---------|---------|---------|
| Parishes                           | 13      | 29      | 41      | 67      | 91      | 118     | 142     |
| Parishes without Priests (i.e., Missions) | 15 | 26 | 41 | 37 | 55 | 28 | 20 |
| National Parishes                  | 1       | 2       | 1       | 2       | 1       | 1       | 2       |
| Parish Schools                     | 3       | 19      | 18      | 39      | 52      | 72      | 80      |
| Diocesan Priests                   | 10      | 21      | 67      | 84      | 156     | 268     | 315     |
| Religious Order Priests            | 18      | 51      | 81      | 40[d]   | 60      | 738     | 671     |
| Women Religious                    | —[b]    | —[b]    | 324     | 414     | 1,208   | 1,427   | 1,024   |
| Catholic Population                | —[b]    | —[b]    | —[b]    | —[b]    | —[b]    | —[b]    | —[b]    |
| Total Population                   | —[b]    | —[b]    | —[b]    | —[b]    | —[b]    | —[b]    | —[b]    |

[b]Insufficient data.
[c]Eastern Shore parishes in the Diocese of Wilmington included.
[d]Does not include priests in education because of insufficient data.

## MARYLAND
### Archdiocese of Baltimore (1789)

|                                    | 1850[a] | 1880[a] | 1900[a] | 1930[a] | 1950    | 1960      | 1980      |
|------------------------------------|---------|---------|---------|---------|---------|-----------|-----------|
| Parishes                           | 16      | 55      | 80      | 106     | 118     | 162       | 151       |
| Parishes without Priests (i.e., Missions) | 14 | 34 | 30 | 55 | 40 | 30 | 11 |
| National Parishes                  | 5       | 6       | 10      | 14      | 9       | 6         | 5         |
| Parish Schools                     | 10      | 65      | 67      | 100     | 89      | 101       | 83        |
| Diocesan Priests                   | 19      | 67      | 84      | 169     | 234     | 266       | 275       |
| Religious Order Priests            | 20      | 159     | 152     | 120[c]  | 281     | 420       | 315       |
| Women Religious                    | 59      | —[b]    | —[b]    | 849     | 2,460   | 2,785     | 1,972     |
| Catholic Population                | —[b]    | —[b]    | —[b]    | —[b]    | 336,000 | 410,714   | 413,321   |
| Total Population                   | —[b]    | —[b]    | —[b]    | —[b]    | —[b]    | 1,691,910 | 2,449,720 |

[a]Excludes the District of Columbia.
[b]Insufficient data.
[c]Does not include priests in education because of insufficient data.

## NORTH CAROLINA
### Diocese of Charlotte (1972)

|  | 1850 | 1880 | 1900 | 1930[c] | 1950[c] | 1960[c] | 1980 |
|---|---|---|---|---|---|---|---|
| Parishes | 0 | 2 | 5 | 18 | 37 | 45 | 62 |
| Parishes without Priests (i.e., Missions) | 0 | 0 | 5 | 6 | 14 | 25 | 21 |
| National Parishes | 0 | 0 | 0 | 0 | 0 | 0 | 0 |
| Parish Schools | 0 | 1 | 2 | 9 | 18 | 20 | 17 |
| Diocesan Priests | 0 | 1 | 1 | 9 | 54 | 48 | 50 |
| Religious Order Priests | 0 | —[b] | 13 | 31 | 81 | 43 | 50 |
| Women Religious | 0 | —[b] | —[b] | 161 | 318 | 235 | 229 |
| Catholic Population | —[b] | —[b] | —[b] | —[b] | —[b] | —[b] | 47,805 |
| Total Population | —[b] | —[b] | —[b] | —[b] | —[b] | —[b] | 2,850,000 |

[b]Insufficient data.
[c]Includes the Abbatia Nullius of Belmont Abbey.

## NORTH CAROLINA
### Diocese of Raleigh (1924)

|  | 1850 | 1880 | 1900 | 1930 | 1950 | 1960 | 1980 |
|---|---|---|---|---|---|---|---|
| Parishes | 3 | 3 | 7 | 18 | 53 | 62 | 58 |
| Parishes without Priests (i.e., Missions) | 9 | 8 | 12 | 35 | 34 | 10 | 18 |
| National Parishes | 0 | 0 | 0 | 0 | 0 | 0 | 0 |
| Parish Schools | 0 | 4 | 6 | 12 | 23 | 34 | 19 |
| Diocesan Priests | 4 | 4 | 7 | 21 | 34 | 58 | 51 |
| Religious Order Priests | 0 | 0 | 2 | 9 | 50 | 40 | 27 |
| Women Religious | 0 | —[b] | —[b] | 36 | 110 | 278 | 125 |
| Catholic Population | —[b] | —[b] | —[b] | —[b] | —[b] | —[b] | 46,691 |
| Total Population | —[b] | —[b] | —[b] | —[b] | —[b] | —[b] | 2,970,022 |

[b]Insufficient data.

## SOUTH CAROLINA
### Diocese of Charleston (1820)

| | 1850 | 1880 | 1900 | 1930 | 1950 | 1960 | 1980 |
|---|---|---|---|---|---|---|---|
| Parishes | 5 | 15 | 9 | 23 | 42 | 58 | 75 |
| Parishes without Priests (i.e., Missions) | 7 | 6 | 14 | 24 | 26 | 30 | 5 |
| National Parishes | 0 | 1 | 0 | 0 | 0 | 0 | 0 |
| Parish Schools | 0 | 6 | 5 | 10 | 17 | 31 | 32 |
| Diocesan Priests | 9 | 16 | 15 | 39 | 55 | 71 | 67 |
| Religious Order Priests | 0 | 0 | 0 | 4 | 41 | 58 | 54 |
| Women Religious | 20 | 50 | 69[a] | 138[a] | 230 | 340 | 272 |
| Catholic Population | —[b] | —[b] | 8,000 | 9,570 | 17,508 | 31,702 | 59,027 |
| Total Population | 668,507 | 995,577 | 1,340,316 | 1,738,765 | 2,117,027 | 2,382,594 | 2,876,000 |

[a]Includes novices and postulants.
[b]Insufficient data.

232

## VIRGINIA
### Diocese of Arlington (1974)

|  | 1850 | 1880 | 1900 | 1930 | 1950 | 1960 | 1980 |
|---|---|---|---|---|---|---|---|
| Parishes | 3 | 4 | 6 | 13 | 21 | 31 | 57 |
| Parishes without Priests | | | | | | | |
| (i.e., Missions) | 1 | 5 | 9 | 20 | 15 | 11 | 5 |
| National Parishes | 0 | 0 | 0 | 0 | 0 | 0 | 1 |
| Parish Schools | 0 | 2 | 1 | 4 | 9 | 18 | 24 |
| Diocesan Priests | 2 | 4 | 5 | 17 | 34 | 44 | 71 |
| Religious Order Priests | 1 | 2 | 2 | 1 | 28 | 30 | 99 |
| Women Religious | 0 | 8 | 13 | 36 | 115 | 175 | 293 |
| Catholic Population | —[b] | —[b] | —[b] | —[b] | —[b] | —[b] | 174,150 |
| Total Population | —[b] | —[b] | —[b] | —[b] | —[b] | —[b] | 1,317,500 |

[b]Insufficient data.


## VIRGINIA
### Diocese of Richmond (1820)

|  | 1850[c] | 1880[c] | 1900[c] | 1930[c] | 1950[c] | 1960[c] | 1980 |
|---|---|---|---|---|---|---|---|
| Parishes | 7 | 15 | 19 | 45 | 66 | 80 | 100 |
| Parishes without Priests | | | | | | | |
| (i.e., Missions) | 12 | 7 | 23 | 36 | 22 | 35 | 28 |
| National Parishes | 3 | 1 | 1 | 4 | 3 | 2 | 0 |
| Parish Schools | 1 | 23 | 16 | 24 | 27 | 34 | 26 |
| Diocesan Priests | 8 | 21 | 31 | 58 | 91 | 115 | 118 |
| Religious Order Priests | 0 | 2 | 7 | 17 | 59 | 72 | 53 |
| Women Religious | 17 | —[b] | —[b] | 313 | 362 | 631 | 414 |
| Catholic Population | —[b] | —[b] | —[b] | —[b] | —[b] | —[b] | 111,011 |
| Total Population | —[b] | —[b] | —[b] | —[b] | —[b] | —[b] | 3,685,720 |

[b]Insufficient data.
[c]Excludes West Virginia parishes assigned to Richmond; includes Virginia parishes assigned to the Wheeling and Wilmington dioceses.

## WEST VIRGINIA
### Diocese of Wheeling-Charleston (1850)

| | 1850[d] | 1880[d] | 1900[d] | 1930[d] | 1950[d] | 1960[d] | 1980 |
|---|---|---|---|---|---|---|---|
| Parishes | 2 | 23 | 33 | 74 | 83 | 90 | 114 |
| Parishes without Priests (i.e., Missions) | 9 | 37 | 52 | 82 | 67 | 65 | 54 |
| National Parishes | 1 | 2 | 1 | 6 | 5 | 6 | 0 |
| Parish Schools | 1 | 24 | 12 | 39 | 44 | 49 | 34 |
| Diocesan Priests | 4 | 31 | 41 | 95 | 101 | 99 | 113 |
| Religious Order Priests | 1 | 1 | 4 | 22 | 38 | 75 | 88 |
| Women Religious | 20 | 146[c] | —[b] | 453 | 515 | 756 | 453 |
| Catholic Population | —[b] | —[b] | —[b] | —[b] | —[b] | —[b] | 102,192 |
| Total Population | 302,313 | 618,457 | 958,800 | 1,729,205 | 2,005,552 | 1,860,421 | 1,744,237 |

[b]Insufficient data.
[c]Includes postulants and novices.
[d]Excludes Virginia parishes assigned to Wheeling; includes West Virginia parishes assigned to Richmond diocese.

# PART THREE

# Modest and Humble Crosses: A History of Catholic Parishes in the South Central Region (1850–1984)

Charles E. Nolan

# Contents

# Preface

"There is always something fascinating about the history of a Catholic parish," wrote Archbishop Joseph F. Rummel in 1948. "Usually modest and humble in its beginnings, it grows larger, more dignified, and more efficient with the years. It is almost human in its development, and quite understandingly so, for it is composed of vibrant human beings and is intimately influenced by their genius, their moods, and their fortunes. Equally true is it that a parish reflects the conditions, civic, social, economic, as well as religious, that prevail at various stages of its existence and development."[1]

The crosses on the Catholic churches that gradually appeared throughout the South Central region between 1850 and 1980 were often like the parish beginnings themselves—modest and humble. Most of these new crosses stood atop country churches that served small Catholic communities in predominantly Protestant areas. Others stood atop spacious churches in New Orleans, Louisville, Houston, and other new or expanding cities.

The same tension that Archbishop Rummel pointed out between environmental influences and the genius, moods, and fortunes of the people who formed Mater Dolorosa Parish in New Orleans is reflected even more vividly in the 2,362 Catholic parishes that existed in the South Central region of the United States between 1850 and 1980. The pages that follow provide a generic portrait of these parishes, the influences that shaped them, and the people who composed them.[2]

The skeleton of this portrait of parish expansion and development in Alabama, Arkansas, Kentucky, Louisiana, Mississippi, Oklahoma, Tennessee, and Texas is a data base of core information (parish name, city, county, state, diocese, date of foundation, ethnic origin, changes in parish status, and sources of information) on 2,362 parishes. This data base provides an accurate picture of the geographical expansion of Catholic parishes at a county, city, diocesan, and state level decade by decade. A profile of Catholic parish expansion, based on this data, is found in Appendix 3.[3]

These county-level data also allow an accurate analysis of the urban-rural balance of the parishes. The data clearly reveal the twofold direction of parish foundations in the region: the gradual expansion of Catholic parishes into rural, Protestant counties and the multiplication of Catholic parishes in urban areas such as New Orleans, Louisville, Mobile, Memphis, and Houston. The urbanization (and suburbanization) of the region's parish life began to accelerate significantly in the early twentieth century, reaching into newer or smaller cities such as Lafayette, Brownsville, Biloxi, Birmingham, and Tulsa. The Catholic parish experience in the South Central region, however, was centered in the rural, Protestant countryside.

This skeleton of parish development is fleshed out by several additional themes. The first is the region's rich ethnic heritage, which is rooted in Spain, France, the American colonies, and Africa; this heritage also includes a large segment of the nation's native American Indians. Immigrants from throughout Europe as well as European colonies such as Santo Domingo, Canada, Mexico, and Cuba are found in early Texas, Louisiana, Alabama, and Mississippi. Immigrants later came in large numbers and established parishes that are identified as Austrian, Polish, German, Irish, Italian, Lebanese, Syrian, Hungarian, Czechoslovakian, Alsatian, and Belgian. This same immigrant tradition is found in recently formed Korean and Vietnamese parishes.[4]

A second theme is the great variety of complementary roles that priests and laity played in the formation and development of the region's parishes. Although several noteworthy examples of these roles are examined, only the most generic patterns of clerical-lay relationships in parish development are summarized.

A third theme examines the rapport between local Catholic parishes and their Protestant neighbors. With a few geographical exceptions, the region's Catholics were a distinct minority in a Protestant culture. At times, Catholics were the objects of the violent outbreaks of anti-Catholicism by the Know-Nothings, the American Protective Association, the Ku Klux Klan, and the bigots of the 1928 presidential election. In the 1920s, Catholics in Alabama and Arkansas found themselves the object of convent-search laws. The Oregon case that attempted to require compulsory attendance of all children in public schools threatened the very existence of Catholic schools throughout the nation. Numerous parish histories, however, recount a different pattern of Catholic-Protestant relations. In many cities and towns, Protestants played an important role in establishing Catholic congregations, and Protestant-Catholic rapport remained cordial and even cooperative.

Parish size and organizational complexity form another theme. The great variations between parishes and the absence of accurate, diocesan census data allow for only the most general observations on parish size.

A fifth theme touches on the role of the Catholic school system and later the Confraternity of Christian Doctrine (CCD) and Catholic Youth Organization (CYO) in incorporating youth into parish life. The Catholic school was an ideal, if not a reality, in almost all Catholic parishes down through the years. Unfortunately, scholarly histories of Catholic education in the region's eight states are lacking, although most parish histories include information about local schools and/or related educational programs.

The final theme—parish devotional practices—is usually poorly documented in regional parish histories. A few examples and trends are incorporated into this study.

This study is based on diocesan lists of parishes with their foundation dates, special diocesan newspaper supplements, state and diocesan histories that detail parish development, the annual *Catholic Directories,* published parish histories, and personal visits to more than 90 parishes in Alabama, Louisiana, and Mississippi over the past decade. Most parish histories and even more newspaper sketches are at best introductory sources of information. These parish histories usually concentrate on a few themes: the main accomplishments of pastors and school principals; the financing and construction of the buildings that housed and symbolized the congregation's life and work; the impact of major events such as war; parish organizations; and the early families mentioned in the sacramental registers. More recent histories frequently explore the impact of change and the parish's sense of community and service. These parish histories range in size from a page or two in a dedication booklet to Father Donald Hebert's 747 page history of St. Anthony Parish in Eunice, Louisiana.[5] Information used in this study was based on the most reliable sources that were available for each parish, beginning with the diocesan list of parishes and culminating with personal research on individual parishes.[6]

A special word of thanks must be added to the many archivists, administrative assistants, and chancellors who sent parish lists, histories, and newspapers; this material was indispensable for this study. Monsignor Larry J. Droll of San Angelo, Sister Lois Bannon, O.S.U., of Dallas, Ofelia Tennant of San Antonio, Sister Mary Kay Veillon, M.S.C., of Alexandria-Shreveport, Father Michael Zilligen of Brownsville, Father James Geraghty of Lafayette, Martha L. Byrd of Fort Worth, Father Dan Scheel of Galveston-Houston, Mrs. Una Daigre of Baton Rouge, and Mrs. Rita Burns of Tulsa sent material from their respective dioceses. Sister Dolores Kasner, O.P., of the Catholic Archives in Texas sent parish lists with foundation dates from five dioceses. Mrs. Okla McKee sent out a special questionnaire to all parishes in the El Paso Diocese to gather information for this project. Sister Catherine Markey, M.H.S., of Little Rock added many helpful observations to the material she sent. Father John Lyons spent two days with me, sharing his marvelous collection of parish material and, more importantly, his great knowledge of the Kentucky Church. Archbishop Oscar H. Lipscomb, whose biographies of Bishops Michael Portier and John Quinlan are among the best in the region, sent information on the later Mobile parishes. Ann Nicholson and Thomas Stritch assisted me during my visit to the Nashville archives. Father J. Edgar Bruns, my colleague at the New Orleans Archdiocesan Archives, provided many helpful suggestions on the early pages of this manuscript and shared the results of his own research. Monsignor Earl C. Woods, chancellor of the Archdiocese of New Orleans, shared with me his own experiences in planning for future parish development and encouraged me to pursue this research. Dr. Jay Dolan carefully examined the early drafts of this manuscript and provided valuable suggestions that have been incorporated into these pages. Finally, my father,

Charles E. Nolan, Sr., despite his personal grief following the deaths of his youngest son and, soon afterward, his wife, proofread and improved the final manuscript.

## Notes

1. Preface to *The Catholic Church in Carrollton, 1848–1948. Church of the Nativity of the Blessed Virgin Mary, 1848–1899, Mater Dolorosa German Church, 1871–1899, Mater Dolorosa Church, 1899–1948* by Roger Baudier, (New Orleans: 1948). Archives of the Archdiocese of New Orleans.

2. In this study, the criterion for establishing the foundation date for parishes was the appointment or arrival of a resident pastor. Parishes often use and celebrate many other events as the origin of their communities: the first baptism, the beginning or completion of the first church or chapel, the first Mass, the first cemetery, or the first parish organization. When diocesan parish lists were re-evaluated against the criterion of the appointment of a resident pastor, many early foundation dates were changed—some by several decades. The terminology used in the early *Catholic Directories* further confuses the issue because these directories listed churches rather than parishes. In this study, however, directory criteria for station (community visited regularly by a priest but without a chapel), mission (community with a church or chapel but without a resident priest), and church/parish (community with a resident pastor) are used. The formal establishment of a parish is a clearer and more frequent criterion in recent decades.

3. The core of this study is a data bank of information (called "Parish") on 2,362 Catholic parishes that existed in the South Central region between 1850 and 1980. Earlier parishes such as St. Bernard in Galveztown, Louisiana, and several Texas missions that were already closed by 1850 were not included; parishes founded after 1980 were likewise omitted. The basic information on each parish included the name, diocese, city, county, state, ethnic identity, date of establishment, as well as the nature and dates of major status changes such as closure or merger with another parish, and the source of this data. The data were gathered in five stages: (1) all Catholic parishes in the *1982 Catholic Directory* and diocesan directories were listed and, where foundation dates were given, these were included; many dioceses do not have current lists of foundation dates; (2) earlier *Catholic Directories* were used to determine the date of establishment (and, where necessary, closing date) by assigning the year previous to the first or last appearance in the directory; subsequent research indicated this methodology is generally accurate, particularly in the twentieth century; (3) printed summaries of parish histories—either in the form of separate books or special newspaper editions—supplemented and corrected the original data and added many details concerning other themes in this study; in many cases, these printed histories also provided more accurate establishment dates; (4) individual parish histories were consulted or information from personal parish research was incorporated; (5) the *1936* and *1955 Catholic Directories* were examined parish by parish to identify parishes no longer in existence; other directories were used to establish the opening and closing dates of these parishes. In all, 164 closed parishes were identified in this study. The most difficult

parishes to trace were those founded in the nineteenth century. Diocesan summaries often omit early closed parishes, while the shift of parishes from one locality to another, the assignment of one priest to several communities, and changes in parish names make it difficult to use the *Catholic Directories* as a guide. There were, no doubt, additional early parishes that were not identified in this study.

4. There were several reasons why a Southern parish was called Polish, German, Mexican, black, or Irish. The majority of ethnic parishes were identified as such because they exclusively or primarily served one ethnic group, used a language other than English for sermons, popular devotions, meetings, and school instruction, and often had a priest of the same background and language. One problem with this designation in the South Central region is that "Americans" were originally a minority in Acadian, Mexican, and Indian sections of the region. In addition, many rural Indian, Mexican, and Acadian parishes were simply listed as local parishes without any ethnic designation. In this study, ethnic parishes were identified through parish or diocesan histories and/or the *Catholic Directories;* these sources did not identify many Hispanic and Acadian parishes as such. In addition, several parishes proudly point to their dual national origins: German and Irish, Czech and Polish, French and African. The question of ethnic designation becomes still more complicated when national parishes are discussed. National parishes were canonically established in urban areas to serve and protect specific ethnic communities. The majority of parishes in the South Central region were small-town parishes that served all who lived within the cities or towns as well as the surrounding countryside, regardless of ethnic background. Even in urban areas, parishes that served distinct ethnic groups were most often not canonically established national parishes. In New Orleans, St. Mary Italian Church did not become a national parish until 1921 after more than a century of serving Creole, German, Irish, African, and Italian communities at different times. The nearby St. Anthony Church also served the Italian community, but without official status as a national parish. In 1947, the status of all San Antonio parishes was changed from national to territorial, while in New Orleans many French-speaking parishes were considered simply as territorial parishes as early as the 1860s.

5. Donald J. Hebert, *History of St. Anthony Parish, Eunice, Louisiana, 1902–1983, Including a History of St. Edmond School, 1911–1983* (Eunice: Hebert Publications, 1983).

6. Five major sources of data on the region's 2,362 parishes were identified. For the parishes founded before 1940, the major sources of data were: diocesan lists with foundation dates (221), first appearance in the *Catholic Directories* (150), brief parish sketches that appeared in state histories or diocesan newspapers (530), a combination of the *Catholic Directories* and parish sketches (136), and published parish histories or personal visits to parishes (209). For parishes founded after 1940, the breakdown on sources is: diocesan lists with parish foundation dates (515), first appearance in the *Catholic Directories* (228), state histories or diocesan newspapers (288), a combination of *Catholic Directories* and parish sketches (50), and published parish histories or personal visits (35). The weakest data are from parish lists with foundation dates for the 221 parishes founded before 1940. Information on the ethnic character of parishes, particularly the Hispanic parishes of Texas and the French parishes in Louisiana, is also incomplete.

# CHAPTER ONE

# Catholic Parishes in 1850

By 1850, 318 identified Catholic communities were spread across Alabama, Arkansas, Kentucky, Louisiana, Mississippi, Tennessee, Texas, and the future Oklahoma. More than two-thirds of these pockets of Catholicism were either small stations or missions; only 101 Catholic communities had reached parish status.[1]

These parishes and communities already reflected a long and diverse heritage that dated back 170 years to the Spanish mission of Corpus Christi de Ysleta in the El Paso Valley (1680). Two modern El Paso parishes trace their origin to this original settlement and its missions: Our Lady of Mount Carmel (1682) and La Purisima (1683). The Spanish also established a chain of missions from El Paso to Los Adaes near Natchitoches in Louisiana. The Spanish mission system, however, was gradually abandoned and the missions were completely secularized by 1794. A long period of neglect followed under the Spanish, Mexican, and Texan regimes. The rebirth of the Catholic Church in Texas began in 1838 when Bishop Antoine Blanc of New Orleans sent Father John Timon, C.M., as his vicar for the newly independent Texas nation. By 1850, some of the early mission sites were in ruins, while others had become the centers of rejuvenated missions or parishes. In addition to the El Paso missions, Sacred Heart Parish in Nagocdoches (1716), St. Patrick in Lufkin (1717), as well as San Jose de Bexar (1720) and San Francisco Espada (1731) in San Antonio all trace their origin to the early Spanish years.

Another set of parishes descended from the French who established colonies at Old Biloxi (1699), Mobile (1703), and New Orleans (1718). The Mississippi Valley's oldest existing parish—Immaculate Conception in Mobile—was founded in 1703. In 1716, a priest was appointed to the French military post at Natchez. The French and later Spanish colony of Louisiana became the region's major center of permanent Catholic parish development between 1720 and 1785. St. Louis Church at New Orleans was established in 1720, two years after the city's founding. The French assigned priests to settlements at La Balize in 1722, the German Coast above New Orleans in 1723, and Pointe Coupee and Natchitoches in 1728. The Spanish later established eleven additional parishes in Louisiana. The most significant factor in these Spanish-era parishes, a factor that shaped Louisiana's Catholic future, was the settlement of exiled Acadians in the rural areas surrounding Bayou Lafourche, Attakapas, and Opelousas.[2]

The Louisiana Church's early dependence on colonial governments for support was, at best, a mixed blessing that left a long, debilitating legacy of lack of parish financial support.[3] It also was in large part responsible for the long, acrimonious controversy that erupted in 1842 between Bishop Antoine Blanc and the church wardens of St. Louis Cathedral in New Orleans over ownership and management of the cathedral.[4] The trustee controversy had a major influence on parish development in mid-nineteenth century Louisiana. Bishop Blanc refused to send a pastor to the community at Plaquemine until the church property was signed over to the diocese in 1850. The same was true in other rural Louisiana parishes. In addition, the cathedral church wardens tried to block the establishment of new city parishes that would dilute their influence.[5]

In the late eighteenth and early nineteenth centuries, the center of parish growth shifted dramatically to Kentucky. Here, Catholic communities with a different character began to emerge along the creeks that formed an arc around Bardstown. Holy Cross on Pottinger's Creek in 1785 was the first. These new Kentucky settlements were founded by native Americans from the Eastern states who joined in the beginning of the great Western migration. Catholic pioneers moved to Kentucky and, to a lesser degree, other areas in the region, in search of better land. They often traveled as a family or group, bringing their traditions and religion with them. Of the twenty-nine parishes that trace their origin to the half century between 1780 and 1830, seventeen were in Kentucky. The four future bishops born in the region before 1850—Ignatius Reynolds, Martin J. Spalding, John L. Spalding, and George Montgomery—were all natives of Kentucky.

The decade preceding 1850 witnessed a rapid increase in the number of Catholic parishes in the South Central region. During this period, forty-seven new parishes were established; almost half the existing parishes in 1850 were less than a decade old.[6]

Several new urban and rural parishes of the 1840s were formed by German and Irish immigrants. The South Central region, however, always numbered far fewer immigrants than its Northern and Eastern neighbors. In 1850, Alabama, Arkansas, Mississippi, and Tennessee all numbered less than 2% foreign-born residents; only Louisiana was above the national average (11.5%) for the nation's white residents. The absence of large numbers of immigrants played a major role in the area's slow Catholic parish development.[7]

Geography largely determined the location of the region's pioneer parishes. The South Central region covered more than 620,000 square miles—an area larger than the combined size of modern France, Spain, Italy, Portugal, Switzerland, and the Benelux countries. Texas alone, with an 1850 population of less than 213,000, was larger than the future Poland, Germany, or Czechoslovakia.

Many parts of this vast region were still sparsely settled in 1850. At least 4,303,000 inhabitants (18.6% of the nation's total population) resided in the South Central region's seven states; the census for that year did not include Indian Territory (Oklahoma). Tennessee with 1,003,000 residents was the region's most populous state; Texas was the least populated. The region's largest ethnic group was of African descent. Approximately 45.4% of the nation's slave population resided in the South Central region; Alabama, Kentucky, Louisiana, Mississippi, and Tennessee all numbered more than 200,000 slaves.[8]

The region was blessed with abundant natural resources. The powerful Mississippi River and its tributaries flow down from the North and bisect the region as they move toward the Gulf of Mexico. The area's numerous rivers, streams, lakes, and bayous produced some of the world's most fertile farmland, provided the pioneer paths of transportation and commerce, offered their banks for early settlements, and served as plentiful sources of food. The very names of these rivers evoke much of the region's history: the Pecos and the Rio Grande, the Pearl and the Tombigbee, the Arkansas and the Tennessee. The early parishes in the Mississippi Valley were located along these major rivers and bayous.

By 1850, cities, towns, and farms had moved beyond the waterways; the Natchez Trace and the National Road were among the roads that opened new paths of migration and settlement. The nation's 9,000 miles of railroad stretched into the South and already were attracting immigrant laborers who would become the core of many Catholic parishes. The Irish railroad crew with which Bishop Richard Miles spent a week in Athens during his initial pastoral visit to Tennessee in 1837 later helped form Chattanooga's first Catholic parish. Irish laborers flocked to New Orleans to work—and often die—on the city's expanding network of canals.

The region also contained other natural wealth besides its fertile farmland and abundant waterways. Countless longhorn cattle grazed on Texas' vast prairie lands and soon became a source of wealth, power, and American folklore. The area's untapped natural gas and oil deposits became a major factor in shaping the region's economy and parish development during the twentieth century.

Catholics were influenced by the same powerful social, economic, and political forces that also shaped the region. Although they stood apart from their Protestant neighbors in religious belief, practice, and affiliation, Catholics tended to mirror the prevailing acceptance of slavery, devotion to the South, conservatism, and slow acceptance of education. Most Southern Catholics became ardent Confederates during the forthcoming war.[9]

In 1850, the region's political boundaries were still evolving. Seven of the region's eight states had already entered the union. Oklahoma formed part of Indian Territory and did not become a state until 1907. The region's county (parish in Louisiana) structure was still in a formative stage. The 1850 census listed 468 counties in seven states; 289 additional counties would be formed in these states plus seventy-seven counties in Oklahoma.

The region's Catholic hierarchy was well-organized.[10] Each of the seven states had its own diocese. New Orleans had been established by the Spanish in 1793 as the vast Diocese of Louisiana and the Floridas. An administrative vacuum had followed Bishop Luis Penalver y Cardenas' transfer to Guatemala in 1801. The appointment of Father Antoine Blanc as Bishop of New Orleans in 1835 not only began a new period of stability in ecclesiastical leadership in Louisiana, but also provided a remarkable man to guide the Mississippi Valley and Texas for a quarter century. Under Bishop Blanc's direction, the Mississippi Valley witnessed the largest percentage increase in new parishes that the region ever experienced. When the hierarchical reorganization of 1850 raised New Orleans to an archdiocese with Antoine Blanc as its first archbishop, Alabama, Arkansas, Mississippi, and Texas became part of the new province.

The Diocese of Bardstown, Kentucky, was established in 1808 as the region's second major administrative center. The original diocese was also immense and included all or part of ten future states outside Kentucky. By 1838, the diocese was limited to the state of Kentucky and, in 1841, the see city was moved to Louisville. In 1850, Louisville became part of the new Province of Cincinnati. At the time, one small part of Kentucky in and around Covington was included in the Diocese of Cincinnati, an unsatisfactory situation that was resolved by the creation of the Diocese of Covington in 1853.

In 1825, Father Michael Portier was appointed to the new Vicariate of Alabama and the Floridas; four years later, he became the first bishop of the Diocese of Mobile. Other new dioceses soon followed: Nashville and Natchez in 1837, Little Rock in 1843, and Galveston in 1847. Only the western tip of Texas—the El Paso area—was not included in the latter.

Parish development during the Antebellum period owes much to Rome's policy of sending missionary bishops to Alabama, Arkansas, Mississippi, Tennessee, Texas, and, in 1853, northern Louisiana and eastern Kentucky, where few identified Catholic communities existed. This policy was a response to the Third Provincial Council of Baltimore, which, in 1837, not only petitioned for new dioceses at Natchez, Nashville, and Dubuque, but also observed, "Necessity demands action and there is danger without doubt in delay; for experience shows that in these new regions, when Episcopal Sees are founded from the very beginning of the new settlements themselves, it is much easier and safer to build churches, and religion can be spread in every way, due to the few obstacles placed in the way by sectaries and also because one can procure at a reasonable price ground and estates for the erection and support of churches, colleges, and seminaries."[11]

The Antebellum bishops became key figures in the advancement of existing parishes and the formation of new communities. They contacted remote families and groups of families, recruited and appointed priests, gathered money to raise buildings and support programs, and offered a personal example of unselfish service to the Church. These men, with the exception of Archbishop Blanc, initially found themselves alone (or almost alone) in vast geographical areas. They were truly remarkable men: Benedict Joseph Flaget of Bardstown, Antoine Blanc of New Orleans, Michael Portier of Mobile, Richard Miles of Nashville, Jean Marie Odin of Galveston, Andrew Byrne of Little Rock, and John Chanche of Natchez. One characteristic of the Antebellum Church in the South Central region was its great stability in episcopal leadership from 1830 to the Civil War.

Michael Portier was typical of these missionaries. When Bishop Portier arrived at Mobile on December 20, 1826, he found only two priests and three churches in all of Florida and Alabama. Shortly after the bishop's arrival, both priests left; in October of 1827, the church in Mobile burned down. Bishop Portier personally had to lay the foundation of Alabama parish life, making long, arduous missionary journeys to contact pockets of Catholic families, traveling to Europe to recruit priests and obtain needed financial resources, and balancing basic parish needs with a concern for schools, orphanages, and hospitals. [12]

One week after his installation as Nashville's first bishop on October 15, 1838, Bishop Richard Miles, O.P., with Father Elisha J. Durbin, set out on horseback to find and visit his new flock. The two clerics traveled more than 500 miles visiting scattered Catholic families at Murfreesboro, Walden's Ridge, and other settlements. They spent a week instructing and ministering to an Irish railroad crew at Athens. Soon after their return to Nashville, Father Durbin returned to Kentucky and Bishop Miles found himself alone with a responsibility for 42,000 square miles. When the weather improved the following spring, the bishop set out alone on another journey that took him almost 700 miles. [13]

Ferdinand von Roemer, a scholar and scientist who met Bishop Jean Marie Odin in 1846 at New Braunfels, recorded his impression of Galveston's first ordinary: "Bishop Odin lives as did the early Christian evangelists. He journeys incessantly up and down the country in order to tend a flock scattered in all directions. Knowing neither fear nor fatigue, he crosses the lonely plains and prairies on horseback. By his energetic labors and unaffected amiability he has won the respect even of those who do not share his beliefs." [14]

Although comprehensive information about the region's Antebellum clergy is still lacking, many pioneer pastors exhibited the same missionary zeal as their bishops. Father Elisha J. Durbin in Kentucky and Tennessee, Father Francis Donahoe in Arkansas, and Father Gabriel Chalon in Alabama were among the priests who traveled great distances to serve many small clusters of Catholic families.

One characteristic of the region's Antebellum clergy is clear: most, outside of Kentucky and Tennessee, were foreign-born, a fact that stood in stark contrast to the region's lack of immigrants. This dependence on foreign clergy continued well into the twentieth century, with notable differences between states such as Louisiana and Kentucky. The region's lack of clergy was due in part to the fact that European priests were frequently called to serve those communities—both rural and urban—where their fellow-countrymen and women resided and where language was a minimal barrier. The Dutch clergy who came to Mississippi and Louisiana in the late nineteenth century were exceptions to this pattern.[15]

The region's Catholic parish life was centered mainly in rural areas. In 1850, three out of every four Catholic parishes in the South Central region were located in cities, towns, or villages of less than 3,500 people. Eighty percent were the sole Catholic parishes in their respective cities or towns; only five cities had more than one parish. This predominately rural character of Southern parish life set the region apart from the urban, immigrant experience of the Northern Catholic Church. The Southern Catholic Church in 1850 faced an immense challenge to extend its presence into the region's rural areas; Catholic parishes existed in only 67 (8%) of the region's 834 future counties.

The *Catholic Directory's* distinction between parish (sometimes more vaguely listed as "church"), mission, and station provides a useful framework for tracing the main stages in the development of Southern parish life, particularly in rural areas. In addition, there was frequently a preliminary stage—the family or extended family—although this phase of parish formation is too often poorly documented. Many missionaries recorded the discovery of scattered Catholic families whose very existence they had to seek out and whose retention of their Catholic allegiance was often remarkable. The joy and hospitality with which the priests and bishops were greeted were an indication of the faith that these families had preserved without the benefit of clergy or a larger Catholic community.

These families, when discovered, often became the gathering place for the second stage of parish development—the station. During this phase, priests began to visit families, ranches, towns, or small clusters of Catholics on a regular basis. In 1850, Father Joseph Anstaett, pastor of Cummings' Creek in Austin County, Texas, visited such stations at Columbus, Lagrange, Bastrop, Austin, Dof, Ellinger, Buchel's Settlements, and Washington. Father Thomas Grace of Memphis attended Bolivar, Jackson, Somerville, "and other stations in West Tennessee."[16]

The building of the first chapel—sometimes a small wooden structure that the community itself erected on donated land, sometimes a well-financed brick edifice on purchased land—marked the next stage of parish development. The chapel became a place of worship and instruction, a community gathering place, a place of lodging for the visiting priest, and a concrete expression of the community's Catholic faith to their Protestant neighbors.

The assignment of a priest to the community was the culmination of local parish development. On occasion, a priest took up residence before a church was constructed or even planned, thus skipping the intermediate mission stage. In the

South Central region, a city or town often shared its priest with many surrounding communities. Priests were frequently away on a mission circuit that formed an integral part of parish life. Many Catholic parishes in the South Central region were small in numbers but vast in areas.

Although most of the region's people lived in rural areas, the 1850 census tentatively indicated the country's major cities. The South Central region had only eight cities with populations of more than 3,500. New Orleans with 116,000 residents was the nation's fifth largest city; Louisville numbered 43,000 residents; Mobile, 21,000; and Nashville, 10,000; Natchez, Vicksburg, Galveston, Memphis, and Lexington, more than 3,500. Each of these urban areas had at least one Catholic parish, a pattern that remained consistent throughout the succeeding years. By the time that southern communities reached urban status, a Catholic parish was already established there.[17]

As late as 1830, no city in the region had more than one formal parish, although New Orleans had St. Mary's chapel at the archbishop's residence in addition to St. Louis Cathedral. During the next two decades, the rapid expansion of parish life in New Orleans and, to a much lesser degree, Mobile, Covington, and Louisville, was an expression not only of urban growth but also of a new component of Southern Catholic life—the Irish and German immigrant. By 1850, New Orleans, with thirteen parishes, was the region's sole major urban Catholic center.[18]

The new urban parishes reflected an ethnic diversity that would typify city parishes into the twentieth century. The region's first Irish parish was St. Patrick in New Orleans, established in 1833. St. Boniface in Louisville (1837) was the first German parish. During the 1840s, additional German parishes were also established at Louisville and Covington, Kentucky; in New Orleans; and at New Braunfels, Castroville, and Fredericksburg, Texas.

In New Orleans, clusters of neighboring parishes were established to serve German, French, and English-speaking congregations. The first was just below the Vieux Carre—the original French city; St. Vincent de Paul served the French; Holy Trinity, the Germans; and Sts. Peter and Paul, the Irish and "Americans." Across the city, the Redemptorist Fathers lived in a single rectory while serving three ethnic communities: the English-speakers at St. Alphonsus, the Germans at St. Mary Assumption, and the French at Notre Dame de Bon Secour. Each Redemptorist parish had its own imposing brick church by 1860.

The rural character of the majority of the region's Catholic communities shaped the size and complexity of parish life. Many parishes served less than a hundred families, often scattered over many miles. Parish budgets were small and goods as well as money helped support the pastor and church. Parishioners helped build churches, prepare meals for the pastor, provide elementary religious instruction for the young, and assist the needy. The new, imposing brick churches that began to appear in both urban and rural areas marked an increase in both parish size and complexity. In many parishes, men assisted with parish construction, management, and finances, while women fostered liturgical devotion, personal piety, and education through altar societies, sodalities, and religious instruction. A visiting priest who preached or lectured well could attract large audiences of both Catholics and Protestants in remote areas.

By 1850, the region's Catholic parishes already included a diverse ethnic heritage. Seven major ethnic groups or categories can be identified. Africans and their descendants formed the region's largest ethnic group. In 1850, there were 1,453,000 slaves and 38,000 free persons of color in the region's seven states (excluding the future Oklahoma).[19] The region included the largest concentration of Catholic slaves and free persons of color. Louisiana's Code Noir legislated that Catholic slaveholders must see that their slaves were baptized and instructed in their religion and that families not be separated. The provision concerning baptism was better observed than those concerning family life and education. During the first two decades of the nineteenth century at St. Louis Cathedral in New Orleans, more than twice as many slaves and free persons of color were baptized as whites.[20] Despite harsh state laws restricting free persons of color, one Catholic parish—St. Augustine in Isle Brevelle between Alexandria and Natchitoches—was founded by and for free persons of color before 1850. Free persons of color also played a significant role in the early history of New Orleans' St. Augustine Parish.[21]

The second major ethnic group originated in Texas with the early Spanish missions; the original Spanish settlers were soon augmented by Spanish colonials and their descendants from Mexico. By 1836, however, when Texas revolted against Mexico, Mexicans numbered only 7% of Texas' population.[22]

A third group was composed of the colonial French who settled in the Mississippi Valley at Old Biloxi (1699), Mobile (1703), Natchez (1716), and New Orleans (1718). This group was epitomized in the Catholic Creole life of New Orleans that Roger Baudier so vividly depicted.[23]

The first Catholic settlers of Holy Cross, St. Mary, Fairfield, White Sulphur, and Bardstown in Kentucky represent a fourth ethnic group. These parishes were established by American-born pioneers from the East Coast and, with the exception of Bardstown, represented a minority religion in a predominantly Protestant culture. This minority pattern was common in most areas of the region.

A fifth major ethnic group—sometimes confused with Louisiana's first French settlers—consisted of transplanted French immigrants from Acadia and Santo Domingo. These two groups entered Louisiana in the late eighteenth and early nineteenth centuries and made substantial contributions to Louisiana's unique Catholic role in the South. The Santo Domingans quickly became assimilated into New Orleans Creole life, while the Acadians generally pioneered the rural areas of southwest Louisiana where they maintained a distinctive culture that still endures.

The Indians who were found mainly in Indian Territory represent a sixth major ethnic group in the region. The process of relocating the Indians to this area continued throughout the Antebellum period. In 1850, Father Theopholus Marivault of Fort Smith in Arkansas was responsible for Fort Gibson in the Cherokee Nation and also had "lately commenced a mission among the Cherokees and Choctaws."[24]

The newly arrived immigrants formed the final generic ethnic group, although this category included many nationalities. By 1850, the Irish and Germans were the largest immigrant groups in the South. The Germans congregated especially in New Orleans, Covington, and Louisville, as well as several rural areas in Kentucky and Texas. Several 1850 parishes in Kentucky, Louisiana, Mississippi, and Tennessee were identified as Irish. However, immigrant Catholics did not come to the South in the same large numbers as to northern cities.

Each of these major ethnic groups included a great mixture of nationalities, tribes, outlooks, and traditions. The later stereotype of the Indian, the Irishman, the Mexican, and the Frenchman obscured the great diversity that existed between individual segments within these groups. Great differences even existed between similar Indian tribes such as the Sioux, the Cheyenne, and the Comanche.[25] In Louisiana, established Creole and Acadian families looked upon newly arrived immigrants from revolutionary and Napoleonic France more as aliens than fellow-countrymen.

Thus, by 1850, the South already had an ethnically complex parish life that extended throughout seven states, was concentrated in rural parishes that often served as centers for long circuits to neighboring Catholic communities, and, with the exception of southern Louisiana and selected areas of Alabama, Kentucky, Mississippi, and Texas, was a minority religion in a Protestant culture. Parish communities provided familiar language, devotions, and customs for newly arrived immigrants en route to their new American way of life. European devotions, prejudices, and customs were also still strong among the descendants of the colonial populations of Louisiana, Alabama, and Texas. Finally, one vital factor in early parish development was unquestionably the strong sense of Catholic faith that led small groups of men and women to make extraordinary sacrifices to maintain their inherited beliefs and practices, build a place of Catholic worship, and request a pastor of their own. This strong religious faith appears frequently in parish histories as the driving force in the development of new parishes.

## Notes

1. *1850 Catholic Directory* lists 166 "churches," thirteen missions, and 139 stations; cf. Appendix A for a more accurate number of parishes based on the appointment of a resident pastor. Of the 101 original parishes, eleven would be closed, reduced to missions,

or merged with newly formed parishes during the next 130 years. Only 4% of the region's 1980 Catholic parishes were founded before 1850.

2. Spanish colonial parishes were St. Martinville, St. James, St. Gabriel, Donaldsonville, Edgard, Opelousas, Galveztown on the Amite River below Baton Rouge (established during the American Revolution as an outpost against the British), St. Bernard, Baton Rouge, Plattenville, and Mansura.

3. Observations by Msgr. Francis Leon Gassler, cited in Charles Nolan, *Mother Clare Coady: Her Life, Her Times and Her Sisters* (New Orleans: Academy Enterprises of New Orleans, 1983), 38–39.

4. Research notes of Father J. Edgar Bruns, historian of the Archdiocese of New Orleans, on Archbishop Antoine Blanc. On the complex role of trustees, cf. also *Catholics in the Old South: Essays on Church and Culture,* edited by Randall M. Miller and Jon. L. Wakelyn (Macon: Mercer University Press, 1983), 20–26, 35, 83–87.

5. Personal research notes for *A Southern Catholic Heritage: Volume II, The Ante-Bellum Parishes of Alabama, Louisiana and Mississippi.*

6. *1840* and *1850 Catholic Directories* and "Parish" data base.

7. J. D. B. DeBow, *Statistical View of the United States. . . . Being a Compendium of the Seventh Census* (1850). Texas numbered 18,000 foreign-born white residents (11.4%), while Kentucky listed 31,000 (4.1%). In Louisiana, 67,000 foreign-born residents formed 26.3% of the white population. The percentage for the smaller states was: Alabama (1.7%), Arkansas (0.9%), Mississippi (1.6%), and Tennessee (0.7%).

8. *Ibid.* Kentucky had 982,000 inhabitants; Alabama, 772,000; Mississippi, 606,000; Louisiana, 518,000; Arkansas, 210,000.

9. Miller and Wakelyn, 13–17.

10. *Ibid.,* 53–76.

11. George J. Flanigen, ed., *Catholicity in Tennessee: A Sketch of Catholic Activities in the State, 1541–1937* (Nashville: Ambrose Printing Company, 1937), 26.

12. Oscar H. Lipscomb, "The Administration of John Quinlan, Second Bishop of Mobile, 1859–1883" in *Records of the American Catholic Historical Society of Philadelphia,* LXXVIII (March–December, 1967), 8–9.

13. George J. Flanigen, compiler, *The Centenary of Sts. Peter and Paul's Parish, Chattanooga, Tennessee* (Chattanooga: 1952), 4–5. Archives of the Diocese of Nashville. A detailed description of Father John D. Maguire's journeys in Middle and East Tennessee is found on pages 5–7.

14. Carlos E. Castaneda, *Our Catholic Heritage in Texas* (Austin: Boeckmann-Jones Company, 1958), VII:106. Also cf. VII:16–28 for Bishop Timon's first visit to Texas.

15. Cf. Roger Baudier's unpublished essays on the Dutch clergy in Louisiana and Mississippi, Baudier Papers, 2:7, Archives of the Archdiocese of New Orleans.

16. *1850 Catholic Directory.*

17. J. D. B. DeBow, *Statistical View of the United States. . . . Being a Compendium of the Seventh Census* (1850).

18. In New Orleans, new parishes included St. Patrick (1833), St. Vincent de Paul (1838), St. Augustine (1841), St. Joseph (1844), Annunciation (1844), Holy Name of Mary (1847), Holy Trinity (1847), St. Teresa of Avila (1848), Sts. Peter and Paul (1848), and St. Stephan (1849). In Louisville, St. Boniface (1837) and Our Lady (1839) were founded, while St. Vincent de Paul (1847) was established in Mobile. In Covington, As-

sumption (1837) and Mother of God (1841) were founded. St. Thomas and St. Joseph in Bardstown trace their origins to 1812 and 1816, respectively.

19. J. D. B. DeBow, *Statistical View of the United States. . . . Being a Compendium of the Seventh Census* (1850).

20. St. Louis Cathedral Baptismal Registers, 1800–1820. Archives of the Archdiocese of New Orleans.

21. Concerning the Isle Brevelle community, cf. Gary B. Mills, *The Forgotten People: Cane River's People of Color* (Baton Rouge: Louisiana State University Press, 1977); also cf. the same author's essay in Miller and Wakelyn, 171–194; Concerning St. Augustine, cf. personal research notes for Volume II of *A Southern Catholic Heritage*.

22. Joe B. Frantz, *Texas: A Bicentennial History* (Nashville: American Association of State and Local History, 1976), 59.

23. Roger Baudier, "Historic Old New Orleans," in *Catholic Action of the South, 1932–1960.*

24. *1850 Catholic Directory.*

25. Lawrence Goodwyn, *The South Central States: Arkansas, Louisiana, Oklahoma, Texas; Time Life Library of America,* Oliver E. Allen, Senior Ed. (New York: Time Incorporated, 1967), 58–59.

## CHAPTER TWO

# Plantations, War, and Reconstruction (1850–1880)

The three decades from 1850 to 1880 have special significance in Southern history. They witnessed the final years of Antebellum culture, the fratricidal War Between the States, and the harsh experience of political Reconstruction that so shaped and scarred Southern life and thought for decades. The three decades formed sharply contrasting backgrounds for Catholic parish development.

The 1850s began with the great compromise concerning the extension of slavery into newly formed territories. The compromise was not a lasting one and the slavery debate moved inexorably toward Secession and the confrontation at Fort Sumter in 1861. Throughout the decade, the South Central region remained a rural, plantation society where cotton was king. By 1850, about 60% of all the slaves in the United States were employed in growing cotton. New Orleans was the major exception to this rural pattern.[1]

The 1850s also saw the continued arrival of large numbers of immigrants, particularly from Germany and Ireland. These new immigrants soon fanned nativist animosity that took concrete form in the Know-Nothing Party of the 1850s. In addition to local and state officers, the party nationally elected seventy-five congressmen in 1854. The same year, pitched battles took place in St. Louis between native Americans and immigrant Irish.[2]

Several Catholic parishes became victims of this nativist hostility. In 1852, the small Catholic community at Knoxville, Tennessee, purchased land and, in March, began the construction of its first church. When a wave of bigotry "threatened the structure," two Protestant gentlemen, Mr. Swan and Mr. Nelson, intervened to help protect the Catholic property.[3] In 1854, the Catholic Church in Helena, Arkansas, was burned down; around the same time, hostile Protestants in Fort Smith, Arkansas, instituted an unsuccessful lawsuit to block Bishop Andrew Byrne's purchase of property for the city's Catholic community.[4]

In 1855, nativist bigotry erupted into violence and death in Louisville. The election of a Know-Nothing mayor and incitement by the local newspaper created a tense atmosphere among the city's 55,000 citizens, half of whom were Irish and German immigrants. On August 6, election day, hostile nativist mobs attacked immigrant Catholics; 22 people died in the violence and many more were

253

wounded. St. Martin of Tours Church was attacked during the riot.[5] In San Antonio, Catholic Mayor Thomas J. Devine helped disperse a Know-Nothing mob; one death resulted; Catholics in New Orleans, Nashville, and Galveston were also attacked.[6] The Know-Nothing movement was soon swallowed up in the events that led to the Civil War.

Five of the original Confederate states—Alabama, Arkansas, Mississippi, Texas, and Louisiana—came from the South Central region. Tennessee voted to join the seceding states after Fort Sumter. Many Indians in the future Oklahoma sided with the South—a factor that was later used to justify further expropriation of their land. Even Kentucky, the region's only state that did not join the Confederacy, felt the impact of the war. Bishop Martin J. Spalding of Louisville

> . . ."soon saw the educational establishments of the diocese either closed or languishing from the effects of the all-pervading disaster that was sweeping the country from the Ohio River to the gulf. He saw his own people divided and warring against each other, as was indeed the case with his separated brethren all over the state. Himself a non-combatant . . . , he left nothing undone that it was possible for him to do to assuage suffering and to lessen woes that were irremediable through any human agency. 'My diocese,' he wrote about this time, 'is cut in twain; I must attend to souls without getting into angry political discussion.' "[7]

The war devastated many areas of the South. Tennessee was a major battleground; many towns and rural areas throughout the region witnessed the arrival of invading armies. Early in 1862, Union forces took Forts Henry and Donelson in Tennessee. On April 6–7, 1862, both Union and Confederate armies suffered immense losses at Shiloh. Less than three weeks later on April 26, Captain David Farragut accepted the surrender of New Orleans, which became an occupied city for the next fifteen years. The Vicksburg campaign, including the lightning attack on Jackson, occupied much of the first half of 1863. Grant laid siege to Vicksburg on May 22 and accepted its surrender on July 4; five days later, Port Hudson, Louisiana, surrendered, thus clearing the Mississippi River of Confederate defenses. The Battle of Chattanooga, on November 24, 1863, opened the way for Sherman's destructive march toward the sea. In August of 1864, the Union fleet entered Mobile Bay and assaulted the city on March 17, 1865; Confederate defenders evacuated the city on April 12.

Many Catholic parishes witnessed bloodshed and destruction during the war. St. Mary Church in Galveston was riddled with bullets; the city's Ursuline Nuns cared for the wounded of both sides. Alexandria, Natchitoches, Monroe, Donaldsonville, and Thibodaux were among the many Louisiana cities that were occupied by Federal troops. Assumption Church in Nashville was commandeered and pillaged in 1864 by Federal troops, while St. Mary Church served for a time as a hospital. The Catholic community in Jackson, Mississippi, had its place of worship destroyed or pillaged three times by Federal troops; the early parish registers were destroyed in the July of 1863 fire. The Catholic Church in Selma, Alabama, was among the buildings destroyed when Union troops set fire to the city in 1863. The churches or schools in Alexandria, Hydropolis, Donaldsonville, and Patterson in Louisiana, Vicksburg and Yazoo City in Mississippi, and Chattanooga were among those partially damaged or occupied by Northern troops. The Catholic churches in Bay St. Louis, Mississippi, and Alexandria, Louisiana, were saved only through the intervention of local priests.[8]

In addition to physical destruction, many churches found themselves in occupied cities. New Orleans became an occupied city in 1862; Mobile, in 1865. These occupations made contact between the region's bishops and their flock difficult. Sections of Louisiana were cut off for several years from New Orleans. Bishop John Quinlan of Mobile was placed in prison overnight in Columbus by a zealous Confederate guard who thought the bishop's papers were not in order.[9] This occupation status also insinuated itself in the very fabric of parish life. When Jefferson Davis ordered prayers and fasting for the success of the Confederacy in 1862 and again in 1863, Louisiana's military governors forbade such observances.

The war drained parishes both of men of fighting age and the region's limited number of priests. Eight priests from Spring Hill College in Mobile served as Confederate chaplains; three had official commissions.[10] When Archbishop Odin asked for volunteer chaplains in New Orleans, every Redemptorist and Jesuit in the city volunteered together with many diocesan priests. The most famous of those whom Archbishop Odin allowed to serve was French-born Father Isidore Francois Turgis. Father Turgis' personal courage on the battlefield and unselfish devotion to his men won him the lasting respect of New Orleans' war veterans. His funeral in 1868 was among the largest the city had ever witnessed.[11]

Many Southern pastors who defiantly proclaimed their loyalty to the Confederacy found themselves imprisoned, under house arrest, or at least under surveillance. Father James Ignatius Mullon of St. Patrick in New Orleans openly defied General Benjamin Butler and prayed "as he saw fit." Butler did not imprison the priest for fear of antagonizing the Irish, including those among his own troops. Father Napoleon Perche of New Orleans was placed under house arrest and his paper, *Le Propagateur Catholique,* was suspended. Father Francis Mittelbronn at Pointe Coupee proudly blessed the Confederate flag of his departing parishioners despite the nearby presence of Federal troops; he was promptly arrested, imprisoned in Baton Rouge, tried, and then returned to his parish under guard. When Bishop William Henry Elder of Natchez refused to follow a military order concerning prayers for Union civil and military authorities in Catholic churches, he was briefly sent into exile in Vidalia, Louisiana, in July of 1864. Father Emmeram Bliemel, O.S.B., the pastor of Assumption Church in Nashville from 1861 to 1863, was arrested by Northern troops and charged with treason for carrying medical supplies to Confederate soldiers. Father Bliemel was later released, re-arrested, and again released; he died on August 31, 1864, while administering the Sacraments during the battle of Jonesboro.[12]

In addition to draining parishes of their men and dioceses of their priests, the war also brought economic hardship throughout the South. Schools particularly suffered. Spring Hill College's enrollment dropped from 233 in 1861 to sixty-three in 1862. Many Catholic academies that depended on revenue from boarders faced difficult times. The chronicler of Mt. Carmel Academy in Thibodaux, Louisiana, noted that the school had flourished until the war. "At the beginning of September, 1862, we had only twelve boarding students and this number remained more or less the same until 1866. Due to these unfortunate times we lost the sum of $2,000.00 due on the tuition of the students."[13]

The war had a dramatic effect on the foundation of new parishes. No five-year period between 1850 and 1980 saw fewer new parishes established than between 1861 and 1865. Only twenty-two new parishes in Alabama, Kentucky, Louisiana, Mississippi, and Texas were founded during the war. Two of these new parishes—Patterson and Lakeland in Louisiana—returned to mission status in 1862 and remained without pastors until the end of the war. No new parishes were established in Arkansas and Tennessee during the war.

By the war's end, the South was devastated politically, socially, and economically. The cotton crop did not again equal its 1860 size until 1879. Louisiana's sugar cane industry was in ruins. While property values increased rapidly in the North during the Reconstruction years, they decreased significantly in the South. In Texas, land values fell to 20% of their 1860 valuation. Roads, bridges, railroad tracks, and levees were in ruins or at least disrepair. The banking system was in chaos. The war had also brought havoc to the South's modest educational system, draining teachers, students, and resources. In the Diocese of Natchitoches, "when the men in gray straggled back, it was to find ruin, poverty and distress all through North Louisiana, to which soon were added the racial question and the scheming carpetbaggers with their Reconstruction plans . . . [Two Catholic schools closed.] Building of new churches and mission chapels halted for a long time. Funds were lacking. Priests suffered want—parishioners had little for themselves."[14]

Emancipation placed the South's black population at the center of Reconstruction. "Never before in the history of the world had civil and political rights been conferred at one stroke on so large a body of men."[15] While the promised social and economic benefits of emancipation did not materialize, the changing Southern culture was reflected in the fact that more than 600,000 blacks were enrolled in elementary schools in the South by the end of Reconstruction.[16] Reconstruction in the South ended in 1877 with the withdrawal of the last Federal troops from Louisiana. Many of the political, economic, social, and educational benefits that the emancipation had promised to the South's black population were soon diluted or destroyed.

The impact of the war and Reconstruction on Catholic parishes was evident in the small Catholic community at New Gascony, Arkansas. The congregation had built a church to accommodate almost 200 people before the war. Most of the town's men served in the Confederate army and many did not return. In 1867, scarcely twenty people attended Sunday Mass.[17] The economic hardships of the Reconstruction years were also partially responsible for the large debts that Bishop John Quinlan of Mobile and Archbishop Napoleon Perche of New Orleans contracted to meet the expanding needs of their dioceses. Both left debts that their successors had to deal with for many years.[18]

In Texas, the harshness of Reconstruction was mitigated by a unique American phenomenon that began in 1866. That year, the first major cattle drive from near the mouth of the Rio Grande River headed north for the railroad junction at Sedalia, Missouri. The following year, cattle headed for the newly created railroad junction at Abilene, Kansas. Thus began the quarter century of the great cattle drives that added a new source of wealth and power to Texas and Oklahoma's already rich farmlands. The drives also formed the basis of a new American folklore and mythology, for the cowboy reflected some of the fundamental aspirations of the American spirit.[19]

Against this grim background, it is surprising that Catholic parish life continued to expand in the South Central region throughout these thirty years. Additional parishes were formed, the number of priests increased, and new Catholic schools and institutions appeared throughout the region. During these thirty years, the number of Catholic communities more than doubled to 685; the number of Catholic parishes increased 243% to 345—a growth rate unparalleled during any other period in this study.[20]

The pattern of parish expansion followed that of the preceding decades. The region's typical new Catholic communities were not the large urban parishes such as St. John the Baptist in New Orleans or St. Paul in Louisville, but rather the small, rural communities such as Sacred Heart Mission in Winchester, Tennessee, Immaculate Conception Parish in Panna Maria, Texas, or St. Paul Parish in Florence, Kentucky. By the end of the period, three out of every four Catholic parishes were the sole Catholic communities in their respective cities or towns.

One measure of this extension of a Catholic presence into the countryside between 1850 and 1880 is the fact that Catholic parishes were established in 106 new counties; in 1850, only sixty-seven counties had Catholic parishes. Again and again, parish histories recount two overlapping patterns in the formation of these new parishes. In the first pattern, the priest on his mission circuit searched out isolated Catholic families and became the catalyst in forming a community. He said Mass, administered the Sacraments, instructed both adults and children, and provided a tangible link with the universal Catholic Church. He returned on a regular basis, informed neighboring families of these visits, and encouraged the construction of a chapel. On occasion, the priest then chose such a community as the new center of his mission circuit.

Fathers Ghislain Boheme of Mississippi and Charles Menard of Louisiana epitomized this pattern of parish formation. When Father Boheme was assigned to Paulding, Mississippi, in 1843, his territory stretched from Tennessee to the Gulf of Mexico and from Alabama to near the Pearl River. Father Boheme began visiting the area's Catholic families and persuaded about 200 Catholics, mostly Irish, to move near the church to form a Catholic nucleus for the area. By 1857, Father Boheme, in addition to caring for his small Paulding community, made a regular circuit of 350 miles on horseback to visit individual Catholic families throughout the area. Father Boheme died near Ashland, Virginia, on June 2, 1862, less than two months after he volunteered as a chaplain in the Confederate army.[21] Father Charles Menard of Thibodaux, Louisiana, is still remembered as the "Apostle of Bayou Lafourche." His remarkable journal, covering his half century (1842–1894) as pastor of this small community on Bayou Lafourche, recounts his frequent, long journeys to outlying areas and his personal role in the foundation of every new parish established in the area before 1894.[22]

The second pattern of Catholic expansion saw these same isolated families as the primary force in the formation of new stations, missions, and parishes. These pioneer Catholic settlers sought out a priest to come and celebrate Mass, administer the Sacraments and preach. They banded together to donate or purchase a small piece of land, build a chapel and, finally, requested a pastor of their own. The early stages of these Catholic communities are usually inadequately documented with emphasis on the purchase of land, the subscription list, the building of the chapel, the first names in the sacramental registers, and, perhaps, the names of the first trustees.

A few parish histories provide a glimpse at how these rural Catholic families—and they were legion in the South—preserved and strengthened their faith during these early stages of parish formation. The first Catholics of St. Florian, Alabama, gathered in the small frame church they erected in 1872 where John B. Locker, a blacksmith and wagonmaker who had migrated from Ohio, led the community in the Rosary and other prayers, while Mrs. Annie Schaut took care of the sacristy, taught Catechism and music, and directed the community brass band.[23]

At Mon Louis Island below Mobile, Maximilian Colin, a native of France and the island's first resident, built a small chapel in 1853. Maximilian and his wife "were steeped in Catholic faith and they set out to live every phase of that faith." Each morning and evening, Mr. Colin gathered the area's small community of residents at the chapel "to pray, sing and worship." About 1861, priests from Mobile began to occasionally visit the Mon Louis community. When the Civil War began, every man on the island was conscripted into the Confederate army. "Then followed the practice of the Rosary every day to bring back the husbands and men who had 'gone to war.' " When every man from Mon Louis Island returned alive from the war, the community continued the practice of the daily Rosary in thanksgiving through the late 1940s.[24]

The first settlers came to Tours, Texas, in 1873 from Illinois and Austria, just two years after the area had been opened for settlement. They immediately built a small log chapel and residence for visiting priests. For many years, John Jupe acted as "lay pastor" on feast days and Sundays, reading and explaining the Gospel as well as leading the congregation in the recitation of the Rosary. Tours did not have a resident priest until 1886. When Bishop Dominic Mauncy of Brownsville made a Confirmation tour of his vicariate in 1879, he confirmed 2,862 adults and children at eighty ranches in the area; the bishop was struck by "the simple generosity of the hardworking rancheros" he encountered.[25]

This same pattern was evident in a more urban setting at Bellevue, Kentucky. In 1873, the German Catholic community in Bellevue was attending Mass at nearby Newport. On February 2, 1873, these Bellevue men formed a society to purchase land and build a church. Weekly meetings were held and enthusiasm ran high. Since the number of Irish and German Catholics in Bellevue was about even, an invitation was extended to the Irish to join in a common effort for a new church. "A few responded." The Catholic women of Bellevue also formed a society with the same aim.

> "The Catholics of Bellevue in those days were not blest with earthly goods; they belonged to the humbler walks of life. Large families were the rule. They had, however, a strong, solid faith; and courage and generosity, and above all, loyalty to their spiritual superiors, were characteristic of them. They gave generously of their meagre means, and hand in hand they worked and toiled to raise the necessary funds to erect a place of worship."

On March 9, Bishop Augustus Toebbe of Covington met with the men and approved their building proposal, adding a substantial donation of his own. Land was purchased in April and paid for by the following May. In April of 1874, a census revealed that Bellevue had forty Catholic families with one hundred adults and ninety-two children. In July, a building committee was chosen and work began immediately on a one-story brick building to serve as church and school. "Considerable work, such as excavating, hauling, etc., was done gratuitously by the members." The completed building, "humble in appearance yet withal a house of God," was dedicated under the name of Sacred Heart of Jesus on November 22, 1874. Passionist Fathers from Cincinnati served the new congregation on Sundays for a year before Father Bernard Hillebrand was appointed the first pastor in 1875; the same year, Sisters of Notre Dame from Cleveland, Ohio, opened a Catholic school. Church wardens were chosen "to assist the pastor in the administration of the temporalities of the church." The congregation grew rapidly and by 1890 numbered 200 families.[26]

Parish growth was not limited to the countryside. By 1880, eight cities had three or more Catholic parishes. New Orleans with twenty-nine parishes and Louisville with eighteen were the region's only large urban Catholic centers. Covington, Newport, Nashville, Memphis, Mobile, and San Antonio numbered between three and seven parishes. Seven other cities and towns had two parishes.

One new urban parish was unique. St. Augustine was established for Louisville's black Catholic community in 1869. The number of black Catholics in Louisville increased significantly after Lincoln's 1863 emancipation. The opening of several black non-Catholic Churches after the war posed both a model and a threat to the Catholic community. In 1869, Bishop William McCloskey appointed Father John Lancaster Spalding to establish a parish for the city's black Catholics. Father Spalding, in a letter to his uncle, Archbishop Martin J. Spalding of Baltimore, wrote, "I am finally persuaded that it is the duty of the Church in this country to make greater efforts than have been made for the conversion of Negroes, not for their sake alone but for the general welfare of the Church and the nation." The new community first used the cathedral for its organizational meetings and worship. The seventy-five members of St. Augustine Parish attended the blessing of their completed school-church building on February 20, 1870. One Mass each Sunday was set aside for the neighborhood's white Catholics who regularly attended St. Augustine until the completion of their new church—Sacred Heart—in 1873.[27]

Much has been written about the possible number of "strayed sheep" among the South's Catholics. Around 1813, Bishop Flaget, who spoke from experience as well as conviction, noted the future path that Southern priests needed to follow:

> "It is almost impossible to form an idea of the Catholics who forget their religion on account of lack of priests, or the lack of zeal of priests who have charge of these congregations. Not a day passes that we do not find great numbers of these strayed sheep, who, because they do not see the real shepherd, become Baptists, Methodist [sic], etc., or at least nothingists. To remedy this great evil it would be necessary that a priest, filled with the spirit of God, and convinced of the value of souls, should often get away from his accustomed route, and going out into the country, ask if there are not Catholics in these regions. The discovery of a single one will lead to the discovery of ten others. If he found only one family he could say Mass there, preach, catechise, and pray. Let him show a great desire for the salvation of souls and a contempt for their money. With such dispositions a priest would have the consolation of bringing to the bosom of the Church millions of his children who never will enter it unless we go after them."[28]

Many Catholics in the South abandoned the religion of their forefathers to join local Protestant churches, although accurate figures are difficult to establish. When Bishop John Quinlan visited Eutaw, Alabama, in 1861, he found few Catholic descendants among those who remained from the Napoleonic exiles who had settled there between 1818 and 1820.[29]

Of special interest, however, is how isolated Catholic families and small communities who seldom saw a priest retained their Catholic faith and allegiance. One such group of Catholics was found in Winchester, Tennessee. Father Joseph Stokes from Charleston first visited the community in 1829 in response to a request made via Dublin, Ireland. Among the Catholics who welcomed Father Stokes was James Dardis who had not seen a Catholic priest in thirty years. For the next forty years, the Catholics at Winchester remained a mission station and were periodically visited by priests who celebrated Mass in a local home, the county court house, or a Protestant church. In 1866, John Henry Erwin, a Presbyterian minister, became a Catholic and joined the community. The small group of Catholics received another boost in 1868 when a dozen Catholic families were brought to Winchester to work in a factory. Although the factory soon failed, a few families remained. Around the same year, the community built St. Martin Church, named in honor of the patron of one of its members, Martin Scharber. Each family contributed $40.00 and helped with the actual construction. At the time, the congregation was a heterogeneous group of French, Swiss, German, Irish, and English ancestry. Winchester remained a mission for another two decades until the arrival of the Paulist Fathers in 1890.[30]

A poignant, public 1868 letter from the small community at Bastrop in Morehouse [Civil] Parish, Louisiana, reflects the struggle and frustration of Catholics in multi-denominational towns. While their Jewish, Methodist, Baptist, and Episcopalian neighbors each had their own church and religious school, the Catholics had only a lot for a future building. The potential for conversions as well as internal community growth was evident during the semi-annual visits of Father Louis Gergaud from Monroe: ''The people are delighted when there are Catholic services, and the whole town turns out when they hear of his coming to preach.'' The community requested a resident priest who could also offer needed religious instruction for both adults and children. In a public reply, the Louisiana Catholic paper, *The Morning Star,* commented that the Reconstruction-era Church was ''prostrated in material resources.'' Money and priests were simply not available to respond to the community's request. Bastrop did not receive a resident pastor until 1943.[31]

A number of factors contributed to the expansion and growth of Catholic parishes during these thirty years. The first important factor was the region's continued population growth. By 1880, 8,919,000 people resided in the South Central region (excluding the future Oklahoma), more than double the region's population in 1850. The region's 3,012,000 black residents represented 45.8% of the nation's total black population.[32]

The absence of a large foreign-born population continued to retard the region's parish development. The 1880 census listed only 274,000 foreign-born residents in the South Central region—less than the number of foreign-born residents in the states of California, Massachusetts, Michigan, New York, Ohio, Pennsylvania, or Wisconsin. New York State alone had more than four times the total foreign-born population of the South Central region.[33] The Irish and Germans were the two largest immigrant populations in the South Central region and both made significant contributions to the region's parish growth. Irish and German parishes were established in both urban and rural areas. The 1880 census also included national figures for two other foreign-born groups that contributed much to Catholicism in the South: the French (107,000) and the Mexicans (68,000).[34]

Another important factor was the increasing number of priests who served in the area. From 1850 to 1880, this number increased almost threefold to 558. The most impressive growth took place in Texas where the number of priests jumped from sixteen to 115 in thirty years. In contrast, Alabama had twenty-two priests in 1880, an increase of only two over 1850.[35]

Only two states—Kentucky and Mississippi—reported the breakdown of religious-diocesan priests in 1880. In these states, diocesan priests formed three-quarters of the clergy. The percentage working in parishes was even higher. Religious communities such as the Jesuits in Louisiana and Alabama, the Benedictines in Central Arkansas, and the Oblates of Mary Immaculate in the lower Rio Grande Valley made significant contributions to parish development.[36]

This increase in the region's clergy took place despite the devastating number of priests who died from yellow fever, cholera, and other diseases, as well as the many priests whose ministry in individual states was a transitory one. Several of Bishop John Quinlan's priests in Alabama died soon after ordination. In a twelve week period between August 11 and October 30, 1878, eleven priests in the Archdiocese of New Orleans died. Most were victims of yellow fever; they ranged in age from 27 to 48. The yellow fever epidemic at Memphis that same year claimed the lives of an estimated 2,000 Catholics, including twelve Sisters, ten priests, and three brothers.[37]

Parish histories particularly honor the memory of priests, sisters, and brothers who have sacrificed themselves for the congregation. Many gave generously of their time, their talents, and even their health. The memories of dedicated men and women who sacrificed their very lives are especially precious. One of many examples of the self-sacrificing work by priests and religious during times of suffering took place in 1873 at Shreveport, Louisiana. When a violent yellow fever epidemic broke out on August 18, almost half the city's 9,000 residents fled. All three of Shreveport's priests—Fathers Jean Pierre, Isidore Queremais, and Jean Marie Biler—together with the Daughters of the Cross from the local academy ignored their personal safety and dedicated themselves to assisting the sick and dying. Father Queremais died on September 15, Sister Martha on September 16, Sister Angela on September 23, and Father Pierre on September 24. When the dying Father Biler wrote to Father Louis Gergaud of Monroe for help, Father Gergaud left immediately, telling his assistant, "Please write to the bishop and tell him that I am going to my death." Father Biler died on September 26 and Father

Gergaud, on October 1. Father Francois LeVezouet of Natchitoches who was also summoned to assist his confreres died on October 9. Father J. J. Duffo, S. J., a veteran of yellow fever epidemics at New Orleans, answered Bishop Auguste Martin's plea for help and remained in Shreveport for the last days of the tragedy; 759 people died at Shreveport during the epidemic.[38]

Father Peter Keralum, O.M.I., "the lost missionary," epitomized another type of heroic pastoral service; he was one of the Oblates of Mary Immaculate who served in Texas' Rio Grande Valley. Father Keralum disappeared in November of 1872, while on a mission circuit out of Mercedes. For a decade, his disappearance was the object of much speculation. On November 30, 1882, his remains, saddle bags, and Mass kit were found under mesquite and brush by five cowboys looking for wild calves. A confrere noted, "He had died a natural death from exhaustion, all alone in a desolate country."[39]

The establishment of five new ecclesiastical jurisdictions also fostered parish development. In 1853, the Antebellum policy of creating new dioceses in sparsely Catholic-populated areas continued with the establishment of the dioceses of Covington in Kentucky and Natchitoches (now Alexandria-Shreveport) in Louisiana. The unsettled times that followed are reflected in the fact that more than two decades passed before the creation of the next diocese—San Antonio in 1874. That same year, the vicariate apostolic of Brownsville—the forerunner of the Diocese of Corpus Christi—was established. Two years later, the prefecture apostolic of the Indian Territory was created and placed under the direction of French Benedictines.

A final factor in parish development was the substantial financial assistance that European missionary societies provided to new, struggling dioceses in the region. *La Societe de la Propagation de la Foi,* the *Leopoldinen Stiftung,* and the *Ludwig Missionsverein* all provided needed funds for new churches and schools, seminary training for priests, and ship passages for European priests and sisters to come to the area. The Diocese of Galveston alone received almost a quarter million dollars from these three societies between 1846 and 1901.[40]

Several general observations about parishes during this period can be gleaned from parish and diocesan histories. Parishes varied greatly in size. Many parishes in New Orleans and Louisville served several thousand people. In the countryside, parish size was measured in distance rather than people. Many rural parishes began with only a handful of people. The Dallas Catholic community, in 1868, consisted of the Maximo Guillot family and two single men; six years later, Dallas had a resident priest.[41] When Father James O'Kean arrived in Pocahontas, Arkansas, in 1868 to take up residence and begin construction of Randolph County's first Catholic Church, only two Catholics resided in the town and none in the surrounding countryside. Before he was called to Little Rock in 1870, O'Kean had received seventy-five converts into the Catholic community.[42]

The new parishes of this period reflect the region's diverse ethnic character.

Most southern rural Louisiana parishes used French for their records and sermons. A similar Spanish character appeared in areas of Texas. The South, however, was also becoming a melting pot of its own, though to a lesser degree than the North. San Antonio in 1880 reflected the region's new ethnic composition. In addition to San Fernando Cathedral, the city's other three parishes served English, German, and Polish communities.

The largest number of immigrant parishes identified in this study for this period were German. Irish parishes are more difficult to identify from general histories. Other ethnic minorities also appear during these three decades. Panna Maria in Texas (1858) prides itself as the nation's oldest Polish parish.[43] St. Michael in San Antonio and Annunciation in St. Hedwig, Texas, were founded in 1866 to serve Polish residents. In 1865, St. Mary in Prada was established for Slovak immigrants. Holy Rosary in D'Hanis, Texas, was an Alsatian parish, while Nativity of the Blessed Virgin Mary in High Hill, Texas (1870), served mainly Austrians. The South's first Italian parish, the Church of the Resurrection, was established in New Orleans in 1873; two years later, the parish was transferred to the old mortuary chapel on Rampart Street and renamed St. Anthony.[44]

The region's largest ethnic group were those of African descent. The revolutionary change in their status as citizens during these years offered the Catholic Church as well as other Christian denominations a new challenge to evangelize. Father James Hennesey, S.J., observed that the Second Plenary Council of Baltimore in 1866 decided to leave this challenge to individual bishops rather than adopt a comprehensive program. He added, "one serious consequence of internal dissension was the failure to adopt a cohesive and vigorous program for evangelization of the four million freed black people. Specific action plans fashioned by Spalding and recommended by Roman authorities were watered down to the level of pious exhortation with implementation left to local choice."[45] The basic pattern that emerged after the council was a continuation of the existing practice of serving black Catholics in their present parishes. As social lines hardened, this meant that blacks' participation in parish life was limited to worship, the Sacraments, and their own organizations; St. Augustine in Louisville was the exception.

In most areas of the South, Catholics remained a religious minority. Catholics in the South often bore the brunt of interdenominational rivalry, territoriality, and hostility, although the early correspondence from missionaries of the American Home Missionary Society (founded in 1826) included as many objections to the Disciples of Christ and Mormons as to Catholics. In 1845, seven Protestant ministers in Louisville joined together "to awaken the attention of the community to the dangers which threaten the liberties . . . of these United States from the assaults of Romanism." The patterns of interdenominational bigotry or cooperation varied greatly from area to area, from period to period. Bishop John Quinlan of Alabama reported in 1881 that there was "no organized hostility to the Church, no bitter hostility manifesting itself in violence of any kind; but, on the contrary, a kindly readiness to listen to instruction. The missions of the Diocese of Mobile are at perfect peace—no persecution whatever.'' In Kentucky, the pioneer work of Father Stephen Badin contributed much to religious toleration.[46]

Most parish histories have little to say about Protestant prejudice during these years. These same parish histories also provide many examples of a different pattern of early Catholic-Protestant relations. Protestants often offered the hospitality of their churches to visiting Catholic priests and donated land and/or money to help their Catholic neighbors build a church. Two Methodist ministers and Dr. Robert L. Keenan, a Baptist minister, were among those who contributed to the building fund for Tuscaloosa's first Catholic church in 1845. Earlier, Protestants also contributed to the establishment of the first Catholic churches in Mobile, Nashville, and Memphis. Non-Catholics joined their Catholic neighbors in rebuilding the Catholic church in Selma, Alabama, after its destruction during the war. When Catholic priests first began visiting the Catholic families at Independence, Kentucky, between 1858 and 1865, ''It seems that many non-Catholics also took advantage of these rare visits to be present at the services.''[47]

Florence, Kentucky, was an example of a small town where Catholics and Protestants not only lived in peace, but also helped and respected one another. Although the first pastor was not named to Florence until 1874, the congregation traced its origin to 1851, when Cornelius Ahern, a stonemason, came to Florence with his family. He found three other Catholics in the town. ''The Aherns naturally felt lonely without the Mass and invited Father Thomas R. Butler from Covington to say Mass.'' Father Butler arranged to come in the latter part of 1851 and said Mass at the Ahern log cabin on Shelby Street; the Ahern home became the community's first place of worship and the family shared its hospitality with those who came from the countryside or nearby towns. ''The village people took very kindly to him [Father Butler] and invited him up to the Christian church to explain Catholic doctrine, which invitation Father Butler accepted.'' In 1855, Ezra Fish, a non-Catholic, donated land for a Catholic church. Mr. Ahern, with the help of other parishioners, built the stone foundation for the church. When the Know-Nothings in the countryside threatened to burn down the unfinished building, John Bradford, a prominent non-Catholic, warned his Catholic neighbors of the danger; twenty Catholic men gathered to guard the church that night. Colonel H. Buckner, also a non-Catholic, courageously ''went to the meeting of the Know-Nothings and, laying a revolver on the table and calling God to witness, stated he would shoot the man who put a match to the Catholic church. He was known to be a man of his word. . . .'' The townspeople also pledged that they would help defend the church. No harm was done to the chapel, which was dedicated in June of 1856. Florence became part of the mission circuit out of Mt. Sterling, Kentucky, until it reached parish status in 1874.[48]

Much anti-Catholic prejudice was rooted in ignorance and the unquestioning acceptance of fanciful portraits of "the Roman Church" as the whore of Babylon, the Vatican army poised for an invasion of Florida, or the superstitious worshiper of idols. Around 1880, Taylor Jackman, the local tax collector, first approached the home of Father B. Maria Ziswyler at Altus, Arkansas, with great fear and trembling; he had never personally met a Catholic priest and had been raised with a portrait of Catholic clergymen "as men with horns and claws and tails, etc." Mr. Jackman was later able to share these baseless fears with the priest.[49] Father Eugene Weibel of Pocahontas, Arkansas, liked to repeat an incident that occurred during one of his frequent missionary journeys to search out isolated Catholic families. When the priest asked if there were any Catholics in the area, one gentleman hesitated a moment and then replied, "Any what? Any Catholics? No, we don't raise'm."[50]

Catholic priests often set aside time during their infrequent visits to outlying Catholic settlements to explain to Protestant audiences the true nature of Catholicism and refute the outrageous portraits that abounded. Business and social contact as well as friendship also helped combat this ignorance. Protestants frequently attended Catholic services or lectures in rural areas. Many non-Catholics attended the Catholic Easter services at Altus, Arkansas.[51] Attendance of Protestant children in the growing number of Catholic schools also helped break down ignorance and prejudice. When Father Weibel opened a Catholic school in Pocahontas, Arkansas, in 1880, only two of the original twenty-five students were Catholics.[52] In the early 1860s, three-fourths of the students at St. Cecilia School in Nashville were non-Catholics.[53]

Father A. P. Gallagher of Mena, Arkansas, encountered another factor that softened Protestant hostility toward Catholics. Mrs. Louck, a staunch Baptist, always had a hot meal awaiting the priest at her hotel when he returned from visiting nearby missions or stations. Her hospitality to Father Gallagher was due in part to the priest's respect for her Baptist beliefs, but also in part to the kind care her husband had received from Catholic sisters after he was wounded in the war.[54]

The growing role of the Catholic school during these years was also evident. Although the reporting of school statistics varied widely among the region's dioceses, these figures indicate that the total number of schools increased from forty to 307 during these three decades. Most of the dioceses did not include enrollment figures. Many schools, however, were obviously small rural institutions. Only in the Archdiocese of New Orleans among the five dioceses reporting enrollment totals was the average school size more than one hundred pupils.[55]

Many parishes of this period were simply organized. Annual budgets of less than a thousand dollars reflected a simple, country life where goods and services were exchanged rather than money. Men acted as trustees and formed building and subscription committees, while women formed altar societies, sodalities, devotional groups, taught in the school or Catechism program, and led the singing.

German, Irish, and Polish societies were formed in many parishes to keep alive ties with their ancestral homes as well as assist in the transition to a new life.

The European and Mexican heritage was also evident in parish devotions, although parish histories generally say little of these practices. In Louisiana, the Italians brought with them devotion to St. Anthony, St. Rosalie, and St. Joseph, while the parishioners of Holy Trinity built a chapel to St. Roch in thanksgiving for being spared during the 1867 yellow fever epidemic. Devotion to the Blessed Virgin played a vital role in Acadian spirituality; the daily Rosary together with *"la Societe du Rosaire,"* the Children of Mary, and the Brown Scapular were familiar parts of Acadian religious life.[56]

Bishop Jean Marie Odin encountered Mexican devotions to St. Rita outside Brownsville at the beginning of this period. Almost the whole population took part in the evening procession in which a jeweled statue of Mary Immaculate was carried and the Rosary and litany of the Blessed Virgin were chanted. Devotion to Our Lady of Guadalupe was a powerful force in the development of the Texas Church.[57]

Toward the end of this period, three significant events took place that foreshadowed major changes in the complexion of the region's Catholic parishes. In 1869, St. Augustine Parish was established in Louisville to provide better service to the city's black community, as well as to offer new opportunities for leadership that were not available in existing parishes. In 1875, Father Isidore Robot, O.S.B., took up residence at Atoka in Indian Territory and initiated a new era in the evangelization of the future Oklahoma. The third event, though less distinct, was equally important. During the 1870s, almost 30% of the region's new parishes were established in Texas; this decade marked the beginning of Texas' emergence as the center of Catholic parish growth.

## Notes

1. Samuel Eliot Morison, Henry Steele Commager & William E. Leuchtenburg, *The Growth of the American Republic* (New York: Oxford University Press, 1969), I:568.

2. Morison, Commager & Leuchtenburg, I:587–588. Of the 2,598,000 immigrants who entered the country during the 1850s, 952,000 came from Germany and 914,000, from Ireland. Gerald Shaughnessy, S.M., *Has the Immigrant Kept the Faith? A Study of Immigration and Catholic Growth in the United States, 1790–1920* (New York: The MacMillan Company, 1925), 140.

3. James J. Lorigan, *Church of the Holy Ghost, Knoxville, Tennessee* (Knoxville: n.d.). Archives of the Diocese of Nashville.

4. Historical Commission of the Diocese of Little Rock, *The History of Catholicity in Arkansas* (Little Rock: *The Guardian*, 1925), 9–10. Courtesy of the Archives of the Diocese of Little Rock.

5. *The Centenary of the Church of Saint Martin of Tours, Louisville, Kentucky, 1853–1953* (Louisville: 1953). Parish booklet in the private collection of Father John Lyons, Louisville, Kentucky.

6. Miller and Wakelyn, 228; Walter Brownlow Posey, *Religious Strife on the Southern Frontier* ([Baton Rouge]: Louisiana State University Press, 1965), 109.

7. Ben J. Webb, *The Centenary of Catholicity in Kentucky* (Louisville: Charles A. Rogers, 1884), 486.

8. Personal research notes for Volume II of *A Southern Catholic Heritage.* Lipscomb, 63, 65–66; Webb, 45–49; Castaneda, VII:125, 288–289, 359–360; *Centenary, Church of the Assumption, Nashville, Tennessee, 1859–1969* (Nashville: 1969). Archives of the Diocese of Nashville.

9. Lipscomb, 54–57.

10. *Ibid.*, 48–49.

11. Roger Baudier, *The Catholic Church in Louisiana* (New Orleans: A. W. Hyatt Stationery Mfg. Co., Ltd., 1939), 425–426; Nolan, *Mother Clare Coady,* 3.

12. Baudier, *The Catholic Church in Louisiana,* 425–428; James Pillar, *The Catholic Church in Mississippi, 1837–1865* (New Orleans: The Hauser Press, 1964), 297–343; *Centenary, Church of the Assumption, Nashville, Tennessee, 1859–1969* (Nashville: 1969). Archives of the Diocese of Nashville.

13. Lipscomb, 44; Charles Nolan, *Bayou Carmel: The Sisters of Mount Carmel of Louisiana, 1833–1903* (Kenner, Louisiana: 1977), 50–51.

14. Morison, Commager & Leuchtenburg, I:726–729; Lipscomb, 119; Historical Commission of the Diocese of Little Rock, 13; Frantz, 123; Roger Baudier, *The Catholic Church in North Louisiana* (Alexandria: 1953), 37.

15. Morison, Commager & Leuchtenburg, I:729.

16. Morison, Commager & Leuchtenburg, I:732.

17. Historical Commission of the Diocese of Little Rock, 13.

18. Lipscomb, 117–119; Baudier, *The Catholic Church in Louisiana,* 446, 461–467.

19. Goodwyn, 75–84.

20. *1850* and *1880 Catholic Directories.*

21. Personal research notes for Volume II of *A Southern Catholic Heritage;* Pillar, 10, 25, 33–34, 93–95, 122–123, 137, 140, 143, 217–221, 285.

22. *Annales de L'eglise de St. Joseph, P.sse Lafourche, etat de La Louisiane [1842–1892].* Manuscript in St. Joseph Parish, Thibodaux, Louisiana.

23. Rose Gibbons Lovett, *Catholic Church in the Deep South* (Birmingham: The Diocese of Birmingham in Alabama, 1980), 66.

24. *The Catholic Week* (November 23, 1979), 61.

25. Castaneda, VII:136; *St. Martin's Church, Tours, Texas, 100th Anniversary Celebration, December 1, 1874* (Tours: 1974). Courtesy of the Catholic Archives of Texas at Austin.

26. *Golden Jubilee, Sacred Heart Church Bellevue, Kentucky, 1874–1974* (Bellevue: 1974). Parish Collection, Archives of the University of Notre Dame.

27. "St. Augustine, Louisville," typed manuscript in Parish Collection, Archives of the University of Notre Dame.

28. F. Herman Schauinger, *Cathedrals in the Wilderness* (Milwaukee: The Bruce Publishing Company, 1952), 101.

29. Lovett, 31.

30. *Church of the Good Shepherd, Decherd, Tennessee, Dedicated May 13, 1969* (Decherd: 1969). Archives of the Diocese of Nashville.

31. *The Morning Star,* February 16, 1868.

32. *Statistics of the Population of the United States at the Tenth Census (June 1, 1880).* Henceforth referred to as 1880 census. From 1850 to 1880, the total population of the United States also doubled to 50,156,000.

33. The 1880 census listed 6,680,000 Americans (13.3% of the total population) as foreign-born. However, the 1880 census also noted, "with three exceptions only, viz, the states of Florida, Louisiana and Texas, the Southern states are practically without any foreign element." Comparisons with the earlier 1850 census figures are not appropriate since the 1850 percentages were for white residents only. However, the statistics of individual states confirm the accuracy of the census bureau's observation. Texas had the region's largest number and percentage of foreign-born residents: 115,000 (7.2%). Kentucky with 60,000 (3.6%) and Louisiana with 54,000 (5.7%) followed. Arkansas (1.3%), Tennessee (1.1%), Mississippi (.8%), and Alabama (.8%) had few foreign-born residents.

34. Shaughnessy, 159.

35. *1850, 1860, 1870* and *1880 Catholic Directories.* The number of priests serving in the region increased by 113 during the 1850s, 118 during the 1860s and 136 during the 1870s.

36. *1880 Catholic Directory.*

37. Lipscomb, 107–108; Charles Nolan, *St. Maurice Parish of New Orleans* (New Orleans: 1982), 30–31; George J. Flanigen, "Historical Notes," undated newspaper series in the Archives of the Diocese of Nashville.

38. Baudier, *The Catholic Church in Louisiana,* 437–439.

39. *A Parish Remembers [Our Lady of Mercy Parish, Mercedes, Texas], Fifty Years of the Oblate Endeavor in the Valley of the Rio Grande, 1909–1959,* 38–48. Courtesy of the Archives of the Diocese of Brownsville.

40. Castaneda, VII:173.

41. *Souvenir, Dedication of Sacred Heart Cathedral, October 26, 1902, Dallas, Texas.* Parish Collection, Archives of the University of Notre Dame.

42. *The Catholic Missions of North-East Arkansas from Their Opening in 1868 to the Fire Which Destroyed the Church, Convent and Rectory of Jonesboro, May the 16th, 1896* (St. Louis: 1896). Parish Collection, Archives of the University of Notre Dame.

43. Edward J. Dworaczyk, *Church Records of Panna Maria, Texas* (Chicago: Polish Roman Union of America, n.d.). Parish Collection, Archives of the University of Notre Dame.

44. Personal research notes on Resurrection Church in New Orleans.

45. James Hennesey, S.J., *American Catholics: A History of the Roman Catholic Community in the United States* (New York: Oxford University Press, 1981), 160.

46. Lipscomb, 128. "The good relations between Catholics and Protestants he [Father Stephen Badin] established set the tone for the subsequent years, despite occasional outbreaks of unchristian bigotry." John B. Bohes, *Religion in Ante Bellum Kentucky* (Lexington: The University Press of Kentucky, 1976), 58–59; Posey, 76–112, particularly 101 and 107.

47. *Souvenir, Golden Jubilee Celebration, St. Cecilia Parish, Independence, Ken-*

*tucky, 1880–1930* (Independence: 1930) in Parish Collection, Archives of the University of Notre Dame; Lipscomb, 83; Lovett, 24; Historical Commission of the Diocese of Little Rock, 17, 77.

48. *Souvenir, Diamond Jubilee Celebration, St. Paul Church, Florence, Kentucky, 1856–1931* (Florence: 1931). Parish Collection, Archives of the University of Notre Dame.

49. Placidus Oechsle, O.S.B., *Historical Sketch of the Congregation of Our Lady of Perpetual Help at Altus, Arkansas . . . Founded November 21, [1879]* (n.p.: 1930). Parish Collection, Archives of the University of Notre Dame.

50. *The Catholic Missions of North-East Arkansas from Their Opening in 1868 to the Fire Which Destroyed the Church, Convent and Rectory of Jonesboro, May the 16th, 1896.*

51. Placidus Oechsle, O.S.B., *Historical Sketch of the Congregation of Our Lady of Perpetual Help at Altus, Arkansas . . . Founded November 21, [1879].*

52. *The Catholic Missions of North-East Arkansas from Their Opening in 1868 to the Fire Which Destroyed the Church, Convent and Rectory of Jonesboro, May the 16th, 1896.*

53. Miller and Wakelyn, 106.

54. *Souvenir of the Golden Jubilee of the Rt. Rev. Msgr. A. P. Gallagher . . . as Pastor of St. Agnes Church, October 16, 1897* (Mena, Arkansas: 1947). Parish Collection, Archives of the University of Notre Dame.

55. *1850* and *1880 Catholic Directories;* also cf. Harold A. Beutow, *Of Singular Value: The Story of U.S. Catholic Education* (New York: The Macmillan Company, 1970), 108–117, 146–163.

56. Roger Baudier, "The Acadians—Catholiques Toujours," unpublished manuscript in the Baudier Papers, 9:7, Archives of the Archdiocese of New Orleans.

57. Castaneda, VII:114.

# CHAPTER THREE

# "That Sacred Inheritance of their Faith" (1880–1920)

The description of the first settlers of Holy Family Parish in Tulsa aptly characterized the populations of many new Catholic communities that were carved from prairie lands, riverbanks, and woods during this period. The parish history noted, "The population was made up, like well nigh all of them, of persons and families of various creeds and no creed." Among these early settlers were Catholics "who though they had ventured far to the frontiers, had nevertheless brought with them that sacred inheritance of their faith."[1] The frontier and rural areas were the focal points of Catholic parish expansion and development in the South Central region throughout these four decades.

The period from 1880 to 1920 was, in many respects, a continuation of the region's earlier rural development. By 1920, 74.1% of the region's residents still lived in rural areas, while only 48.8% of the nation's total population was classified as rural. Although Birmingham became "the Chicago of the South" and Louisville developed into a center of the cigar industry, industrialization and its consequent urbanization took place much more slowly in the South Central region than it did in the nation as a whole.

Parish development during these years reflected this rural, agrarian way of life. Urban parishes increased both in number and size so that by 1920 the number of cities with two or more Catholic parishes had quadrupled over 1880. The center of parish expansion, however, remained the countryside. Almost two-thirds (366) of the period's new Catholic parishes were pioneer parishes in cities or towns where no Catholic parish had previously existed. By 1920, Catholic parishes had spread to 42% (353) of the region's future counties—more than double the number in 1880.

Many new parishes represented a maturing of earlier Catholic missions and stations. In 1890, Winchester, Tennessee, became a mission center for the Paulists with Father Elias P. Younan as the first superior and pastor. Three years later, a school was opened under the direction of Dominican Sisters from Nashville; by the end of the first session, sixty pupils were enrolled. In 1905, increased enrollment necessitated a major addition to the school building. In 1906, construction of a new, brick church began. "Again the parishioners did much of the

271

construction, hauling sand from the riverbeds and making moulds from which concrete blocks were made.'' The new church, with a seating capacity of 275, was dedicated on December 30, 1907. The community then numbered 132 communicants, including twelve black converts, plus seventy-five children preparing for First Communion. Father James Duffy who became pastor about 1905 was an innovative farmer; he developed one of the finest Holstein herds in Tennessee and helped found, in 1909, the first cooperative creamery in the South.[2]

Simultaneously, new missions and stations were established to serve more isolated Catholic settlements. Small groups of Catholic families continued to live far distances from the nearest resident priest. When Bishop Nicholas Gallagher of Galveston proposed around 1889 that Dallas become the see city of a new Texas diocese, he observed that North Texas numbered only 15,000 Catholics among the area's one million residents: ''They are widely scattered through the country so as to make it difficult to reach them and this is one reason why so many are indifferent and the cause of many having fallen away from the faith in years past. . . .'' The bishop also noted some prejudice, ''due more to ignorance than malice.''[3]

The Vincentian Fathers established their mission at St. Mary in Opelika, Alabama, in 1910; the mission included eight counties, 5,300 square miles, and 120 known Catholics in a population of 210,000. The area was larger than Connecticut.[4] When the Diocese of El Paso was established in 1914, priests from Marfa regularly made a twenty-six-day circuit of eight missions and twenty-three stations on horseback. They rested only three days at Marfa before setting out again on the circuit.[5] Father E. F. Callahan established Johnson City as the center of the East Tennessee mission field in July of 1904; his territory consisted of thirty-four counties, 12,000 square miles, and a total population of a half million; only 300 Catholics lived in the area.[6]

This same picture emerges from a 1925 commentary on Bishop John Morris's first eighteen years in Little Rock (1907–1925):

> ''One of the first cares of the Bishop was to reach the scattered Catholics of the vast diocese, and while the force of men has not always been sufficient to reach all with the regularity that he wishes, he has instituted a system of mission work that has done much to handle this problem, and the lapse of a few more years will see every Catholic of this jurisdiction given regular opportunity to practice his religion, and due arrangement for the Catholic training of his children.''[7]

These vast mission areas often demanded heroic sacrifices of the priests who served them. Many letters from these missionaries are eloquent, unassuming witnesses to the finest examples of pastoral service. In 1882, 33-year-old Father J. A. Foppe was appointed pastor of Pascagoula, Mississippi. For three years, he zealously sought out isolated Catholic families and villages in addition to his work at the parish church. At Murray Station, he found ten Catholics who had not seen a priest in seven years. In 1885, Father Foppe was transferred to Holly Springs where "his parish territory was designated not by miles or even by towns and villages, but by counties." A decade before, the pastor here had died "from want of proper nourishment." In 1878, six sisters died while nursing the victims of yellow fever.

> "If there had been fatiguing journeys, endless work, and little subsistence at Pascagoula for Father Foppe, all of these difficulties were multiplied manyfold at Holly Springs. But he carried on doggedly in this vast area of few villages and scattered farms, until, like his predecessors, he succumbed to the privations and arduous labors."

In 1893, Father Foppe returned to Holland "a broken man" who neglected his own health to serve his parishioners.[8]

In 1896, Father Brocard Ecken, O. Carm., wrote to his superior of his visits to the missions in Texas' Big Bend area:

> "I have been here [Fort Davis] for three years. It is hard work. I have been in danger of death, as three times Freemason fanatics have attempted to shoot me. We are prepared to die for the Faith! There aren't even churches here in the area and sometimes we must celebrate Mass for the people in caves. We serve some twenty-five mission stations over a wide area. We are so poor that on our trips the only thing we have to eat are tortillas. . . ."[9]

In 1906, Father Celestin Cambiaire of Creole, Louisiana, invited newly arrived Archbishop James H. Blenk to visit his Gulf Coast parish. He suggested that the archbishop allow at least fourteen days to administer confirmation to the outlying chapels that were reached "through swamps, bayous and quick-sand." The priest then continued, "During three years, I have been living in the swamps in untold fatigues and privations, entirely isolated from the civilized world and deprived not only of the most simple comforts but also of mental and spiritual satisfactions. There is nobody to talk to, nobody to trust and confide in." The priest added that he tried to battle without complaint, fear, or weakness against ignorance, indifference, loneliness, malaria, rheumatism, and lack of companionship.[10]

Several events during this period merit special mention because each influenced parish development in a unique way. The first was the discovery of black gold—oil. In Texas, the first, modest discoveries by Corsicana town officials were overshadowed in 1901 by the state's first great gusher—the Lucas well at Spindletop near Beaumont. Additional fields were discovered over the next three years. In 1930, the discovery of the vast East Texas oil field irrevocably altered the region's future and became a significant factor in Texas' rapid growth. Oklahoma and Louisiana also became leading oil-producing states. These new discoveries changed patterns of population growth, political power, and the distribution of wealth.

The second event was the opening of Indian lands to white settlement. Families and individuals literally gathered at a starting line and raced to stake out new claims on these fertile lands. Guthrie (Oklahoma) changed from an unclaimed prairie to a town of 15,000 people in a single day—April 22, 1889. The town's new settlers came from thirty-two states and three territories in the United States as well as six foreign countries. Simultaneously, the federal government's 1870 "Peace Policy" that had placed 80,000 Catholic Indians under Protestant control was reversed and, in 1883, Indians were allowed full religious freedom.[11]

Bartlesville was one of the new parishes that was formed from former Indian lands. The area was still a prairie in the Cherokee Nation in 1884 when Indian traders first established themselves on the south bank of the Caney River. By 1901, four Catholic families—"small in number but strong in faith"—resided here; all were storekeepers. Two families were of Irish ancestry, one of French, and one of German. In the fall of 1901, Father Edward Van Wesberghe of Pawhuska, twenty miles west in the Osage Nation, first came to say Mass at a millinery store. He visited the community on a monthly and later bimonthly basis. The discovery of oil in 1903 brought many Irish families to Bartlesville. The population—white and Indian—soon numbered about 200. In 1903, plans for a church began. Land was donated and a subscription raised funds for the small brick building. The completed church was dedicated by Bishop Theophile Meerschaert on January 22, 1905. The following year, Father John Van den Hende was appointed the first resident pastor. His parish included not only Bartlesville but all of Washington and Nowata counties. In 1912, a school was opened under the direction of Ursuline Nuns from Paola, Kansas.[12]

The third event was the violence, political unrest, and later religious persecution that began in Mexico with the 1910 revolution. Many priests, brothers, and sisters who fled Mexico settled in such diverse areas as New Iberia in Louisiana, Hartshorne in Oklahoma, and San Antonio in Texas. A great number of lay men and women also crossed the border to form a growing Mexican presence in the Texas Church.

The fourth event was the *Plessy vs. Ferguson* decision (1896) with its judicial approval of "separate but equal" facilities for blacks and the hardening of racial attitudes that the decision both reflected and fostered. The decision and the social climate it helped create became part of the stimulus to found separate parishes for black, Mexican, and Indian Catholics in large cities and also in smaller towns and rural areas.

The fifth event was more generic. The vast distances that individual parishes covered made contact with outlying families dependent on available transportation. Pastors visited their flock on foot, on horseback, and by boat or piroque during the preceding period and, in many areas, well into the twentieth century. But the railroad and later automobile changed the way parishes were created and outlying communities were served. This period included much of the Golden Age of railroad building that began in 1865 and lasted until America's entry into World War I. By 1910, Texas surpassed Illinois' lead in total miles of railroad track. In the 1880s alone, more than 70,000 miles of new track were constructed in the country. Henry Ford's production of his first low cost automobile in 1908 ushered in still another new age in transportation.

The community at Marienfeld (changed to Stanton by Protestant neighbors in 1890) was one of the many new Catholic parishes that followed the paths of the railroads. On August 15, 1882, four Carmelites and one farmer from Kansas stepped off the Texas and Southern Railroad at Grelton Station halfway between Fort Worth and El Paso. The railroad had just completed the track, and the station included little more than a telegraph office and a pumping station. Father Anastasius Peters, Adam Konz, and their companions pitched two large tents as temporary living quarters and a chapel; they immediately set about constructing a wooden church and planting crops. Thirty German families joined these pioneers the first year and a small farming town quickly sprang up. The railroad extolled the possibilities of the area in handbills that attracted additional settlers from Europe as well as the North. By 1884, there were sufficient residents to petition successfully for the establishment of a new county—Martin County. Nature was not always kind to the new settlers whose crops suffered from drought and sandstorms; the *Leopoldinen Stiftung* and the *Ludwig Missionsverein* provided financial assistance to the struggling community.

With the arrival of additional priests, Marienfeld became the center of mission work for the area. Between 1882 and 1895, ten stations from Colorado City to Van Horn were established along the Texas and Southern Railroad line, forming "a parish 200 miles long and only one township cite [site] wide." Six of these stations, including Midland and Odessa which grew rapidly after discovery of oil, became parishes between 1885 and 1953.[13]

When young Father A. P. Gallagher arrived at the newly established St. Agnes Parish in Mena, Arkansas, on October 16, 1897, "he found ten Catholic families, a very small, poorly constructed church and parish house, and a fourteen hundred dollar debt awaiting him." His parish included missions that stretched a hundred miles to the north and south of Mena. Father Gallagher spent much time in the cabooses of the Kansas City Southern, the main road to his missions, although he had to make the trip from Wilton to White Cliffs by handcar. Father Gallagher always retained a special fondness for the "rough and ready [railroad] men with big hearts" who shared many of his days and nights on the road.[14]

Another generic event was the emergence of national Catholic organizations, such as the Holy Name Society and the Knights of Columbus. Both organizations had a profound impact on parish life with their emphasis on practical Catholicism; frequent Mass and Communion; local, state, and national meetings; public processions; and a new sense of Catholic fellowship for men. The first Holy Name Societies in New Orleans were established at St. Vincent de Paul (1899), St. John the Baptist (1901), St. Cecilia (1901), and St. Alphonsus (1904) parishes following missions by Redemptorist Fathers. In 1907, the area's combined Holy Name Societies held their first public rally. By 1909, New Orleans had twenty parish societies with a membership of 2,500 men.[15]

The final event was World War I. The nation's Catholic bishops patriotically backed America's effort after the declaration of war and were conscious of the importance of a full Catholic participation in the war. Catholics served in the armed services in great numbers, and the Knights of Columbus and women's committee of the NCWC assisted at military camps both at home and abroad. One by-product of the war was the great movement of men and women back and forth between the nation's diverse regions; many Northerners were introduced to the South for the first time and vice versa. Military camps—which often housed large numbers of Catholics—placed new demands for parish services.

The war also changed Europe's ability to provide financial and personnel assistance to the United States. As late as 1914, 89% of the diocesan clergy in the Archdiocese of New Orleans were foreign-born; the war impelled Archbishop James H. Blenk and his successor, Archbishop John Shaw, to hasten the establishment of a major seminary for the area.[16]

Much Catholic parish expansion during these years represented the Church's efforts to serve the region's rapidly growing population. While the United States doubled its population between 1880 and 1920, the population in the South Central region grew at an even more rapid rate. By 1920, 19,136,000 people (18% of the nation's total) resided in the region.[17]

The pattern of parish expansion largely reflected the demographic differences in population growth among the region's eight states. During the 1880s and 1890s, the greatest population growth took place in Texas where the number of residents almost doubled to 3,048,710, making it the sixth largest state in population. By 1920, Texas' population had tripled its 1880 size.

The most spectacular growth during the first two decades of the twentieth century occurred in Oklahoma where the number of residents almost tripled in twenty years to 2,028,000. The populations of Kentucky, Mississippi, and Tennessee all grew at a significantly slower pace than the nation as a whole during these four decades.[18]

During these years, more than 23,600,000 immigrants entered the country; the first decade of the twentieth century alone saw an unprecedented arrival of 8,800,000 immigrants. There was a great shift, however, in the origin of the new immigrants. While Germans, English, Irish, and Swedes constituted the largest number of immigrants in the 1880s, Italians, Russians, Austrian-Hungarians, Canadians, English, and Mexicans predominated in the 1910s. Some of these national groups—Russians, Swedes, and Greeks—were hardly represented in the South. As during previous periods, the number of immigrants in the South Central region was far below the national average. By 1900, Arkansas only had 1.1% foreign-born residents; Alabama, Mississippi, and Tennessee had .8% or less. By 1920, the foreign-born population in these states decreased still further.[19]

In 1900 for the first time, all the region's dioceses submitted Catholic population statistics. These estimates represented, at best, educated guesses rather than accurate census figures. The *Catholic Directory* for 1900 listed the Catholic population of the South Central region as 791,000—5.7% of the region's population and 7.8% of the nation's total Catholic population. The largest concentration of Catholics (365,000) resided in Louisiana where 26.4% of the population were Catholic; 170,000 Texas Catholics represented only 5.6% of the state's population, while Kentucky's 150,000 Catholics formed 7% of its residents. Arkansas, Alabama, Mississippi, Tennessee, and Indian Territory-Oklahoma each numbered less than 30,000 Catholics.[20]

The Catholic presence in the South Central region increased during the first two decades of the twentieth century. By 1920, an estimated 1,450,000 Catholics lived in the region—an 83.3% increase over 1900. Catholics constituted 7.6% of the region's population and 8.1% of the nation's total Catholic population.[21]

The number of Catholic communities grew rapidly during these four decades. By 1900, the region included 1,814 Catholic communities; less than a third were parishes. By 1920, the number of Catholic communities increased to 2,764, including 883 parishes.[22]

During this period, the center of Catholic parish growth shifted from Louisiana and Kentucky to Texas and Oklahoma. This trend began in Texas in the 1870s and in Oklahoma in the 1880s. In Texas, the number of parishes jumped from sixty-five in 1880 to 156 in 1900 and to 296 in 1920. During these forty years, 43% of the region's new parishes were established in Texas.

Oklahoma-Indian Territory traces the origin of its parish development to 1875 when the Atoka mission was established. In 1886, parishes were founded at Krebs and Pawhuska. Two years later, Sacred Heart was established. Guthrie, Oklahoma City, Edmond, and El Reno were founded in 1889—the year of the first great run to claim newly opened land in the future state. By 1900, twenty-five parishes had been established in this territory where only one mission center had existed in 1885; by 1920, Oklahoma numbered fifty-five parishes.

Much of this parish expansion was made possible by the growing number of priests who served in the region. While 558 priests labored in the region in 1880, there were 887 priests here in 1900 and 1,567 in 1920.[23]

Despite the impressive expansion of Catholic parishes during these years, this expansion was accompanied by only modest hierarchical development. Three of the new dioceses were in Texas: Dallas (1890), Corpus Christi (1912), and El Paso (1914); Corpus Christi had previously been the prefecture of Brownsville. In 1891, the prefecture of Indian Territory was raised to a vicariate apostolic with

Bishop Theophile Meerschaert as its first head; the area became the Diocese of Oklahoma in 1905. The Diocese of Lafayette, Louisiana, was established in 1918.

Much of the region's parish history during this period is found in the small, rural communities that struggled to maintain and nourish "the sacred inheritance of their faith." One remarkable community history began in the latter years of this period. St. John the Baptist Church in Grand Bay, Alabama, traces its origin to the conversion of one man. On April 16, 1912, Virgil Davis, a 62-year-old farmer, was baptized by Father Emmett Kennedy, pastor at nearby Bayou La Batre. Twenty family members and relatives followed Mr. Davis into the Catholic Church during the following months. Although Virgil Davis died on February 16, 1913, his home became the local mission station. In 1924, a small chapel was built on Davis' land and turned over to the diocese. Grand Bay became a parish in 1972.[24]

A Kentucky mission community experienced a different fate. St. Joseph Mission at Golden Pond in Trigg County was established by German immigrants who first arrived in this iron foundry area in 1878. They came from Pittsburgh where they traded their homes for "barren land in the Laura Furnace precinct." In 1882, a log chapel was constructed under the supervision of Father Charles Haesley, a priest of the Diocese of Nashville, on land donated by the Hillman Land Company. The community numbered eight families at the time. When the chapel was destroyed by a cyclone, a new one was built in 1894. During the 1880s, the community was visited from Hopkinsville or Franklin and, during the 1890s, from Paducah. In later years, priests from Minta, Adrian, Princeton, and Hopkinsville served the community. Around 1909, the community was listed as a station of Henshaw and then of Morganfield. The colonists suffered severe economic hardship, particularly after Laura Furnace closed. They were also ethnically and religiously unacceptable to their Baptist and Methodist neighbors. "The colony was a strange phenomenon for the local puritans [sic] because they had never been exposed to Catholicism, and as a result the colonists seemed a weird lot to the onlookers." By 1914, some families had already begun to move away and the church fell into disrepair; it was sold around 1925. Until about 1937, Mass was celebrated only occasionally by a visiting priest at the home of one of the handful of remaining Catholics. With the passing years, some families joined local Protestant churches while a few retained their Catholic faith. The small, passing immigrant community produced several vocations to the priesthood and sisterhood.[25]

Rural communities were very vulnerable to local conditions. This fact is evident in the Italian community that was established first at Sunnyside and then Tontitown in Arkansas. In 1895 and 1896, 250 families were brought from Italy to work on a large cotton plantation at Sunnyside. The community soon had a church, school, and resident pastor. Malaria, the boll weevil, and discontent with the plantation management led many families to move to Mississippi and Missouri. Father P. Bandini, the pastor, however, purchased land at Tontitown in Washington County and encouraged some families to join him there. While another priest served at Sunnydale for about a decade, the Catholic population continued to dwindle. By 1925, only three families remained and Sunnydale became "hardly more than an empty name." At Tontitown, Father Bandini started a profitable grape-growing industry for the new community, had the town incorporated, was instrumental in attracting the railroad, and even acted as mayor for two terms. When he died in 1917, "he died poor, having sacrificed whatever he had for the benefit of his beloved colony."[26]

Local industry was mainly responsible for the formation of two Mississippi parishes. Immaculate Conception Parish in Laurel (1904) owed its existence in large part to the lumber industry and sawmills that attracted many Catholics from Michigan, Louisiana, and Iowa. St. Michael Parish in Biloxi (1917) was composed of Austrians, Poles, Bohemians, and Acadians who were recruited to work in local fish canning factories.[27]

One essential factor in this expansion of the rural Catholic Church was the assistance provided by the newly founded (1905) Catholic Church Extension Society. Between 1905 and 1921, 315 chapels in Texas alone were built with help from the society; 80% of Amarillo's early churches, schools, and rectories were built with society assistance.[28]

One unique program of the society utilized modern transportation to continue the tradition of parish missions and Catholic revivalism that Jay Dolan so well portrayed. The society funded three chapel cars—"churches on wheels"—that operated in the West and the South. The 1916 and 1917 mission circuits of the chapel car "St. Paul" in Louisiana revealed much about the hunger of isolated, rural Catholics for the Sacraments and solid instruction, as well as the potential for improved relations with non-Catholics.

At Egan, 610 people attended the closing service; the mission resulted in 204 confessions, 289 Communions, twenty-four children and adult First Communions, two baptisms, one convert, three revalidated marriages, and a local resolution to build a chapel. At McElroy, many non-Catholics as well as Catholics attended the mission; one adult woman made her First Communion and her husband asked for baptism. At Sorento, the number of attendees at the mission increased from 110 the first day to 230 the last day. The mission at Gonzales was so successful that the priest remained there twelve days. Average attendance at daily Mass was 400, while 950 attended instructions for the married and single and 178 attended the children's mission. Six Baptists and one Methodist were received into the Church. At Krotz Springs, ten of the forty-five persons who attended the nightly missions were Protestants. Two Catholics returned to the Church, although several families who had drifted into Methodism remained hostile. Father Byron Krieger, C.Ss.R., one of the car's chaplains, recalled,

"Naturally in most of these places, the unfortunate Catholics were in woeful ignorance of the most elementary doctrines of the Church. While in most localities, the chapel car and the missionary Father were received joyously and enthusiastically, and shown every mark of esteem and courtesy by the townspeople, non-Catholics as well as Catholics, in some instances the priest had to contend against the most aggressive bigotry. . . . In most places, the non-Catholics who came to hear the discourses, at first perhaps through curiosity, became attentive listeners; and in the end, even if they were not converted to the truth, they went away less prejudiced against their Catholic fellow-citizens; and thus the spirit of bigotry and intolerance was greatly allayed."[29]

Parallel to this rural parish development, expanding urban areas also made new demands for Catholic parishes. In 1900, only eighteen of the nation's 161 cities with more than 25,000 citizens were located in the South Central region. Every one of these cities had at least one Catholic parish. New Orleans with a population of 287,000 and thirty-three Catholic parishes was the region's largest city. Louisville with 205,000 residents and thirty-two Catholic parishes was second in size; Memphis with 102,000 residents and six Catholic parishes was third.[30] By 1920, almost seventy communities in the region had two or more Catholic parishes. The greatest Catholic parish growth was concentrated in six cities: New Orleans, Louisville, Birmingham, El Paso, San Antonio, and Houston; all had nine or more new parishes. Biloxi, Nashville, Fort Worth, Mobile, and Dallas followed with four to six new parishes. This urban growth was a prelude to the rapid urbanization and suburbanization of the region's parishes during the next period.

These new urban parishes also evolved a more complex parish structure and organization. One such new parish was St. Andrew Parish in Montgomery, Alabama, where Father Philip English was appointed the first pastor in 1910.

"Father English set to work organizing the Junior and Senior Holy Name Societies, the Ladies of Charity, Young Ladies' Sodality, Sunday School Association, Altar Society, the Choir and the Guild, a social organization for single men and women, all of which flourished under his capable leadership. . . . Many parishioners recall the genuine love, concern, and interest which prevailed among all members of the parish at all the many church services besides Sunday morning Masses; such as Benediction, Stations of the Cross, May devotions, and missions. Many young Catholic servicemen stationed in the area during the war years found their way for Sunday Mass and were invited home for dinner. Several marriages resulted from these associations."[31]

This period also witnessed the gradual "Americanization" of many of the region's Catholics. World War I, improved transportation and communication, the birth of a new generation of American Catholics, and the foundation of national Catholic organizations such as the Knights of Columbus and the Catholic Educational Association (later the NCEA) were great catalysts in awakening a national consciousness among Catholics and in overcoming a preoccupation with local interests. The process of "Americanization" took several different forms in the South Central region. In Oklahoma, Bishop Theophile Meerschaert (1891–1924) personified the identification of the Church with the new frontier society that so quickly emerged. An acquaintance thus described this remarkable pastor:

"His was a simple life. He lived it with the pioneers, breaking bread with them, sleeping in their homes or out under the stars. His hands were rough from driving ponies the length and breadth of a land that needed a shepherd. When rivers were up, he slept under wagons with only a blanket over him. . . . His words were always that of encouragement to his few priests and his scattered people. Yet those words were always golden for they carried so much hope and charity and love. Then, too, he never tired of speaking of the great days to be in Oklahoma. . . . He loved the handclasps of those whose hands were tilling the soil of a new territory; loved to stoop and take the hand of a bright-eyed child who might help build the Church in future days. He left behind a monument in the hearts of the Faithful that endures today."[32]

Roger Baudier succinctly described another type of "Americanization" that took place in Louisiana under Archbishop James H. Blenk (1906–1917), particularly among the Creole parishes:

"The breaking away from the traditions of the past and the permeating of the American attitude and view in all classes became accelerated. Many old views and traditions were abandoned, and with them the old school and the old aristocracy waned. English as the common tongue gained ground and French began to be neglected. This transition was evident also in the government of the Church in Louisiana, and the administration of Archbishop Blenk saw this change quite tangibly effected. In fact, that period may be regarded as the era of Americanization, the final breaking away of the venerable archdiocese from the old French school of thought and views, attachments and influence. Attention turned sharply to Catholic affairs and activities in this country, and finally there began full participation of the archdiocese in American church activities."[33]

Still a different type of "Americanization" took place among immigrant communities, particularly the Germans. The events surrounding World War I placed the German communities under a cloud of suspicion and hastened the transition from German to English in both school and church. As early as 1897, Bishop William McCloskey of Louisville commented about the city's four German parishes, "Practically speaking, St. Boniface's and the Immaculate Conception are today English-speaking Congregations. In fifteen years, the other two German Churches [St. Martin and St. Joseph] will have become English-speaking." In fact, the transition from German to English at Immaculate Conception was a gradual one. The minutes of the board of trustees were kept in German until 1914. In 1920, church announcements and the sermon at High Mass changed from German to English. By 1925, all parish prayers were in English.[34]

While some existing communities became Americanized, new immigrant communities were also being established. St. Anthony Parish in Bryan, Texas, was established in 1896 to serve a large Italian community that moved to the area from Louisiana to work on cotton plantations.[35] In 1884, Bishop Edward Fitzgerald donated three lots to the German community at Little Rock to build their own church; the previous year, Father Regidius Henneman, O.S.B., had come to St. Andrew Cathedral to serve the German Catholics of Little Rock's only parish. The new St. Edward Church was dedicated on August 26, 1885. In 1901, the cornerstone for a new church was laid. At the time, the *Arkansas Gazette* commented,

> "Wherever a German settles, be it in the country or in the city, on a farm or in business, he at once exerts his energies and his zeal to accomplish the end in view. His target is success, and he rarely fails to reach his goal. Prosperity marks the German path. . . . Humble was the beginning of St. Edward's Church. Nearly all the members of the congregation at first found employment as dependent laborers. They did not shirk from labor. They arrived here with little or nothing to their name, but they came to build themselves a home. They began, they persevered and they succeeded. Ten years ago only a few owned their homes. Today those who have no homes are newcomers.
>
> "The Germans are a religious people. In God they always trust. The greater glory of God and the salvation of souls are the two great and primary principles which our German Catholics imbibed from their very infancy. These principles are a spur to duty and they are the key to success. Guided by these principles, the German Catholics are regularly attending the services at their place of worship in full numbers. Every Sunday, early in the morning, service begins, and the church is always filled three and four times a day."[36]

A decreasing number of new parishes, founded during this period, were ethnic. Most of the new parishes identified as Irish and German were former missions or stations with large ethnic components among their early residents. A scattering of Czech, Italian, Belgian, and Polish parishes also appear during these years. Bishop John Shaw's 1912 letter to a priest who applied to work in the Diocese of San Antonio reflected the continued need to provide for ethnic communities: "I find myself unable to accede to your request as I am well-supplied at present with German priests and have no need of English-speaking priests; what I chiefly need being Poles, Bohemians, and Spaniards."[37]

In 1880, the region had only two parishes that were founded by or for black Catholics. The oldest was St. Augustine at Isle Brevelle, Louisiana; in 1869, St. Augustine was founded in Louisville for the city's black Catholics.[38] This era marks a new and concerted effort to serve the region's black Catholics by establishing independent parishes for them. In 1888, St. Peter Claver Parish was founded in San Antonio. In 1889, Holy Rosary Church was established in Galveston and, in 1890, Holy Family Parish was founded in Natchez. During the following decade, parishes for black Catholics were established in Pine Bluffs (Arkansas), New Orleans, LeBeau (Louisiana), Mobile, and Nashville; thirty-six additional parishes were founded by 1919. These early parishes marked both a new effort to evangelize and serve the region's black Catholics as well as the hardening lines of racial separation that were embedded in the nation's law by the *Plessey vs. Ferguson* decision. Of the 329 new parishes that were opened between 1900 and 1919, thirty-eight were established for black Catholics. When John Gillard computed the number of exclusively Catholic parishes as of January 1, 1928, sixty-four of the country's 121 parishes and thirty-five of the fifty-three missions were in the South Central region; 65.4% of the nation's black Catholics resided here.[39] These new parishes owe much to the assistance of Mother Katherine Drexel as well as the zealous work of the Josephite Fathers, Society of the Divine Word, Society of St. Edmund, Sisters of the Blessed Sacrament, and Holy Family Sisters.

Many Acadian, Mexican, and Indian parishes in Louisiana, Texas, and Oklahoma are not identified as such in secondary sources; ethnic figures on these parishes are incomplete. As late as 1887, French was still used as the primary language in all but a dozen of the Archdiocese of New Orleans' 120 churches.[40] When Bishop Paul Nussbaum became bishop of Corpus Christi in 1913, 70,000 of the diocese's 83,000 Catholics were of Mexican ancestry.[41]

Bishop John Shaw of San Antonio welcomed Mexican refugees into his diocese and made a special effort to serve this growing population. On January 20, 1911, he wrote to Archbishop Blenk of New Orleans:

"I have now seen a good deal of the work; what there is, is good but we shall have to increase it very much as soon as possible. I feel very strongly that the first duty of the Church here is to these poor souls, who are full of faith, wonderfully responsive to kindness and generous as far as their slender means permit. . . . We have at least 20,000 Mexicans in the city [San Antonio] yet we have only eight fathers and of these some are always absent on the country missions. . . . I have also laid down a rule that for the future no student will be ordained until such time as he can speak Spanish fluently."[42]

One Mexican community that moved toward separate parish status during this period was Our Lady of Guadalupe in Cuerco, Texas. This railroad town, founded in 1873, included Catholics from Iowa, Pennsylvania, Louisiana, Mississippi, England, and Germany among its early citizens. St. Michael Church was completed in 1876 and Father V. L. Manci, S.J., became the first resident pastor. By 1923, 435 Mexicans resided in the Cuerco area. Few of them attended St. Michael for "lack of space, language difficulties, and other reasons." Land for a church for these Catholics was purchased and Catholics and non-Catholics in Cuerco, together with the Catholic Church Extension Society, provided funds for a new church. The church was blessed on May 4, 1925, and Dominican Fathers took charge of the congregation.[43]

During these years, several radical changes in Catholic parish life took place. The most significant change is unfortunately overlooked in most parish histories. Pope Pius X provided Catholics with a deeper understanding of the Eucharistic mystery and pointed out the erroneous attitudes that kept Catholics away from Holy Communion. The annual reports of St. Maurice Parish in New Orleans reflect the impact of this change on parish life. Although the estimated number of parishioners remained between 3,000 and 3,500 from 1890 through 1920, there was a dramatic growth in the reported number of annual Communions. In 1890, 750 annual Communions were reported; many obviously did not even make their Easter Duty that year. The number of Communions increased to 3,215, in 1906; 8,000, in 1908; and 17,000 by 1922. During a two-week mission in 1933, Father Charles Greco, the future bishop of Alexandria, noted with pride that 6,600 people received Holy Communion.[44]

This period also experienced a new growth in one essential element of the local parish—the school. The Third Plenary Council of Baltimore in 1884 insisted that each parish establish its own parochial school within two years—a goal that was never realized. At the time, about 40% of all parishes had their own schools.

The response to the council's directive in the South Central region was phenomenal. The 1880 *Catholic Directory* listed 307 Catholic schools. By 1900, the number of schools rose to 575 and enrollment stood at 53,241. By 1920, 796 schools were educating 133,332 elementary and secondary students—a more than sevenfold increase in forty years. Enrollment in the region's Catholic schools increased at a faster pace than that of the nation's Catholic schools as a whole. Compulsory attendance laws and child labor laws were significant factors in increased attendance at both public and private schools during this period.[45]

The growth was more than simply one of numbers. Improved pedagogy, centralized management, a more varied curriculum, and better teacher training became issues of this period. In New Orleans, Archbishop James H. Blenk, himself a former professor and president at Jefferson College above New Orleans, took a keen interest in education. In September of 1906, Archbishop Blenk established the first archdiocesan school board and appointed Father Leslie Kavanagh, a respected educator, pastor, and organizer, as the first superintendent. As Roger Baudier observes, previous to this "revolution" in Louisiana's Catholic education, "it was more or less everyone-on-his-own, except for Archbishop [Francis] Janssens who did make an effort." Father Kavanagh soon brought to New Orleans some of the nation's best educational theory, curriculum, textbooks, and pedagogy. He established a Catholic teacher's institute, a uniform course of studies for Catholic schools, and uniform examinations. In many cases, however, parents had to be convinced of the value of Catholic education. Within the New Orleans Catholic schools in 1921, enrollment dropped from 6,000 for the first grade to 1,400 in the third grade to 637 in the eighth grade.[46]

Most of this Catholic school growth was accomplished by the many communities of religious sisters who formed the core of the region's teaching staff. The role of these sisters, who often worked in the most primitive circumstances, forms an integral part of most parish histories.

During this period, Louisiana experimented with several Catholic–Public School ventures that attracted much less attention and opposition than Bishop John Ireland's programs at Fairbault and Stillwater, as well as similar ventures in New Mexico, New York, and Pennsylvania. When Father Antoine Borias brought the Sisters of Perpetual Adoration to Breaux Bridge in 1891, they first staffed the local public school. In 1905, the sisters moved to the newly opened St. Bernard Free Parochial School. In Plattenville, Father Jules Bouchet served as a trustee of the local school board and the Sisters of Mt. Carmel at Plattenville's Catholic school received salaries from the local school board from 1895 until 1912; Sister Lucy Dobbins, O.Carm., was the first Plattenville sister to pass the state teacher examination and thus qualify for a public school salary.[47]

Organizations always formed the main avenue for active lay participation in parish life. The types, sizes, and roles of these organizations varied greatly from parish to parish. Certain general patterns, however, emerge during this period. Men served as trustees and financial advisors throughout the nineteenth century, while women formed altar societies, sodalities, and organizations to help the needy. German, Irish, and Polish societies such as the Ancient Order of Hibernians served as links with the past as well as bridges to the future. When Arkansas' German Catholic societies merged in 1890, local societies from ten different parishes and cities comprised the new organization.[48] The Total Abstinence Societies, the Holy Name Societies, and the St. Vincent de Paul Societies all offered additional means of parish participation.

The growing role of parish organizations is evident in New Orleans' parishes. In 1890, only five organizations—the St. Vincent de Paul Society, the altar society, the Children of Mary, a purgatorial society, and a rosary society—were active in more than a quarter of the city parishes. A variety of other organizations reflected the period's emphasis on private devotions and mutual aid: Total Abstinence Society, St. Anna Verein, the Society of the Holy Family, Holy Face Society, and St. Alphonsus Beneficial Society. By 1920, more than half of these same parishes had a Senior Holy Name Society, St. Vincent de Paul Society, an altar or sanctuary society, the League of the Sacred Heart, the Children of Mary, and an ushers' society. In addition, the Junior Holy Name Society, St. Margaret's Daughters (a women's charitable organization), and Holy Angels or Guardian Angels society were present in a quarter or more of the parishes.[49]

In the 1890s, the newly formed Knights of Columbus came South and had an immense impact on parish life. The Knights included Louisville (1898), Nashville (1901), El Paso (1902), Covington (1902), Mobile (1902), New Orleans (1902), and Vicksburg (1904) among their early councils. The Knights' emphasis on "practical" Catholicism was soon visible. When over 1,000 "earnest, sterling Catholic gentlemen" received Holy Communion as a body at St. Alphonsus Church in New Orleans in 1908, the local Catholic paper called the event "one of the grandest and most impressive sights ever witnessed in this city." From among these Knights came the future lay leaders of the Archdiocese of New Orleans—a phenomenon that was not unique to Louisiana. When the Nashville Knights of Columbus and the Catholic Club were consolidated in July of 1915, their combined membership totaled 569 men. When the local council at Cuero, Texas, was organized in 1914, forty-nine men became charter members. Concerning the Cuerco council, the parish history notes, "The local council has done much for the spread of information about the Church, youth work, and support of local and national Christian education and activities."[50]

In 1916, the Texas Knights of Columbus who were themselves the object of open, venomous attacks by the Ku Klux Klan voted to sponsor a traveling missionary who would undertake to explain Catholic religion to non-Catholics. Throughout the 1920s, men such as Father Charles McCarty, C.M., and Father Roberto Libertini, S.J., criss-crossed the state and did much to break down the barriers of ignorance, bigotry, and intolerance. In 1930, the Knights turned to the radio as a means of continuing this work.[51]

The pastor's critical role in the presence and growth of parish organizations was evident at St. Rose of Lima Parish in New Orleans. Father Francis Mittelbronn (1866–1896), the former ardent Confederate pastor of Pointe Coupee, shared his French colleagues' suspicion and fear of Catholic lay organizations; the secularization and anti-clericalism that were occurring in France left scars on Louisiana's French clergy. Canon Mittelbronn gave little attention to the parish's few existing organizations. His successor, Dutch-born Father Alphonse Janssens (1897–1939) "felt he could get better cooperation from the parishioners, more interest in parish affairs, and closer contact with the Church by formation of such groups." Father Janssens reorganized the existing altar and St. Vincent de Paul societies; he also established an ushers' society, a Holy Name Society, the Catholic Boy Scouts, the League of the Sacred Heart, St. Margaret's Daughters, the Children of Mary, a senior sodality of the Blessed Virgin Mary, and, after a 1913 fire destroyed the church, a building fund association. In the 1930s, Father Janssens added a CYO, CCD, a chapter of the Archdiocesan Council of Catholic Women, and a drama club.[52]

Parishes continued to offer great contrasts in size and geographical limits. Rural parishes had small congregations spread over large distances, while urban parishes had greater concentrations of Catholics in smaller areas. By 1920, New Orleans' parishes differed greatly in size from less than 1,000 parishioners to more than 10,000.[53] A census of the Catholic community at Greenwood, Mississippi, in 1912, revealed twenty-six families with 100 people of American, Austrian, German, French, Irish, Italian, and Syrian ancestry.[54]

This period ended with World War I. Catholics had patriotically volunteered for military service in large numbers and were outstanding in their service to military personnel. The National Catholic War Council became the forerunner to a more structured and centralized American hierarchy. The war also became a catalyst for the profound social, economic, and demographic changes that marked the next era.

## Notes

1. *Historical Sketch; A Quarter Century's Incipience, Growth and Development of the Holy Family Parish, Tulsa, Oklahoma, 1899–1924.* Parish Collection, Archives of the University of Notre Dame.

2. *Church of the Good Shepherd, Decherd, Tennessee, Dedicated May 13, 1969.*

3. Castaneda, VII:139; concerning the status of many small Texas communities at the turn of the century, cf. P. F. Parisot and C. J. Smith, *History of the Catholic Church in the Diocese of San Antonio, Texas, 1685–1897* (San Antonio: Francis J. Bowen, 1897), *passim.*

4. *The Catholic Week* (November 23, 1979), 33.

5. *Anniversary of the Foundation of the Diocese of El Paso, March 3, 1914, and of the Consecration of the Most Reverend Sidney M. Metzger, Bishop of El Paso, April 10, 1940* (El Paso: Diocese of El Paso, 1965), 25. Courtesy of the Archives of the Diocese of El Paso.

6. Flanigen, "Historical Notes."

7. Historical Commission of the Diocese of Little Rock, 25.

8. Roger Baudier, "Priests from the Netherlands," unpublished manuscript in Baudier Papers, 2:7, Archives of the Archdiocese of New Orleans.

9. Franz B. Lickteig, "Commissariate of the South," *The Sword,* XXVI (October, 1966), 53; also cf. Parisot and Smith, 199–202.

10. C. P. Cambiaire to Archbishop Blenk, Cameron, Louisiana, July 17, 1906. Archbishop Blenk Papers, Archives of the Archdiocese of New Orleans.

11. Goodwyn, 68, 97–110; Hennesey, *American Catholics,* 192.

12. *The Southwest Courier,* October 8, 1955, 26.

13. Lickteig, *The Sword,* XXV (February, 1965), 38–45; (June, 1965), 19–24; XXVI (February, 1966), 10–12; Parisot and Smith, 206–207.

14. *Souvenir of the Golden Jubilee of the Rt. Rev. Msgr. A. P. Gallagher . . . as Pastor of St. Agnes Church, October 16, 1897.*

15. Paul J. Sendker, "History of Holy Name Society in New Orleans," *Catholic Action of the South,* December 5, 1935.

16. Nolan, *Mother Clare Coady,* 39, 43–45.

17. *Twelfth Census of the United States, 1900,* and *Fourteenth Census of the United States, 1920.* In 1920, 86.6% of Mississippi's residents lived in rural areas; the percentage in Arkansas was 83.4%. Alabama, Kentucky, Oklahoma, and Tennessee had rural populations that varied from 73.5% to 78.3%. Texas had a rural population of 67.6%, while Louisiana (65.1%) had the region's lowest percentage of rural dwellers.

18. *Fourteenth Census of the United States, 1920.* By 1920, Texas had 4,663,000 residents; Alabama, Kentucky, Oklahoma, and Tennessee all numbered between 2,000,000 and 2,500,000 residents; Arkansas, Louisiana, and Mississippi all numbered between 1,752,000 and 1,791,000 residents.

19. Shaughnessy, 254, 275. Kentucky had only 31,000 foreign-born in 1920, while there were 60,000 in 1880. Tennessee had 16,000 in 1920, slightly less than the 17,000 in 1880. Alabama had only 9,000 foreign-born in 1920, down from 18,000 in 1880. Mississippi registered a slight decrease from 9,000 to 8,400.

20. *1900 Catholic Directory.* Cf. "Ecclesiastical Statistics" in *New Catholic Encyclopedia; 1850 Catholic Directory;* John Tracy Ellis and Robert Trico, *A Guide to American Catholic History* (Santa Barbara, California: ABC-Clio, 1982), pp. 15–16. The debate on the validity of estimates of Catholic population is well known. As early as 1850, the editors of the *Catholic Directory* pleaded for a more accurate way of determining Catholic population—either by pegging such statistics to baptisms, marriages, and funerals or by taking an accurate Catholic census. Neither of these paths was followed. In fact, it was not until 1900 that all the dioceses of the South Central region submitted estimates of Catholic population. It was not until 1920 that all the dioceses submitted baptismal, marriage, and funeral statistics. Gerald Shaughnessy's attempt to determine more accurately Catholic growth in terms of immigration, natural growth, and conversions remains the only major study of pre-1920 Catholic population statistics, although his methodology and figures are now questioned. Note that the *Catholic Directory* for 1980 gives the region's total population as 35,854,000 or 2,559,000 below the actual census figure.

21. *1920 Catholic Directory.*

22. *1900* and *1920 Catholic Directories.* The *Catholic Directory* for 1920 listed 864 parishes; 883 of the communities identified in this study reached parish status by 1920.

23. *1880, 1900* and *1920 Catholic Directories.* El Paso statistics include part of New Mexico until 1983; Mobile figures include part of Florida until 1967.

24. *The Catholic Week* (November 23, 1979), 79.

25. Roger Futrell, "St. Joseph's: the Parish of the Rivers," manuscript in Parish Collection, Archives of the University of Notre Dame. For the contrasting histories of two small Slovakian Catholic communities in Arkansas, cf. Historical Commission of the Diocese of Little Rock, 73 and 181.

26. Historical Commission of the Diocese of Little Rock, 112–113, 128–130.

27. Richard O. Gerow, *Catholicity in Mississippi* (Natchez: Hope Haven Press, 1939), 292, 305–307.

28. Castaneda, VII:194.

29. Roger Baudier, "The Chapel Cars of the Catholic Church Extension Society in the Louisiana Dioceses," unpublished manuscript (1956) in Baudier Papers, 1:19. Archives of the Archdiocese of New Orleans. On nineteenth century parish missions, cf. Jay Dolan, *Catholic Revivalism: The American Experience, 1830–1900* (Notre Dame: University of Notre Dame Press, 1978).

30. *Twelfth Census of the United States, 1900.*

31. *The Catholic Week* (November 23, 1979), 63.

32. *The Southwest Courier* (October 8, 1955), 7.

33. Nolan, *Mother Clare Coady,* 41.

34. Webb, 93–94.

35. *Diamond Anniversary, St. Anthony Church, Bryan, Texas, 1896–1971* (Bryan: 1971). Courtesy of the Catholic Archives of Texas in Austin.

36. *Diamond Jubilee of St. Edward's Church, Little Rock, Arkansas, 1884–1959* (Little Rock: 1959). Courtesy of the Archives of the Diocese of Little Rock.

37. *Archdiocese of San Antonio, 1874–1974* (San Antonio: Archdiocese of San Antonio, 1974), 26.

38. Mills, *The Forgotten People: Cane River's Creoles of Color;* "St. Augustine, Louisville."

39. John T. Gillard, S.S.J., *The Catholic Church and the American Negro* (Baltimore: St. Joseph's Society Press, 1929), 58–59.

40. A. Magnien, S.S., to Dr. [Louis P. Chapelle], Baltimore, February 20, 1887. Chapelle Papers in the Archives of the Archdiocese of New Orleans.

41. Castaneda, VII:147–148.

42. *Archdiocese of San Antonio, 1874–1974,* 25.

43. *History of St. Michael's Parish, Cuerco, Texas, Centennial Souvenir, 1875–1975* (Cuerco: 1975), 1–15. Parish Project field research material, University of Notre Dame.

44. Nolan, *St. Maurice Parish of New Orleans,* 37, 40, 54.

45. *1880, 1900* and *1920 Catholic Directories;* Beutow, 164–217.

46. Nolan, *Mother Clare Coady,* 89–90.

47. Roger Baudier, *Breaux Bridge Centennial of St. Bernard's Church, 1847–1947* (Breaux Bridge: 1947), 38–40; Nolan, *Bayou Carmel,* 100–103; Beutow, 170–177.

48. Flanigen, "Historical Notes."

49. Archdiocese of New Orleans annual parish reports for 1890 (ten parishes), 1889 (one parish), 1891 (three parishes), and 1895 (initial report for St. Katherine) and 1920 for fifteen city parishes including French, German, Irish, Italian, African, and cosmopolitan congregations; the city had thirty parishes in 1890. Concerning devotional practices, cf. Dolan, 174–179.

50. *History of St. Michael's Parish, Cuerco, Texas, Centennial Souvenir, 1875–1975,* 36; Flanigen, "Historical Notes"; Roger Baudier and Millard F. Everett, *Knights of Columbus in Louisiana, 1902–1962* (New Orleans: Louisiana State Council, Knights of Columbus, 1965), 1–28.

51. Castaneda, VII:427–431, 451–454.

52. Roger Baudier, *Centennial, 1857–1957, St. Rose of Lima Parish, New Orleans* (New Orleans: 1957), 28–57.

53. Archdiocese of New Orleans annual parish reports on January 1, 1920, for fifteen city parishes. Records Center of the Archdiocese of New Orleans.

54. Gerow, 292.

# CHAPTER FOUR

# "A Builder of Churches and Schools" (1920–1960)

The four decades from 1920 to 1960 spanned the gala 1920s, the Great Depression of the 1930s, World War II, and the postwar prosperity. Regionalism declined as new means of communication and transportation brought national events and trends to the most remote rural areas. People moved more freely from one region to another on vacation, conventions, job transfer, or retirement. While the Great Depression and early war years slowed down the expansion of Catholic parishes in the South Central region, the postwar years witnessed the establishment of an unprecedented number of new parishes.

Urbanization profoundly changed the South Central region between 1920 and 1960. In 1920, less than 5 million of the region's 19,136,000 residents (25.9%) lived in urban areas of 2,500 or more. By 1960, more than 17 million South Central residents (59.7%) were no longer classified as rural. In Texas alone, more than 7,150,000 residents lived in urban areas—a number that exceeded by 2 million the region's total urban population in 1920.[1]

During these four decades, the region's population grew by almost 10 million (51%). Texas far outstripped all other states in population growth, accounting for half of the region's total increase. By 1960, however, the region accounted for only 16.2% of the nation's total population, down from 18% in 1920 when Alaska and Hawaii were not yet states.[2]

By 1960, an estimated 3,607,000 Catholics lived in the South Central region—an increase of 2,157,000 (149%) in forty years that far outpaced the region's population growth rate. By 1960, Catholics comprised 12.4% of the region's total population—a significant jump from 7.6% in 1920. The South Central region now accounted for 8.8% of the nation's total Catholic population—up from 8.1% in 1920.[3]

During these four decades, the role of the mission and station declined as many smaller communities received a resident pastor. Between 1920 and 1960, the total number of Catholic communities in the region increased modestly from 2,764 to 3,076; the number of parishes doubled to 1,757. While the number of missions remained about the same, the number of stations decreased from 978 to 322. By 1960, 57% of the region's Catholic communities were parishes—a significant increase over 1920. These increases took place despite the slowdown in the establishment of new parishes during the Great Depression and early World War II years.[4]

This period also witnessed the beginning of "the golden era" of new Catholic parishes—a twenty-three-year span beginning in 1947 and ending in 1969 when 767 parishes were established—almost one-third of all the region's parishes. Many of these new parishes were founded in rapidly expanding suburban areas. In Jefferson [Civil] Parish outside New Orleans, the number of Catholic parishes increased from two to eighteen; in Harris County, Texas (Houston), the number jumped from ten to forty-six.[4]

Despite the growing number of parishes, only three new dioceses were created: Owensboro (1937) in Kentucky as well as Amarillo (1926) and Austin (1948) in Texas. San Antonio (1926) and Louisville (1937) became the see cities of new ecclesiastical provinces.

One key factor in the parish growth and expansion was again the concurrent increase in the number of priests serving the region. The number of priests—like the number of new parishes—doubled between 1920 and 1960. By 1960, more than 3,000 priests were serving the region's 3,607,000 Catholics.[5]

The most surprising aspect of parish expansion during this period was the continuing number of new rural and small-town parishes. Despite the region's rapid urbanization and suburbanization, 428 of the period's new parishes (48%) were opened in cities and towns where no Catholic parish formerly existed. Catholic parishes were established in 181 additional counties; by 1940, half of the region's counties had at least one Catholic parish.

Our Lady of Mercy Parish at Mercedes, Texas, in the Rio Grande Valley exemplified this continuing Catholic expansion into small towns. The parishioners were mainly of Mexican birth or ancestry. Before Mercedes received its first pastor in 1909, the area already had a Catholic heritage that dated back sixty years. The Oblates of Mary Immaculate had begun visiting the scattered ranches and settlements of the area as early as 1859. They came first from Brownsville and, in 1899, from La Lomita. The first chapels in the area were at Santa Maria (1882) and Toluca (1899).

Mercedes appeared suddenly on the map in 1907 as part of the expansion of the St. Louis, Brownsville, and Mexican Railroad as well as the Rio Grande Land and Irrigation Company. These two companies donated land for a church in 1908 and Nuestra Senora de la Merced was blessed the following year. Fathers Adrian Bornes, O.M.I., and Paul Hally, O.M.I., were assigned to Mercedes the same year, with Father Hally responsible for the surrounding mission territory.

The mission territory developed rapidly with a chapel usually preceding by a decade the assignment of a resident pastor. St. Joseph at Donna became a parish in 1915; St. Joseph at Alamo, in 1924; St. Francis Xavier at La Feria and St. Theresa of the Child Jesus at Edcouch, in 1930. In Raymondville, Our Lady of

Guadalupe dates from 1927 and St. Anthony from 1950. Sacred Heart at Harlingen became an independent parish in 1927; in 1940, St. Anthony was opened in Harlingen for English-speaking residents and, in 1958, Assumption of the Blessed Virgin Mary became the city's third parish. St. Joan of Arc in Weslaco was founded in 1929, and St. Pius X was opened here in 1955 for English-speakers. Eleven parishes were thus carved from the Mercedes missions by 1960.

Parish development at Mercedes was not only geographical. In 1909, the Sisters of Mercy arrived in Mercedes. For the first six years, they taught in the local public schools. In 1915, a parochial school was established and a new school building was erected in 1926. In 1922, a new church and rectory were completed. Sacred Heart filial chapel for English-speakers was built in 1930.

In 1953, a CCD program was established; the Sisters of Divine Providence arrived in 1955 to assist with this work. In 1957, two catechetical centers were erected near public schools; by 1959, 2,000 children were receiving instruction twice a week at these centers.

By 1959, Mercedes was a city of about 12,000 people, including 10,000 Catholics. The church was filled at all five Sunday Masses and the number of Communions was "vast." Two days were required to hear all the confessions before each First Friday. Other active parish societies included the Holy Name Society— "a large body of men faithful to their weekly meetings and their monthly Communion. The example that these devoted men have given to the Parish has been a vertiable [sic] inspiration, and there is no one who does not feel the impact of their loyalty, devotion, and good example." A Junior Holy Name Society, Parent-Teacher Organization, Mothers Club of the Parish Confraternity, an altar society, *Las Hijas de Maria,* the Knights of Columbus (1958), and the parish choir completed the list of parish organizations.

The parish history concludes, "Thus, the work of the early Fathers has borne fruit; numerous parishes now cover the former mission territory, many of which have more parishioners than the whole territory had in 1909."[6]

Another example of a small town that received its first Catholic parish during this period was Tallassee, Alabama, in Elmore County. The small Catholic community here experienced a great influx of veterans and their brides after World War II. In 1950, the celebration of Mass was moved from private homes to the Veterans of Foreign Wars' hall. In 1953, Mrs. Robert Blount donated a parish site. The following year, ground was broken for a new combination church and rectory, and, in September, Father Walter Meniz, C.M., was appointed the first resident pastor. Mass was first celebrated in the new church on October 30, 1955.[7]

The tradition of lay leadership in small mission towns was continued during the 1920s by Mr. T. J. Gallagher of Camden, Arkansas. Mr. Gallagher was a state senator, attorney, and member of the public school board.

"When the clergy were not available, he took upon himself as much of their duties as was consistent with the lay state. Despite a life of great activity, he would be found many a Sunday teaching the little children their Catechism. He was never found wanting when called upon in behalf of the church. There is no doubt that his kindly influence has much to do with the church's high standing in South Arkansas today."[8]

More than half of the period's new parishes were in urban and suburban areas. By 1960, Louisville, New Orleans, and San Antonio had more than fifty parishes; Houston, Mobile, Dallas, Birmingham, El Paso, Memphis, and Oklahoma City all had more than twenty Catholic parishes. Forty-two counties had concentrations of ten or more Catholic parishes.

Dallas was one city that experienced spectacular parish growth during this period. In 1900, Dallas had only one Catholic parish. By 1929, Dallas proper had five parishes while Dallas County had seven. By 1960, this number jumped to twenty-five with the establishment of sixteen new parishes in Dallas and new parishes at Garland (1944) and Richardson (1956).

St. Pius X Parish in Dallas was part of this urban growth. The parish was established in 1954 during the population explosion that followed World War II. The local Chamber of Commerce noted in 1954 that Dallas' postwar growth "had been the equivalent of dropping the entire population of Toledo, Ohio, on the city of Dallas." Bishop Thomas K. Gorman "was a bishop of his times. He was a builder of churches and schools, of universities and seminaries. He was a man sent by the Holy Spirit to respond to the demands of a changing city, one whose Catholic population was increasing more rapidly than anyone had anticipated."

In 1954, Bishop Gorman established five new parishes in Dallas, including St. Pius X. When Father Vincent Wolf first visited the site of his new parish, he found "black gumbo soil . . . located far out on a country road"; 192 families composed the new congregation. Parishioners later recalled those early days: daily Mass in the rectory chapel, the portable altar for Sunday Mass at Casa View School auditorium, the bingo games in the rectory backyard, and the constant influx of new parishioners. During the first year, the Men's Club, the Ladies' Society, the Holy Name Society, and the choir were established.

The parish history notes,

"But there was one central thought in everyone's mind—to build a church and a school. It was a thrill to see the cotton field come to life and begin to grow concrete and steel buildings instead of cotton. Another tradition was begun. Fund-raising to meet the needs of our parish. . . . It was a community of struggling young families, all strapped with mortgages, fence notes, the expenses of starting and rearing a family. But there was also the realization that all shared in the responsibility of providing for the parish's needs."

In 1955, St. Pius X School opened with five classrooms and an auditorium where Mass was first celebrated on May 29, 1955. That same year, an extensive scouting program for boys and girls was established.

When Father Thomas Weinzapfel became pastor in 1956, the parish had increased from 192 to 700 families and a fund-raising program had already begun. The parish continued to grow at a rapid rate. By 1958, the parish had 900 families, and, by 1961, 1,100 families. Like many new suburban parishes, St. Pius X gave priority to its school over a permanent church. In 1957, ground was broken for eleven new classrooms. Six additional classrooms and office space were added around 1961. Ground was not broken for the permanent church and rectory until 1967.

The parish also began exploring new dimensions of Catholic community. In 1957, Operation Understanding saw the parish host 200 visitors from other denominations. The Christian Family Movement was organized and the parish nurses helped establish a school health program. In 1961, the parish sponsored two parishioners, Jim and Pat Speak, who left for three years as papal volunteers in Bolivia. In 1964, Operation Otomi linked the parishioners of St. Pius X to the Otomi Indian villages in Mexico's Valle de Mezquital.[9]

Urban parish priorities of this period were also reflected in the building program of St. John the Evangelist Parish that was established in Memphis, Tennessee, on February 5, 1947: a school, temporary church, and home for sisters in 1949; a permanent rectory in 1953; a school addition in 1955; a combination cafeteria, gymnasium, and auditorium in 1962; and, finally, the dedication of a new church on December 27, 1962. The pattern was a familiar one in rapidly expanding urban and suburban areas.[10]

St. Francis Xavier Parish in Tulsa, Oklahoma, was an example of suburban development during the early years of this period. In 1926, Father Francis C. Kelley was appointed to establish Tulsa's fifth Catholic parish. "In his first sermon [on April 11 in a local theatre], the pastor outlined his policy of letting the people of the parish carry on its work." Among the infants baptized that same afternoon was the granddaughter of one of Tulsa's pioneer Catholic families who had often provided hospitality to visiting missionaries. In the evening, the pastor met with his newly appointed trustees "to organize, institute surveys, and make an analysis of parish requirements." The first priority was to find a small house to use as a rectory and parish center. "Father Kelley believed that the best way to build a real parish was to keep his parishioners well-informed," so he immediately initiated a parish newsletter. To better understand the parish, its people, and its needs, the men of the parish, working late into the night, completed a parish census in ten days. When the census identified 162 children of school age, most of whom were receiving no Catholic instruction, the parish priorities were set: school first, rectory second, church third. In August, ground was broken for the new school-church building. In October, Father Kelley celebrated the parish's first Mass in the new edifice. The new school, under the direction of Benedictine Sisters, opened with 150 children. These accomplishments all took place before the parish's first anniversary.[11]

An example of urban development in an already-existing parish took place at St. Maurice in New Orleans; the parish had been established in 1852 and included the 1815 battlefield on which Andrew Jackson and his men defended the city against the British. In 1926, Father Charles Greco, the future bishop of Alexandria, Louisiana, became the first American-born pastor of St. Maurice. During the next eighteen and one-half years, Father Greco became the major force in helping his parishioners deal with the vast social, economic, political, and demographic changes that spanned the Great Depression and a world war. He insisted again and again on the primacy of the spiritual in daily life and created an extraordinary parish spirit to support families during times of crisis and change.

During Father Greco's pastorate, the parish almost doubled in size to 5,600 Catholics. Father Greco directed much of his activity toward organizing and reorganizing the many parish societies and activities that waxed and waned during these two decades. The St. Maurice Progressive Association became the spearhead of Father Greco's financial plans for the parish. Despite the Great Depression, the church was completely remodeled, the rectory was improved, a new brick school was constructed, and a gymnasium was built.

Other organizations already in existence when Father Greco arrived were the St. Vincent de Paul Society, the Altar Society, the ushers, the Children of Mary, the Catholic Knights of America, and the Junior Holy Name Society. During Father Greco's pastorate, many new parish organizations and societies were founded: girl scouts (1927), St. Margaret's Daughters (1930), baseball league (1933), seminary club (1935), the CCD (1935), the CYO (1936), the PTA (1939), school band (1941), the USO (1942), and Newman Club for public school students (1944), among others. Summer picnics began in 1927 and the drama club began its presentations in 1930. Frequent missions offered opportunities for communal and individual renewal. During the mission periods, Father Greco constantly exhorted his parishioners to "be apostles" and bring others to these missions.

In 1944, the school playground offered supervised morning activities for neighborhood children. Year after year, the parish generously responded to Father Greco's Thanksgiving and Christmas drives for food and clothing, for the area was not affluent and the Great Depression caused widespread need. Father Greco saw that no child was deprived of a Catholic education because of financial reasons. In February of 1935, Father Greco asked his parishioners to use Brotherhood Day "to bring forcefully home that we are all brothers, no matter to what religion we belong, that consequently there be more love and tolerance."

St. Maurice Parish was the center of the neighborhood's social as well as religious life during these years. Annual fairs, missions, and the long list of weekly activities brought a constant flow of people to the parish buildings. Father Greco left a memory that is still revered by his former parishioners. One parishioner recalled, "Father Greco was a great man. He was a priest who pulled the congregation to him. He had the power to bring people together. Everybody loved him. We were like one big family."[12]

This period witnessed two different trends in the establishment of parishes for black Catholics. New parishes for blacks multiplied through the 1950s. More than 120 parishes for black Catholics were founded between 1920 and 1959; these figures are unquestionably incomplete. One such parish was Our Lady of the Rosary in Jeanerette, Louisiana. The parish was established in 1947 with Father Cosmos Schneider, S.V.D., as the first pastor. A parish school was soon opened and enrollment stood at 120 by January of 1950.[13] Another of these new parishes was St. Vincent de Paul Parish, established in 1940 in Nashville, Tennessee; the parish served Fisk University, Meharry Medical Center, and Tennessee State University. By 1960, St. Vincent de Paul numbered 900 parishioners. The Easter liturgy of 1960 when fifty adults were baptized into the church was symbolic of the parish's early years; between 1940 and 1960, 575 converts and 400 infants were baptized into the community.[14]

A shift in this policy of establishing separate black parishes began in the 1950s. In 1954, the separate but equal policy that *Plessy vs. Ferguson* had made law in 1896 was struck down by the Supreme Court in *Brown et al. vs. Board of Education of Topeka*. Separation became symbolic of a past segregation and ingrained racial prejudice that stood in opposition to the Gospel call to treat all men as brothers. The concrete expression of this new awareness, however, was not uniform among the region's black parishes. While many black and white parishes were merged to form single Catholic communities, other black parishes retained their own identity and separate existence. Our Lady of the Rosary in Jeanerette continued to grow as a distinct Catholic community.

A similar set of contrasting trends took place among Hispanic Catholics, particularly in Texas. In some cases such as Mercedes, the Hispanic parish was the parent parish; in other cases such as Cuerco, new parishes were formed to serve the Hispanic minority. Concern for Hispanic Catholics prompted the 1943 seminar in San Antonio on the problems of Spanish-speaking Catholics, and led to the establishment of the Catholic Council for Spanish-speakers. In 1945, Archbishop Robert Lucey of San Antonio was named chairman of the Bishop's Committee for Spanish Americans—a position he held until his retirement in 1969. Unfortunately, most of Texas' Hispanic parishes are not identified as such in diocesan summaries or Catholic Directories.[15]

Every period in this study can be characterized as a time of great church building. Parish histories devote much space to their churches, schools, rectories, convents, parish halls, and catechetical centers. These buildings demanded great sacrifice on the part of all and became, in turn, a source of justifiable parish pride.

This emphasis on buildings, however, sometimes overwhelmed all other aspects of parish life. This distortion is epitomized in a 1953 comment by Father Bernard Spoelker of St. Martin of Tours Parish in Louisville. Writing of his predecessor, Father Louis Ohle (1905–1917), Father Spoelker observed,

> "There were few events of great importance to take place during these years. That is explained somewhat by the fact that there was little left to be done in the way of further building or expansion of the parish facilities already constructed by the year 1905. And so the events of these years were concerned primarily with the functions of the various organizations and societies of the parish."[16]

The parish construction that took place from 1920 to 1959 was extraordinary. Bishop Thomas Gorman of Dallas was not the only great bishop-builder of this period. Bishop Anthony J. Schuler, S.J., of El Paso (1915–1942) was "a dynamic man" who "spent most of his efforts in building." In San Antonio, Archbishop Robert Lucey completed more than 400 building projects between 1941 and 1969, including 135 new or renovated churches, about eighty new or renovated school buildings, seventy-eight rectories, and thirty-six convents. When Bishop Thomas Toolen came to Mobile in 1927, most of Alabama's sixty-seven counties lacked a Catholic church or chapel. During the next forty-two years, the bishop built 189 churches and chapels, eighty-four grammar schools, and seventeen high schools.[17]

Many of these new buildings provided facilities for the rapidly expanding Catholic educational endeavor. While the number of Catholic elementary and secondary schools increased from 796 in 1920 to 1,473 in 1960, the number of students in these schools more than tripled from 133,000 to 413,000. The 1950s were the high point in student enrollment in Catholic schools.[18]

By 1960, regional CCD programs were educating 333,000 public and private school students—44.7% of all elementary and secondary students receiving Catholic instruction.[19] These programs demanded great lay participation as teachers, helpers, fishers, etc. When St. Lawrence the Martyr Parish was formed in suburban Metairie in 1958, a CCD program was immediately established side by side with the Catholic school. The original core of twenty adults increased to forty in 1959, 200 in 1960, and 315 in 1962. By 1962, 969 students were enrolled in the program, a slightly larger number than were attending the rapidly expanding Catholic elementary school. Many early parish workshops and adult education programs were geared toward these adults who were working with CCD.[20]

Catholic educational programs changed greatly, particularly during the postwar years. An increasing number of state-certified and degreed sisters, brothers, and priests staffed the schools, while many lay teachers joined parish, religious, and diocesan faculties. Catholic high schools increased in number and offered complete curricula that vied with local public schools. The goals of education, the role of religion in the public schools, and government aid to private schools became the subject of philosophical debates and major judicial decisions that shaped the future of American education.[21]

There was also a new emphasis on improved religious instruction and a movement away from rote memorization of the Catechism. The need for change was reflected in a 1923 report by Father Francis Badeaux of St. Ann Parish in New Orleans. Only 400 of the parish's 1,100 school age children attended Catholic schools; 123 additional children attended (often irregularly) weekly preparation classes for Confirmation or First Communion. In the Catholic school, the sisters "restrict themselves to giving a definition of words and hear[ing] the memorized lessons," while in the Confirmation classes "it is impossible to teach Catechism according to any method, as the number of pupils is too great." Father Badeaux was well aware of the deficiencies of such a program and pointed out its remedies. Parents must live their faith, accept their obligation to see that their children receive sound religious instruction, and cooperate in maintaining better classroom discipline. Sisters need training in Catholic doctrine and catechetics so they can explain the faith rather than monitor rote memory of definitions.[22]

There were also other forces at work in American parishes during these years. The liturgical movement, though still small, was already emphasizing the concept of the Church as Mystical Body and the need for more active participation in the Mass and sacramental celebrations. A growing concern to integrate youth into parish life saw the CYO and CCD movements attract large numbers of adults to share in making young people more a part of parish life. Emphasis on the church's social teaching—particularly in regard to workers and unions and, later, racial integration—was a prelude to more general social concerns. Organizations like CFM strengthened family life. The Great Depression years made many parishes centers for food, clothing, and rent as well as spiritual help and fellowship.

The early years of this period also witnessed a new outbreak of anti-Catholicism that was fanned by the 1928 election and took its most violent form in the Ku Klux Klan. *The Morning Star,* New Orleans' Archdiocesan paper, carried an article on December 11, 1920, by Charles P. Sweeney that had first appeared in *The Nation.* Sweeney noted with concern "the growing menace of racial and religious intolerance in the United States. . . . [Thomas] Watson's election [to the United States Senate] is essentially the victory of a Fifth Estate, of the sinister forces of intolerance, superstition, prejudice, religious jingoism, and mobism." Sweeney observed that Thomas E. Kilby was elected governor of Alabama "because he induced the voters to believe him a stauncher foe of Catholicism than his opponents." In Alabama, the True American Society voted to eradicate Catholicism. In 1914, a Catholic church in Birmingham and a school in Pratt were burned down; two years later, armed guards at Birmingham's Catholic churches drove off attackers. Sweeney concluded, "All the while Watson and his associates are ranting about safeguarding liberty and American institutions they are largely responsible for the widespread belief existing in the South today that lynch law is God's law—if the party to be lynched is black of face, goes to confession, or reads the Talmud!''[23]

National attention focused on this violent bigotry when Father James Coyle, pastor of St. Paul's Parish in Birmingham, was murdered in front of witnesses as he sat on his front porch on August 11, 1921. His assailant was Edwin Stephenson, a Methodist minister who was outraged that Father Coyle had officiated at the marriage of Stephenson's daughter to a Catholic. Stephenson, whose defense lawyers included future Supreme Court Justice Hugo Black, was found not guilty by reason of insanity. Hugo Black argued that Stephenson had acted on an ''uncontrollable impulse'' while temporarily insane over his daughter's action in marrying a Catholic and adopting the Catholic faith. Stephenson's actions were not condoned by local Protestant ministers. Rev. Henry M. Edmonds, pastor of the Independent Presbyterian Church, publicly decried the crime: ''This is a deplorable thing. We in America have many things to learn; one of them is to respect the sanctity of life. A minister of the Gospel has done this thing; matters are sadly perverted when the gentle Jesus is represented by a man with a smoking pistol in his hand and his victim lying dead at this feet.''[24]

Catholics, however, even in small, rural, Protestant areas did not always meet this same hostility. Parish histories continue to point out the many Protestant benefactors who helped build Catholic churches and schools and who came occasionally to hear a good sermon or lecture. World War II also became a mitigating force in this anti-Catholic bigotry as Catholic men served loyally in the service and the world began to impinge in new and forceful ways on the small rural areas of the South.

Parishes continued to vary greatly in size and complexity. One detailed profile of parish size in the postwar era is found in the Diocese of Owensboro, Kentucky. In 1952, the diocese numbered 33,000 Catholics out of a population 592,000 and had sixty-seven Catholic communities—thirty-eight parishes, twenty-four missions, and five stations. There were no listed Catholics in seven of the diocese's thirty-two counties, while another thirteen counties each had less than 300 Catholics. Ten small parishes had 250 or less members, while the ten largest parishes numbered 1,000 or more parishioners. Only three parishes had more than 2,000 members. Twenty-two of the missions had less than 225 members; the two largest missions numbered 325 and 360, respectively. All the stations listed seventy-five or fewer Catholics.[25]

Father Joseph Fichter's 1951 sociological study of a Southern parish quantified individual participation in parish devotional and sacramental life. The list of devotions was typical of the era: Forty Hours, May crowning, Lenten services, novenas in honor of Our Lady and various saints, annual missions, the Rosary, Stations of the Cross, Benediction, processions, retreats, and special celebrations such as the St. Joseph Altar that reflected various ethnic backgrounds.[26]

One remarkable example of local parish devotional practice began in 1950 at

Christ the King Parish in Dallas; the parish was established in 1941. During the Korean War, a group of parish women began meeting in their homes to pray for world peace. In October of 1954, the group set up an eight-hour schedule of prayer in church before the Blessed Sacrament; as the number of women who joined in this prayer increased, the devotion was extended to two days a week, three days, and then the whole week. In January of 1951, a group of parish men began a similar evening vigil. By the spring of 1952, parishioners of Christ the King Parish were praying before the Blessed Sacrament for world peace around the clock, seven days a week. This continuous prayer was still in practice thirty years later.[27]

The 1950s saw many pastors and parishioners looking critically at parish life and seeking ways to better form community, serve the poor, gain a better understanding of their faith, and grow spiritually. Father J. B. Gremillion's fascinating journal of the mid-1950s reflects his personal struggle as pastor of suburban St. Joseph in Shreveport, Louisiana, to meet the new challenges that faced postwar parishes: inadequate Catholic education for the parish's high percentage of college graduates; an inability to transfer Christian faith and values to business, professional, and scientific fields; a need to assist and strengthen families; a lack of sense of neighborhood among men and women who often shared little more than an ability to buy or rent housing in a similar price range; a high percentage of families in which one parent was non-Catholic; an inherited racism and lack of social awareness; a widespread desire for deeper personal spirituality, community, and opportunities for service; outdated forms of parish worship and devotions; and narrow church organizations that failed to look beyond parish and denominational boundaries. Much of Father Gremillion's work centered around making his parish a "family of families" and empowering his parishioners to assume a new and more vital role in both church and society. The cooperation and enthusiasm of his parishioners was a gauge of how accurately he perceived and met their needs. Many of the concerns and directions that are associated with the Vatican Council II find initial expression in this journal.[28]

By 1960, 1,740 Catholic parishes were active in 521 counties in the South Central region. New parishes were being founded at an unprecedented rate, both in rapidly growing cities and in small towns. The Catholic presence in the South Central region was expanding significantly, particularly in Texas, as a new era of change suddenly and, in many cases, unexpectedly arrived.

### Notes

1. Statistical data from the articles on the eight regional states in the *Encyclopedia Americana*. In 1960, Texas alone among the region's states had a lower percentage of rural population (25%) than the nation as a whole (26.5%). Mississippi's rural population in

1960 was still 62.3%—the highest in the region. More than half of the residents of Arkansas and Kentucky were also still classified as rural.

2. *Ibid.* By 1960, the nation's population stood at 179,323,000. From 1920 to 1960, the region's population increased from 19,136,000 to 29,001,000. Texas' population increased by 4,926,000.

3. *1920, 1930, 1940, 1950* and *1960 Catholic Directories.*

4. *1920* and *1960 Catholic Directories.* The 1,740 parishes identified in this study were in existence at the beginning of 1960.

5. *Ibid.*

6. *A Parish Remembers [Our Mother of Mercy Parish, Mercedes, Texas], Fifty Years in the Valley of the Rio Grande (1909–1959).*

7. *The Catholic Week,* November 23, 1979, 77.

8. Historical Commission of the Diocese of Little Rock, 193.

9. *St. Pius X Catholic Church, 25th Anniversary, 1954–1979* (Dallas: 1979). Courtesy of the Archives of the Diocese of Dallas.

10. *St. John Evangelist Catholic Church, Dedication and School Yearbook, December 27, 1962. Memphis, Tennessee* (Memphis: 1962). Parish Collection, Archives of the University of Notre Dame.

11. *The Southwest Courier,* October 8, 1955, 19.

12. Nolan, *St. Maurice Parish of New Orleans,* 46–58.

13. *Our Lady of the Rosary Dedication Mass, Jeanerette, Louisiana, May 22, 1983.* Parish Project field research material, University of Notre Dame.

14. *Dedication, St. Vincent de Paul Church, Nashville, Tennessee, April 28, 1960* (Nashville: 1960). Parish Collection, Archives of the University of Notre Dame.

15. *Archdiocese of San Antonio, 1874–1974,* 32.

16. *The Centenary of the Church of Saint Martin of Tours, Louisville, Kentucky,* 1853–1953.

17. Castaneda, VII:153; *Archdiocese of San Antonio, 1874–1974,* 33; *The Catholic Week,* November 23, 1979, 9.

18. *1920, 1930, 1940, 1950* and *1960 Catholic Directories.*

19. *1960 Catholic Directory.*

20. Personal research notes for historical booklet on St. Lawrence the Martyr Parish, Metairie, Louisiana.

21. Concerning Catholic education in general, cf. Beutow, 218–280.

22. *Ibid.,* 278. 1923 Parish Visitation Report, St. Ann Parish, New Orleans. St. Ann File, Records Center of the Archdiocese of New Orleans.

23. Nolan, *Mother Clare Coady,* 46–47.

24. Lovett, 59–60.

25. *Yearbook, 1952, Diocese of Owensboro and Review, 1937–1952.* Parish Collection, Archives of the University of Notre Dame.

26. Joseph H. Fichter, *Dynamics of a City Parish; Southern Parish, Volume I* (Chicago: The University of Chicago Press, 1951).

27. *Church of Christ the King, Dallas, Texas, Its History, Its Symbolic Beauty, Its Devotion* (Dallas: 1982). Courtesy of the Archives of the Diocese of Dallas.

28. J. B. Gremillion, *The Journal of a Southern Pastor* (Chicago: Fides Publishers Association, 1957).

## CHAPTER FIVE
# The Challenge of Change (1960–1984)

The decades that began in 1960 witnessed unparalleled changes in American Catholic parish life. In 1960, John F. Kennedy was elected the first Catholic president of the United States; he carried Arkansas, Louisiana, Texas, and part of Alabama. His election represented in part a victory over the forces of anti-Catholic bigotry that had played a recurring role in the South's history.

The largest segment of America's black population continued to live in the South. Much of the struggle for equal rights under the law in the early 1960s took place in the South Central region: the confrontation between freedom riders and hostile Alabama whites in 1961 that led to the desegregation of interstate buses; the dispatching of federal marshalls to accompany James Meredith to the University of Mississippi in 1962; the desegregation of all major hotels and motels in Nashville in 1963; and the confrontation with Governor George Wallace at Tuscaloosa the same year.

The struggle for racial equality and equal opportunity for all men and women took place in men's hearts as well as in courtrooms and legislative halls. As early as 1953, Archbishop Joseph Rummel of New Orleans had exhorted his flock to desegregate Catholic parish services and organizations—an exhortation that was not followed in many parishes. A decade later, on March 15, 1963, the archbishop wrote,

> "Ever mindful, therefore, of the basic truth that our colored Catholic brethren share with us the same spiritual life and destiny, the same membership in the Mystical Body of Christ, the same dependence on the Word of God, the participation in the Sacraments, especially the most Holy Eucharist, the same need of moral and social encouragement, let there be no further discrimination, but they should not be harassed when they attend services in any parish church or mission, or when they apply for membership in parish organizations."[1]

Events in Rome were to have more far-reaching effects on the South's Catholic parishes. The election of Pope John XXIII in 1958 and his subsequent convocation of a new Vatican Council affected every aspect of parish life. The world's bishops first gathered in Rome in September of 1962. Before the close of the council in 1965, the first dramatic impact of this historic gathering was felt in all American parishes. The implementation of a simpler ritual at Mass and the introduction of the vernacular affected the very heart of parish life. A new era of dramatic change in parish life had begun. The council also re-examined every aspect of Catholic life and thought. It reshaped the way Catholics thought about themselves, about other Christians, and about the world in general. It supplemented a juridical self-understanding with a more pastoral understanding of the Church as service to all men, as the place where God's Word is proclaimed, as the community of God's people, and as the mystery of salvation. The concept of collegiality that was proposed for the universal Church was also soon applied to diocesan and parish life.

The council also brought theology in a new and forceful way to the living room as well as to the rectory. Birth control, the role of Mary and the Saints, and the historicity of the Genesis accounts of creation became more frequent topics of discussion. These discussions revealed the wide divergence of beliefs, practices, and opinions that existed among American Catholics. The controversy that followed the publication of the encyclical, *Humanae Vitae,* was certainly novel to American Catholics—respected theologians declaring their opposition to a basic papal pronouncement and episcopal directives. Most dissenting theologians remained within the Catholic Church and even retained their teaching positions. Catholics joined on both sides of the dispute. The long-term effect was the realization that such basic theological and pastoral disagreements could exist within the one Catholic Church.

This period also witnessed the rapid growth of several movements that significantly impacted parish life: the *Cursillo* movement, Marriage Encounter, and the Catholic Charismatic Movement. Each of these affected parish life indirectly by providing men and women with an experience of personal change, growth, and conversion that most often spilled over into more active participation in parish life. At one of the initial town hall meetings called in the Archdiocese of New Orleans by Archbishop Philip Hannan, in 1980, to help examine archdiocesan needs and set local priorities, almost every participant had experienced one of the three above movements.

The Catholic Charismatic Movement in New Orleans exemplifies the impact of these movements. In 1969, Father Harold Cohen, S.J., began hosting charismatic prayer meetings in New Orleans at private homes and soon afterward at Loyola University. When the gatherings outgrew the university meeting facilities, they moved to St. Edward the Confessor Church in Metairie, the first of several parishes that have hosted the meetings over the years. During the early 1970s, Father Cohen was often invited to surrounding dioceses where he helped in the formation of many charismatic groups. By 1984, more than half of the dioceses in the South Central region had a charismatic office or official liaison person to work with the movement. Since the early 1970s, the Archdiocese of New Orleans has had a permanent charismatic office headed by Father Cohen with Al Mansfield as full-time administrative assistant. Mr. Mansfield is also one of the country's four "traveling Timothies" who regularly visit regional charismatic groups. In 1975, the Center of Jesus the Lord was opened under the direction of Father Emile Lafranz as a charismatic spiritual center.

Mr. Mansfield observed,

> "The Charismatic Movement is both a gift of God and an observable movement of men. I believe that the charismatic gifts are indeed the love of God given to the Church for its upbuilding in our day. Like all things we humans do, our response to this gift—the Charismatic Movement—has both its strengths and weaknesses. Sometimes we have splintered into small groups that lack adequate gifts of leadership, teaching, or healing. On the other hand, literally thousands of people have been touched by the Charismatic Movement to a greater or lesser degree. It is difficult to give exact figures but we have many indicators of the widespread outpouring of the charismatic gifts. In our archdiocese alone, we have more than sixty active charismatic groups. Our 1984 regional conference attracted 4,500 people. More than 500 people a year participate in our main charismatic meeting's Life-in-the-Spirit seminars and these seminars have been held continually for more than fifteen years. Many other local charismatic groups also sponsor these seminars. Although it would be incorrect to say that the Charismatic Movement has transformed any parish in our archdiocese, these charismatic gifts have enabled countless adults as well as young people to take new and active roles in their parishes. The charismatic experience has given Catholics a new hunger to read the Bible, a new freedom to express their faith, a new eagerness to talk about their relationship to God, and a new ability to witness to others. Those men and women, both young and old, who have received the charismatic gifts offer parishes new opportunities for listening to the Word of God as well as service and evangelization."[2]

In the mid-1970s, another adult movement that emphasized the new spirit of the Vatican Council began in Little Rock, Arkansas. The Diocese of Little Rock Scripture Study Program was begun by Fred and Tammy Woell. Their own experience in the interdenominational Bible Study Fellowship prompted them to begin a similar program for their fellow Catholics. With the help of Dr. and Mrs. Carl Wengar of the Bible Study Fellowship, Father Al Schneider, and Father Jerome Kodell, O.S.B., a new program was developed that combined prayer and Scripture study in a powerful way that centered around a leadership of "praying people, believing people, and prepared people." The program was more than "an academic endeavor or an adult education class"; it was rather "a dynamic outreach of God's Word that touches hearts and changes lives."

Participation in the initial meetings at St. John Catholic Center in Little Rock far exceeded the planners' expectations. Parishes immediately began requesting the training, support, and excellent materials that the program rapidly developed.

In June of 1977, Bishop Andrew McDonald adopted the program as the Diocese of Little Rock's main adult education program; the bishop prayed with the leadership and assisted at the presentation of the program in each deanery later in the year. Each parish was asked to initiate a Scripture Study program. By 1980, the program was in place in most Arkansas parishes; in addition, it was being used in forty other states as well as such countries as Australia, Brazil, and Nigeria. In many Arkansas parishes, the program became a major factor in revitalizing parish life and fostering a new sense of community.[3]

Parish expansion between 1960 and 1980 continued to reflect the region's population growth. During these twenty years, the South Central region's population increased by more than 9,000,000 to 38,413,000, outpacing the national growth rate. The region was the home of 17% of the nation's residents—up from 16.2% twenty years earlier.[4] By 1980, an estimated 4,551,000 Catholics lived in the South Central region—an increase of 944,000 in twenty years; the region was now the home of 9.1% of the nation's Catholics—up from 8.1% in 1960.[5]

The region's rapid urbanization continued during these decades. By 1980, more than 25,000,000 of the region's residents—two out of every three—were classified as urban.

The rapid expansion of new parishes that marked the postwar era continued through 1969. In the early 1970s, a significant decrease in the establishment of new parishes began and became more pronounced toward the end of the decade. The annual rate of opening new parishes dropped to fifteen by the late 1970s— less than half the figure during the years of rapid growth from 1947 to 1969. Texas far outpaced the other regional states in parish growth. More than half of the period's new parishes were in Texas; another 15% were in Louisiana.

The small city and town continued to be the focal points of parish expansion, despite the decline in rural population. More than 49% of the 551 parishes founded during these years were the first Catholic parishes in cities or towns where no Catholic parish had previously existed. Parishes were established for the first time in eighty-seven new counties. New parishes were founded in such unfamiliar places as Iowa Park, Texas, and Kleinwood, Louisiana; Prattville, Alabama, and Lorman, Mississippi; Springdale, Arkansas, and Monticello, Kentucky; Watonga, Oklahoma, and Martin, Tennessee.

St. Joseph Parish in Prattville, Alabama, was officially established in 1966 with the appointment of Father Patrick O'Connor as the first resident pastor. The parish owes its existence to the women who formed the St. Andrew Altar Society in 1956 to bring a Catholic church to their small town. These women raised funds, purchased land, and arranged for temporary facilities for Mass. In March of 1962, ground was broken for the city's first Catholic church, which was completed in October. Prattville at the time numbered 6,600 people; thirty-five Catholic families composed this mission community. Four years later, the mission was raised

to a parish. The early 1970s saw the formation of a parish council and the implementation with "dignity and good taste" of liturgical and architectural changes.
Father Patrick Nicholson, pastor from 1975 to 1978, was especially remembered
"for what he did for our relationship with the other community churches. He
spoke and taught at local Protestant churches and civic clubs. He invited their
clergy to speak to us." By 1975, the parish numbered 264 families.[6]

Significant parish expansion also took place in the region's urban areas. Six
or more new parishes were established in Houston, San Antonio, Louisville, Corpus Christi, El Paso, Baton Rouge, Lafayette, New Orleans, Brownsville, Dallas,
Fort Worth, and unincorporated Metairie. With the exception of Louisville, all
these areas were in Texas or Louisiana. By the end of the period, Houston had
surpassed New Orleans and Louisville for the first time as the city with the greatest concentration of Catholic parishes. Many of these new parishes were in newly
developed suburban sections where young families were all, in a sense, newcomers.

At the same time, many older parishes were closed or merged with existing
parishes. Of the 164 parishes identified in this study that are no longer in existence, one hundred were closed between 1960 and 1983. This figure is certainly
misleading for many earlier, closed parishes were simply not identified. The reasons for closing parishes are usually not discussed in diocesan parish summaries.
In fact, many ethnic parishes, including parishes for blacks and whites or Hispanic
Americans and whites, were merged. In some instances, such as in Madisonville,
Louisiana, both existing parishes were suppressed and a new parish formed. In
other cases, such as Holy Redeemer in New Orleans where the parish church and
school were destroyed by Hurricane Betsy in 1965, the parishioners became part
of nearby Sts. Peter and Paul Parish. In addition to the closed parishes, another
105 existing parishes no longer had a resident pastor by 1980.

Black and Hispanic parishes were not the only ones to be closed. Some older
ethnic parishes in urban areas followed the same path. In New Orleans, Holy Trinity (German), St. Mary (Italian), St. Ann (French), and St. Michael (Irish) were
among the parishes that were closed during this period. The major new ethnic
parishes that were established during these years served refugees from Southeast
Asia. Parishes were established for the Vietnamese in Amarillo (1976), Port Arthur (1978), Morgan City (1981), and New Orleans (1983); a Korean Parish was
established in Dallas (1977).

The growing Hispanic presence, especially in Texas, is reflected in the four
national offices that were established in the Archdiocese of San Antonio during
the 1970s. *Padres* was founded in 1970 as an organization of Spanish-speaking
priests; *Las Hermanas* was founded in 1971 by Hispanic-speaking Religious
Women. In 1972, the National Foundation for Mexican-American Vocations was
organized in San Antonio by Bishop Patrick Flores; the same year, the Mexican-

American Cultural Center was founded here by the Texas Catholic Conference in cooperation with the *Padres* and *Las Hermanas* as "a center of research, education, leadership formation, and publications dedicated to the liberation and integral development of the Hispanic-American population."[7]

Ethnic consciousness also came to the fore with the appointment of bishops from ethnic minorities. Bishop Harold Perry was consecrated as auxiliary bishop of New Orleans in 1966, thus becoming the first black bishop since the 19th century. In 1977, Bishop Joseph Howze, then auxiliary to Bishop Joseph Brunini of Jackson, was appointed the first modern black ordinary of an American diocese when the Diocese of Biloxi was created in Mississippi. New bishops of Hispanic ancestry were likewise appointed. Bishop Patrick Flores was named auxiliary bishop of San Antonio in 1970, bishop of El Paso in 1978, and archbishop of San Antonio in 1979. Bishop Raymundo Pena was named auxiliary bishop of San Antonio in 1975 and bishop of El Paso in 1980. Bishop Ricardo Ramirez was consecrated as auxiliary bishop of San Antonio in 1981. Bishop Rene Gracida became Corpus Christi's bishop in 1983 after serving in the dioceses of Miami and Pensacola-Tallahassee. Texas' bishops brought the needs of Hispanic Americans to the attention of their fellow ordinaries. El Paso's Bishop Sidney Metzger asked all American bishops to support the striking Hispanic Farah workers, while Bishop Humberto Madeiros of Brownsville asked his fellow bishops to provide field ministries for Mexican migrant workers.[8]

Another significant change that followed Vatican Council II was the break-up of large dioceses and the establishment of new, smaller dioceses at a rate unmatched since the Antebellum period. These new dioceses brought the bishop and his administration closer to individual parishes and provided an episcopal presence in the region's growing urban centers. San Angelo (1961), Brownsville (1965), Beaumont (1966), Fort Worth (1969), Victoria (1982), and Lubbock (1983) were formed in Texas. Baton Rouge (1961), Houma-Thibodaux (1977), and Lake Charles (1980) were established in Louisiana. Birmingham was founded in Alabama in 1969; Biloxi in Mississippi, in 1977. Memphis, Tennessee, became a diocese in 1971 and Tulsa, Oklahoma, in 1977. In all, thirteen new dioceses were created. In 1980, Mobile became an archdiocese with Birmingham, Jackson, and Biloxi as suffragans.

Change is the catchword that appears continuously in parish histories of this period. Sacred Heart of Jesus Parish in New Orleans, a parish dating back to 1879, documented and reflected on the impact of these years of change. Many former parishioners had moved to the suburbs during the postwar years; by the late 1970s, Sacred Heart of Jesus Parish was composed mainly of several minority groups as well as a large number of the poor and elderly. In the wake of Vatican Council II, the concept of collegiality was expressed locally in the formation of an active, policy-making parish council with committees or departments for human relations, parish life, finance/administration, religious education, community development, and liturgy. A team ministry was established and expanded to include deacons, sisters, and laity. The parish history observes,

> "The struggle here in Sacred Heart Parish, while it is still going on, is for unity. Individuals, groups, and organizations have tried to band together to make the parish a living Faith Community. This they have done when they have come together. The potluck Thanksgiving dinner for which a special invitation went out to those who had no one with whom to eat their Thanksgiving meal; the Confirmation Mass for the Vietnamese at which the church was filled to overflowing; a Mass of Thanksgiving for a newly ordained priest in the black, white, and Spanish traditions; the multi-cultural liturgies to relate to the ethnic groups of the parish; the family type baptism and socials in which the congregation really participates; the paraliturgical devotions for special seasons that continue to furnish life-giving blood to the people; the neighborhood Masses celebrated in the various areas of the parish; and the personalized weddings in which the couples exchange meaningful vows of their own composition—all these speak of the struggle for unity. A Spanish altar cloth, a dashiki, a black, green, and red stole, a red rose on the altar of sacrifice: symbols of culture, they are signs of unity. They . . . speak of the parish logo with the black, white, and brown hands interlocking in Christ to tell of faith, unity, and love which the people have chosen as their watchwords. They celebrate in faith, in oneness, and in love."[9]

Holy Trinity Parish in Dallas was another older parish that responded positively to the challenge of change and whose liturgy became an expression of the parish's life and faith. Founded in 1907 as a rural parish, Holy Trinity was "in the heart of suburbia" by the 1930s. In the 1960s, the population of the parish changed ethnically and economically. The parish history noted,

> "By the time the changes of Vatican II reached us, many people were wondering if a parish encompassing so many minorities, single people, elderly people, and—more paradox—residents of Highland Park could survive. . . . But the mix of neighborhoods and the mix of people caused a strange kind of combustion. . . . Holy Trinity embraced the spirit as well as the letter of Vatican II. Holy Trinity revived the idea of a Catholic community that worshiped together to supplant the old reality of a community of Catholics who happened to live near one another. Holy Trinity itself started to become a symbol in many Catholic minds of how a community of Christians should worship—which is why fully 50% of our pews are filled every Sunday by people from outside the parish."[10]

In 1980, Father Frank Uter of St. Mary Parish in New Roads, Louisiana, pinpointed the heart of these changing patterns of parish life. St. Mary is the daughter parish of the French colonial parish of St. Francis of Assisi that was founded in 1728. The parish received its first native pastor, Father A. J. LeBlanc, in 1962; Father LeBlanc established integrated school facilities, implemented the new liturgical changes, and "helped the congregation grow with the changes." Father Uter was appointed pastor in 1976; in October of 1980, he reflected on the profound change he saw taking place among his parishioners:

> "Look back into the recent past. Remember how we were always studying the Church, changes in the Church and the Sacraments? Remember the Lenten study groups we had only four years ago? This is good and there is nothing wrong with study. We will always have to do this, but contrast it with the past year as we have initiated new ministries and grown in others. What we studied in the 1970s is happening in the 1980s.
>
> ."Last week I had a most vivid and beautiful example of this. A parishioner returned from the hospital where he had been undergoing treatment and called one of our lay ministers of the Eucharist, a friend, and asked her if she would bring him Communion. This was most touching and moved me greatly to see parishioners turn to each other and ask for ministry. . . . But isn't it wonderful to see and hope for the day when *all* of us feel free enough to minister to and be ministered to by each other?
>
> "On that day we will be Church in the fullest sense of the word. And that day is coming. We have changed and are continuing to change. Let us always thank God for what he is doing with us."[11]

One area of parish life where the changes of these decades was most evident was in the parish school. In the South Central region in 1950, Catholic schools (including seminaries and universities) were staffed by 9,102 teachers; 76.8% of these were religious sisters; only 11.8% of the teachers were lay men and women. The rapid expansion of CCD programs for Catholic children in private and public schools made parishes turn increasingly to lay men and women to take responsibility for the education of the young. This same lay role was also evident in the CYO and scouting programs. Many study groups and adult education programs provided opportunities for these new Catholic teachers to understand better their faith and enrich their understanding of the laity's role in the church. The laity's increasing responsibility for the education of youth soon moved from the CCD and the CYO to the Catholic school. Between 1950 and 1980, a dramatic change in the staffing patterns of the Catholic school took place. By 1960, lay teachers formed 33.3% of the teaching staff in all Catholic schools in the region; ten years later, they constituted 54.1% By 1980, 75.4% of all Catholic teachers in the region were lay men and women; only 19.8% of the Catholic school teachers were sisters and another 4.8% were brothers and priests. The challenge of enabling and helping lay teachers to pass on the Catholic heritage became one of the major challenges of parish life in the 1980s.[12]

Side by side with staffing changes in Catholic schools, there was an equally significant change in the number and percentage of Catholic children who attended these schools. While 413,000 children attended Catholic schools in the region in 1960, this number decreased to 295,000 in 1980. During this period, the number of Catholic elementary and secondary schools declined from 1,473 to 982.

In 1960, 44.7% of all Catholic elementary and secondary students who were receiving religious instruction in the South Central region were enrolled in religious education programs rather than Catholic schools. By 1980, the percentage was 62%. Again, there were significant variations within the region's dioceses.[13]

At the same time, the percentage of Catholic children receiving formal Catholic education in the United States was declining. In 1965, 35.5% of all Catholic school age children were receiving no formal religious instruction. In 1980, this percentage stood at 43.6%. Almost two-thirds of all Catholic secondary school age children were receiving no formal religious instruction in 1980. A similar picture emerged on the elementary level. Regional figures are not available. Thompson and Hemrick point out that the increase in children who receive no formal instruction stabilized around 1977. While noting with encouragement this stabilization, they comment that this decline "will have powerful implications for church life during the latter decades of this century. That sharp decline in program participation by youth suggests there has been a considerable weakening of the socialization process by which youth participate in, are nurtured by, contribute to, and become familiar with the meaning of Catholic values."[14]

In most dioceses of the region, Catholics have formed a minority in a Protestant culture. One aspect of this minority status has been the large number of mixed marriages between Catholics and Protestants. In 1950, almost one Catholic marriage in four in the South Central region (23%) included one Protestant partner. These figures remained fairly stable in 1960 (23.1%) and 1970 (26.6%). A decade later, there was a significant increase in Catholic-Protestant marriages in the region. More than one out of every three Catholic marriages (34.6%) included one Protestant partner. In more than half of the region's dioceses in 1980, there were more Catholic-Protestant marriages than marriages between two Catholics. In the dioceses of Mobile, Birmingham, Little Rock, Tulsa, Jackson, Oklahoma City, Memphis, and Nashville, two-thirds of all Catholic marriages included one Protestant partner. These figures also imply new challenges to parish administrators as the family becomes more important in providing religious training to children, sharing in parish planning and operation, and fostering community spirit.[15]

In every period, the great diversity that exists among parishes is evident. Neighboring parishes often followed divergent paths while new pastors often brought in new eras—both better and worse than their predecessors. The great changes in parish life that followed Vatican Council II provided for more local choices and responsibility and thus opened the door to even greater diversity. Parishioners crossed parish (and even denominational) boundaries with much greater ease than in the past, seeking communities where they could share their faith, devotion, desire for service, and aspirations. This same diversity is reflected in recent parish histories. One of the main points of the RENEW program, already in progress in several dioceses of the region, is to encourage model parishes to share their experiences with other parishes. A few examples illustrate this diversity.

St. Mary Parish was established in Jackson, Mississippi, in 1948 at the beginning of the postwar expansion. Construction of a school and convent began the following year, while the rectory and church were begun in 1955. A school addition was needed in 1957.

St. Mary numbered 1,650 parishioners in 1971. However, the neighborhood began to change socially, economically, and racially. By 1976, the Catholic population had dropped to 1,094 and by 1981, to 680. Many parishioners who moved away from the neighborhood continued to form part of the St. Mary community. Parish evening meetings were eventually dropped, thus greatly reducing the opportunities for parish participation.

In 1967, a formal parish council was established for "the guidance, instruction, and spiritual welfare of the parishioners." Of the seventeen lay members of the council, twelve were elected and five appointed. By 1982, the council's purposes had become more specific: (1) determine parish and community needs; (2) establish goals and priorities; (3) discover and utilize all the parishioners' talents; (4) bring all parishioners into closer spiritual communion through parish activities, prayer, and renewal; (5) make the parish more outgoing and caring, especially toward those in need; and (6) establish a sound financial plan.

The parish school continued, although the percentage of Catholic students decreased. By 1981, the school had ninety-four Catholic and seventy-three non-Catholic students. A decade before, there had been only two non-Catholic children among the school's 246 pupils.

Although the parish was reduced in numbers and changed in population, parish life continued to be expressed in a variety of committees and programs that reflected its priorities and concerns. Active committees in 1981 included property management, community service, education, evangelization, finance, and liturgy. In addition, parish groups include the prayer group, the Rite of Christian Initiation, Catholic Women's Association, the CYO, the Junior CYO, *Cursillo,* Religious Education for Children, Vacation Bible School, and Marriage Preparation.[16]

In 1977, St. Joseph Parish in Clarksville, Texas, received Deacon Ben Comisky as its first non-priest pastor. Clarksville is one of North Texas' oldest Catholic parishes. As early as 1846, the few families at Clarksville were visited occasionally by priests from Little Rock, Arkansas, and later from Nacogdoches. In 1871, Father Theodore Buffard became Clarksville's first pastor. Over the years, several groups of sisters conducted Catholic schools in the town; the last school was closed in 1929. Five years later, the CCD program was formally established in the parish. In 1935, the first vacation religion school was held. In the

1950s, doctrinal and pedagogical classes were initiated for religion teachers; the parish history noted, "The pastor and people expect great things from a more integral application of the works of the CCD in the parish."

The parishioners always remained a small Catholic minority in a Protestant county; Catholics in 1983 comprised less than 2% of the county's population. Between 1914 and 1937, the number of families in the parish varied between fifty and seventy. In 1955, there were forty-eight Catholic families in the parish; eighteen of these included one Protestant parent. In 1960, the parish numbered sixty-six families including twenty-eight with one Protestant parent; by 1970, the number of families decreased to thirty with eighteen including one Protestant parent. In 1980, the number of parish families was fifty-two.

While the parish had a Holy Name Society and altar society for many years, the local Knights of Columbus were not organized until 1950. In recent years, the number of parish organizations and groups multiplied. New organizations and groups included the St. Vincent de Paul Society and Bible study groups. Deacon Comisky also became active in the ministerial association and civic groups, encouraged adult education classes, and increased liturgical participation during his tenure in the parish.[17]

Unlike many rural parishes for black Catholics, Our Lady of the Rosary in Jeanerette, Louisiana, did not merge with a nearby parish. Although the school closed as many outlying families with school-age children transferred to other parishes, the small Jeanerette community remained strong. Under Father Thomas A. Mullally (1975– ), parish organizations such as lay ministers, youth choir, and the Knights of Peter Claver were established or revived. Spiritual growth was actively encouraged through retreats, days of recollection, engaged and marriage encounter weekends, and parish renewal. In 1976, the parish fair was re-established and in 1978, the parish hall was re-purchased from the local school board.

On May 22, 1983, the community of Our Lady of the Rosary participated in the dedication of its new church. Many had contributed not only money but also their time and talents to help with the construction of the new edifice. On this occasion, Father Mullally observed,

> "About forty years ago, many black Catholics migrated to churches of other faiths for various reasons. The forefathers of this parish banned together for prayers and a deepening of faith as they envisioned the development of their own parish. Many obstacles had to be overcome, but their faith in God gave them the strength and guidance needed in founding Our Lady of the Rosary Parish. These same families and their offspring have faithfully supported and carried out many projects at Rosary, which exemplify and deepen their Christian love, charity, and faith. Their faith is now bearing fruit as the dream of a new church is fulfilled today. You, the present generation, have kept the faith and ran the race well. This new house of the Lord is a testimony of a faith built not on sand, but on good soil."[18]

St. Bernadette Soubirous in Clear Lake City in suburban Houston was established with 400 families on August 1, 1977. The boundaries were cut from St. Paul Parish, which gave its entire July 31 Sunday collection to the new parish. On August 7, Father Franklin Tasker, O. Carm., founding pastor, celebrated the parish's first Masses at Armand Bayou Elementary School, the temporary location of Sunday liturgies for the next three years. On August 10, sixty-five people attended the first parish meeting where an interim parish council and the basic committees that guided the next years were established: architecture, religious education, liturgy, and finance.

The interim parish council and its committees concentrated on fostering individual participation. Town hall meetings explained goals and asked for suggestions. Home Masses brought neighbors together spiritually and socially. Participation in Sunday liturgies was encouraged and a Christian Action committee immediately turned the parish's attention to the ministry to the needy. One of the parish council's first decisions was to set aside 5% of all Sunday collections for use by the Christian Action committee. When the parish held its first picnic in September of 1978, more than 800 people attended.

Ground was broken for the new church on January 7, 1979. Simultaneously, a rectory and multi-purpose building were begun. A ladies' society, a family life committee, and youth committee were established. The parish council set as its main goal for 1980 to strengthen the sense of community within the parish. By June of 1980, when the new church was dedicated, the parish already numbered 840 families. In the dedication book on that occasion, the parish reflected: "All of us—our old and our young, our distressed and our fortunate—are Church. So, as we dedicate our 'church,' our new home, we also dedicate ourselves as a faith community within the Universal Church."[19]

In an unusually candid history, St. Joseph the Worker Parish in Marrero, Louisiana, summarized the impact of the radical changes of the 1960s and 1970s on parish life. St. Joseph the Worker, located in metropolitan New Orleans, was a mission station for Italian truck farmers at the turn of the century. In 1923, a chapel was constructed in Amesville, as the area was then called; this original wooden chapel remained the center of parish life for fifty-five years. During the next three decades, new residents of French and African descent moved into the area in large numbers. The area maintained "a rural and small town character" despite new industry.

In 1938, a new building replaced the two sacristy classrooms as the mission school; five years later, two Sisters of Mt. Carmel from the neighboring parish at Westwego began teaching at the Amesville school. In 1951, the black parishioners purchased land that eventually became the site of the present parish church.

In 1955, St. Joseph the Carpenter [sic] Parish was officially established with Father Anthony Russo as the first pastor. Soon, school enrollment increased and new parish organizations were formed.

The parish history describes the events that began on January 18, 1959, when two black youths sat in the front of the church as the parish's "wanderings in the desert." During the following weeks, tensions increased. On February 8, Archbishop Rummel wrote directly to the parishioners denouncing "the manifestations of ill temper, harsh words, threats of violence, and even show of arms [one usher had come to church armed the previous Sunday]." The archbishop continued,

> "[Christ] teaches us that everyone is our neighbor, equally to be loved. Christ makes our love of our neighbor the yardstick of our love of him and true discipleship with him. . . . No, my dearly beloved. . . . We cannot despise our fellowman just because his race or nationality, his features or the color of his skin are different from our own. Certainly, the house of God . . . is not the place to show prejudice or contempt, or to violate justice or charity, or to cause humiliation or pain."

Despite the archbishop's plea, violence erupted in March. Mass attendance dropped dramatically, although parishioners gradually began to return to St. Joseph. An uneasy peace settled over the now-integrated church services. Separate parish organizations for blacks and whites continued.

When the school was integrated in 1962, racial violence, tension, and fear again erupted. The school was picketed and enrollment dropped from 250 to one hundred pupils. The annual fair for 1963 was canceled as was the traditional St. Joseph procession.

In 1964, Father Maurice Gubler was named pastor; his pastorate was a very difficult one. School enrollment remained low; parish organizations struggled with periods of growth and decline, relying on "the old faithful." These years also saw a new set of changes in the parish. The parish history continues,

> "The parishioners of St. Joseph the Worker, still reeling from and not yet coping with the social and cultural shock of integration, were faced with yet another set of major changes in the practice of their religion. Familiar ways of worshiping had become like a pair of old shoes, perhaps outdated and worn, but comfortable. You weren't even conscious of them. All of a sudden, things were different, more changes were happening, more adjustment was needed. Mass was in English, the priest was facing the people, songs were being sung in English, by the congregation, and even at 'low masses.' "

Amidst all this change and turmoil, new signs of life appeared. By 1965, the St. Joseph procession was revived and, by 1966, the school was sponsoring a minifair. "Old devotions and religious practices were still maintained, as they are today, but the new was accepted, if not yet embraced. . . . More people became active participants in Sunday worship, gradually beginning to understand the profound significance of liturgical change."

In 1967, Father Ignatius Roppolo was appointed pastor. Parishioners recall Father Roppolo's style of leadership. One observed, "He got people to sit down and talk and dialogue. . . . The church came alive at the time." Noted another, "We began to have pot-luck suppers and began to eat each other's food—that's when it began to happen.'' Still another recalled, "You couldn't really tell him no . . . 'you are a parishioner, this is your parish, you have to participate.' " Great care was taken in the preparation of the liturgies. More emphasis was given to individuals and families in the parish bulletin. In 1967, a parish finance committee was established, composed of both black and white parishioners; part of the committee's responsibility was long-range planning. Parishioners were encouraged to set aside "one hour's wage" each week to the Lord. Weekly income jumped from $489 in 1967 to $1,300 in 1970. "But most of all the increased income represented a deeper commitment to God and the parish."

Father Roppolo also called on his parishioners "to put off the racial prejudice, the fear, the intolerance of the past and come together as a real parish family where people truly loved and cared for one another." Home visits, home Masses, and neighborhood coffees fostered opportunities for parishioners to get to know one another. The Ladies' Altar Society was integrated, followed soon afterward by other parish activities and organizations. Former parishioners again began to become active in the parish and school enrollment increased. Programs for adults, youths, and children multiplied.

The changes initiated by Vatican Council II continued to filter into the parish. A parish liturgical commission was established. In 1969, the vigil Mass was initiated. Adult and youth choirs were formed. While new programs, such as a Mass for World Peace, were introduced, the traditional St. Joseph procession and St. Joseph Altar were also fostered. At the same time, the parish bulletin encouraged parishioners to greater participation in local and world concerns. The parish adopted and subsidized a catechist in Guatamala. In 1969, Father Roppolo, after careful planning, established a representative parish council and gave it responsibility for the "overall care, planning, and management of the parish."

Father Roppolo's three year pastorate was a time when parishioners "were enabled to grow in a sense of what it really means to be a faith-community, to be the Church. What for many people would have remained a source of division and possibly destruction—being a multi-cultural and multi-racial parish—became instead for the people of St. Joseph the Worker a rich and beautiful blessing."

In 1970, Father Douglas Dousson was appointed St. Joseph's fourth pastor. The next decade was one of continuous growth for the parish. Religious education programs, missions, Scripture study groups, convert classes, home religion classes for high school students, and sacramental seminars multiplied. The school also grew and an integrated, active PTA reinstated the annual fair in 1972. Commented one parishioner after the successful fair, "It was a great feeling seeing all people of the parish working with such cooperation and genuine togetherness for the common cause. . . . It marks a milestone in our ability to live as one people of God."

In 1971, Father Doussan, his two assistants, three sisters, and a lay couple,

Ron and Jan Schulte, officially established a team ministry for the parish. They began by meeting daily to pray, study, and plan together. This team ministry became part of St. Joseph's style of leadership, although team composition has changed over the years.

A new social responsibility manifested itself in Senior Citizens' programs, Thanksgiving and Christmas drives for the poor, a community relations' committee and, in 1973, a decision to give 4% of the weekly parish income to the poor. This percentage was later raised to 8%. When the first Vietnamese family came to church in May of 1975, they were quickly adopted by the parish, as were other Vietnamese, both Catholic and Buddhist.

On January 15, 1978, ground was broken for a new Church of St. Joseph the Worker on the land that the black parishioners had purchased almost forty years earlier. The first Mass was celebrated in the new church on December 3, 1980. The parish history concludes,

"This day, this church was a powerful symbol of the people's dedication and commitment to the Lord and of the Lord's abundant blessing on them, leading them into a new era in their history. They ritualized this new covenant with the Lord not only through the first Mass in the new church but also by gathering together that very same day in a Parish Assembly to take their new dreams and create new goals from them for the future of the parish. . . . The dreams and goals were those of the people. The Spirit of the Lord was powerfully at work in the midst of his people that day as they formed a new covenant with him, dared to dream new dreams, and walked with hope into the future."[20]

## Notes

1. Archbishop Joseph Rummel's Pastoral Letter of March 15, 1953. Rummel Collection, Archives of the Archdiocese of New Orleans.

2. Interview with Al Mansfield, Metairie, July 17, 1984.

3. Marilyn Howley Smith, *Hearts Changed; Lives Arranged Through the Power of the Word of God: The Story of the Scripture Study, Diocese of Little Rock* (Siloam Springs, Arkansas: God Provides Publishing Company, 1980).

4. 1980 census data from articles on the eight states in the *Encyclopedia Americana*. By 1980, Texas numbered 14,229,000 residents; Louisiana and Tennessee both had more than 4,000,000 inhabitants. Halvorson and Newman have shown that almost two-thirds of the changes in church membership and affiliation between 1952 and 1971 in thirty-five major white religious groups can be traced to general demographic changes. The changing patterns of where people live is the single most important factor in changing patterns of religious affiliation throughout the country. The writers, at the same time, recognize that other human factors are also involved in these changes and raise intriguing questions about the nature and complexity of these factors. Peter L. Halvorson and William M. Newman,

1952–1971, *Patterns in Pluralism; A Portrait of American Religion* (Washington, D.C.: Glenmary Research Center, 1980).

5. *1960* and *1980 Catholic Directories.* Cf. Bernard Quinn, Herman Anderson, Martin Bradley, Paul Goetting, and Peggy Shriver, *Churches and Church Membership in the United States, 1980* (Atlanta: Glenmary Research Center, 1982), 10–25; the region's total Catholic population in 1980 is computed here as 4,492,000.

6. *The Catholic World* (November 23, 1979), p. 39.

7. *Archdiocese of San Antonio, 1874–1984,* 46.

8. Hennesey, 314, 326; Gilberto Rafael Cruz and Martha Oppert Cruz, *A Century of Service: The History of the Catholic Church in the Lower Rio Grande Valle* (Harlingen, Texas: United Printers & Publishers Inc., 1979), 36. Courtesy of the Archives of the Diocese of Brownsville.

9. *Sacred Heart of Jesus Parish, 1879–1979, New Orleans* (New Orleans: 1979). Archives of the Archdiocese of New Orleans.

10. George Weber, C.M., *Learning to Love; 75 Years of Growth in the Trinity; Holy Trinity Church [Dallas], 1907–1972* (Dallas: 1972). Courtesy of the Archives of the Diocese of Dallas.

11. October 5, 1980, St. Mary's Parish Bulletin; *St. Mary's Church, New Roads, Louisiana* (New Roads: 1978). Parish Project field research material, University of Notre Dame.

12. *1950, 1960, 1970,* and *1980 Catholic Directories.*

13. *1960, 1970,* and *1980 Catholic Directories.*

14. Andrew D. Thompson and Eugene F. Hemrick, *The Last Fifteen Years: A Statistical Survey of Catholic Elementary and Secondary Formal Religious Education, 1965–1980* (Washington, D.C.: United States Catholic Conference, 1982).

15. *1980 Catholic Directory.*

16. St. Mary Parish, Jackson, Mississippi. Parish Project field research material, University of Notre Dame.

17. St. Joseph Parish, Clarksville, Texas. Parish Project field research material, University of Notre Dame.

18. Our Lady of the Rosary Parish, Jeanerette, Louisiana. Parish Project field research material, University of Notre Dame.

19. *St. Bernadette Catholic Church, Dedication, June 7, 1980* (Clear Lake City, Texas: 1980). Courtesy of St. Bernadette Parish.

20. Sister Kathleen Pittman, C.S.J., with design by Sister Catherine Martin, O. Carm., *The Story of Saint Joseph the Worker, Commemorating Its Twenty-Fifth Anniversary* (Marrero, Louisiana: 1981), 27 and *passim.* Archives of the Archdiocese of New Orleans.

# Conclusion

During Vatican Council II, Bishop Ernest Unterkoefler of Charleston, South Carolina, pointed to the Catholic experience in the South during the nineteenth and early twentieth centuries as a persuasive argument in favor of the restoration of the permanent diaconate. The bishop noted that the shortage of priests made it difficult for scattered Catholic communities and families to maintain their faith; he added that permanent deacons could have played a major role in administering the Sacraments and instructing both young and old.[1]

Bishop Unterkoefler rightly pointed out the basic pattern of Catholic parish life in the South Central region—small communities scattered over large geographical areas. In 1850, the Catholic Church faced an immense challenge to extend its presence into the Southern countryside; Catholic parishes existed in only 8% of the region's future counties. During each decade from the 1870s to the 1960s, new Catholic parishes were established in at least 5% of the region's counties; the one exception was the Great Depression decade of the 1930s when parishes were founded in only twenty-four new counties (3%).

Most of the region's Catholic communities were missions or stations well into the twentieth century. In 1920, less than three out of every ten Catholic communities in the region had a resident priest. Much of the effort at parish development during the succeeding decades was directed toward these small communities. Despite the region's rapid urbanization and suburbanization, 48% of all Catholic parishes established between 1920 and 1980 were new Catholic parishes in cities and towns that had not previously had a resident priest. Simultaneously, Catholic parishes were established in new or expanding urban centers, so that every city had at least one Catholic parish. The frequent identification of the American Catholic experience with immigrant, urban populations does not adequately describe the Southern Catholic experience where numerous small, rural and frontier communities preserved and nurtured their faith, often under difficult circumstances.

Many Catholics in these isolated settlements drifted into other religions. The nineteenth-century observations of Bishop Flaget concerning Kentucky and Bishop Gallagher concerning Texas were based on long years of pastoral experience. Leakage, however, was not exclusively a rural or nineteenth-century problem. Father Joseph Fichter, in 1951, documented the significant percentage of Catholics in an urban Southern parish who were "nominal or dormant Catholics"; more than a third of the children baptized in this parish between 1930 and 1950 apparently had no further contact with the Church during their upbringing.[2]

The patterns of parish expansion and development differed significantly among the region's eight states. The expansion of Catholic parishes was far different in Louisiana and Kentucky than in Tennessee and Arkansas. The Mexican revolution, the Civil War, and the discovery of oil influenced Oklahoma and Texas differently than Mississippi and Alabama. The statistical tables in Appendix A clearly indicate the different patterns in new parish establishment among the region's eight states.

Much parish expansion and development followed demographic trends. This study, in a general way, confirms Newman and Halvorson's conclusions concerning the strong statistical relationship between religious adherence and population trends.[3] The rapid expansion of Catholic parishes in Oklahoma around 1900 and shift of the region's Catholic center from Louisiana to Texas are explained in large part by demographic trends. The establishment of new parishes often followed by years and even decades the arrival of new Catholic communities in more isolated areas. Small clusters of Catholics lacked the resources to support a resident priest and, even when such support was possible, priests were always in short supply.

Other factors also contributed to parish expansion and development. The appointment of missionary bishops during the Antebellum period, the strong Catholic faith and allegiance among individual families and small communities, the financial help of both foreign and American Catholic societies, the zealous labors of many priests, the dedicated work of countless religious sisters and brothers, and parish revivals were key elements in both establishing new parishes and nurturing existing parishes. Racial attitudes and laws, the region's abundant natural resources and waterways, foreign and domestic wars, economic trends, and new means of transportation and communication played major roles in determining where and when parishes were established. Vatican Council II was the major catalyst for the profound changes that have characterized parish life since the 1960s.

The lack of immigrant Catholics was a major factor in the slow Catholic expansion in the South Central region. Alabama, Arkansas, Mississippi, and Tennessee all had very small immigrant populations throughout the nineteenth and early twentieth centuries, while the other states had immigrant communities that were usually far smaller than in the North.

The South Central region has its own unique ethnic heritage. The French, Spanish, Africans, and Indians were the original inhabitants in areas where "Americans" were first considered newcomers. While many Germans, Irish, Italians, Czechs, and Poles formed their own parishes, their numbers did not parallel those in the North. In most small, rural congregations, however, Catholics of many ethnic backgrounds formed a single community. Parishioners of Mexican, English, German, and American backgrounds founded the Catholic parish in Cuerco, Texas; St. Michael in Biloxi, Mississippi, included Austrians, Poles, Bohemians, and Acadians among its founders. Many urban parishes also reflected this same ethnic mixture. The impact of this cosmopolitan character on early Southern parishes has not been adequately examined. Most parish histories poorly document the gradual weakening of national consciousness among European immigrants and the replacement of ethnic parishes by geographical communities based more on economics than national origin.

The South Central region was and is the home of a large segment of the country's black, Indian, and Hispanic Catholic populations. These minorities first formed part of larger white congregations. The Second Plenary Council of Baltimore reached no consensus on a unified plan of evangelizing the emancipated slaves. In the late nineteenth and early twentieth centuries, separate parishes and schools for black, Indian, Hispanic, and white (where they were in the minority) Catholics multiplied. This trend reversed itself dramatically in the 1950s when segregation became a symbol of un-Christian racism. Not all minority parishes were willing to be assimilated into larger congregations. The black Catholic community at Jeanerette, Louisiana, continues to flourish as a separate parish.

The complementary roles of priest and laity have differed greatly over the years, sometimes within a brief period in a single parish. Individual personalities shape this relationship as much as general trends. Parish histories recall priests, religious, and laypersons who generously gave of themselves and whose example and work shaped future generations. Father Charles Menard in Louisiana, John Jupe in Texas, Father Eugene Weibel in Arkansas, Cornelius Ahern in Kentucky, and the women of the St. Andrew Altar Society in Alabama were all strong forces in the early years of their respective parishes.

Lay participation in parish life expressed itself in many organizations, devotions, and programs. Trustees, sodalities, children's societies, national organizations, and altar societies were part of most early parishes. The Knights of Columbus, the Knights of Peter Claver, the Holy Name Society, St. Margaret Daughters and other women's charitable organizations, temperance and mutual benefit societies, and a host of devotional societies became vehicles for greater participation in parish life in the late nineteenth and early twentieth centuries. The CYO, the CCD, and the Christian Family Movement furthered this process and occasioned much sound adult education. In more recent times, the *Cursillo* movement, the married and engaged encounter weekends, the charismatic renewal, creative programs of sacramental education and participation, innovative youth retreat programs, study groups, and educational programs for parish religion teachers have contributed to parish growth. During the past two decades, parishes have begun new programs to call upon, train, and commission a great variety of parish ministers: lectors and music ministers, youth ministers and religious education directors, eucharistic ministers and social action directors. Many parishes now have permanent deacons as part of their staff.

Most parish histories poorly document the great liturgical changes of the twentieth century, especially the earlier changes that resulted in more frequent reception of the Eucharist and a growing consciousness of the Church as the Mystical Body of Christ. Parish bulletins and, to a lesser degree, parish histories, trace the more recent introduction of the vernacular, new forms of architectural expression, new rites for the Mass and Sacraments, and growing community participation in the liturgy.

The parish school has formed part of the reality or the aspirations of all parishes over the years. Catholic school enrollment peaked during the post-World War II years. Fewer modern parishes have a parish school, and many parishes now place great emphasis on general religious education programs for adults and youths alike. The growing role of lay men and women as religious educators is a significant trend of the past three decades. One major pastoral challenge that parishes now face is the need to provide these lay teachers with adequate intellectual training and opportunities for spiritual growth so they can indeed help to pass on the faith to the next generation. Likewise, the large number of children and youth who continue to receive little or no religious instruction is a grave parish concern.

In most parts of the region, Catholics have been a religious minority. In 1980, Catholics constituted less than 5% of the populations of Alabama, Arkansas, Mississippi, Oklahoma, and Tennessee.[4] In the 1850s and the 1920s, anti-Catholic bigotry burst forth with sometimes violent consequences for local Catholics. Catholics and Protestants, however, have also lived together in peace and friendship in many towns and cities. Parish histories often mention their Protestant benefactors and friends with great pride. A large percentage of Catholic families includes one Protestant parent—a trend that has significantly increased in recent years and offers new pastoral challenges as families are brought increasingly into parish planning, education, worship, and service.

Patterns of popular piety are more difficult to determine from parish histories. At any given time, they are a blend of traditional devotions and practices, often with strong ethnic ties, popular trends, and the parish's own individual character. The daily communal Rosary that began at Mon Louis Island, Alabama, during the Civil War and the continuous prayer for peace that started at Christ the King Parish in Dallas during the Korean conflict are outstanding examples of local parish devotion. Devotion to Mary is expressed in the 550 regional churches that are dedicated to her under her many geographical, national, devotional, and doctrinal titles.

Few parish histories have reflected on the significance of the "modest and humble" crosses they erected over their churches. St. John the Evangelist community in Luling, Texas, was an exception. The community originated in 1876 and became a parish in 1938. In 1945, the parish numbered 146 Hispanic and twenty-nine non-Hispanic families out of a population of 5,000. On the occasion of the dedication of its new church that same year, the parish reflected on its new and old churches:

"The religious consciousness of a people lies at the base of all community progress, serving God and expressing allegiance by building beautiful tabernacles to his glory, rendering thereby a service to all mankind.

"The Church of St. John the Evangelist is now one of the most outstanding church edifices in Caldwell County. It is an architectural achievement of the highest interest. Primarily designed for the worship of God by its congregation, St. John the Evangelist's Church is an enduring inspiration to everyone. Here is an example of community spirit and cooperation. It points the way to civic pride and the desire for the finer things of life. This edifice is destined to become prosperous in culture and religion, and will attract the best qualities of citizenship. The strong faith of the good people of St. John the Evangelist Parish has been displayed in this beautiful monument of God dedicated to his service."[5]

## Notes

1. Bishop L. Abel Caillouet, *Journal of the Second Vatican Council,* unpublished manuscript in the Archives of the Archdiocese of New Orleans.
2. Fichter, 18–20, 33–40.
3. Newman and Halvorson, 15 and *passim.*
4. Quinn, Anderson, etc., 10–25.
5. *Dedication Souvenir, St. John the Evangelist Church, Luling, Texas, October, 1945* (Luling: 1945). Courtesy of the Catholic Archives of Texas at Austin.

## For Further Reading*

*Archdiocese of San Antonio, 1874–1974.* San Antonio: The Archdiocese of San Antonio, 1974.

Baudier, Roger, *The Catholic Church in Louisiana.* New Orleans: A. W. Hyatt Stationery Mfg. Co., Ltd., 1939.

Castaneda, Carlos E., *Our Catholic Heritage in Texas, Volume VII (1836–1950).* Austin: Boeckmann-Jones, Company, 1958.

*The Catholic Week,* November 23, 1979. Sesquecentennial, 1829–1929, Diocese of Mobile, Alabama.

*Changing Times: The Story of the Diocese of Galveston-Houston in Commemorating Its Founding.* Houston: The Diocese of Galveston-Houston, 1972.

*Clarion Herald,* June 2, 1977. Diocese of Houma-Thibodaux Edition.

Flanigen, George J., editor, *Catholicity in Tennessee: A Sketch of Catholic Activities in the State, 1541–1937.* Nashville: Ambrose Printing Company, 1937.

Gerow, Richard O., *Catholicity in Mississippi.* Natchez: Hope Haven Press, 1939.

* All works contain many brief parish histories.

Historical Commission of the Diocese of Little Rock, *The History of Catholicity in Arkansas.* Little Rock: *The Guardian,* 1925.

Lipscomb, Oscar H., *The Administration of John Quinlan, Second Bishop of Mobile, 1859–1883* in *Records of the American Catholic Historical Society of Philadelphia, LXXVIII* (March–December, 1967).

Lovett, Rose Gibbons, *Catholic Church in the Deep South.* Birmingham: The Diocese of Birmingham, 1980.

*The Morning Star,* June 1, 1914, and December 25, 1915. These issues include historical sketches of dioceses and parishes in Alabama, Arkansas, Georgia, Louisiana, Mississippi, Oklahoma, and Texas.

Parisot, P. F. and Smith, C. J., *History of the Catholic Church in the Diocese of San Antonio, Texas, 1685–1897.* San Antonio: Francis J. Bowen, 1897.

Pillar, James J., *The Catholic Church in Mississippi, 1837–1865.* New Orleans: The Hauser Press, 1964.

Ryan, Paul E., *History of the Diocese of Covington, Kentucky.* Covington: The Diocese of Covington, 1954.

*The Southwest Courier,* October 8, 1955. Golden Jubilee, 1905–1955, Diocese of Oklahoma City and Tulsa.

*Texas Concho Register,* March 25, 1966. Consecration and Installation of Thomas A. Tschoepe as Bishop of San Angelo.

Webb, Ben J., *The Centenary of Catholicity in Kentucky.* Louisville: Charles A. Rogers, 1884.

# Parish Expansion—Statistical Summary

## TOTAL PARISHES BY STATE AND DECADE

|        | AL  | AR  | KY  | LA  | MS  | OK  | TN  | TX  | Total |
|--------|-----|-----|-----|-----|-----|-----|-----|-----|-------|
| 1850   | 4   | 3   | 34  | 40  | 6   | 0   | 3   | 11  | 101   |
| 1860   | 5   | 5   | 54  | 69  | 12  | 0   | 8   | 25  | 178   |
| 1870   | 13  | 7   | 74  | 87  | 19  | 0   | 10  | 36  | 246   |
| 1880   | 15  | 14  | 100 | 110 | 22  | 1   | 18  | 65  | 345   |
| 1890   | 17  | 23  | 123 | 120 | 24  | 6   | 20  | 104 | 437   |
| 1900   | 25  | 34  | 137 | 136 | 27  | 25  | 25  | 156 | 565   |
| 1910   | 36  | 43  | 162 | 156 | 35  | 45  | 31  | 210 | 718   |
| 1920   | 49  | 48  | 175 | 184 | 43  | 55  | 33  | 296 | 883   |
| 1930   | 61  | 55  | 186 | 229 | 47  | 84  | 42  | 372 | 1,076 |
| 1940   | 68  | 60  | 192 | 262 | 50  | 86  | 50  | 433 | 1,201 |
| 1950   | 89  | 72  | 208 | 326 | 67  | 106 | 63  | 506 | 1,437 |
| 1960   | 109 | 84  | 241 | 397 | 85  | 128 | 79  | 617 | 1,740 |
| 1970   | 120 | 84  | 274 | 453 | 105 | 132 | 80  | 781 | 2,029 |
| 1980   | 136 | 84  | 274 | 479 | 115 | 126 | 94  | 873 | 2,181 |
| 1981   | 137 | 84  | 275 | 482 | 116 | 127 | 95  | 882 | 2,198 |
| Closed | 14  | 11  | 23  | 39  | 1   | 23  | 14  | 39  | 164   |

Total parishes identified in study. 2,362

Totals as of the beginning of the year indicated.

## PERCENTAGE INCREASE IN NEW PARISHES BY DECADE

|        | AL      | AR      | KY    | LA   | MS      | OK      | TN      | TX    | Total |
|--------|---------|---------|-------|------|---------|---------|---------|-------|-------|
| 1850   | —       | —       | —     | —    | —       | —       | —       | —     | —     |
| 1860   | 25.0*   | 66.7*   | 58.8  | 72.5 | 100.0*  | —       | 166.7*  | 127.3 | 76.2  |
| 1870   | 160.0*  | 40.0*   | 37.0  | 26.1 | 58.3    | —       | 25.0*   | 44.0  | 38.2  |
| 1880   | 15.4    | 100.0*  | 35.1  | 26.4 | 15.8    | —       | 80.0    | 80.6  | 40.2  |
| 1890   | 13.3    | 64.3    | 23.0  | 9.1  | 9.1     | 600.0*  | 11.1    | 60.0  | 26.7  |
| 1900   | 47.1    | 47.8    | 11.4  | 13.3 | 12.5    | 316.7*  | 25.0    | 50.0  | 29.3  |
| 1910   | 44.0    | 26.4    | 18.2  | 14.7 | 29.6    | 80.0    | 24.0    | 34.6  | 27.1  |
| 1920   | 36.1    | 11.6    | 8.0   | 17.9 | 22.9    | 22.2    | 6.5     | 41.0  | 23.0  |
| 1930   | 24.5    | 14.6    | 6.3   | 24.5 | 9.3     | 52.8    | 27.3    | 25.7  | 21.9  |
| 1940   | 11.5    | 9.1     | 3.2   | 14.4 | 6.4     | 2.4     | 19.0    | 16.4  | 11.6  |
| 1950   | 30.9    | 20.0    | 8.3   | 24.4 | 34.0    | 23.3    | 26.0    | 16.9  | 19.7  |
| 1960   | 22.5    | 16.7    | 15.9  | 21.8 | 26.9    | 20.8    | 25.4    | 21.9  | 21.1  |
| 1970   | 10.1    | 0.0     | 13.7  | 14.1 | 23.5    | 3.1     | 1.3     | 26.6  | 16.6  |
| 1980   | 13.3    | 0.0     | 0.0   | 5.7  | 9.5     | –4.5    | 17.5    | 11.8  | 7.5   |
| 1981   | —       | —       | —     | —    | —       | —       | —       | —     | —     |

*percentage based on less than ten parishes.

**PARISH ESTABLISHMENT BY NEW COUNTIES**

| | AL | AR | KY | LA | MS | OK | TN | TX | Total new co. | Total to date |
|---|---|---|---|---|---|---|---|---|---|---|
| 1850 | 3 | 3 | 18 | 24 | 6 | 0 | 3 | 10 | — | 67 |
| 1860 | 0 | 2 | 6 | 7 | 3 | 0 | 3 | 11 | 32 | 99 |
| 1870 | 5 | 2 | 9 | 2 | 6 | 0 | 0 | 6 | 30 | 129 |
| 1880 | 2 | 5 | 7 | 3 | 2 | 1 | 4 | 19 | 43 | 172 |
| 1890 | 1 | 4 | 5 | 2 | 1 | 5 | 0 | 21 | 39 | 211 |
| 1900 | 3 | 5 | 2 | 2 | 2 | 15 | 3 | 24 | 56 | 267 |
| 1910 | 1 | 5 | 4 | 2 | 3 | 11 | 3 | 14 | 43 | 310 |
| 1920 | 2 | 5 | 4 | 0 | 3 | 4 | 1 | 24 | 43 | 353 |
| 1930 | 3 | 3 | 5 | 2 | 1 | 7 | 3 | 16 | 40 | 393 |
| 1940 | 3 | 3 | 1 | 4 | 0 | 1 | 1 | 11 | 24 | 417 |
| 1950 | 6 | 6 | 4 | 9 | 6 | 7 | 8 | 10 | 56 | 473 |
| 1960 | 3 | 5 | 5 | 1 | 8 | 4 | 7 | 15 | 48 | 521 |
| 1970 | 3 | 1 | 12 | 0 | 9 | 4 | 2 | 21 | 52 | 573 |
| 1980 | 8 | 2 | 5 | 0 | 3 | 0 | 6 | 8 | 32 | 605 |
| 1981 | 1 | 0 | 1 | 0 | 0 | 0 | 1 | 0 | 3 | 608 |
| Total | 44 | 51 | 88 | 58 | 53 | 59 | 45 | 210 | 608 | |

Total counties with no Catholic parishes:

| | 23 | 24 | 32 | 6 | 29 | 18 | 50 | 44 | 226 | |
|---|---|---|---|---|---|---|---|---|---|---|

Total counties:

| | 67 | 75 | 120 | 64 | 82 | 77 | 95 | 254 | 834 | |
|---|---|---|---|---|---|---|---|---|---|---|

Total counties that once had a Catholic parish but with no parish in 1981:

| | 2 | 1 | 5 | 0 | 1 | 3 | 4 | 0 | 14 | |
|---|---|---|---|---|---|---|---|---|---|---|

**APPENDIX 4:**

# Diocesan Statistics

## ALABAMA
### Diocese of Birmingham (1969)

|  | 1850 | 1880 | 1900 | 1930 | 1950 | 1960 | 1980 |
|---|---|---|---|---|---|---|---|
| Parishes | — | — | — | — | — | — | 55 |
| Parishes without Priests (i.e., Missions) | — | — | — | — | — | — | 15 |
| National Parishes | — | — | — | — | — | — | + |
| Diocesan Priests | — | — | — | — | — | — | 68 |
| Religious Order Priests | — | — | — | — | — | — | 57 |
| Women Religious | — | — | — | — | — | — | 191 |
| Catholic Population | — | — | — | — | — | — | 53,000 |
| Total Population | — | — | — | — | — | — | 2,200,000 |

( ) = year diocese was established.
— = diocese not yet established.
+ = reliable data not available; cf. Footnote 4, Preface.

## ALABAMA
### Archdiocese of Mobile (1829)

|  | 1850 | 1880 | 1900 | 1930 | 1950 | 1960 | 1980 |
|---|---|---|---|---|---|---|---|
| Parishes | 18# | 26# | 27 | 67 | 100 | 126 | 73 |
| Parishes without Priests (i.e., Missions) | * | * | 33 | 41 | 62 | 62 | 19 |
| National Parishes | + | + | + | + | + | + | + |
| Diocesan Priests | 20## | 22## | 34 | 70 | 124 | 189 | 95 |
| Religious Order Priests | ## | ## | 32 | 83 | 178 | 217 | 77 |
| Women Religious | * | * | * | * | 660 | 768 | 173 |
| Catholic Population | 11,000 | 16,000 | 20,000 | 50,000 | 71,000 | 107,000 | 56,000 |
| Total Population | * | * | * | * | * | 3,256,000 | 1,351,000 |

( ) = year diocese was established.
+ = reliable data not available; cf. Footnote 4, Preface.
* = data not provided in *Catholic Directory*.
# = listed as churches.
## = combined figure for diocesan and religious priests.
NB diocese included part of Florida until 1967.

# ARKANSAS
## Diocese of Little Rock (1843)

| | 1850 | 1880 | 1900 | 1930 | 1950 | 1960 | 1980 |
|---|---|---|---|---|---|---|---|
| Parishes | 7# | 30# | 31 | 50 | 67 | 75 | 74 |
| Parishes without Priests (i.e., Missions) | 1 | * | 20 | 61 | 36 | 41 | 47 |
| National Parishes | + | + | + | + | + | + | + |
| Diocesan Priests | 6## | 15## | 21 | 58 | 108 | 121 | 110 |
| Religious Order Priests | ## | ## | 22 | 33 | 52 | 64 | 64 |
| Women Religious | * | * | 150 | 608 | 599 | 830 | 534 |
| Catholic Population | * | 5,000 | 10,000 | 27,000 | 37,000 | 45,000 | 57,000 |
| Total Population | 210,000 | 803,000 | 1,312,000 | 1,854,000 | 1,910,000 | 1,750,000 | 2,186,000 |

( ) = year diocese was established.
+ = reliable data not available; cf. Footnote 4, Preface.
* = data not provided in *Catholic Directory*.
# = listed as churches or churches and church buildings.
## = combined figure for diocesan and religious priests.
NB 1850–1950 total population from U.S. Census.

**KENTUCKY**
**Diocese of Covington (1853)**

|                              | 1850 | 1880   | 1900   | 1930   | 1950   | 1960      | 1980      |
|------------------------------|------|--------|--------|--------|--------|-----------|-----------|
| Parishes                     | —    | 52#    | 47     | 66     | 69     | 79        | 85        |
| Parishes without Priests (i.e., Missions) | —    | 23     | 29     | 17     | 29     | 20        | 25        |
| National Parishes            | —    | +      | +      | +      | +      | +         | +         |
| Diocesan Priests             | —    | 52     | 63     | 101    | 124    | 196       | 193       |
| Religious Order Priests      | —    | 4      | 7      | 8      | 23     | 15        | 20        |
| Women Religious              | —    | *      | *      | 735    | 795    | 886       | 1,081     |
| Catholic Population          | —    | 42,000 | 50,000 | 65,000 | 72,000 | 87,000    | 109,000   |
| Total Population             | —    | *      | *      | *      | *      | 1,354,000 | 1,500,000 |

( ) = year diocese was established.
— = diocese not yet established.
+ = reliable data not available; cf. Footnote 4, Preface.
* = data not provided in *Catholic Directory*.
# = listed as churches.

**KENTUCKY**
**Archdiocese of Louisville (1808)**

|                              | 1850   | 1880    | 1900    | 1930    | 1950    | 1960    | 1980      |
|------------------------------|--------|---------|---------|---------|---------|---------|-----------|
| Parishes                     | 46#    | 102#    | 93      | 112     | 88      | 106     | 119       |
| Parishes without Priests (i.e., Missions) | 10     | *       | 40      | 50      | 25      | 24      | 30        |
| National Parishes            | +      | +       | +       | +       | +       | +       | +         |
| Diocesan Priests             | 57##   | 76      | 108     | 126     | 160     | 228     | 255       |
| Religious Order Priests      | ##     | 43      | 56      | 105     | 133     | 171     | 124       |
| Women Religious              | *      | *       | *       | *       | 1,416   | 1,557   | 1,462     |
| Catholic Population          | 35,000 | 150,000 | 100,000 | 117,000 | 132,000 | 163,000 | 210,000   |
| Total Population             | *      | *       | *       | *       | *       | 951,000 | 1,302,000 |

( ) = year diocese was established (Bardstown).
+ = reliable data not available; cf. Footnote 4, Preface.
* = data not provided in *Catholic Directory*.
# = listed as churches or churches and church buildings.
## = combined figure for diocesan and religious priests.
NB 1880 total Catholic population as listed.

## KENTUCKY
### Diocese of Owensboro (1937)

| | 1850 | 1880 | 1900 | 1930 | 1950 | 1960 | 1980 |
|---|---|---|---|---|---|---|---|
| Parishes | — | — | — | — | 37 | 40 | 53 |
| Parishes without Priests | | | | | | | |
| (i.e., Missions) | — | — | — | — | 26 | 26 | 23 |
| National Parishes | — | — | — | — | + | + | + |
| Diocesan Priests | — | — | — | — | 50 | 66 | 77 |
| Religious Order Priests | — | — | — | — | 10 | 16 | 18 |
| Women Religious | — | — | — | — | 438 | 482 | 280 |
| Catholic Population | — | — | — | — | 31,000 | 38,000 | 50,000 |
| Total Population | — | — | — | — | * | 629,000 | 678,000 |

( ) = year diocese was established.
— = diocese not yet established.
+ = reliable data not available; cf. Footnote 4, Preface.
* = data not provided in *Catholic Directory*.

## LOUISIANA
### Diocese of Alexandria-Shreveport (1853)

| | 1850 | 1880 | 1900 | 1930 | 1950 | 1960 | 1980 |
|---|---|---|---|---|---|---|---|
| Parishes | — | 13# | 19 | 27 | 70 | 82 | 79 |
| Parishes without Priests | | | | | | | |
| (i.e., Missions) | — | 17 | 19 | 53 | 61 | 66 | 59 |
| National Parishes | — | + | + | + | + | + | + |
| Diocesan Priests | — | 17## | 20 | 28 | 65 | 114 | 120 |
| Religious Order Priests | — | ## | 0 | 17 | 58 | 52 | 42 |
| Women Religious | — | * | 67 | 216 | 315 | 359 | 226 |
| Catholic Population | — | 30,000 | 30,000 | 48,000 | 52,000 | 79,000 | 83,000 |
| Total Population | — | * | * | * | * | 939,000 | 1,033,000 |

( ) = year diocese was established. (Natchitoches)
— = diocese not yet established.
+ = reliable data not available; cf. Footnote 4, Preface.
* = data not provided in *Catholic Directory*.
# = listed as churches.
## = combined figure for diocesan and religious priests.

## LOUISIANA
### Diocese of Baton Rouge (1961)

|  | 1850 | 1880 | 1900 | 1930 | 1950 | 1960 | 1980 |
|---|---|---|---|---|---|---|---|
| Parishes | — | — | — | — | — | — | 69 |
| Parishes without Priests (i.e., Missions) | — | — | — | — | — | — | 23 |
| National Parishes | — | — | — | — | — | — | + |
| Diocesan Priests | — | — | — | — | — | — | 97 |
| Religious Order Priests | — | — | — | — | — | — | 64 |
| Women Religious | — | — | — | — | — | — | 125 |
| Catholic Population | — | — | — | — | — | — | 174,000 |
| Total Population | — | — | — | — | — | — | 646,000 |

( ) = year diocese was established.
— = diocese not yet established.
+ = reliable data not available; cf. Footnote 4, Preface.

## LOUISIANA
### Diocese of Houma-Thibidaux (1977)

|  | 1850 | 1880 | 1900 | 1930 | 1950 | 1960 | 1980 |
|---|---|---|---|---|---|---|---|
| Parishes | — | — | — | — | — | — | 34 |
| Parishes without Priests (i.e., Missions) | — | — | — | — | — | — | 9 |
| National Parishes | — | — | — | — | — | — | + |
| Diocesan Priests | — | — | — | — | — | — | 57 |
| Religious Order Priests | — | — | — | — | — | — | 8 |
| Women Religious | — | — | — | — | — | — | 73 |
| Catholic Population | — | — | — | — | — | — | 130,000 |
| Total Population | — | — | — | — | — | — | 182,000 |

( ) = year diocese was established.
— = diocese not yet established.
+ = reliable data not available; cf. Footnote 4, Preface.

## LOUISIANA
### Diocese of Lafayette (1918)

|  | 1850 | 1880 | 1900 | 1930 | 1950 | 1960 | 1980 |
|---|---|---|---|---|---|---|---|
| Parishes | — | — | — | 63 | 100 | 131 | 153 |
| Parishes without Priests |  |  |  |  |  |  |  |
| (i.e., Missions) | — | — | — | 47 | 97# | 80 | 51 |
| National Parishes | — | — | — | + | + | + | + |
| Diocesan Priests | — | — | — | 75 | 118 | 154 | 197 |
| Religious Order Priests | — | — | — | 34 | 76 | 103 | 106 |
| Women Religious | — | — | — | * | 380 | 498 | 410. |
| Catholic Population | — | — | — | 192,000 | 295,000 | 388,000 | 399,000 |
| Total Population | — | — | — | * | * | 590,000 | 774,000 |

( ) = year diocese was established.
— = diocese not yet established.
+ = reliable data not available; cf. Footnote 4, Preface.
* = data not provided in *Catholic Directory*.
# = missions and chapels listed together as chapels.

## LOUISIANA
### Diocese of Lake Charles (1980)

|  | 1850 | 1880 | 1900 | 1930 | 1950 | 1960 | 1980 |
|---|---|---|---|---|---|---|---|
| Parishes | — | — | — | — | — | — | — |
| Parishes without Priests (i.e., Missions) | — | — | — | — | — | — | — |
| National Parishes | — | — | — | — | — | — | — |
| Diocesan Priests | — | — | — | — | — | — | — |
| Religious Order Priests | — | — | — | — | — | — | — |
| Women Religious | — | — | — | — | — | — | — |
| Catholic Population | — | — | — | — | — | — | — |
| Total Population | — | — | — | — | — | — | — |

( ) = year diocese was established.
— = diocese not yet established.

# LOUISIANA
## Archdiocese of New Orleans (1793)

| | 1850 | 1880 | 1900 | 1930 | 1950 | 1960 | 1980 |
|---|---|---|---|---|---|---|---|
| Parishes | 60@ | 94# | 107 | 132 | 155 | 180 | 133 |
| Parishes without Priests | | | | | | | |
| (i.e., Missions) | * | 34@@ | 54 | 97 | 102 | 85 | 11 |
| National Parishes | + | + | + | + | + | + | + |
| Diocesan Priests | 74## | 162## | 130 | 140 | 210 | 219 | 230 |
| Religious Order Priests | ## | ## | 81 | 210 | 288 | 350 | 316 |
| Women Religious | * | * | * | * | 1,692 | 2,001 | 1,275 |
| Catholic Population | 170,000 | 250,000 | 325,000 | 344,000 | 458,000 | 618,000 | 530,000 |
| Total Population | 518,000 | * | * | * | * | 1,446,000 | 1,263,000 |

( ) = year diocese was established.
+ = reliable data not available; cf. Footnote 4, Preface.
* = data not provided in *Catholic Directory*.
# = includes churches and church buildings.
## = combined figure for diocesan and religious priests.
@ = includes churches and chapels.
@@ = includes missions and stations.
NB 1850 total population from U.S. Census.

334

**MISSISSIPPI**
**Diocese of Biloxi (1977)**

|  | 1850 | 1880 | 1900 | 1930 | 1950 | 1960 | 1980 |
|---|---|---|---|---|---|---|---|
| Parishes | — | — | — | — | — | — | 42 |
| Parishes without Priests (i.e., Missions) | — | — | — | — | — | — | 13 |
| National Parishes | — | — | — | — | — | — | + |
| Diocesan Priests | — | — | — | — | — | — | 66 |
| Religious Order Priests | — | — | — | — | — | — | 30 |
| Women Religious | — | — | — | — | — | — | 93 |
| Catholic Population | — | — | — | — | — | — | 52,000 |
| Total Population | — | — | — | — | — | — | 579,000 |

( ) = year diocese was established.
— = diocese not yet established.
+ = reliable data not available; cf. Footnote 4, Preface.

**MISSISSIPPI**
**Diocese of Jackson (1837)**

| | 1850 | 1880 | 1900 | 1930 | 1950 | 1960 | 1980 |
|---|---|---|---|---|---|---|---|
| Parishes | 9# | 41# | 26 | 45 | 66 | 84 | 72 |
| Parishes without Priests (i.e., Missions) | * | * | 42 | 64 | 65 | 64 | 28 |
| National Parishes | + | + | + | + | + | + | + |
| Diocesan Priests | 7## | 19 | 30 | 54 | 88 | 95 | 77 |
| Religious Order Priests | ## | 6 | 3 | 18 | 94 | 104 | 43 |
| Women Religious | * | * | 150 | 267 | 660 | 407 | 324 |
| Catholic Population | 7,000 | 13,000 | 18,000 | 34,000 | 51,000 | 64,000 | 43,000 |
| Total Population | 607,000 | 1,132,000 | 1,551,000 | 2,010,000 | 2,179,000 | 2,179,000 | 1,700,000 |

( ) = year diocese was established. (Natchez)
+ = reliable data not available; cf. Footnote 4, Preface.
* = data not provided in *Catholic Directory*.
# = listed as churches or churches and church buildings.
## = combined figure for diocesan and religious priests.
NB 1850–1950 total population from U.S. Census.

## OKLAHOMA
### Diocese of Oklahoma City (1905) ∧

|                                        | 1850 | 1880  | 1900    | 1930   | 1950      | 1960      | 1980      |
|----------------------------------------|------|-------|---------|--------|-----------|-----------|-----------|
| Parishes                               | —    | 0     | 30      | 80     | 105       | 127       | 67        |
| Parishes without Priests (i.e., Missions) | —    | 0     | 34      | 87     | 100       | 82        | 53        |
| National Parishes                      | —    | —     | +       | +      | +         | +         | +         |
| Diocesan Priests                       | —    | 0     | 22      | 89     | 118       | 186       | 108       |
| Religious Order Priests                | —    | *     | 26      | 54     | 93        | 89        | 38        |
| Women Religious                        | —    | *     | 150     | 462    | 714       | 790       | 278       |
| Catholic Population                    | —    | 4,000 | 18,000  | 55,000 | 74,000    | 97,000    | 67,000    |
| Total Population                       | —    | —     | 790,000 | *      | 2,233,000 | 2,300,000 | 1,625,000 |

( ) = year diocese was established.
— = diocese not yet established.
+ = reliable data not available; cf. Footnote 4, Preface.
* = data not provided in *Catholic Directory*.
∧ = established in 1876 as Prefecture Apostolic of Indian Territory.
NB 1900 and 1950 total population from U.S. Census.


## OKLAHOMA
### Diocese of Tulsa (1973)

|                                        | 1850 | 1880 | 1900 | 1930 | 1950 | 1960 | 1980      |
|----------------------------------------|------|------|------|------|------|------|-----------|
| Parishes                               | —    | —    | —    | —    | —    | —    | 53        |
| Parishes without Priests (i.e., Missions) | —    | —    | —    | —    | —    | —    | 28        |
| National Parishes                      | —    | —    | —    | —    | —    | —    | +         |
| Diocesan Priests                       | —    | —    | —    | —    | —    | —    | 63        |
| Religious Order Priests                | —    | —    | —    | —    | —    | —    | 27        |
| Women Religious                        | —    | —    | —    | —    | —    | —    | 224       |
| Catholic Population                    | —    | —    | —    | —    | —    | —    | 50,000    |
| Total Population                       | —    | —    | —    | —    | —    | —    | 1,160,000 |

( ) = year diocese was established.
— = diocese not yet established.
+ = reliable data not available; cf. Footnote 4, Preface.

**TENNESSEE**

**Diocese of Memphis (1971)**

|                                          | 1850 | 1880 | 1900 | 1930 | 1950 | 1960 | 1980      |
|------------------------------------------|------|------|------|------|------|------|-----------|
| Parishes                                 | —    | —    | —    | —    | —    | —    | 35        |
| Parishes without Priests (i.e., Missions)| —    | —    | —    | —    | —    | —    | 10        |
| National Parishes                        | —    | —    | —    | —    | —    | —    | +         |
| Diocesan Priests                         | —    | —    | —    | —    | —    | —    | 59        |
| Religious Order Priests                  | —    | —    | —    | —    | —    | —    | 24        |
| Women Religious                          | —    | —    | —    | —    | —    | —    | 173       |
| Catholic Population                      | —    | —    | —    | —    | —    | —    | 47,000    |
| Total Population                         | —    | —    | —    | —    | —    | —    | 1,500,000 |

( ) = year diocese was established.
— = diocese not yet established.
+ = reliable data not available; cf. Footnote 4, Preface.

**TENNESSEE**

**Diocese of Nashville (1837)**

| | 1850 | 1880 | 1900 | 1930 | 1950 | 1960 | 1980 |
|---|---|---|---|---|---|---|---|
| Parishes | 6# | 29# | 19 | 34 | 54 | 66 | 55 |
| Parishes without Priests (i.e., Missions) | * | * | 15 | 20 | 31 | 36 | 24 |
| National Parishes | + | + | + | + | + | + | + |
| Diocesan Priests | 9## | 27## | 18 | 43 | 81 | 113 | 77 |
| Religious Order Priests | ## | ## | 5 | 20 | 30 | 31 | 41 |
| Women Religious | * | * | * | * | 461 | 502 | 168 |
| Catholic Population | 3,000 | * | 28,000 | 29,000 | 38,000 | 73,000 | 66,000 |
| Total Population | 1,003,000 | 1,542,000 | 2,021,000 | 2,617,000 | 3,292,000 | 3,468,000 | 2,766,000 |

( ) = year diocese was established.
+ = reliable data not available; cf. Footnote 4, Preface.
* = data not provided in *Catholic Directory*.
# = includes churches and chapels
## = combined figure for diocesan and religious priests.
NB 1850–1950 total population from U.S. Census.

339

**TEXAS**
**Diocese of Amarillo (1926)**

|                                      | 1850 | 1880 | 1900 | 1930   | 1950   | 1960      | 1980    |
|--------------------------------------|------|------|------|--------|--------|-----------|---------|
| Parishes                             | —    | —    | —    | 22     | 42     | 51        | 58      |
| Parishes without Priests (i.e., Missions) | —    | —    | —    | 29     | 29     | 57        | 31      |
| National Parishes                    | —    | —    | —    | +      | +      | +         | +       |
| Diocesan Priests                     | —    | —    | —    | 25     | 45     | 66        | 67      |
| Religious Order Priests              | —    | —    | —    | 8      | 27     | 38        | 23      |
| Women Religious                      | —    | —    | —    | *      | 187    | 244       | 168     |
| Catholic Population                  | —    | —    | —    | 31,000 | 49,000 | 91,000    | 89,000  |
| Total Population                     | —    | —    | —    | *      | *      | 1,154,000 | 800,000 |

( ) = year diocese was established.
— = diocese not yet established.
+ = reliable data not available; cf. Footnote 4, Preface.
* = data not provided in *Catholic Directory*.


**TEXAS**
**Diocese of Austin (1948)**

|                                      | 1850 | 1880 | 1900 | 1930 | 1950   | 1960    | 1980    |
|--------------------------------------|------|------|------|------|--------|---------|---------|
| Parishes                             | —    | —    | —    | —    | 53     | 73      | 82      |
| Parishes without Priests (i.e., Missions) | —    | —    | —    | —    | 45     | 38      | 34      |
| National Parishes                    | —    | —    | —    | —    | +      | +       | +       |
| Diocesan Priests                     | —    | —    | —    | —    | 54     | 85      | 101     |
| Religious Order Priests              | —    | —    | —    | —    | 46     | 50      | 51      |
| Women Religious                      | —    | —    | —    | —    | 199    | 245     | 190     |
| Catholic Population                  | —    | —    | —    | —    | 79,000 | 121,000 | 137,000 |
| Total Population                     | —    | —    | —    | —    | *      | 875,000 | 991,000 |

( ) = year diocese was established.
— = diocese not yet established.
+ = reliable data not available; cf. Footnote 4, Preface.
* = data not provided in *Catholic Directory*.

## TEXAS
### Diocese of Beaumont (1966)

|  | 1850 | 1880 | 1900 | 1930 | 1950 | 1960 | 1980 |
|---|---|---|---|---|---|---|---|
| Parishes | — | — | — | — | — | — | 44 |
| Parishes without Priests (i.e., Missions) | — | — | — | — | — | — | 13 |
| National Parishes | — | — | — | — | — | — | + |
| Diocesan Priests | — | — | — | — | — | — | 57 |
| Religious Order Priests | — | — | — | — | — | — | 34 |
| Women Religious | — | — | — | — | — | — | 121 |
| Catholic Population | — | — | — | — | — | — | 84,000 |
| Total Population | — | — | — | — | — | — | 587,000 |

( ) = year diocese was established.
— = diocese not yet established.
+ = reliable data not available; cf. Footnote 4, Preface.

## TEXAS
### Diocese of Brownsville (1965)

|  | 1850 | 1880 | 1900 | 1930 | 1950 | 1960 | 1980 |
|---|---|---|---|---|---|---|---|
| Parishes | — | — | — | — | — | — | 60 |
| Parishes without Priests (i.e., Missions) | — | — | — | — | — | — | 50 |
| National Parishes | — | — | — | — | — | — | + |
| Diocesan Priests | — | — | — | — | — | — | 49 |
| Religious Order Priests | — | — | — | — | — | — | 71 |
| Women Religious | — | — | — | — | — | — | 170 |
| Catholic Population | — | — | — | — | — | — | 318,000 |
| Total Population | — | — | — | — | — | — | 443,000 |

( ) = year diocese was established.
— = diocese not yet established.
+ = reliable data not available; cf. Footnote 4, Preface.

**TEXAS**
**Diocese of Corpus Christi (1912)^**

|                                 | 1850 | 1880   | 1900   | 1930    | 1950    | 1960    | 1980    |
|---------------------------------|------|--------|--------|---------|---------|---------|---------|
| Parishes                        | —    | 12#    | 13     | 46      | 69      | 86      | 76      |
| Parishes without Priests        |      |        |        |         |         |         |         |
| (i.e., Missions)                | —    | 12     | 36     | 101     | 93      | 111     | 49      |
| National Parishes               | —    | +      | +      | +       | +       | +       | +       |
| Diocesan Priests                | —    | 22##   | 11     | 35      | 58      | 84      | 83      |
| Religious Order Priests         | —    | ##     | 11     | 50      | 89      | 138     | 90      |
| Women Religious                 | —    | *      | *      | *       | 413     | 546     | 226     |
| Catholic Population             | —    | 40,000 | 60,000 | 248,000 | 454,000 | 525,000 | 178,000 |
| Total Population                | —    | *      | *      | *       | *       | 914,000 | 545,000 |

( ) = year diocese was established.
— = diocese not yet established.
+ = reliable data not available; cf. Footnote 4, Preface.
* = data not provided in *Catholic Directory*.
^ = established in 1874 as Vicariate Apostolic of Brownsville.
# = listed as churches.
## = combined figure for diocesan and religious priests.

**TEXAS**
**Diocese of Dallas (1890)**

|                                 | 1850 | 1880 | 1900   | 1930   | 1950   | 1960      | 1980      |
|---------------------------------|------|------|--------|--------|--------|-----------|-----------|
| Parishes                        | —    | —    | 32     | 56     | 83     | 97        | 59        |
| Parishes without Priests        |      |      |        |        |        |           |           |
| (i.e., Missions)                | —    | —    | 40     | 55     | 54     | 47        | 16        |
| National Parishes               | —    | —    | +      | +      | +      | +         | +         |
| Diocesan Priests                | —    | —    | 34     | 56     | 87     | 122       | 107       |
| Religious Order Priests         | —    | —    | 10     | 26     | 74     | 121       | 104       |
| Women Religious                 | —    | —    | *      | *      | 555    | 672       | 355       |
| Catholic Population             | —    | —    | 22,000 | 46,000 | 67,000 | 119,000   | 165,000   |
| Total Population                | —    | —    | *      | *      | *      | 2,974,000 | 2,779,000 |

( ) = year diocese was established.
— = diocese not yet established.
+ = reliable data not available; cf. Footnote 4, Preface.
* = data not provided in *Catholic Directory*.

## TEXAS
### Diocese of El Paso (1914)

|  | 1850 | 1880 | 1900 | 1930 | 1950 | 1960 | 1980 |
|---|---|---|---|---|---|---|---|
| Parishes | — | — | — | 46 | 51 | 63 | 78 |
| Parishes without Priests (i.e., Missions) | — | — | — | 113# | 68 | 63 | 35 |
| National Parishes | — | — | — | + | + | + | + |
| Diocesan Priests | — | — | — | 33 | 47 | 93 | 92 |
| Religious Order Priests | — | — | — | 56 | 73 | 80 | 78 |
| Women Religious | — | — | — | * | 344 | 385 | 370 |
| Catholic Population | — | — | — | 120,000 | 145,000 | 200,000 | 224,000 |
| Total Population | — | — | — | * | * | 440,000 | 800,000 |

( ) = year diocese was established.
— = diocese not yet established.
+ = reliable data not available; cf. Footnote 4, Preface.
* = data not provided in *Catholic Directory*.
# = stations and missions listed together.
NB The Diocese of El Paso also included part of New Mexico until 1983.

## TEXAS
### Diocese of Fort Worth (1969)

|  | 1850 | 1880 | 1900 | 1930 | 1950 | 1960 | 1980 |
|---|---|---|---|---|---|---|---|
| Parishes | — | — | — | — | — | — | 54 |
| Parishes without Priests (i.e., Missions) | — | — | — | — | — | — | 25 |
| National Parishes | — | — | — | — | — | — | + |
| Diocesan Priests | — | — | — | — | — | — | 69 |
| Religious Order Priests | — | — | — | — | — | — | 40 |
| Women Religious | — | — | — | — | — | — | 165 |
| Catholic Population | — | — | — | — | — | — | 91,000 |
| Total Population | — | — | — | — | — | — | 1,524,000 |

( ) = year diocese was established.
— = diocese not yet established.
+ = reliable data not available; cf. Footnote 4, Preface.

## TEXAS
### Diocese of Galveston-Houston (1847)

|  | 1850 | 1880 | 1900 | 1930 | 1950 | 1960 | 1980 |
|---|---|---|---|---|---|---|---|
| Parishes | 20# | 40# | 42 | 72 | 90 | 115 | 142 |
| Parishes without Priests (i.e., Missions) | * | * | 21 | 84 | 41 | 40 | 15 |
| National Parishes | + | + | + | + | + | + | + |
| Diocesan Priests | 16## | 48## | 49 | 109 | 123 | 169 | 202 |
| Religious Order Priests | ## | ## | 15 | 35 | 104 | 160 | 254 |
| Women Religious | * | * | 320 | * | 1,183 | 1,294 | 649 |
| Catholic Population | * | 25,000 | 40,000 | 135,000 | 205,000 | 412,000 | 437,000 |
| Total Population | * | * | * | * | * | 2,290,000 | 2,960,000 |

( ) = year diocese was established.
+ = reliable data not available; cf. Footnote 4, Preface.
* = data not provided in *Catholic Directory*.
# = listed as churches.
## = combined figure for diocesan and religious priests.

## TEXAS
### Diocese of Lubbock (1983)

|  | 1850 | 1880 | 1900 | 1930 | 1950 | 1960 | 1980 |
|---|---|---|---|---|---|---|---|
| Parishes | — | — | — | — | — | — | — |
| Parishes without Priests (i.e., Missions) | — | — | — | — | — | — | — |
| National Parishes | — | — | — | — | — | — | — |
| Diocesan Priests | — | — | — | — | — | — | — |
| Religious Order Priests | — | — | — | — | — | — | — |
| Women Religious | — | — | — | — | — | — | — |
| Catholic Population | — | — | — | — | — | — | — |
| Total Population | — | — | — | — | — | — | — |

( ) = year diocese was established.
— = diocese not yet established.

## TEXAS
### Diocese of San Angelo (1961)

|                                          | 1850 | 1880 | 1900 | 1930 | 1950 | 1960 | 1980    |
|------------------------------------------|------|------|------|------|------|------|---------|
| Parishes                                 | —    | —    | —    | —    | —    | —    | 43      |
| Parishes without Priests (i.e., Missions) | —    | —    | —    | —    | —    | —    | 32      |
| National Parishes                        | —    | —    | —    | —    | —    | —    | +       |
| Diocesan Priests                         | —    | —    | —    | —    | —    | —    | 53      |
| Religious Order Priests                  | —    | —    | —    | —    | —    | —    | 24      |
| Women Religious                          | —    | —    | —    | —    | —    | —    | 38      |
| Catholic Population                      | —    | —    | —    | —    | —    | —    | 77,000  |
| Total Population                         | —    | —    | —    | —    | —    | —    | 557,000 |

( ) = year diocese was established.
— = diocese not yet established.
+ = reliable data not available; cf. Footnote 4, Preface.

## TEXAS
### Archdiocese of San Antonio (1874)

|                                          | 1850 | 1880   | 1900   | 1930    | 1950    | 1960      | 1980      |
|------------------------------------------|------|--------|--------|---------|---------|-----------|-----------|
| Parishes                                 | —    | 50#    | 41     | 102     | 103     | 125       | 162       |
| Parishes without Priests (i.e., Missions) | —    | *      | 32     | 100     | 103     | 93        | 69        |
| National Parishes                        | —    | +      | +      | +       | +       | +         | +         |
| Diocesan Priests                         | —    | 45##   | 52     | 91      | 128     | 187       | 204       |
| Religious Order Priests                  | —    | ##     | 16     | 116     | 174     | 199       | 263       |
| Women Religious                          | —    | *      | *      | *       | 1,070   | 1,600     | 1,500     |
| Catholic Population                      | —    | 47,000 | 70,000 | 181,000 | 260,000 | 380,000   | 575,000   |
| Total Population                         | —    | *      | *      | *       | *       | 1,201,000 | 1,376,000 |

( ) = year diocese was established.
— = diocese not yet established.
+ = reliable data not available; cf. Footnote 4, Preface.
* = data not provided in *Catholic Directory*.
# = listed as churches.
## = combined figure for diocesan and religious priests.

**TEXAS**
**Diocese of Victoria (1982)**

|                                           | 1850 | 1880 | 1900 | 1930 | 1950 | 1960 | 1980 |
|-------------------------------------------|------|------|------|------|------|------|------|
| Parishes                                  | —    | —    | —    | —    | —    | —    | —    |
| Parishes without Priests (i.e., Missions) | —    | —    | —    | —    | —    | —    | —    |
| National Parishes                         | —    | —    | —    | —    | —    | —    | —    |
| Diocesan Priests                          | —    | —    | —    | —    | —    | —    | —    |
| Religious Order Priests                   | —    | —    | —    | —    | —    | —    | —    |
| Women Religious                           | —    | —    | —    | —    | —    | —    | —    |
| Catholic Population                       | —    | —    | —    | —    | —    | —    | —    |
| Total Population                          | —    | —    | —    | —    | —    | —    | —    |

( ) = year diocese was established.
— = diocese not yet established.

# General Index

Acadians, 243, 249–250, 267, 279, 283, 319
Adult education, 18, 28, 48–49, 56–58, 97, 99, 160, 198, 204, 297, 304–305, 309, 315
Ahern, Cornelius, 265, 320
Alsatian-Americans, 264
Altar and Rosary Societies, 49, 68, 159
American Catholic Missionary Union, 39
American Home Missionary Society, 264
American Protective Association, 48
Americanization (inculturation), 67, 75–76, 78–79, 84, 86, 174, 280–282
Ancient Order of Hibernians, 285
Anstaett, Joseph, 247
Apostolic Mission House, 173
Augustinians, 29, 67, 86
Aust, Richard, 42
Austrian-Americans, 264, 276, 279

Bacon, David, 21
Badeaux, Francis, 298
Baden, Stephen, 121
Baltimore, Diocesan Synod of 1791, 158; First Plenary Council of, 22; Second Plenary Council of, 136, 182, 264, 320; Third Plenary Council of, 22, 284; First Provincial Council of, 22; Third Provincial Council of, 245
*Baltimore Catechism*, 50, 97, 168, 202
Bandini, P., 279
Barry, Patrick, 166
Baudier, Roger, 249, 281, 284
Beaven, Thomas D., 44
Benedictine nuns, 295
Benedictines, 136, 138, 255, 262–263, 267, 282, 304
Bible Study Fellowship, 304
Biler, Jean Marie, 262
Bishops, see Clergy
Black, Hugo, 299
Black Americans, 46–48, 70, 76–77, 85, 87, 96, 124, 130–131, 134, 136–139, 142–144, 147–148, 160, 163, 169, 172, 174, 177, 182–186, 194, 197, 214–218, 238, 244, 249, 256–257,

260–261, 264, 267, 272, 274, 282–283, 296, 302, 306–308, 312–315, 319–320
Blake, James, 57
Blanc, Antoine, 242–243, 245–246
Blenk, James H., 273, 276, 281, 283–284
Blessed Sacrament Fathers, 53
Bliemel, Emmeram, 255–256
Blount, Mr. Robert, 292
Boheme, Ghislain, 258
Bohemian-Americans, 180, 183, 279, 282, 319
Borias, Antoine, 285
Bornes, Adrian, 291
Bouchet, Jules, 285
Boy/Girl Scouts, 49, 69, 97, 286, 294–295
Bresnahan, Patrick J., 173
Brosman, Mary L., 167
Brothers of the Holy Cross, 23
Browne, Henry J., 18, 97
Brownson, Orestes, 121
Brunini, Joseph, 307
Buffard, Theodore, 311
Butler, Benjamin, 255
Butler, Thomas, R., 265
Byrd, Harry, 147
Byrne, Andrew, 246, 253
Byrne, Pierce, 94
Byzantine Catholics, see Eastern Rite Catholics

Callahan, E.F., 272
Cambiaire, Celestin, 273
Canon Law, Revised Code of, 121
Capuchins, 137–138
Carmelite sisters, 285
Carmelites, 273, 275, 313
Carrell, George A., 161
Carroll, Coleman, 212
Carroll, John, 12, 121
Carthusians, 29
Castro, Fidel, 212
Catholic Church Extension Society, 39, 279, 286
Catholic Interracial Council, 77
Catholic Knights of America, 295

Catholic War Veterans, 73
Catholic Welfare Bureau, 167
Catholic Women's Association, 311
Catholic Youth Organization (CYO), 69, 97, 99, 160, 238, 286, 295, 298–299, 311, 320
Catts, Sidney J., 141
Chaldean Catholics, 182
Chalon, Gabriel, 246
Chanche, John, 246
Charismatics (Catholic), 93–94, 202, 207, 303–304, 320
Children of Mary, 285–286, 295
Chinese-Americans, 67
Christian Brothers, 212
Christian Family Movement (CFM), 201, 294–295, 320
Church Unity Octave, 74
Civil Rights Movement, 87, 147, 194, 198, 210
Civil War, 1, 5, 13, 15, 20, 30–31, 75, 132–134, 140, 165, 171–172, 180, 244, 253–256, 258–259, 319, 321
Clark, Dennis, 22
Clergy, roles of, 10–12, 18–20, 24, 29–32, 58–60, 67, 84–85, 98, 100, 138, 155, 157, 163–166, 199–202, 210, 257–258, 320
Cohen, Harold, 303–304
Colin, Maximilian, 258
Comisky, Ben, 311–312
Communal life of parishes, 168, 203–210
Confraternity of Christian Doctrine (CCD), 70–71, 95, 97–99, 169, 204–205, 212, 238, 286, 292, 295, 297–298, 309, 320
Connelly, James, 73
Coughlin, Charles E., 121
Council of Trent, 11–12, 18
Cox, Harvey, 79
Coyle, James, 299
Cuban-Americans, 135, 140, 180–181, 197, 212–213, 238
Cullinane, Michael, 163
Cunnie, Edward F., 77
Curley, Michael J., 142, 166
Curran, John J., 58–59
*Cursillos de Christiandad*, 94, 201, 207–208, 210, 212, 302, 311, 320

Dardis, James, 261
Darragh, James A., 29–30
Daughters of the Cross, 262
David, John B., 134

Davis, Jefferson, 255
Davis, Virgil, 278
Day, Dorothy, 121
Deacons, 95, 97, 200, 311–312, 318, 320
Depression (Great Depression), 66, 68–70, 73, 143–144, 161, 167, 176, 290–291, 295, 298
Devine, Thomas J., 254
Devlin, Francis, 128
Devotional and liturgical practices, 4, 10, 25–27, 29, 31, 49–52, 60, 68–69, 73–74, 78, 80, 88–89, 93–95, 100, 129, 160, 168, 174–176, 179, 197, 202, 208–210, 218, 238, 267, 280, 284, 299, 320–322
Dillon, Agnes, 144, 167
Directors of Religious Education, 201
Divine Word Fathers, 184, 283, 296
Dobbins, Lucy, 285
Dolan, Jay P., 139, 239, 279
Dominican sisters, 144, 167, 271
Dominicans, 283
Donahoe, Francis, 246
Donnelly, Arthur J., 24
Donohue, James F., 158
Dougherty, Dennis, 67–68, 75
Dousson, Douglas, 315
Dower (Rev.), 41
Downey, Daniel, 177
Draft riots (NYC), 31
Drexel, Katherine, 47, 283
Duffo, J.J., 263
Duffy, James, 272
Durbin, Elisha J., 246
Dutch-Americans, 247
Dutkiewicz, Julian, 40

Eastern Rite Catholics, 42, 115, 182; also see Melkites, Maronites, Ruthenians
Eccleston, Samuel, 177
Ecken, Brocard, 273
Ecumenism, 71, 74, 91, 168, 173–174, 203, 207–208, 265, 294
Edmundites, 283
Education, see Parochial Schools, Adult Education, Confraternity of Christian Doctrine
Eisenhower, Dwight D., 72
Elder, William H., 132, 255
Elliott, Walter, 173
Ellis, John Tracy, 121, 194
England, John, 162
English, Philip, 280

Erwin, John H. 261
Ethnicity, 4, 9–12, 16, 18, 31, 37, 40, 72, 92, 100, 123, 130, 140, 144, 159, 177–186, 204, 210–217, 238, 276, 282, 306–307, 319–320; also see specific ethnic groups
Evangelization, 58, 214
Ever, Luke J., 39–40

Farragut, David, 254
Felician sisters, 180
Fichter, Joseph, 299, 318
Finances, 5, 24–25, 41, 53–56, 58–59, 69–70, 77, 87, 92,100, 129, 133, 143, 158, 160–162, 164, 170, 178, 196–197, 206, 217, 257, 266, 294–295, 315
Fitzgerald, Edward, 282
Flaget, Benedict J., 246, 260, 318
Flores, Patrick, 306–307
Foppe, J.A. 272–273
Ford, Henry, 275
Freedman's Aid Society, 137
French-Americans, 2, 9, 16–17, 43–45, 75–76, 85, 87, 90, 92, 98–99, 128, 134, 138, 162, 171, 174, 242, 248–249, 258, 261–263, 274, 283, 286–287, 306, 313, 319
Fundamentalism, 203, 207
Furfey, Paul Hanley, 121

Gagnier, Louis, 17
Gallagher, A.P., 266, 275, 318
Gallagher, Nicholas, 272
Gallagher, T.J. 292
Gallitzen, Dimitri, 121
Garreau, Joel, 90
Gartland, Francis X., 165
Georgia Catholic Laymen's Association, 142–143, 160
Gergaud, Louis, 261–263
Gerhardinger, Theresa, 178
German-Americans, 13, 16–17, 19, 21, 24–26, 37, 40–41, 45, 47, 60–61, 75, 86, 127–128, 130–131, 135, 138, 142, 144, 148, 162, 169, 177–180, 183, 211, 238, 243, 248, 250, 253, 259, 261–262, 264, 267, 274–276, 278, 281–282, 285, 287, 306, 319
Gibbons, James, 121, 166, 180
Gillard, John, 283
Gorman, Thomas K., 293, 297
Grace, Thomas, 247
Gracida, Rene, 307

Grant, Ulysses S., 22, 254
Greco, Charles, 284, 295–296
Greek-Americans, 276
Greeley, Andrew M., 95, 100
Gremillion, J.B., 300
Grifferty, Joseph, 86
Gross, William, 133, 135–137
Guadalupanas sisters, 212
Gubler, Maurice, 314
Guillot, Maximo, 263

Haesley, Charles, 278
Haitian-Americans, 130, 148, 174, 208, 211, 214
Hally, Paul, 291
Handlin, Oscar, 16
Hannan, Philip, 303
Hayes, Patrick, 47
Healy, James A., 163
Hebert, Donald, 239
Henneman, Regidius, 282
Hennesey, James, 264
*Hermanas*, 306–307
Hill, Samuel, 124
Hillebrand, Bernard, 259
Hilterman, (Rev.), 47
Hispanics, 5, 9, 46, 85–87, 92, 94, 140, 148, 197, 205, 208, 211–214, 282, 296, 306–308, 319–321; also see specific national groups
Hodur, Francis, 42
Hogan, William, 121
Holy Family sisters, 283
Holy Ghost Fathers, 47
Holy Name Society, 27, 67–68, 72, 99, 160, 201, 275–276, 285–286, 292–293, 295, 312, 320
Howze, Joseph, 307
Hughes, John J., 15, 17, 19–22, 121
*Humanae Vitae*, 201, 203, 303
Hungarian-Americans, 37, 42, 238, 276
Huyler, Victoria, 144, 167

Independent Czechoslovak Church, 43
Indians, see Native Americans
Ireland, John, 121, 285
Irish-Americans, 2, 12–13, 16–18, 20–21, 24, 30–31, 37, 40–42, 44–45, 55, 59–61, 75–76, 86, 90, 99, 127–128, 130, 135, 141, 162–163, 165, 174, 177, 179, 183, 211, 238, 243–244, 248, 250, 253, 255, 258–259, 261–262, 264, 267, 274, 276, 281, 285, 287, 306

# Index of Places and Parishes